THE SPATIAL TURN IN THE LITERATURE AND ART
OF EARLY MODERN SPAIN

The Spatial Turn in the Literature and Art of Early Modern Spain

EDITED BY MARY E. BARNARD
AND FREDERICK A. DE ARMAS

UNIVERSITY OF TORONTO PRESS
Toronto Buffalo London

© University of Toronto Press 2026
Toronto Buffalo London
utppublishing.com
Printed in Canada

ISBN 978-1-4875-6533-6 (cloth)   ISBN 978-1-4875-6535-0 (EPUB)
                                   ISBN 978-1-4875-6534-3 (UPDF)

Library and Archives Canada Cataloguing in Publication

Title: The spatial turn in the literature and art of early modern Spain / edited
   by Mary E. Barnard and Frederick A. de Armas.
Names: Barnard, Mary E., 1944– editor | De Armas, Frederick A., 1945– editor
Series: Toronto Iberic.
Description: Series statement: Toronto Iberic | Includes bibliographical
   references and index.
Identifiers: Canadiana (print) 20250301032 | Canadiana (ebook) 20250301091 |
   ISBN 9781487565336 (cloth) | ISBN 9781487565343 (PDF) | ISBN 9781487565350 (EPUB)
Subjects: LCSH: Spanish literature – Classical period, 1500–1700 – History and criticism. |
   LCSH: Space in literature. | LCSH: Space – Social aspects – History. | LCSH: Art and
   literature – Spain – History. | LCSH: Art, Spanish – 16th century. | LCSH: Art,
   Spanish – 17th century.
Classification: LCC PQ6066 .S63 2025 | DDC 860.9/003–dc23

Cover design: Tamara Hawkins
Cover image: Diego Velázquez, *Las Hilanderas*, 1657–8, Museo del Prado, Madrid. The
Picture Art Collection / Alamy Stock Photo

Ornament: iStock ID: 1414772456 Vasiliyart

The manufacturer's authorised representative in the EU for product safety is Mare
Nostrum Group B.V., Mauritskade 21D, 1091 GC Amsterdam, The Netherlands.
Email: gpsr@mare-nostrum.co.uk.

We wish to acknowledge the land on which the University of Toronto Press
operates. This land is the traditional territory of the Wendat, the Anishnaabeg, the
Haudenosaunee, the Métis, and the Mississaugas of the Credit First Nation.

University of Toronto Press acknowledges the financial support of the Government of
Canada, the Canada Council for the Arts, and the Ontario Arts Council, an agency of
the Government of Ontario, for its publishing activities.

Contents

List of Illustrations   vii

Introduction: The Spatial Scene   3

**Part One: Spaces of Voicing, Intellectual Enquiry,
and the Sublime**

1 Acoustic Spaces: Vocal Performance and Trauma in Sonnets by
Fernando de Herrera   17
MARY E. BARNARD

2 "Ward off this Gloomy Darkness": Spaces of Conflict and
Sublimity in Calderón's *La vida es sueño*   31
FREDERICK A. DE ARMAS

3 The Space of Memory: Three Sixteenth-Century
Iberian Examples   44
MARINA S. BROWNLEE

4 Geographic Games: Cosmic Miniatures and Creative Play
from Jewish Theology and Medieval Alexander Romances to
Cervantes's Modern Fiction   68
KEITH BUDNER

Part Two: Spaces for the Performance of Alternate Realities

5 Early Modern Geotagging in Cervantes's "El coloquio
de los perros"   93
CAROLYN A. NADEAU

6 Eluding Surveillance and Repression in Early Modern Madrid:
   Manufacturing Safety through Street Performances in
   Cervantes's *La gitanilla*   110
   MATÍAS A. SPECTOR

7 Performance Space in Cervantes's *Pedro de Urdemalas*   127
   EDWARD H. FRIEDMAN

8 The Person of a King: Sovereignty, Performance, and Court Spaces
   in Three Royal Impostor Plays   142
   CHRISTOPHER WEIMER

Part Three: Sacred Spaces

9 Poeticizing Spaces in Seventeenth-Century Religious Poetry   161
   MARÍA CRISTINA QUINTERO

10 Mirrors, Self Portraits, and Visionary Exemplarity: An Analysis
   of the Guadalupe Chapel, Royal Discalced Convent, Madrid   180
   ROSILIE HERNÁNDEZ

11 The Spatial Display of Poetry in the *Recibimiento al
   obispo Pimentel* (1629)   197
   VÍCTOR SIERRA MATUTE

12 Spaces of Death: The Virgin of the Arch and the Cult of the Dead in
   María de Zayas's *La fuerza del amor*   216
   RYAN D. GILES

Works Cited   229

Contributors   255

Index   259

Illustrations

1.1. *Odysseus and the Sirens*, Attic red-figured vase, ca. 480–470 BCE   28

4.1. Raphael, *School of Athens* fresco (detail), 1508–11   80

4.2. Alfonso X el Sabio, *Libro de juegos, o Libro del ajedrez, dados y tablas*   83

5.1. Louis de Meunier's rendition of La plaza de San Francisco, 1668   97

5.2. Louis de Meunier's rendition of La Lonja, 1668   101

11.1. Cover of the *Recibimiento al obispo Pimentel*   199

11.2. Sketch of the third emblem included in the collection   208

11.3. Acrostic sonnet that displays the motto "Pastor Vigilans"   210

12.1. Fifteenth-century painting of Virgin with Child   219

12.2. *Madonna delle Anime Purganti*, 1638–42   226

THE SPATIAL TURN IN THE LITERATURE AND ART
OF EARLY MODERN SPAIN

Introduction: The Spatial Scene

O God, I could be bounded in a nutshell and count myself a king of infinite space, were it not that I have had bad dreams.

Shakespeare, Hamlet, act 2

Shakespeare was fully attuned to the new cosmologies proposed by Copernicus, by Tycho Brahe's new architecture of the universe, and especially by Thomas Digges, the English mathematician and astronomer, who claimed that the stars were not held fast in crystal spheres but extended throughout an infinite space.[1] Written at a time of changing cosmologies, Shakespeare's *Hamlet* discarded earth's central position in the cosmos, its unique place in the universe, to view with awe an unbounded and dangerous space: "Hamlet's conceit sets up a polarity between containment and infinity ... an acknowledgment of the decisive victory of the spatial paradigm over the Aristotelian placial paradigm" (Gillies 2023, 177–8). Partly for his belief in a heliocentric cosmology of infinite space, Giordano Bruno (1548–1600) was condemned by the Inquisition and burned at the stake in Rome about the time that *Hamlet*, with its stark contrast between containment and unbounded space, was first performed.[2]

The spatial turn in cosmological theories was accompanied by new ways of conceiving space more broadly in sixteenth- and seventeenth-century Spain, a time when traditional conceptions of space were challenged, when new lands were discovered by Europeans, a time of religious and political unrest, of advances in the science of anatomy, and of remarkable inventions and artistic and literary production.[3] Ways of conceiving space encompass the many spheres of human activity, where cultural memory and identity are constructed and contested, and where epistemological enquiries are tested. Advances in cosmological thought were made possible by the invention of the telescope, an instrument that became central to the new theories of the cosmos and optics. As a tool of high culture, it played an important role in Baroque fiction, as in the interplay between scientific and political discourses in Francisco de Quevedo's satire *La Hora de todos y la Fortuna con seso*, where the spheres of cosmography and optics combine to offer a critique, no matter how ambiguous, of Spain's colonial project.[4]

Cartography offered a novel way of conceiving space beyond the cosmological sphere. Although Iberian cartographers did not benefit from the innovative projection maps of the Flemish Gerardus Mercator, the famous cartographer in Charles V's service who dedicated his 1540 map of Flanders to the Habsburg emperor, they staged their own cartographic revolution by merging a geometric cartography, occasioned by the rediscovery of Ptolemy's second-century *Geographia* (translated into Latin in 1412), with a linear spatiality inherited from the late Middle Ages, as it appears in Hernán Cortés's "Segunda carta de relación" [Second letter from Mexico] (Padrón 2004, 92–3). The mapping of the world following the discovery of "new" lands made possible the "invention" of America as a new space for Spanish colonialism.

Early modern Spain was also involved in a mapping of a different kind. Philip II (1556–98), who was well versed in astronomy, architecture, mathematics, and geography – including the indispensable *Geographia* by Ptolemy, which inspired his cartographic and geographic projects – commissioned the leading topographical artist in Europe, the Flemish Anton van den Wyngaerde, to paint a series of views of cities and towns, which were executed in drawings and paintings with pen and ink (Kagan 1989). Although Wyngaerde's cityscapes were not published at the time or put on display in public spaces like Madrid's royal palace, following the European tradition of exhibiting maps and topographical views in palaces, such as the Villa Farnesina or the Villa Medici in Rome (Kagan 1989, 50–1), they provided Philip with a new framework for conceiving and legitimizing his empire as a space of cities, with his diverse lands in Europe, America, the East Indies, and Northern Africa dubbed an "empire of cities."[5]

Cities themselves were composed of micro spaces, spheres of human interaction defined by the characteristic activities within them: the newly created anatomy theatres, public theatres, the royal court, royal prisons, private art collections and libraries, and religious institutions, which acquired new prominence in early modern Spain. The oldest anatomy theatre, constructed at the University of Salamanca in 1552–4 during the reign of Charles V (1516–56), was followed by anatomy theatres in Alcalá, Saragossa, Valencia, Barcelona, and Madrid, where the dissection of the human body became a privileged space of exploration for the construction of an evidence-based knowledge of the body's inner realm (Martínez-Vidal and Pardo-Tomás, 2005).[6] Like the anatomy theatres, public theatres (*corrales de comedias*) were spaces of staged performances with galleries for seated audiences and areas for standing spectators. The Habsburg court similarly functioned like a theatre, and as in a *corral de comedias*, alternate, contested, and conflicted realities were staged. Philip IV's court at the Buen Retiro, a royal retreat and pleasure palace in the outskirts of Madrid, was a "magnificent theater" where the monarch, "permanently onstage," played his exalted role (Brown and Elliott 1986, 31). Another royal space, an infamous prison in Seville, produced so much noise that Philip II had to stop in front of it to listen with amazement, as if he were in a theatre. Cervantes, who was imprisoned there, includes it as a space of disharmony in *Don Quixote*, conjoining it with harmonious and idealized locations in his novel, thus inserting the spaces and places of architecture as a key facet in his writings (de Armas 2022).

The Habsburg kings and nobles displayed paintings, artefacts, and exotic curiosities in what were in effect private museums, performative spaces where learned spectators brought their own knowledge to engage the objects in dialogic exchange.[7] Philip II amassed a large collection of relics at the Escorial; Philip III (r. 1598–1621) acquired an immense collection of paintings (between 1500 and 2747) and luxurious objects; Philip IV (r. 1621–65) displayed his prized paintings by Velázquez and other premier artists of his day in the Buen Retiro for his private viewing. And the *curioso* Vincencio Juan de Lastanosa (1607–82) was widely known for his famous Wunderkammer (Barnard and De Armas 2013, x–xiii).

Libraries, enriched by the arrival of the printing press in the early 1470s, became privileged spaces for creating a shared cultural memory. Many market towns and cities acquired printing presses, with Madrid setting up its own in 1566 after Philip II made it Spain's capital (Bass 2008, 150). The availability of printed books allowed nobles, writers, and universities to acquire substantial collections of printed books. Private libraries were the norm for learned nobles, like Íñigo López de Mendoza, Marquis of Santillana, and Diego Hurtado de Mendoza, Count of Melito. Philip II, an eminent bibliophile, built the Escorial Library in 1584, which contained one of the largest collections of Greek, Latin, and Arabic manuscripts, and printed books, in part by the acquisition of entire private libraries from Benito Arias Montano and the Hieronymite friar José de Sigüenza, among others. Garcilaso de la Vega (1501?–36), Miguel de Cervantes (1547–1616), and Juan de Arguijo

(1567–1622) were among the notable writers with significant collections of printed books. Wealthy women writers had access to libraries of their male family members. Aristocrat and art collector Mencía de Mendoza, Marquise of Cenete (1508–54), inherited a library that had belonged to her father and her grandfather, and had access to the extensive library of her husband, the Duke of Calabria; Luisa de Carvajal y Mendoza (1566–1614), aristocrat, mystic, and activist, read widely from the impressive library of her uncle, Francisco Hurtado de Mendoza (Cruz 2011, 45–53).[8]

Libraries also contained works of art, as in the well-known astronomical ceiling fresco, *El cielo de Salamanca* [*The sky of Salamanca*], painted for the old university library[9] and the *Assembly of the Gods* ceiling painting in the library of Juan de Arguijo, which served as a setting for his academy, attended by distinguished writers like Lope de Vega and Fernando de Herrera. The academy was an important venue of networking beyond the royal court, where the reading of literary texts and the viewing of the ceiling painting created an intimate collective experience that transformed the material site of books and painting into a space of cultural exchange (Barnard 2022, 91–3, 106, 107).

Monasteries and convents offered traditional venues for sacred cultural exchange through teaching and oral reading, for self-reflection and self-realization in the writing of chronicles, literature, and letters, and for composing music. Like royal courts and libraries, they also were spaces for the production and display of works of art. The Monasterio de las Descalzas Reales, a convent for aristocratic Franciscan nuns belonging to the order of Poor Clares – founded by Philip II's sister, Juana de Austria, in 1559 – owned an exceptional collection of reliquaries, sculptures, and paintings, many brought as part of dowries, others commissioned, making the convent one of the richest in early modern Europe. Sor Ana Dorotea, the illegitimate daughter of Emperor Rudolph II, commissioned numerous paintings from court painter Sebastián de Herrera Barnuevo for the convent's chapel Our Lady of Guadalupe, with twenty-one scenes for the walls surrounding the altar representing women from the Old Testament as described in Martín Carrillo's *Elogios de mujeres insignes del viejo testamento* [In praise of illustrious women of the Old Testament] (1627), creating an intimate space of contemplation and religious instruction within the convent (Hernández 2011, 226, 235).

From shifting cosmologies and new mappings of imperial lands to performances at court and in public theatres, dissections of the human body in anatomy theatres, private encounters with material objects and works of art in collections and with printed books in libraries, each interaction, whether in public or in private, was an exercise in the creation of a new and often revisionary cultural memory that existed unbounded by physical place, as Hamlet would have understood it.

The place/space paradigm, which began in human geography in the 1950s, has enriched a number of scholarly disciplines, including art history, anthropology, sociology, literary studies, and even popular culture.[10] The foundational insights of Gaston Bachelard, Henri Lefebvre, Paul Zumthor, and Michel de Certeau have led to a certain consensus about the relationship between place and space, with space connoting the cultural meaning attached to a fixed, physical place.

Space encompasses the sphere of human activity, performance, and interaction. For Lefebvre, space is *produced* by a specific activity in a dynamic, interconnected triad of perceived, conceived, and lived spaces. Lived space is particularly relevant here. Produced by social interaction and cultural practices, it is the space of "inhabitants" and "users" that "the imagination seeks to change and appropriate" (1991, 38–9). For de Certeau as well, space is a "practiced place" created by everyday activities, in effect, a place put into motion, performed and transformed by "walkers," like the wanderers, the itinerant pedestrians of the city of New York (1984, 92–3, 117–18). That sense of space as a dynamic field of human experience, as opposed to the stability of place, is captured by Yi-Fu Tuan's metaphor of place as security and space as freedom, "we are attached to the one and long for the other" (1977, 3), in a reframing of Hamlet's "bounded" nutshell and "infinite space."

The space/place dynamic that has figured in so many fields in recent decades has failed to fully take hold in the literature of Iberia, and much less in early modern Spain. The twelve essays in this volume illustrate how a reading of early modern Spanish literary texts with that paradigm in mind expands our understanding of the function of space inherent in those works. The essays explore the diverse mechanisms and resources through which literature and culture in general *produce* space: how literature and art can transform our understanding of our place in the world, how poems, prose works, and paintings, as material and symbolic objects, change the sense of the places we inhabit. The essays share a performative approach towards cultural products. They examine instances in which cultural expressions affect our spatial understanding of the world and our sense of ourselves within it: how a story creates a sensual intimacy with the reader; vocal artists carve out acoustic spaces; encyclopedias open up spaces of knowledge as memory; metatheatre redefines a place of performance as a space of contestation; and, in a convent, space is created through visual and aural stimuli.

The Essays

The essays in part 1, "Spaces of Voicing, Intellectual Enquiry, and the Sublime," examine the production of space through voicing, representing the sublime, inquiring into new realms of knowledge, and remodelling theological imagery. In "Acoustic Spaces: Vocal Performance and Trauma in Sonnets by Fernando de Herrera," Mary E. Barnard analyses Herrera's recasting of a cultural memory, the ancient myths of the nightingale and the siren for the production, performance, and reception of voice. Her reading is inspired by Yi-Fu Tuan's insights as to what gives a material place its meaning, its identity and aura, to explain the construction of acoustic spaces. The staging of dynamic vocal performances that reverberate in the soundscape of Philomela's forest and in the seascape of a Homeric siren are examined in the light of Cathy Caruth's theory of trauma. Giving voice to Philomela, who in Ovid silently weaves her story of rape and mutilation, Herrera enables her to wail the trauma of her double wounding and the lyric subject to sing his own trauma. The seductive voice of the siren, conceived as a purely acoustic, disembodied figure of song, lures the Odyssean subject to his doom, which he foresees in the bones of dead sailors who, endowed with voice, sing their trauma. The enchanting power of feminine song is underscored in a different register by an angelic siren, her voice both enticing and divine resounding in her acoustic space of delicate, seductive charm. As these vocal artists activate their places, putting their imprint, their signature on them, they engage the melancholy lyric subject, who seeks the authority of their voice to figure himself in his own acoustic space.

Frederick A. de Armas, in "'Ward off this Gloomy Darkness': Spaces of Terror and Sublimity in Calderón's *La vida es sueño*," evokes pseudo-Longinus's treatise in order to discover hidden spaces in Calderón. The play commences with sublime verses and spaces to set the tone and allow the ensuing action to preserve some of its echoes. Here, a doomed woman is reshaped into a goddess, and a living skeleton allows us to reconstruct a prisoner into a flesh-and-blood human being who is unaware of his potential, his ability to become a perfect prince. The sublime expands the dark horizons of the play, bringing together the natural architecture of mountains, rocky vales, and heavenly heights from which the gods can descend, with the earthly and eerie tower of Segismundo's prison. Sublimity returns and thunders down upon the scene at the end of the second act, disabling space through Segismundo's dream metaphor. Thus, this essay seeks to bring to light how in his philosophical, and tenebrous mode, Calderón compels his audience to see the spaces of terror and the sublime.

Marina S. Brownlee examines innovative spatial categories of three encyclopedists in "The Space of Memory: Three Sixteenth-Century Iberian Examples." The polymath Pedro Mexia's *Silva de varia lección* (1540/1541), the first encyclopedia written in the vernacular and printed as a book, was more than a traditional collection of known information; it created new spaces of knowledge by discussing subjects like the loss of memory through illness, wounds, and old age. Antonio de Torquemada's *Jardín de flores curiosas* (1568), a compendium of ideas, enjoyed an equally large circulation as a discourse on the reception of myths, narratives, and beliefs in the "modern" world of the sixteenth century. It offered not a collection of facts but instead a manual for rethinking old assumptions in the wake of new discoveries and thus as a critique of cultural memory. Huarte de San Juan's *Examen de ingenios para las ciencias* (1575), too, questioned authority and precedent in the face of empirical observation. All three encyclopedists created new, dynamic spaces of enquiry and knowledge set against the space of received knowledge as memory.

In "Geographic Games: Cosmic Miniatures and Creative Play from Jewish Theology and Medieval Alexander Romances to Cervantes's Modern Fiction," Keith Budner tracks down the idea of space-making through acts of play and the imagination, from Jewish premodern theologies to Iberian Alexander romances to Cervantes's *Don Quixote.* The author explores how the Jewish playful creation of the cosmos, as found for instance in the Book of Proverbs, was filtered for Spanish readers through the *Libro de Alexandre* and other Castilian texts, and ultimately reappears in Sancho's spherical thinking and playful miniaturization of the world in the episode of Clavileño. Through this journey, we move from theologies of divine creation to theories of literary fictionality. However, rather than understanding this process as the overcoming of the religious by the secular, Budner proposes an ongoing cultural negotiation, where modern fiction entails the secularization of theological vocabularies.

The essays in part 2, "Spaces for the Performance of Alternate Realities," analyse how public performances, both formal at court and informal in urban settings, created new spatial frames for contesting conventional spatial constructs. In "Early Modern Geotagging in Cervantes's 'El coloquio de los perros,'" Carolyn A. Nadeau follows Berganza's visit to Seville, where Cervantes lived from 1587 to 1600 as a commissary officer responsible for provisioning the royal galleys. Knowing the city's quarters intimately, the author takes his visitor on a tour of the city's notable monuments and districts distinguished by their characteristic activities. The slaughterhouse, the hospital, and the mercantile exchange, each the site of human transactions that define conventional spaces, are also sites of rampant corruption, malfeasance, and violence that characterize an alternative sense of space. Those micro spaces of human activity, made more graphic by Cervantes's own experiences in Seville, enliven Berganza's travel through the city's spaces clustered within the larger, more familiar urban space of Seville. Ultimately, Cervantes's descriptions of specific sites create a sensual intimacy for the reader, who can deeply engage with his narrative structure, social commentary, and artistic concerns.

Matías A. Spector describes a similar transformation of an urban space in "Eluding Surveillance and Repression in Early Modern Madrid: Manufacturing Safety through Street Performances in Cervantes's *La gitanilla*." As gypsies, a marginal group of outsiders, gain temporary control over a public place in Madrid – a rapidly emerging modern city – their entertaining performances not only evade the social and political surveillance under which they live but even redefine the public square as a safe and peaceable space of song and dance. The young gypsy dancer, Preciosa, in particular, appropriates the city with her powerful sense of vision, turning its deceptive, confusing landscape into a secure setting. Spector shows how our perception of urban life in Madrid is far more nuanced if we account for how a metropolitan place of human activity – in contrast to a peripheral city such as Murcia – becomes a space of imagination and control through spontaneous artistic expressions.

Public performance as a means of creating space is also at the centre of Edward H. Friedman's "Performance Space in Cervantes's *Pedro de Urdemalas*." Here we enter the realm of performance by a diverse group of shepherds, gypsies, musicians, dancers, actors, and even a rustic mayor, a miserly widow, and a mistrustful queen, who create multiple realities, in effect, multiple spaces in various settings. Friedman reveals that if the dialectic of identity and performance determines the course of the play – metatheatre built around the motif of acting and unstable roles – physical sites are fundamental to the development of the storyline. Cervantes plays with performance as a means of creating alternate realities, of places infused with human interactions that produce distinct spaces for the interplay of reality and fiction within fiction – "Theater becomes an emblem and a component of reality, an icon and a tangible presence."

Christopher Weimer offers a related study of stages and royal courts as performative venues in "The Person of a King: Sovereignty, Performance, and Court Spaces in Three Royal Impostor Plays." He begins with the observation that a court was a conceptualized political space in orbit around the monarch who served as its centre of gravity through the public performance of their authority. Such performances were mirrored on public and even court stages when actors played the roles of kings and emperors in political *comedias*, and this specular relationship between court and stage reached still greater degrees of complexity in a metatheatrical group of plays that depicted royal impostors, in effect redefining both the court and the stage as spaces of contestation instead of affirmation of royal authority. The result was a stage spectacle of actors impersonating impostors impersonating kings that questioned the political stability and even legitimacy of court spaces so reliant on the convincing performance of sovereignty.

The essays in part 3, "Sacred Spaces," deal with the production of spaces within the physical confines of monastic institutions. In "Poeticizing Spaces in Seventeenth-Century Religious Poetry," María Cristina Quintero examines the poetry of three nuns who, although anchored in a place of confinement and isolation, and under constant surveillance, create interior spaces of creative expression through their lyric poetry. That three accomplished poets – María de San Alberto (1568–1640), Cecilia de Nacimiento (1570–1646), and Marcela de San Félix (1605–87) – could write, in essence perform or "practice" their own emotions and relationships within a hermetic institutional setting that suppressed individuality, is a testament to their capacity to create private spaces of difference that permitted solitude, meditation, and, in many instances, a mystical journey. The space of religious poetry thus became a personal one that stood against the communal, static, enclosed space of the convent.

Rosilie Hernández describes another unique example of conventual self-realization in "Mirrors, Self-Portraits, and Visionary Exemplarity: An Analysis of the Guadalupe Chapel, Royal Discalced Convent, Madrid." She follows a visual-spatial configuration that depicts an encounter with the sacred by splitting the pictorial plane into halves. The top is assigned to the transcendent and the bottom to the immanent human realm. The Guadalupe Chapel's visual program presents a catalogue of Old Testament heroines leading to Marian privilege. Its paintings are unique in that they are executed on mirrors upon which the cloistered nuns, kneeling at the altar in prayer, would see their faces reflected. The play of reflection spatially blurs the limit between their selves, their spiritual foremothers, their earthly fellow nuns, and the eternal Immaculate Mother. Unlike the nuns who expressed their individuality through religious poetry, the nuns of the Guadalupe Chapel confronted themselves visually from the space of pictorial representation while enclosed in their chapel. That visual experience blurred the separation between the self and the sacred images of their female predecessors.

Victor Sierra Matute provides another example of a social space produced within a monastic setting in "The Spatial Display of Poetry in the *Recibimiento al obispo Pimentel* (1629)." It is the study of a manuscript compiled by the Colegio de la Compañía de Jesús de Huete to celebrate the visit of Enrique Pimentel, Bishop of Cuenca, in 1629. The manuscript documents the visit as a spectacle that begins with a child reciting a ballad in honour of the bishop. Poems, written in Latin and Spanish – accompanied by emblems with illustrations – were displayed on wall panels for the bishop to read silently as he walked around the cloister in the presence of the Jesuit brothers, who would in turn read aloud the poems at the banquet that concluded the celebration. The cloister becomes a space of poetic performance in a dynamic interplay of visual, oral, and aural elements. Ultimately, the *Recibimiento al obispo Pimentel* becomes a material testament, representing an event in which inscribed words, spatial arrangement, and physical presence merged, generating a unique experience that transcends the confines of the handwritten page.

In "Spaces of Death: The Virgin of the Arch and the Cult of the Dead in María de Zayas's *La fuerza del amor*," Ryan D. Giles proposes that Zayas's *novela* is informed by both the Neapolitan cult of the fresco Our Lady of the Arch and by the Neapolitan death traditions surrounding the execution of criminals. By focusing on legendary and spatial aspects of both cults, the author explains key elements of the story, such as the abuse suffered by the female protagonist (Laura), the fate of her abuser (her husband Diego), and the crucial notions of martyrdom and salvation. In addition, Giles sheds light on the symbolic and historical meanings interwoven in Zayas's depiction of the macabre roadside chapel in the denouement of the *novela*.

We would like to express our gratitude to Matias Spector (University of Chicago) for his help in assembling and editing this volume. We would also like to thank the Humanities Division and the College at the University of Chicago, and the College of Liberal Arts at the Pennsylvania State University for their generous support.

Notes

1   Harrison (1987), Usher (2010), and Gillies (2023). Usher argues that
    Hamlet is an allegory of the new cosmology where Rosencrantz and
    Guildenstern refer to the astronomer Tycho Brahe. Hamlet's uncle,
    King Claudius, represents Claudius Ptolemy, who developed in ancient

times the Earth-centric model that became a part of the Christian belief system. He even claims that Shakespeare equates Elsinore Castle with Helsingør, which was being built at the same time as Tycho's astronomical observatory at Uraniborg.

2 In *De l'infinito universo e mondi*, Bruno was also the first to propose not only infinite space but that "fixed stars" were actually suns.

3 On the combination of power and riches as well as poverty and economic crisis in early modern Spain, see Feros (2008). On the precariousness of this period, where the quest for certainty reached into the realms of history, science, religion, and politics, with large cultural implications for literature, see García-Arenal (2020).

4 See García Santo-Tomás (2017, 186–94) and Martínez (2006).

5 On the interaction of European and colonial traditions in images of New and Old World cities and towns, see Kagan (2000). See also Osorio (2017).

6 For details on European anatomy theatres, see in particular Sawday (1995), Findlen (2006), and Klestinec (2011).

7 On performing the museum, see Garoian (2001, 237). Mercedes Alcalá Galán used this concept in her paper "Performing the Museum" (2017).

8 On women's libraries and reading practices, see Cátedra and Rojo Vega (2004) and Álvarez Márquez (2017).

9 This fresco of Ptolemaic constellations, zodiac signs, and planets was allegedly painted by Fernando Gallego (ca. 1483–6) for the vaulted ceiling of the old library of the University of Salamanca. It was used to teach astronomy, a science that flourished in the second half of the fifteenth-century at the university. For details, see Tejero Prieto (n.d.), Hiniesta (2007), and Sánchez León and Recio Sánchez (2024).

10 From the extensive bibliography on place and space, see Soja (1996), Warf and Arias (2009), Tally (2013), and Cresswell (2015).

PART ONE

Spaces of Voicing, Intellectual Enquiry, and the Sublime

1 Acoustic Spaces: Vocal Performance and Trauma in Sonnets by Fernando de Herrera

MARY E. BARNARD,
PENNSYLVANIA STATE UNIVERSITY

Und fast ein Mädchen wars und ging hervor
aus diesem einigen Glück von Sang und Leier
und glänzte klar durch ihre Frühlingsschleier
und machte sich ein Bett in meinem Ohr.
Und schlief in mir ...

And almost a girl it was who emerged
from this singular union of song and lyre
and glowed brightly through her springtime veils
and made herself a bed within my ear.
And slept in me ...

Rainer Maria Rilke, Sonnets to Orpheus, #2

Rainer Maria Rilke found inspiration in Orpheus, son of Calliope, the muse with the gift of song, and daughter of Mnemosyne, goddess of memory. As the poet "of song and lyre," Orpheus possessed the magic of voice, the power of the word and music. For the ancient poets, Orpheus's song moved wild beasts, trees, and rocks, and even when decapitated by the Maenads, his head floating down the river Hebrus, his "death-cold tongue" still sang, making nature attend to its call (Virgil 2000, 4.525). For Rilke, it was the Orphic magic of the female voice that moved the male listener, creating an intimate space within his ear.

Like Rilke, Fernando de Herrera (ca. 1534–97) was captivated by the female voice, by its power to persuade, to compel to action, and its singular capacity to perform in music and song. Two figures of myth and legend, the nightingale and the siren, companions to Orpheus in song and in the violence that gives birth to it, occupy a unique place in Herrera's lyric production. In three sonnets – "Suáve Filomela," "Serena

Luz," and "Al mar desierto – Herrera carves out spaces for the performance of their powerful voices, the nightingale in her ritual wailing and the siren in her alluring, deadly song. Performance is understood here as the dynamic quality of vocalization and audition, in the production of voice and its reception in an acoustic space (Dunn and Jones 1994).[1] Aligned in the sonnets with the production of voice as a cultural construct, performance points to the embodiment of song and its reception by a longing male lyric subject. In this essay, I argue that these vocal artists activate a place, be it a landscape or a seascape, marking it with their imprint and engaging the poet/lover, who responds in awe, wonder, or fear. In a revisionary act of cultural transmission and appropriation, Herrera fashions voice from textual fragments of foundational texts, chief among them Ovid's Philomela, Homer's sirens, and Virgil's nightingale, together with variants from Petrarch and Garcilaso de la Vega.[2]

Space as understood in this essay owes much to Yi-Fu Tuan's insight as to what gives a material place its meaning, its identity and aura (1977). Tuan offers an anecdote involving Neils Bohr and Werner Heisenberg, who visit Kronberg Castle in Denmark. As informed readers of Shakespeare, the physicists realize that the castle "changes as one imagines that Hamlet lived there ... The stones, the green roof with its patina, the wood carvings in the church ... the walls and the ramparts speak a quite different language ... a dark corner reminds us of the darkness in the human soul," that of the melancholy Hamlet (Heisenberg 1972, 51). Herrera, as an informed reader of the ancients and Italians, brings his cultural memory to bear on the nightingale and the siren to show how their performance in song endows their material places with movement and meaning, identity and aura, creating in the process distinctive acoustic spaces. In analysing their vocal performance and spaces, I take cues from Roland Barthes's "the grain of the voice," with the grain privileging the body in the production of musical sound (1977), and from Eugène Minkowski's phenomenological notion of *retentir*, the reverberating and echoing sound that creates soundscapes in the material world (1967). Also pertinent is Cathy Caruth's work on voice and the "wound" that causes and energizes trauma, of a "moving and sorrowful voice that cries out, a *voice* that is paradoxically released *through the wound*" (1996, 2; emphasis in the original).

I

Philomela's Voice

Herrera's "Suäve Filomela" adopts Ovid's raped and mutilated Philomela to sing her trauma. In an open landscape, the lyric subject, witness and keeper of her memory, longs for her commanding and effective song to find consolation and to move his beloved to love:

Suäve Filomela, que tu llanto
descubres al sereno i limpio cielo:
si lamentaras tú mi desconsuelo,
o si tuviera yo tu dulce canto,
yo prometiera a mis trabajos tanto,
qu'esperara al dolor algún consuelo,
i se movieran d'amoroso zelo
los bellos ojos cuya lumbre canto.
Más tú, con la voz dulce i armonía,
cantas tu afrenta i bárbaros despojos;
yo lloro mayor daño en son quexoso.
O haga el cielo qu'en la pena mía
tu voz suene, o yo cante mis enojos
buelto en ti, russeñol blando i lloroso. (384–5)[3]

(Sweet Philomela, you who reveal your weeping
    to the serene and limpid sky,
if you lamented my unhappiness
or if I had your sweet song,
I could lessen my burden
and hope for consolation for my pain,
and would move with burning love
the eyes, whose luminosity I sing.
But you, with your sweet voice and harmony,
sing your rape and barbarous remains;
I sing a worse injury in mournful complaint.
May heaven make your voice
resound in my pain, or make me sing my grievance
transformed into you, sweet and weeping nightingale.)

In Ovid's tale, Procne, missing her sister Philomela, asks her husband, the Thracian king Tereus, to bring her from Athens to their home in Thrace. On their way, deep in the woods, Tereus rapes Philomela, severs her tongue, and abandons her. He tells Procne that her sister has died. Philomela weaves her story in a tapestry and sends it to Procne, who brings her sister to Thrace, where in revenge they kill Procne's son, Itys, cut up his body, cook it, and serve it to his father. Ovid ends the story elliptically. Pursued by Tereus, the sisters escape: "As they fly from him you would think that the bodies of the two Athenians were poised on wings: they were poised on wings! One flies to the woods, the other rises to the roof." The fierce Tereus is transformed into a Hoopoe (Ovid 1984, 6.67–9).[4]

Making explicit what Ovid leaves unsaid, Herrera calls the transformed Philomela by name and gives her a voice. As a nightingale, she laments her violation in solitude, perhaps in the woods at the site of her rape. The image of the wailing nightingale and her acoustic space take shape through a layering of images from Virgil, Petrarch, and Garcilaso. In *Georgics* 4, Virgil sets the voice in a space of performance in song as he stages the story of Orpheus, whose Eurydice is lost to the underworld. Mourning the loss of his wife, he weeps like the nightingale that laments the loss of her fledglings, torn from their nest by a farmer: she "weeps all night long, and perched on a spray, renews her piteous song [miserabile carmen], filling the region round with sad laments" (2000, 4.511–15).[5] Herrera builds upon Virgil's unbounded acoustic space for his nightingale's grieving, sweet song (dulce canto), with details which may have been suggested by Petrarch and Garcilaso.

In the *Rime sparse*, Petrarch speaks of the "many grieving, skillful notes" (tante note sì pietose et scorte) of the nightingale's sweet song that accompanies the lover, reminding him of Laura's death (sonnet 311; 1976, 490). Garcilaso extends both Petrarch and Virgil to create a space of song for the shepherd Nemoroso to mourn his dead Elissa:

Cual suele'l ruiseñor con triste canto
quejarse, entre las hojas escondido [...]
y aquel dolor que siente,
con diferencia tanta
por la dulce garganta,
despide, que a su canto el aire suena,
y la callada noche no refrena
su lamentable oficio y sus querellas,
trayendo de su pena
el cielo por testigo y las estrellas,
desta manera suelto yo la rienda
a mi dolor [...] (Garcilaso, 2020, vv. 324–5, 330–9, 331)[6]

(As the nightingale, singing of heartbreak,
complains from where she's hidden in the leaves [...]
and the pain she feels
with such rich variations
pours so profusely forth
from her sweet, tuneful throat, that the air resounds with
her song, and the silent night does not restrain
this office of lament and accusation,

>   as she calls on heaven
>   and the stars to bear witness to her pain:
>   just so do I give free rein to my grief […])

The term "diferencia," which stood for variation in the musical vocabulary of the time (Mele 1930, 221; Rivers 1974, 295), points to the nightingale's skilful song, echoing Petrarch's "many grieving, skillful notes." Virgil's incantatory song resounds in Nemoroso's mournful nightingale, with the magical power of Orpheus's music, which moves nature, receiving an intimate response. The nightingale's "dulce garganta" is at the centre of this musical staging, with the air echoing her song as if sharing in her mourning, and the nocturnal landscape bearing witness to her pain. In appropriating "cielo" from Petrarch and Garcilaso as a spatial marker for a refigured Philomela, Herrera has her voice resound in open air, the epithets serene and limpid (sereno i limpio) magnifying the bird's vocal range, its limitless sonority. These acoustic spaces act as sound chambers for the nightingale's voice. They remind us of Eugène Minkowski's notion of *retentir*, sound as it reverberates and echoes in nature: an imagined wellspring in a sealed vase, its waves echoing against its sides, filling it with their sonority, or the sound of a hunting horn reverberating through its echo, transforming "the forest, filling it to its limits, into a vibrating sonorous world" (1967, chapter 9). Herrera's Philomela animates the Ovidian forest with her lamenting song, a cultural memory transformed into a dynamic, vibrating soundscape that "speaks" her language – like the walls and ramparts of Kronberg Castle that speak Hamlet's – as she performs her trauma before the pained lyric subject, as we see further below.

The sonority of voice in Garcilaso's text, and in turn Herrera's, brings to mind what Roland Barthes calls "the grain of the voice," with the grain pointing to "the body in the voice as it sings" (1977, 188). Writing on the vocal music called "Russian bass," Barthes remarks that "something is there … beyond the meaning of the words … something which is directly the cantor's body, brought to your ears in one and the same movement from deep down in the cavities, the muscles, the membranes, the cartilages … of the performer and the music he sings" (1977, 181–2). Barthes focuses on the throat, the "place where the phonic metal hardens [and is segmented] … bringing not the soul but *jouissance*" (1977, 183). It is in the "dulce garganta" of Garcilaso's nightingale, the bodily instrument that creates song and projects it from "deep down" in her vocal cords, where the avian performer physically executes her song and brings about the pleasure and delight of her music, which has the power to move the listener. In Herrera, the musical and the

performative intersect as the bird becomes an emblem of vocal authority in its power of persuasion. Virgilian Orpheus's incantatory song
resounds subtextually in the harmony of the singular sweet voice of
Herrera's transformed Philomela. Even though her song does not move
nature, it moves the lyric subject, who recognizes a certain magic in her
voice and longs for it to bring him consolation and, more importantly,
to move to love the beautiful eyes whose radiance he sings.

Voicing Trauma

The voice of Herrera's Philomela comes to the lyric subject's ear from
her mutilated body "as it sings" her double wounding, her rape and violent dismemberment, "cantas tu afrenta y bárbaros despojos." She fulfils
what in Ovid's text she had threatened: "I will fill the woods with my
story and move the very rocks to pity" (1984, 6.547–8), and what Tereus
tried to suppress: "But he seized her tongue with pincers, as it protested
against the outrage ... struggling to speak and cut it off with his merciless
blade. The mangled root quivers, while the severed tongue lies palpitat-
ing on the dark earth, faintly murmuring" (1984, 6.556–60). To render his
sonnet's extraordinary scene of voicing, Herrera recasts Ovid's scene of
weaving: she "hangs a Thracian web [barbarica tela] on her loom, and
skillfully weaving purple notes on a white background, she thus tells the
story of her wrongs" (1984, 576–8). With "purple notes" signifying her
bloodied violated body, and using her shuttle as her "pen," she weaves
a text, echoing an ancient notion in which *texere*, to weave or braid, was
connected with writing, "etymologically the text is a cloth; *textus* from
which text derives, means 'woven'" (Barthes 1977, 76).[7]
   Ovid characterizes Philomela's tapestry as "barbarica," from the
Greek noun *barbaros*, meaning the incomprehensible sounds, the babbling of barbarians, as heard by the Greek ear, extended by implication
to her rape and silencing by the barbarous Thracian. But if Philomela's loom is Thracian in origin, she "manages to weave threads that
are 'skillful,' 'expert,' or 'practiced.'"[8] Recasting his Ovidian subtext,
Herrera transfers "barbarica" to his Philomela's dead tongue, "bárbaros despojos," signifying the violent physical wounding that causes
the trauma she now voices as a nightingale, but just as skillfully and
expertly – like her ancient counterpart – through the commanding presence of her song.
   Trauma entails "much more than a pathology, or the simple illness of
a wounded psyche," explains Cathy Caruth, "it is always the story of a
wound that cries out, that addresses us in the attempt to tell us of a reality or truth that is not otherwise available" (1996, 4). Violence, as in all

traumas, "returns to haunt the survivor later on." Philomela's trauma emanates from the wound stored in her memory, a wound that "cries out" through song, which Herrera's lyric subject preserves by transcribing it as speech on paper. What the subject "hears" in her song is Ovid's foundational tale, a cultural memory that – within the fiction of the text, for he is the poet, the singer in the sonnet – he can write because he has read it. Orality and textuality merge. Herrera's scene of writing becomes a scene of voicing, of an acoustic space in another register, for the subject, like Philomela, is a singer, and his text is in effect a song, a sonnet, *soneto* deriving from the Italian *sonetto*, a "little sound or a little song."

The lyric subject's performance in song expresses his profound sense of loss as he voices in melancholy sadness how the wrong committed against him is greater than Philomela's, "yo canto mayor daño en son quexoso" (I sing a worse injury in mournful complaint). Staging his sorrow narcissistically in all his pain, he exhibits his melancholy in terms proposed by Sigmund Freud in "Mourning and Melancholia." According to Freud, melancholy is a condition of self-diminishment as well as one of exhibitionism and self-promotion. Though diminished by his malady, living in grief and emotionally impoverished, the afflicted speaks out in eloquent self-display, exuberant in his eloquence (1978, 14:246). "It is what we could call an *accredited pathology*," writes Juliana Schiesari of Freud's analysis, "justified by the heightened sense of conscience that the melancholic is said to display ostentatiously" (1992, 9; emphasis in the original). The dark and verbally gifted Hamlet is, for Freud, the eminent melancholic. In keeping with the tenor of eros and melancholia, Herrera's troubled subject, living in his own trauma, singing from his own wound, chooses the plaintive, solitary Philomela as his companion and muse in song and lament.

At the end of the sonnet the subject wishes to be transformed into the nightingale to become not just an echo of Philomela but Philomela herself: "buelto en ti, russeñol blando i lloroso" (transformed into you, sweet and weeping nightingale), an acoustic mirroring that serves as the emblem of poetic voice. Herrera's adaptation of an Ovidian figure for his own story follows Petrarch's project in the *Rime Sparse* of interiorizing myth by placing "metamorphosis in the arena of the psyche" (Barkan 1986, 206). If Petrarch's poet/lover is transformed into Daphne, Actaeon, Phaeton, or Echo to represent what he both desires and dreads, the failure of love that triumphs in art, Herrera's poet/lover leaves his story open-ended, his transformation into Philomela but a wish, highlighting his double loss: the absent woman and the absent voice of the nightingale. Yet both subjects follow a similar trajectory. As Juliana Schiesari comments on Petrarch's *Rime*, "The ecstasy and despair of

Petrarch's lyric eroticized lack in terms of a lost object, the bemoaning of whose loss also erected the [melancholy] poetic subject The point is that psychological loss is recuperated as aesthetic and cultural gain" (1992, 167 and n.12).[9] That is the very point of Herrera's excursion into Philomela's space.

II

The Song of the Siren

Grief and trauma enter a new acoustic space in "Al mar desierto," where the lyric subject is seduced by a compelling siren song in a reworking of Homer's *Odyssey* 12:

> Al mar desierto, en el profundo estrecho,
> entre las duras rocas, con mi nave
> desnuda, tras el canto voi suäve,
> que forçado me lleva a mi despecho.
> Temerario desseo, incauto pecho,
> a quien rendí de mi poder la llave,
> al peligro m'entregan fiero i grave,
> sin que pueda apartarme del mal hecho.
> Veo los uessos blanquear, i siento.
> el triste son de la engañada gente,
> i crecer de las ondas el bramido.
> Huir no puedo ya mi perdimiento,
> que no me da lugar el mal presente,
> ni osar me vale en el temor perdido. (359)

> (Out towards the deserted sea, in the deep straits,
> among the hard rocks in my defenseless ship,
> I follow the sweet song
> that pulls me forward, despite myself.
> Bold desire, unsuspecting heart,
> to whom I surrendered the key of my power,
> now deliver me to fierce and great danger,
> unable to steer clear of the damage done.
> I see the bones whiten, and hear
> the wretched song of the deceived sailors,
> and the rising roar of the waves.
> It is too late to flee my own undoing,
> my present suffering leads nowhere,
> and there is no point in daring as I am already lost in fear.)

Homer's Circe had warned Odysseus, "you will come first to the Sirens who beguile and seduce all men" with their sweet but deadly song: sailors now sit in a meadow surrounded by those who came before, who are but a "heap of bones," skin "all shriveled" (1995, 12.44–6). She instructs him to seal his men's ears with wax and have them tie him fast to the mast, so that he can hear but not succumb to the sirens' song. The sirens have speech and knowledge. They sing the exploits they witnessed at Troy and flatter Odysseus by addressing him as the "great war-glory of the Achaeans" (1995, 12.184). But above all their song casts a spell. "Their power depends emphatically on hearing," writes Charles Segal (1994a, 100). "The verb that repeatedly describes the 'hearing' of their song," he continues, "is *akouein* (purely acoustic hearing, used eight times) never *kluein*, the social hearing of fame" (1994a, 105), which the epic bards proclaim. Their very words confirm the power of their voice: "For never yet has any man rowed past the island in his black ship until he has heard the sweet voice from our lips; instead, he has joy of it, and goes his way a wiser man" (1995, 12.192). Easily seduced, Odysseus longs to hear the alluring voice and begs to be untied.

The lyric subject of Herrera's sonnet, too, is drawn to the irresistible siren song as he sails in his vulnerable ship through the rocky straits. He imagines himself in a silent seascape, echoing the *Odyssey*, where Odysseus and his men approach the sirens' island while silence overcomes the ocean, foreshadowing the hero's vulnerability and the danger to come. The sonnet's sweet and gentle siren song, imagined as resounding in a "windless calm," creates the enticing, dangerous aura of this seascape, the site where rhetoric, sexuality, and violence converge. Without a Circe to warn him, or sailors to bind him to the mast, Herrera's subject is seduced by the disembodied sweet song. The sirens episode in the *Odyssey* makes song "into something quite disturbing," writes Adriana Cavarero, "clearly, it is feminine song that is at stake. This is precisely why it is so disturbing … [the feminine] lends it its seductive power" (2005, 105). Unlike the song of the epic sirens who narrate in their singing, uttering words of praise for the war hero, the sonnet's siren song is devoid of speech. Seductive but wordless, deprived of a semantic correlative, it is even more alluring, as it carries the force of pure voice. In Herrera's recasting of Homer's tale, the lyric subject's encounter with this voice – the voice of the beloved, though absent in the poem – causes his trauma, the wound that "cries out" his unmet desire.

In the *Odyssey*, Odysseus sails forth, escaping the sirens. Another fate awaits Herrera's subject, a solitary wanderer and brooder. Amid the roaring of the waves, he sees from afar the bones of dead sailors, those who were swayed by the siren song, and now, endowed with voice, sing their trauma (Veo los uessos blanquear, i siento / el triste son de la engañada gente; 1985, 359). The rotting bones and lamenting voices create a space of ruination – the dangerous site Circe had warned Odysseus of – which now portends the doom of the lyric subject, who is fully aware of his own undoing. Yet, the singing bones are significant in another sense, for the dead sailors have acquired a certain presence in memory through song, a place in history, if not fame something akin to it. In anticipating his own fate in the bones, and unable to escape his undoing, the seduced subject implicitly foresees his future presence in memory and history, and the remembrance of his trauma by those who will hear his words in song, announced to the world on the printed page. With readers as witnesses, he makes the space of the bones his own to cry out his own trauma.

III

The Hybrid Siren

The siren song appears in a different guise in Herrera's "Serena Luz," which recounts a Neoplatonic journey by means of a hybrid figure, at once angel and siren, spiritual and seductive – her physical beauty reflecting her divine beauty – who guides the lyric subject to heaven.

> Serena Luz, en quien presente espira
> divino amor, qu'enciende i junto enfrena
> el noble pecho qu'en mortal cadena
> al alto Olimpo levantar s'aspira;
> ricos cercos dorados, do se mira
> tesoro celestial d'eterna vena;
> armonía d'angélica sirena
> qu'entre las perlas i el coral respira:
> ¿Cuál nueva maravilla, cuál exemplo
> de la inmortal grandeza nos descubre
> aquessa sombra del hermoso velo?
> Que yo en essa belleza que contemplo,
> aunqu'a mi flaca vista ofende i cubre,
> la immensa busco i voi siguiendo al cielo. (396–7)

> (Serene Luz, in whom breathes the presence of
> divine love, which inflames and at once restrains
> the noble heart, which in mortal chains
> aspires to rise to lofty Olympus;

rich circles of gold, which reflect
a celestial treasure of an eternal lode,
the music of an angelic siren,
who glides among pearls and coral.
What new wonder, what image
of immortal greatness is revealed to us
by the shadow of that lovely body.
For I, in that beauty which I contemplate,
though it wounds and hides from my weak vision,
seek the beauty without limits and follow along the road to heaven.)

With her golden hair in curls resembling halos, and her angelic song marking her divine presence, "serena Luz" stands at the centre of a Neoplatonic journey. She is an "angélica sirena," the epithet "angélica" aligning her with the "donna angelicata" of the *dolce stil nuovo*, the beautiful woman as a creature from paradise. Her origins lie in the myth of Er in Plato's *Republic*, where the heavenly spheres, attached to the spindle of Necessity and governed by the Fates, are controlled by sirens who emit pure tones, their singing creating the harmony of the spheres (2013, Book X). But Herrera's "angélica sirena" is also a dangerous enchantress. Singing her siren song among lovely rocks, "las perlas i el coral" (her teeth and red lips) –fetishes from the Petrarchan canon of beauty – she is a veritable "donna petrosa," pointing to the perils of her allure as she calls to mind Odysseus's sirens among their rocks.[10] In the evolution of the siren in the Western tradition as received by Herrera, she functions as a seductress in body and voice. In Cavarero's words, the siren must now "be beautiful, but she must not speak … What she can do, however, is emit pleasing sounds," the voice and the body reinforcing one another (2005, 107). The subject enters the siren's delicate space of seductive charm – which she constructs both by the aura of her beauty and delicacy, and by her vocal performance – sublimated as it is by the Neoplatonic call; it is where the subject finds pleasure and spiritual guidance on his journey to the Divine.[11]

Dante's *Purgatorio* 19 offers a remarkable antecedent of the alluring, menacing hybrid female inhabiting appropriately the liminal space of purgatory. Imagined in a dream by the pilgrim, whose gaze transforms a stuttering and deformed woman into a beautiful, sweet siren, her song so seductive that he cannot turn his eyes from her, as he confesses (1970–5, 17–18). She reveals herself as a Homeric siren: "I am the sweet Siren who leads mariners astray in mid-sea, so full am I of pleasantness to hear. Ulysses eager to journey on, I turned aside to my song, and whoever abides with me rarely departs, so wholly do I

Fig. 1.1. *Odysseus and the Sirens*, Attic red-figured stamnos, ca. 480–470 BCE. British Museum, London. Erich Lessing / Art Resource, NY.

satisfy him" (1970–5, 19–24). The pilgrim is rescued from his dream by a holy woman who rebukes Virgil for not protecting him from the siren. Virgil rips the siren's clothing to expose her belly; the stench makes Dante avert his eyes. Dante's hybrid female, beautiful but deformed and babbling, monstrous in his imagination, echoes in a real sense the familiar scene from the *Odyssey* on a Greek attic vase, now in the British Museum (see figure 1.1). It depicts Odysseus, tied to the mast, his men rowing the boat, while winged sirens hover above. The siren is portrayed as a type of beast, a monster in her hybridity, with a beautiful face but the body of a predatory bird, with claws. The medieval Christian tradition, which inspired Dante, follows this archetype of the siren as half woman, half bird, for moral purposes, a threat to the life journey of men.

Herrera's fascination with the power of voice is displayed in sonnets that stage compelling performances of female songs and their reverberation in acoustic spaces: the soundscape of Philomela's forest, a vibrating world both sonorous and silent, where her voice cries out from a wound that speaks her trauma, which is re-enacted in a nuanced and urgent plea by the lyric subject; the seascape of a Homeric siren, whose seductive voice draws the subject to his death; and the delicate space of a hybrid angelic siren who seduces with her beautiful body and voice among her rocks for a Neoplatonic journey. These voices belong to a cultural world of foundational narratives, of borrowed textual fragments that authorize the lyric subject as the writer of recast tales within new acoustic spaces.

Notes

1 For insights on the importance of voice and sound in the early modern period, see, for instance, Smith (1999), Bouza (2004), and Font-Paz (2022).

2 On Herrera as a humanist, see Torres Salinas (2019) and Schwartz (2016). On Herrera's *Anotaciones* to Garcilaso's poetry, the best source of his knowledge of the classics and contemporary literary and philosophical traditions, see especially, the essays in López Bueno (1997), with bibliography, Navarrete (1991), and Montero (1987). On Herrera's love poetry, see in particular Macrí (1959, 283–422), Torres (2013, 60–94), Navarrete (1994, 168–89), McNair (2003), and Valencia (2021, 83–123), who relies on and extends Middlebrook's poetics of masculinity in early modern lyric texts (2009).

3 Citations from Herrera's poetry come from Cuevas's edition (1985), with page numbers indicated in the text. Translations are mine, except for the translation of "Serena Luz," which comes from Rivers (1974, 124–5), with emendations.

4 Ovid follows the Hellenistic version of the myth of Philomela. The Roman version has Procne transform into the nightingale, whose song mourns her dead son. Philomela is transformed into a swallow, which can only chirp since her tongue has been severed. On Procne, see Segal (1994b).

5 María Rosa Lida wrote long ago on the nightingale's resonant voice in the quiet of Virgil's night, "el ruiseñor doliente se agiganta en la soledad y aislamiento de la noche" (the pained nightingale grows large in the solitude and isolation of the night; 1975, 105). For a study of the nightingale in sonnets by Góngora, with details on Garcilaso's and Herrera's lyric subjects, see Amann (2013).

6 Garcilaso's citation comes from García Aguilar's edition (2020). Translation is from Dent-Young (2009).

7 See also Chartier (2007, 86).

8 Enterline (2000, 4). Enterline argues that "where the narrator stutters at the effort to turn [Tereus's] unspeakable act into verse [revealed in the term *nefas*: "unspeakable"], Philomela is imagined to coax an expert weaving out of an unintelligible, hence 'barbarous,' instrument."

9 Marsilio Ficino, one of the eminent Renaissance melancholics, connects melancholia and creativity in his *De vita libri tres* (1480–9). For Ficino, the melancholic temperament issues from Saturn, a dark and malevolent planet, which is also the "iuvans pater" of men of intellect, of the exclusive subjectivity of men of genius. In a letter to his friend Giovanni Cavalcanti, he defines melancholia as a "unique and divine gift" (1985, 2:34). On Ficino and melancholia's inspiration and gifts of prophesy shared by Spanish early modern physicians and treatise writers like Huarte de San Juan (*Examen de ingenios*, 1575) and Juan Luis Vives (*Tratado del alma*, 1538), see Orobitg (2010). On melancholia, see Klibanski, Panofski, and Saxl's now classic study (1964), Jackson (1986), Soufas (1990), Agamben (1993), Orobitg (1997), Ferri Coll (2006), de la Flor (2007), and Carrera (2010), with an extensive bibliography.

10 On the stony lady, see Dante's *Rime petrose*, in Dante (2014). On Petrarch's canon of beauty, see Vickers (1982).

11 The hybrid female follows a well-established tradition that passes to early modern poets via the blessed and enticing, menacing and alluring Laura of Petrarch's *Rime sparse*. The heavenly siren of the *Rime* is a nuanced representation of the singing sirens of Platonic thought, who inhabit the celestial spheres with the Fates, known to Petrarch through Cicero and Macrobius. But the sweet, angelic voice has another side, for this siren is crafted by Love. She is the seductress who lives on earth and controls the lover's destiny, threading and unwinding the spool "of his appointed life": the sweetness of her song, complains the lyric subject, "binds my senses … reins/my soul, though ready to depart, with the *great desire* for/the blessedness of *hearing*" (Petrarch 1976, sonnet 167, 7–9; my emphasis).

2 "Ward off this Gloomy Darkness": Spaces of Conflict and Sublimity in Calderón's *La vida es sueño*

FREDERICK A. DE ARMAS, UNIVERSITY OF CHICAGO

Distraught by the "disabling darkness" (Longinus 1991, 9:14)[1] in which Zeus has immersed him and his companions as they struggle to recover the body of the fallen Patroclus, Ajax calls upon the god to bring forth the light, to illuminate the space of battle. This will enable them to fight the Trojans, even onto death – "And in the light destroy us, if you must" (Longinus 1991, 9:14; *Iliad* 17.647).[2] *On the Sublime*, an ancient treatise attributed to Longinus, replete with allusions to Homer, invokes the above-cited passage from the *Iliad* as a striking example of human aspiration and its confrontation with the divine, as conveyed in a moment where "greatness appears suddenly" (Longinus 1991, 1:4) as if it were a lightning bolt from above. In reality, Ajax does not fully understand Zeus's purpose – to extend the battle to honour the fallen Patroclus. At the same time, the warrior's prayer shows his piety and his valour. Although the sublime may grip the soul through the verses of the poet, it also moves the emotions through the spaces created by the words. For example, the treatise depicts a land covered in mist in the *Iliad* (Longinus 1991, 9:14); points to threatening towers built by giants in the *Odyssey* (Longinus 1991, 8:11); and etches the gates of a prison in Demosthenes (Longinus 1991, 15:26). Although Longinus's fragments were thought to have "never found a congenial spirit" during the Renaissance and well into the seventeenth century (Curtius 1973, 400), new studies have led us to reconsider this question and foreground Francesco Robertello's first edition of 1554, which soon competed with those of Paolo Manuzio (1555) and Francesco Porto (1569). Latin, Italian, and English translations followed (Refini 2012, 34–5).[3] As newly discovered echoes of Longinus are detected in Montaigne and Shakespeare, in Milton and Racine, it is imperative to look for sublime moments and its spaces in the literature of Renaissance and Imperial Spain. Cervantes, for example, invokes the sublime in his brief history of the theatre published with his *Ocho comedias y ocho entremeses* (*Eight Plays and Eight Interludes*; 1615); while Pedro Calderón de la Barca includes veiled allusions to Longinus as tutor of Queen Zenobia of Palmyra in his early play *La gran Cenobia* (Cenobia the great; de Armas 2019, 50–65).

Taking Longinus as a point of departure, this essay turns to Calderón, *La vida es sueño* (*Life Is a Dream*; ca. 1630) in order to explore the dark, mythical, and ghostly spaces of sublimity. Here we set out to discover how the architectures of the tower or prison, shadowed by mountains, are able to inject the work with an emotional grandeur akin to the disabling and painful darkness that enveloped Ajax. While *La vida es sueño* commences with sublime verses and spaces to set the tone and allow the ensuing action to preserve some of its echoes, we will argue that it dissipates once we pass into the more common realms of courtly endeavours. It returns but briefly to its full sublimity, thundering down upon the scene at the end of the second act, disabling space through Segismundo's dream metaphor. Thus, this essay seeks to bring to light how in his philosophical, tenebrous, comforting, and discomfiting modes, Calderón "compels his audience to see what he has imagined" (Longinus 1991, 15:24), to see the spaces of the sublime.

We will begin then the with the impacting first scenes of the play where grandeur yields to greatness.[4] Here, Calderón's natural and fabricated architectures construct a setting most appropriate for the grandeur of the work and for its flashes of greatness. These elevated spaces point to the sublime. After all, the original Greek title of Longinus's treatise was *Peri Hypsous*, meaning "aloft" or "on high," that is, close to the gods. Thus, elevation in space goes together with a high tone and style for the work. Flashes from above and glances of the underneath lift us with its eminent concepts and notions.[5] As the play opens, we view Rosaura dressed as a man, descending on horseback from the top of a cliff. The very heights in which she finds herself as well as her disguise[6] open the possibility that we are in the presence of a deity envisioned above. Calderón may be recalling here Longinus's example on how Homer magnifies the divine. Citing the *Iliad* (5.772), "The thundering steeds of gods leap at one bound," the Greek treatise praises the "cosmic dimension" as well as the "extravagance and grandeur" of the description (Longinus 1991, 9:13). In Calderón's play, Rosaura is a figure akin to a goddess. After all, she takes on the name of Astraea later in the work as she enters the court in disguise. Astraea was the last of the immortals to leave earth and would be the first to return, heralding a new Golden Age.

However, she does not pause in the realms above to look down. She is not akin to Michel de Certeau's voyeur who looks down from the top of a building; she is not "a solar Eye, looking down like a god" (de

Certeau 1984, 92). She is unaware of her power, since she feels power-less even at such exalted heights. She is riding the cliffs and cannot control her runaway horse.

Rather than a celestial space, the heights are configured as conflictive, as laboured. This initial scene thus inverts a reader's perception, placing the up high as a space not to be desired. I emphasize the term "reader" since the many spaces of performance would lead us in many other directions. Thus, we will stay with the text and not its many dramatizations and representations. Here the reader stands aghast as Rosaura blames the horse that leads her to fall from on high, and fall from the mountains of Muscovy to the rocky plains of Poland. At the same time, this fall could actually be a signal that she has been unable to control her passions; that she has lost her honour; that she comes to Poland in search of justice. Astolfo, prince of Muscovy, has dishonoured her and left her. Let us recall that Astraea is the goddess of justice that will return to earth in its moment of greatest darkness (de Armas 1986, 98–107). Thus, Calderón has interwoven a "nobility of conception" (Longinus 1991, xiv) with the highest and most abstruse aspirations (a goddess in the guise of a fallen woman who will bring about a Golden Age) since, as Longinus asserts, the human being "admires what passes his understanding" (Longinus 1991, 35:48). As the play shows the clash between upwards and downward spaces, it configures Rosaura as a conflictive figure, a woman whose inner psychic space is in turmoil. At the same time, Calderón is invoking the ancient conception of the circularity of time. Humans arise in a Golden Age where they live among the gods, only to lose perfection through the ages, falling gradually to total injustice and constant war as found in the Age of Iron. Astraea heralds the return of the first age at the moment of greatest darkness.[7] The work, then, begins with a doubling of spaces, the material one representing mountain and rocky plain and the cosmic one representing the heavens and the return of a goddess to earth.

The first two words of the play, "hipogrifo violento" ("wild hippogriff"; Calderón de la Barca 1994, v.1; 1873, 7) are of great significance in terms of the sublime, and also open up new spaces.[8] The first translations of the treatise emphasize much more than the Greek original the violence of the sublime. The Latin version of Pietro Pagano points to "the agitation and affecting of souls, which is violent, and rapturing the soul" (Lehtonen 2016, 453). Kelly Lehtonen explains, "With this expansion, Pagano draws particular attention to the violence of emotion, speaking as if the sublime were an abstract power that actively ravishes the soul of the author. [Niccolò] Da Falgano's Italian translation also expands on the original, claiming … an emotional force as violent as

one coming from divine furore and apt to inspire [or inflame] others"
(2016, 453). The violence that surrounds Rosaura's arrival in Poland,
her runaway horse, the creature she rides described in terms of chaotic
elements, her fall, her pseudo-divine arrival seem conjured by a hand
that is passionately inspired, one that fashions dynamic spaces. Even
the similarities between the action and the Homeric gods that gallop
above form a charged atmosphere of violence, a thunderbolt of emotion that can be seen to emerge from the written word and is bound to
agitate not just Rosaura's being, but that of the readers of the play. Inner
turmoil is expressed through a whirlwind of spaces.[9]

If we turn to the second term in the play, the horse as metaphoric hippogriff, a creature of myth, derived from Ariosto's epic, we will soon
come to realize that one of the origins of the initial agitation has to do with
Strife. A hippogriff is in itself an impossibility, since, according to ancient
tales, horses hate gryphons and will not mate with them. Lope de Vega,
Calderón's predecessor, had forbidden the use of this term. Calderón
utilizes it as the first word in the first play of the first volume of his collected works to challenge his predecessor (de Armas 1993, 3–4; Güntert
2002, 495–507). Longinus argues that one of the roads to greatness "is the
emulation and imitation of the great prose writers and poets of the past"
(1991, 13:22). Alluding to Hesiod's *Works and Days*, Longinus explains
that one of two forms of Strife (Eris) is "blessed to men" – that which
leads to emulate other poets, thus echoing his first point (1991, 13:22).

Calderón takes this point to heart and seeks to surpass Lope de Vega,
his famed predecessor, utilizing "hippogriff," a term he had despised,
turning it into the very image of a second type of Strife. Although actually a horse, Rosaura's naming transforms the space into a quasi-myth-
ical landscape that hints at her divinity. The condition of the earth as
she descends or falls is one of confusion, recreating an architecture of
disharmony. The four elements, which according to Empedocles com-
mingle to create cosmos, are out of order, no longer ruled by Love. As
Strife prevails, elements, horses, and humans are in disarray. The play
allows us to glimpse at a cosmic non-space, the space of chaos that
reigned before cosmos.

During her tumultuous descent, Rosaura feels agitated, uncertain,
addressing her emotions to the runaway horse that rushes down with
the speed of the wind (1994, v. 2). In this rather unusual use of apostrophe, she raises the horse to the category of myth just as she scolds a beast
that cannot understand her.[10] By using this figure of speech, she forces
the reader to peer at that which she addresses, almost forcing some kind
of visualization. In doing so, the monstrous becomes one more element
that serves to fashion a chaotic and threatening space. Rosaura directs

her terror and uncertainty to the horse, using a series of animal meta-phors linked to the four elements in order to show that this non-human animal does not even follow his instincts (1994, v. 5). Kenneth Asher reminds us that "Longinus praises the concentration of intense details in which the person's body seems simultaneously alienated and over-whelmingly engaged" (2017, 35). Rosaura may seem, on the one hand, as if she is merely witnessing what is happening to her and narrating it. However, her cries and her irrational questioning of her horse shows her as overwhelmingly engaged. As the horse throws her, she dismisses the beast in a passionate metaphor. The hippogriff transforms into Phaeton. In his edition of the play, José Ruano de la Haza points out that the meta-phor is inappropriate since Phaeton is the charioteer who, guiding the horses of the Sun, through inexperience falls from on high and is killed. Ruano prefers to see Segismundo as a Phaeton, although again the com-parison is not without difficulties (1994, note to v. 10). Longinus refers to a passage in *Phaeton*, a lost play by Euripides, where in the description of the flight and fall "the poet's mind itself travels along in the chariot and shares the perils" (1991, 15:25). Calderón, in many ways, follows Aeschylus and Longinus. The play shows us Rosaura's perils and we seem to travel through her enunciated thoughts, through the spaces of her mind, as she desperately clings to the horse, questions him, falls and is left almost blinded by fear and passion. Space preserves its dynamism and is related to thought, passion, and experience. Downed but not defeated, she asserts that she will follow the path of destiny while "ciega y desesperada" ("benighted, desperate, blind"; 1994, v. 13; 1873, 7). As with Ajax, she wishes for light, but none seems to be forthcoming in the labyrinthine descent from the mountain. She remains in the threatening and unfamiliar space where the gods have placed her.

The natural architecture of heights, and horrors, as Rosaura is plunged headlong down the cliff blinded by nature's "aspereza enmarañada" ("rough mountain"; 1994, v. 14; 1873, 8) is further highlighted by the encroaching gloom.[11] It is twilight. Inspired by Ajax's cry for light, which he quotes, Edmund Burke, many centuries after Longinus, relates dark-ness to the sublime. In the dark all perils are greater, he declares, so that one is "forced to pray for the light" (1998, 172). Rosaura does not pray; she just moves ahead, failing to be distracted by the comic words of her servant, who is constantly afraid, forever hungry, always hop-ing for a soft bed. The comic is a mere distraction that cannot efface the ominous action. Once in Poland, the more open spaces fail to bring relief to the travellers. As Yi-Fu Tuan asserts, "Space is a common sym-bol of freedom in the Western world" since "it suggests the future and invites action." However, it has a negative side: "space and freedom are a threat" (1977, 54). Rosaura has left her home in Muscovy, the "place" of security, albeit marred by Astolfo's dishonourable deeds. She is now in the open spaces where threats abound, as she seeks to find a way to restore her honour. Indeed, the rocky plains are not without danger. Rosaura points out to her servant Clarín that an almost phantom-like structure can be seen beyond: "a la medrosa luz que aún tiene el día, / me parece que veo / un edificio" ("half-lit by the moon's ray / And the declining day, / It seems, or is it fancy? that I see / A human dwelling?"; (1994, vv. 52–4; 1873, 9). If the first sublime moment in the play had to do with a runaway horse, runaway passions and emotions, the presence of deities on high (Astraea and Phaeton), a cosmic fall and the two forms of Strife, this next moment seems more tranquil, while at the same time building suspense. As darkness approaches, an edifice, perhaps a rustic tower, begins to take form beyond – perhaps an echo of the mountains she descended, a human rather than a natural architecture.

Again, much like Ajax, Rosaura would wish for light, even if it were to disillusion her and lead her to a more dangerous and terrifying space. The very description of the building partakes of sublimity in its very rusticity, as the threatening nature around it fabricates and conceals it:

> Con tan rudo artificio
> la arquitectura está de su edificio,
> que parece, a las plantas
> de tantas rocas y de peñas tantas
> que al sol tocan la lumbre,
> peñasco que ha rodado de la cumbre. (1994, vv. 59–64)

> (Of such a rude device
> Is the whole structure of this edifice,
> That lying at the feet
> Of these gigantic crags that rise to greet
> The sun's first beams of gold,
> It seems a rock that down the mountain rolled.) (1873, 9)

In many ways we can regard the building as a kind of reverse tromp l'oeil, where a three-dimensional building appears as if it were one of those grotesque paintings in the Renaissance where animal, vegetable, and human elements intermingle. When Richard A. Etlin used the sublime to speak of the Domus Aurea and the Roman Pantheon, Michael Silk decided to castigate him for trying to link it to "Longinus' citation of Aeschylean passages with architectural reference" (2012, 520).

Nevertheless, we have already noted the continued presence of architectural spaces in Longinus's examples of the sublime. In addition, Etlin understands the sublimity of nature, as he points to the starry heavens as a source for such an emotion.[12] He also notes that the Roman Pantheon renders homage to the cosmos as a celestial temple (2012, 244), as, for example, how the oculus is able to bring in the light of the sun whose shining sphere keeps moving across the temple throughout the day. As night approaches it travels with increasing speed, suddenly disappearing "as if drawn out by the oculus" (Etlin 2012, 246). A similar discomfiting experience brings out the sublime in Calderón, as the outside twilight suddenly turns into the mouth of night born from inside the tower. Calderón's verses place the reader in the midst of nature, offering a discomfiting experience, a moment when reason is overwhelmed by an image, a building, one that unites nature and culture in ways difficult to understand. It becomes a space of uncertainty.

In the architectural passage, Rosaura clearly connects the "natural" edifice with a large rock that has fallen from the top of the mountain. Thus, it partakes of sublime height. After all, towers are often substitutes for high spaces in strategies for battle. At the same time, this rustic eminence creates astonishment at the almost absent differentiation between nature and artifice. The notion that the building has rolled down from the hill also calls to mind the myth of Sisyphus, who is condemned to continuously roll a boulder up to the top of a mountain. Since he never quite makes it, he has to start the task all over again, eternally. The building, then, is associated with a condemned man, thus creating through subtle allusion a feeling of dread. While for Burke poetry's very obscurity partakes of the sublime (1998, 105), Longinus turns to rhetoric to explain that "the best use of figure is when the very fact that it is a figure goes unnoticed" (1991, 17:29). In the case of the rustic building imaged as Sisyphus's rock, the realization comes slowly, hardly noticed, as the text moves ahead to further terrors. As the reader continues to peruse *La vida es sueño*, she is more and more enmeshed in spaces that create uncertainty, fear, and agitation.

From a quasi-natural architecture that astonishes, the edifice becomes even more menacing when its opening is compared to the mouth of a beast, and more than that, a mouth that reveals that night is born within: "desde su centro / nace la noche" ("From which as from a womb / The night is born"; 1994, vv. 71–2; 1873, 9). The uneasiness of twilight turns into the terror of night. Modulating light and darkness transforms spaces, increasing the agitation of the characters and that of the readers. A tremulous light that can be glimpsed within the dark night of the tower further enhances fear and uncertainty. Rosaura's reaction, as she gazes into the tower, is replete with images so palpable and so astonishing that they bring to the reader's mind the very image of horror and shows her own terror and astonishment. Longinus asserts that "great and passionate expressions affect our mind more closely; by a kind of natural kinship and brilliance they are seen before the figures, whose artistry they overshadow and keep hidden" (1991, 17:29). Thus, whosoever hears Rosaura feels the passionate expressions as they come to the mind's eye in a profusion of forms. Mesmerized by the feeble light that emerges out of night and the tower, Rosaura asks,

> ¿No es breve luz aquella
> caduca exhalación, pálida estrella,
> que, en trémulos desmayos,
> pulsando ardores y latiendo rayos,
> hace más tenebrosa
> la obscura habitación con luz dudosa? (1994, vv. 84–90)

> (Is not that glimmer there afar –
> That dying exhalation – that pale star –
> A tiny taper, which, with trembling blaze
> Flickering 'twixt struggling flames and dying rays,
> With ineffectual spark
> Makes the dark dwelling place appear more dark?) (1873, 10)

Her questions, her tentative and obscure language recall once again Ajax's prayer: "Ward off this gloomy darkness" (Longinus 1991, 9:14). She cannot believe that her sight is constructing a paradox, that of a tremulous light that darkens the tower. As with the building itself, which appeared to be made of parts of nature, the dark light within brings to her mind aspects of the heavens. At first, she conceptualizes the dark light as a dying exhalation, thus referring to the strange phenomena that were said to create comets: "Like clouds are formed by humid vapours exhaling from warm water, heated earth releases a hot dry exhalation which ascends to the upper regions of the terrestrial realm. Comets appear when the earthly exhalations reach the fiery region and ignite" (Tessicini 2018, 2). Did the exhalation fail to catch fire? Is this a fire that is now extinguished, leaving behind but a semblance of light? Comets were signs of ill fortune, and thus, Rosaura's image is an inauspicious one. It transforms a darkened space into a menacing one. This is followed by the possibility that the light is a "pale" star. Shining in the night, such a tenuous light would fail to give much comfort. As if connecting the cosmic architecture with her own emotions, Rosaura then conceives of this light as tremulous in fainting, a corporeal response that takes place in times of feebleness or danger. She further attaches cosmos to body when she uses the verbs "pulsando" and "latiendo." Both terms come from Latin, the first meaning to hit or touch and thence the pulsing of veins and arteries, the latter referring to the bark of a dog, coming to mean the beat of the heart. The light, as if in tune with Rosaura, is hitting her, barking at her, creating dread, as her heart and pulse become one with the mysterious and feeble light. The threatening outer space enters her being creating an agitated inner space. It is no wonder, then, that she concludes that this light makes the habitation even more gloomy and dark. Light, then, is a determining factor of this space. The terror of darkness allows her to paint the scene with a faint chiaroscuro where light, rather than enhancing a scene surrounded by darkness, makes it even more obscure and sinister. Not even Hendrik van Cleve III's painting *The Building of the Tower of Babel* can evoke such tempestuousness, dread, confusion, and chiaroscuro.

Regaining her reason, setting aside her fears, Rosaura concludes that this dreaded space is a prison and that it must harbour a "vivo cadaver" ("living corpse"; 1994, v. 94; 1873, 10). This oxymoron and the appearance of a man dressed in skins, a kind of monster of the labyrinth, a ghost that emerges from the darkness with a faint light, points to the gothic sublime of the nineteenth century with the "lofty towers, dark nights, ghosts and goblins ... moans, sighs ... tyranny, incarceration" (Morris 1985, 301). The natural and the supernatural, life and death, come together, providing an experience of terror felt by characters and audience. They have also moved not just through a series of scenes that take us from the mountain tops to the plains and then closer and closer to a tower, but we have also moved through what Javier Rubiera Fernández has called an itinerant space (2002, 1545–54). While this critic applies it to what an audience experiences at a performance, it can also be used to describe readers that move from one space to another as they follow the words of the characters. There is no abrupt change of scene, but an inexorable descent into what lies below, and then a slow approach to the dreaded tower. For Sebastián de Covarrubias, the term *torre* means "edificio fuerte para defenderse del enemigo" (a strong building to defend against the enemy; 1611, 49).[13] He explains that although it can stand alone, it is frequently part of a castle, rising higher and helping in the defence against enemies. In Calderón's play, it is a paradoxical space. Although it may well rise high for defence, the prisoner seems to be situated at the bottom of the tower. He cannot escape, being enchained. Just as the darkness is modulated to bring about an experience of terror, so is the vertical space of the towering edifice where its heights conceal the prisoner who seems to threaten from the ground.

This penumbral space of dread will only be attenuated when Rosaura's beauty strikes Segismundo as something that is beyond his own experience. This unleashes a sublime moment of awe as two characters deprived of justice and considering themselves "infelice" ("wretched"; 1994, vv. 22, 102; 1873, 8, 11) meet each other in the twilight of a fallen world and in the shadow of an "encantada torre" ("enchanted tower"; 1994, v. 83; 1873, 10).[14] Their encounter, too long to detail here, produces another hundred verses of sublime shock and emotion. While at one point, Segismundo would kill her with his "membrudos brazos" ("strong arms gaunt and grim"; 1994, v. 184; 1873, 13), at another he must confess "tu voz pudo enternecerme" ("Strange thy voice can so unbend me"; 1994, v. 190; 1873, 13). His passions and violent temperament are restrained by admiration, as her beauty becomes, for him, the strangest of sights. Beauty, which for neither Longinus nor Burke is in itself a sublime trait, acquires this very quality in Calderón's play since it is out of place, an unknown quality, and the cause of extreme emotion and awe.

Segismundo's reaction to this beauty and the reader's realization that they are both characters that have been brought down by fortune transforms a space of dread, imbuing it with some aspects of place. Let us recall Yi-Fu Tuan's dictum: "Place is security, space is freedom; we are attached to the one and long for the other" (1977, 3). In Calderón, the freedom of space has turned dangerous, menacing. Suddenly, as two human beings form a bond (albeit tenuous), the threatening space acquires some of the qualities of security ascribed to place. It is as if in the midst of a foreign space, the two begin to create a sense of harmony, a kind of imagined place where they can feel less violent or afraid.

Once Clotaldo arrives, the play, albeit calling on the mystery of Rosaura's sword, acquires the rhythmic pace of the dramatic action. The heights of terror and the lights of night dissipate in order to create a space more akin to palace plays. Readers and audiences come to recognize these new spaces. The suspense, amazement, and sublimity of the play's beginning give way to more familiar spaces. The palace only surprises in terms of space when Segismundo defenestrates one of the servants. The once imprisoned prince now abides at the court since his father is testing his ability to rule. Having failed the test, he is returned back to the tower. In this second instance, the space of the tower has lost its initial mystery. It retains it only for Segismundo, who cannot understand how he has awakened again in a space of incarceration. Clotaldo seeks to calm him, explaining that his experience at the palace had been just a dream.

Calderón reserves the full force of his now philosophical greatness for Segismundo's speech at the end of the second act. From it flows the title of the work and the questioning of the meaning of existence. Here we discover, in Longinus's words, humanity's power of "contemplation and reflection" (Longinus 1991, 35:47) as we perceive in awe how far Segismundo has come, from a resentful and brutal figure to one whose "thoughts often pass beyond the boundaries of the surrounding world" (Longinus 1991, 35:47). The spaces beyond, then, are within. His soliloquy on dreams, in a sense, destroys space, effaces both the threatening tower and the pretentious palace, questioning their very existence. It is as if *La vida es sueño* uses the liberating and threatening freedom of space in order to reject its outer manifestations. Sublimity is found in right action, in the inner spaces of the self. Curiously, the play never seems to fully find place, the safety of home and belonging. Only tenuous moments, when Segismundo is astonished by Rosaura's beauty or when Segismundo forgives his father, give us a sense of incipient place, of a harmony and safety yet to come. From the chaos before cosmos as alluded to at the beginning of the play, we travel through sublime and thunderous spaces to arrive at the insubstantiality of space in Segismundo's soliloquy.

The sublime expands the dark horizons of *La vida es sueño*, bringing together the natural architecture of mountains, rocky vales, and heavenly heights from which the gods can descend, with the earthly and eerie tower of Segismundo's prison. Violence and chaos come together with the gallop of the gods, with the fall from the horse. Indeed, Rosaura's passionate fall (as we travel with her thoughts through an itinerant space) takes her to a shadowed landscape and to an enchanted tower that exudes unfathomable mysteries. Spaces are dynamic, from mountain to rocky plain; from threatening twilight to the tower that yields darkest night. Space stretches beyond, with the illumination of mythical allusions (Astraea, Phaeton, Sisyphus) and with Ajax's plea for light. Passionate expressions both hide and foreground the sublime as it mixes with daring images and unexpected metaphors. Intimations of the heavens are embodied in corporeal spaces, while bodies point to the fragility of life. The expansiveness, dynamism, and mysteries of space collide with Segismundo's questioning of the space of this world. In Calderón's canonical play, the sublime resides in a space that may be nothing but illusion, and where light shines at its darkest as if chaos were at the door of humankind.[15]

Notes

1 This "disabling darkness" seems to be a kind of mist that surrounds the warriors. Jonathan Fenno explains that this occurs in three instances in the context of a slain warrior: it occurs in the battle for Zeus's son Sarpedon;

in the battle for Patroclus; and finally in Apollo's covering of Hector
with mist to prevent his body from decaying (2008, 5). The first two are
clearly similar. Indeed, the miraculous mist points to Zeus's sympathy
for Achilles's companion as well as to the later "cloud of grief" that will
envelope and frustrate him (2008, 8). The mist also prevents those outside
its range to know that Patroclus has been slain, and to notify Achilles. It is
thus a moment that allows Ajax to shine with valour in the darkness.

2 I am using G.M.A. Grube's translation of *On the Sublime*, giving the chapter
number and then the page. I have also used his translations of passages
from the classics, in this case *Iliad* 17.645–7. I have also consulted the
translation by W.H. Fyfe and Donald Russell as well as the introduction
and commentary by D.A. Russell of the Greek edition.

3 For an overview of Costa's research, see Mattioli (1988, 139–55). On
Robortello's edition, see also Refini (2012, 35).

4 As the editor of Longinus's text, G.M.A. Grube asserts, through the ancient
author, that "we must learn to differentiate between mere grandeur and
greatness" (1991, xiii).

5 By this I do not mean that the sublime is equated with one of the three
styles of the ancients, the high or sublime style. Kenneth Asher, for
example, asserts that 'Longinus begins by pointedly insisting that no
level of rhetorical proficiency can ever, by itself, explain true sublimity
(*hypsos*) of expression (2017, 33). Contrary to what a number of early critics
thought, the concept of the sublime, even in the Renaissance, moved
well beyond rhetoric. Lehtonen gives as one of many examples a specific
translation: "da Falgano translates 'hypso' as 'un concetto alto et pieno di
vanto' (a lofty concept and full of significance), explicitly classifying the
sublime as an abstract noun, rather than a stylistic quality" (2016, 451).

6 In classical texts, a theophany, the appearance of a deity to a human, often
takes the form of a disguised god or goddess. In Virgil, for example, Venus
appears to Aeneas as a hunter.

7 This constantly repeating circle of time is common to many ancient
societies. In the Bhagavad Gita, for example, Krishna states, "Whenever
dharma is in decay and adharma flourishes, O Bharata, then I create
myself to protect the righteous and destroy the wicked, to establish
dharma firmly, I take birth age after age" (1967, 4.7–8; 262–3).

8 I will be citing from José Ruano de la Haza's 1994 edition of *La vida es sueño*
and will use Denis Florence MacCarthy's translation. I would prefer, in this
particular case, to refer to the hippogriff as "violent" rather than "wild,"
since the former term points to Rosaura's inner passions. The term "wild,"
however, had strong connotations for the Victorian English translators
of the Spanish play. Edward Byles Cowell emphasizes that readers of
Calderón must put away neoclassical precepts. Only then will they be

rewarded: "A wild and grand tone of fiction pervades his poetry, and lifts up all its incidents and details into a high atmosphere of lyric excitement" (1851, 292; de Armas 1987, 50). Going beyond Cowell, Edward FitzGerald, in his translation seeks to tame *La vida es sueño* which he calls a wild drama (de Armas 1987, 54).

  9 "His [Longinus] most famous metaphors for the sublime are the *whirlwind* and the *thunderbolt*, natural images that have a seemingly godlike origin" (Cheney 2018, 40).

10 Longinus also uses apostrophe to raise categories, in this case, from man to gods (1991, 16.4.27)

11 A more literal translation of the phrase would be "tangled roughness."

12 "When Immanuel Kant observed in *The Critique of the Power of Judgment* (1790) that the view of the starry heavens provoked the sentiment of the sublime, he was gazing into the epicenter of the potential relationship of architecture to the sublime" (Etlin 2012, 230).

13 The translation is my own.

14 For Alexander Parker, Calderón in this and other plays creates the "personal myth" of a fatherless son raised in a tower (1982, 247–56).

15 The sublime, then, is writing that takes us aloft, suspends us with admiration, awe, or terror. It thus creates a space within the self that echoes the impacting spaces of the work itself.

3 The Space of Memory: Three Sixteenth-Century Iberian Examples

MARINA S. BROWNLEE, PRINCETON UNIVERSITY

Space – both visual/material and virtual/mental – is inextricably linked to memory. This association is clear whether we think of antiquity with Cicero or Quintilian, Llull from the Middle Ages, Ficino from the Renaissance, or even prehistoric times with cave paintings and pictographs.

The "spatial turn" that is the focus of this volume suggests retrospection, a looking back to consider how space has functioned both historically and culturally. The humanities have, in fact, seen many constructive turns since the "quantitative turn" initiated in the 1960s, the "linguistic turn" a few decades later, and the recent interest in the "animal turn." A number of philosophers, social theorists, and geographers including Henri Lefebvre, Michel Foucault, and Edward Soja have focused their attention on various types of space that exist in our world.[1] And for the purposes of this essay I will reference primarily to Lefevbre's spatial triad of "Perceived Space," "Conceived Space," and "Experiential Space" (Lefevbre 1991, 36).

As to the first type, "Perceived Space," it concerns visible, material, and measurable phenomena. The second, "Conceived Space," is qualitatively different in that it focuses on mental, imagined space. "Experiential Space," by contrast, involves the lived and imagined possibilities and realities of collective experience. Each of these spaces changes from one culture to the next and its variations affect individual experiential space and critical thinking as well.

Sixteenth-century Iberia offers a prime example of each of these three types of spaces, all of which are linked to the production of memory. It was a time of significant scientific, technological, and imperial ventures fuelled by the space of intellectual curiosity and innovation that we associate with the early modern period. Pedro Mexía, the sixteenthth-century Spanish humanist encyclopedist – indeed, the first modern, that is, vernacular encyclopedist – illustrates his readers' urge to learn that stems from curiosity in his massive *Silva de varia lección* (1540) by making hitherto inaccessible learning available for the first time to his new, vernacular reading public. The way in which Mexía, Antonio de Torquemada, and Juan Huarte de San Juan reflect curiosity and modernity is what I would like to discuss here because of their implications for the space of memory. I view these three writers more as proto-encyclopedists than miscellanists, given that a miscellany according to the OED is "a mixture, medley, or assortment; (a collection of) miscellaneous objects or items," while an encyclopedia is defined as "a literary work containing extensive information on all branches of knowledge, usually arranged in alphabetical order."[2] Alphabetical order is lacking in the works of my three authors, but their contributions are definitely more than "an assortment of miscellaneous objects."

We tend to think of encyclopedias as collections of old facts, as documenting curiosity about the past. But, in fact, they always signal curiosity about the present. Indeed, encyclopedism is a constant of any period that perceives itself as modern. Curiosity as Barbara Benedict remarks, is "always the sign of the rejection of the known as inadequate" (2001, 4).

Given that "modernity" involves intellectual thresholds self-consciously exceeding what has come before, it is not surprising that such times document the breadth and newness of their timely perspectives – their "Conceived Space." Philosophers, scientists, and writers labour to discern what is true from what is false based on their updated knowledge. Epistemology is the focus, and encyclopedic projects make the rethinking of ideas and institutions possible by documenting such progress in understanding.

Obsessive information-gathering is obviously a function of curiosity and a mnemonic resource, but it is also essential to any major paradigm shift. In sixteenth-century Spain, from the government's census-taking to the Inquisition's insatiable "saber vidas ajenas" (public surveillance of private lives), to scientific recording of the exotic far reaches of the empire in all its particularity, it was crucial not only in providing a record of politically useful data but also for its contribution to advances in three unanticipated areas. The advances made by early modern information technology to modern encyclopedism, to the history of subjectivity, and to the invention of the novel in the sixteenth century all reflect the shift from passive wonder to active curiosity.

The insatiable sixteenth-century fascination with novel people, places, objects, and events in the early modern period results from both empirical study and actual expression, highlighting to an equal degree the enquiring subject and subjectivity, which is, of course, an eminently modern obsession. This new curiosity is evident also in the advent of the object-based *Wunderkammer* and in the invention of the museum. Curiosity about objects and information-gathering are, as Claude Levi-Strauss observes, central to early modern thought and empire, especially as a result of the discovery of the New World, which he describes as "that critical moment in modern thought when ... a human community which had believed itself to be complete and in its final form suddenly learned ... that it was not alone, that it was part of a greater whole, and that, in order to achieve self-knowledge, it must first of all contemplate its unrecognizable image in this mirror" (1979, 149).

Though modern readers have not viewed them as three interrelated studies in empiricism, it is no accident that Mexía's *Silva de varia lección* (1540/1551), Torquemada's *Jardín de flores curiosas* (1568), and Huarte de San Juan's *Examen de ingenios* (1575) are all obsessed by empiricism and modernity as well as by the epistemological consequences of each. Each of these three authors explicitly addresses the "curioso lector," and this obsession translates into a reconfigured "Thirdspace," the lived and imagined collective experience.

The fascination with miscellanies in sixteenth-century Iberia – and beyond – is clear. Of their popularity as best-sellers, Marcel Bataillon remarks (in a bit of an overstatement),

En el siglo XVI ... todo libro corría el riesgo de convertirse en miscelánea ... les pareció que, considerándolos en un todo, se podía elaborar con ellos una especie de traje de arlequín bastante agradable, que fuera al mismo tiempo un libro provechoso, haciendo que la verdad infinita de los fragmentos ... permitiera alimentar al espíritu, evitando la hartura. (1986, 637)

[In the sixteenth century ... every book ran the risk of being turned into a miscellany ... it seemed to [writers] that, all things considered, the books could be turned into a type of enjoyable harlequin suit that would also be instructive, allowing the infinite truth of the fragments to nourish the spirit without being excessive.][3]

While every single book written in Spanish Golden Age Iberia clearly did not run the risk of being turned into a miscellany, Bataillon is right in signalling the plethora of miscellanies that were published.[4] Moreover, each of these has its particular attitude towards the space of memory, given that each miscellany is inevitably the product of its idiosyncratic author.

Pedro Mexía's *Silva de varia lección*

In the sixteenth, century, Mexía's *Silva de varia lección* (printed in 1540 and revised in 1551) is the "flagship" of Iberia's early modern miscellanies, given that a flagship is the earliest and most important. In the first one hundred years of its existence, the *Silva* went through at least 107 editions and was translated 75 times in foreign languages – two remarkable statistics in any age. Mexía was born in Seville in 1497 and died there in 1551. A writer, humanist, and historian, he corresponded with such luminaries as Erasmus, Juan Luis Vives, and Juan Ginés de Sepúlveda. He became the official chronicler and cosmographer of Charles V, but he is known most widely for his encyclopedic *Silva*.

In terms of perceived, conceived, and experienced space, Mexía is rightfully proud in saying that he is the first to write a miscellany written not in Latin, but in Spanish:

> Aunque esta manera de escrevir sea nueva en nuestra lengua castellana y creo que soy yo el primero que en ella haya tomado esta invención, en la griega y latina muy grandes auctores escribieron así, como fueron Ateneo, Víndice Cecilio, Aulo Gelio, Macrobio, y aun en nuestros tiempos, Pedro Critino, Ludovico Celio, Nicolao Leóncio y otros algunos. (2003, 40)

> [Although this type of writing is new to our Castilian language, and though I believe that I am the first to write this type of book, in Greek and Latin many illustrious authors wrote the same way, e.g., Athenaeus, Cecilius, Aulus, Gellius, Macrobious, and, in our time, Pedro Critino, Ludovico Celio, Nicolao Leóncio and some others.]

In fact, he references a total of thirty ancient as well as six Renaissance (Italian) miscellanists in his own text.

It is significant that with a nod in the direction of Aulus Gellius's *Noctes Atticae* (*Attic Nights*), he writes, "quise dar estas vigilias a los que no entienden libros latinos … yo he procurado hablar de materias que no fuesen muy comunes ni anduviesen por el vulgo" (2003, 40) [I wanted to provide these vigils to those who do not understand books written in Latin … I have attempted to write about things that are uncommon and not known to the public at large]. Mexía's *Silva* (identified by book histories as "the bedside book of the age") offers its readers metaphorical, "intellectual flowers" crammed into his miscellaneous volume because he claims that "en las selvas y bosques están las plantas y árboles sin orden ni regla" (2003, 40) [in the forest there exist plants and trees lacking rule or order]. His is a "forest" in which readers "hunt" for knowledge. This compilation of information offered by the *Silva* constitutes both a celebration of often exotic detail but also a self-conscious violation of the Renaissance sense of order – calculated to engage and provoke his new vernacular readers by challenging their "Conceived Space."

In fact, Mexía owes much more to Aulus Gellius than his mention of nocturnal lucubrations and occasional subtexts and reminiscences. The *Noctes* is unique in ancient literature because of its authorial stance and its organization, and Mexía identifies strongly with both of these original features of the Roman author. Aulus Gellius proclaims his disorderly structure to be "deliberately lack[ing] arrangement by subject, discipline [or] chronology" (Anderson 2004, 105), in order to avoid "mere polymathy." Gellius's strategic disarray is calculated to avoid readerly monotony.

This same type of disorganized sequence is precisely what Mexía boldly proclaims and celebrates in his own text. And, of course, Mexía's emulation of Gellius should come as no surprise given that the Roman author played "a central role in the 15th- and 16th-century revival of learning" as Anthony Grafton reminds us (2004, 320).

Though Mexía was taken to task by a number of readers (such as Torquemada, who explains that his *Jardín de flores curiosas* is superior to the *Silva* because it is carefully organized), he is following the haphazard structure of the *Noctes* for the same reason – to avoid presenting his readers with a dry and predictable text. Neither Gellius nor Mexía seeks to present an organic system of knowledge of universals or general rules. They are both purposely unsystematic.

The original authorial "I" of Aulus Gellius is also unique in the annals of miscellany history because of its tongue-in-cheek nature. He "pays lip service," as Graham Anderson notes, "to traditional *exempla virtutis*, but he is just as likely to be interested or titillated by gossip about lapses of the great and the good" (2004, 106). As Anderson goes on to explain, "Gellius will just as readily cite the sanctity of an oath maintained by Hannibal, perhaps again for the sake of paradox: even the figure who represents the Roman idea of the devil incarnate is still pledged to maintain universal human values" (2004, 106). Historical examples abound, and by their occasional reimagining, Gellius addresses memory in a cagey way. He also includes folk tales and items of his own invention such as whether it is more desirable for a husband to possess two wives or a wife two husbands.

Mexía likewise includes historical figures – with the added advantage that he can draw on historical memory from the third to the sixteenth centuries as well as deploying his tongue-in-cheek allegations amid his serious remarks about the threat of Islam and the Ottoman Empire (e.g., chapters 12–16). It is striking to note the additional similarity of cultural contexts shared by Gellius and Mexía in their advancing the idea that they are both writing short chapters in order to accommodate the needs of "busy people" – a *topos* among Roman miscellanies (Vardi 2004). Busy professionals were the target audience of both authors, and even Augustine approved of "bite-size pieces that one can simply plug into one's own work" (Grafton 2004, 320). Like Gellius, Mexía is visibly concerned with the status of the book as physical, material object, with its production, use, and circulation, though with a significant difference. For Gellius, book rolls were the format while for Mexía books were in codex form. And though consulting the *Noctes* involved unfurling the roll to a particular passage, the *Silva*'s readers simply needed to turn the page.

As such, we see not only the perceived space of the book but also the conceived space of it in historical memory (antiquity to the 2nd century CE versus antiquity to the sixteenth century), and at the same time, the lived interpretative time and space of each individual reader and reading communities. Both authors at times toy with the authority of the *auctores*. Both invite readers to dip into their tomes at will, and to read not from beginning to end, but in the space of any episode or chapter that speaks to their curiosity at that moment. This is a kind of Google search *avant la lettre* – a type of *Rayuela* experience. Each author-figure is playing in the new urban space of readership, thereby endowing himself as well as his readers with a marked degree of individualism and subjectivity. While the proliferation of print is justly cited in connection with Mexía and the originality of his *Silva*, its authorial identity, its disordered presentation of subjects, and its great publication success, we must acknowledge that his use of the *Noctes* and his profound links to Gellius cannot be forgotten.

After a lengthy exploration of the history of writing surfaces such as papyrus, tablets, pergamine, and skins as well as a method of teaching reading to the blind (Mexía 2003, 543–6), Mexía – clearly focusing on a technology that Gellius did not have – foregrounds the importance of print culture, declaring that "printing is the greatest invention in the world":

Hallado el papel que agora usamos, es tanta la facilidad y copia, que ha ayudado infinito a las letras e libros. Pero sobre todo, el imprimir pues con tanta presteza se escriben tantos millares de libros. Fue y es la mejor invención del mundo. (2003, 546)

[The paper we employ these days is so easy to use and to copy that it has enhanced the publication of books infinitely. But above all, printing

is so quick that thousands of books can be written. It was and is the best
invention in the world.]

Clearly, the invention of print changed everything. The ways of
understanding the world were altered appreciably with the advent
of print in the modern world. Print is linked, as Benedict Anderson
observes, to the emergence of the novel and the newspaper in Europe;
and it is "the first modern-style mass-produced industrial commodity" (Anderson 2006, 34). Sold in great quantities yet ephemeral in their
one-day lifespan as bestsellers, modern newspapers, as Hegel notes,
serve as substitutes for morning prayers; they are, in other words, a
new, secular ritual, a medium that, as Elizabeth Eisenstein observes,
"encouraged silent adherence to causes whose advocates could not be
located in any one parish and who addressed the invisible public from
afar" (1968, 42).

The availability of cheap print meant that readers of all classes could
access it provided they were literate. By contrast, all of Gellius's readers
did not have that opportunity, given that his literate, educated reading
public was a much smaller and elite percentage of the population.

Despite this disparity, both authors claim to be obsessed about
space – about not being prolix but at the same time wishing that they
had more physical space on which to add further thoughts and anecdotes to their manuscripts. They both encourage their readers to decide
on the interpretations and degree of truth that they themselves must
choose, to be active critical readers. And each one offers various examples that clearly strain the reader's imagination. Mexía cagily writes
that switching a ring from one finger to another helps the memory: "
aunque paresce de poca importancia, todavía es algún provecho el que
se sigue de los anillos que algunos traen y llaman de memoria, que,
mudándose de un dedo a otro poniéndolos en cierta forma distinta de
como suelen, les son ocasión de reducir a su memoria las cosas de que
quieren acordarse" (2003, 779) [although it seems unimportant, there is,
nonetheless, an advantage to the link that some people make between
rings and memory; that is, by moving the ring from one finger to
another, they recollect those things that they want to remember]. While
Gellius speaks effectively about memory on various occasions, in terms
of thoughts and observations on memory, it is Mexía who stands out.

The eighth chapter of his third book is entirely devoted to many
forms of memory, including neuro-diverse conditions. He devotes all
of chapter 8 of part 3 of the *Silva* to cognitive changes. Many factors
can affect the faculty of memory adversely, as Mexía explains, "como
son enfermedades, heridas y contusiones en la cabeza, vejez, y súbito

miedo y caídas de alto" (2003, 575) [like illness, wounds and cerebral contusions, old age, sudden fear, and falls from heights].

The effects of such events are routinely diagnosed and recognized as leading to memory loss. However, Mexía goes on to report that some of the afflicted lose their memory entirely, while others only a part of it, such as Francisco Bárbaro (the Venetian aristocrat who travelled in Coluccio Salutati's circle). He was reputed to be a "varón muy docto en la lengua griega, de cierta enfermedad que tuvo, olvidó particularmente todo lo que sabía de griego, quedando en lo demás como de antes, que por cierto es cosa maravillosa" (2003, 575) [a very educated man recognized for his command of Ancient Greek who, as a result of an illness, lost all his knowledge of Greek though his memory still functioned perfectly in everything else]. To give another example of memory issues, he recalls how Herodes Atticus, the second-century sophist, was concerned that his son was unable to retain the letters of the alphabet in his memory. The father's original solution consisted of choosing twenty-four boys his son's age "y a cada uno dellos puso por sobrenombre una letra del a. b. c., porque nombrados los muchachos, y conosciéndolos, le quedase la memoria de las letras" (2003, 576) [and each one was given a letter of the alphabet as his nickname, because by naming the boys and knowing them, he retained the memory of the alphabet]. The illustrious orator Demosthenes, by contrast, forgot his oration to be delivered to Philip of Macedon because of stage fright (2003, 577).

On a more optimistic note, however, we learn that we can actually increase our memory, as Quintilian and Cicero affirm. This is done by creating a "memory palace" where space and memory are conflated:

> como si en una casa muy grande o camino o calle señalásemos con la imaginación e tuviésemos en la memoria muchos lugares e puertas. Después, por cada uno destos lugares ya conocidos, se han de poner con el pensamiento las imágenes de las cosas que se quieren acordar, poniéndolas por la orden que tienen señalados los lugares según que después se quieren acordar de las cosas ... Y ciertamente, por este arte y manera se puede decir y acordar grande número de cosas sin errar; y dello yo tengo alguna experiencia. (2003, 577)

[as if in a very large house or road or street we identified in our imagination and remembered many spaces and doors. After that, for each of those familiar places, images are placed of things that should be remembered, putting them according to the spaces that will lead to memory ... And by this method a great number of things can be recalled, and I myself have experienced this].

Finally, Mexía distinguishes the properties of "memory" as opposed to "reminiscence," a distinction made first by Aristotle. Mexía notes that even animals possess the faculty of memory, yet only humans have the power of reminiscence: "la reminiscencia en solo hombre la hay, que es acordarse con discurso y pensar como contemplando la cosa, discurriendo de lo general a lo particular, de la circunstancia y del tiempo, con consideración y entendimiento" (2003, 579) [only man possesses the power of reminiscence, which involves remembering words and contemplating the subject, moving from the general to the specific, the context and time-frame, with attention and understanding]. "La reminiscencia es una manera de investigar despertando a la memoria por algunas cosas que la hagan acordarse" (2003, 579) [Reminiscence is a method for stimulating memory by investigating things that make it remember]. He ends by informing his reader looking for even more insights on the faculty of memory to consult Marsilio Ficino's *De triplici vita*, where the curious can find "grandes receptas y avisos para curar y conservar la memoria" (2003, 579) [great prescriptions and advice to cure and preserve memory].

Though far from cramming thought-bites haphazardly into his forest, Mexía's plan is a very calculated one. A master of many genres and discourses, his accomplished versatility is evident in that he served as the cosmographer of the Casa de Contratación de las Indias, as the Cronista Oficial del Emperador en lengua romance, as *regidor de ayuntamiento* – as well as having written plays, and participated in *justas poéticas*. His chief written contributions were his encyclopaedic, historiographic, and moral works: the 1540 *Silva de varia lección* (it went through more than one hundred editions in the first two hundred years of its existence), the *Historia imperial y cesárea* (1545), and the *Diálogos y coloquios* (1547).

The *Silva* is iconic, representing both curiosity and modernity. It is a "first," as he proclaims with justifiable pride, for being an encyclopedic work written in the vernacular. Mexía is focused on the curious contemporary reader – the reader who does not know Latin, wishing to communicate uncommon subjects that are not generally known to the public ("materias que no fuesen muy communes, ni anduviesen por el vulgo"; 2003, 41), relating them constantly to the present. As such, Mexía foregrounds the variations that develop in terms of "Perceived" and "Conceived" Space as society evolves.

His learnedness is, moreover, admirable, evident in his referencing of Greek, Latin, and medieval authors, though he cites six Renaissance predecessors most of all. He does not simply evoke the erudition of previous sources, however, he criticizes them, very aware of offering new meanings to old texts.

Mexía is surprising because he is committed to dramatizing progress, to inserting irony and a sense of humour into his writing – things we would not expect from an encyclopedist. He is also committed in his 148 chapters – as he frequently remarks – to concision in an effort to please his readers. His narratives are, moreover, fascinated by the art of storytelling.

If we consider some of his references to "curiosity" and "modernity," we see from the beginning of his encyclopedic venture his focus on expanding the space of knowledge and thus, of memory. He is explicit in proclaiming the newness of his venture – to being the first to author a new invention in Castilian, as quoted above (2003, 40).

In his commitment to modernity, Mexía repeatedly focuses on his "modern" moment in a number of ways. He speaks of "los más doctos modernos," among them Antonio de Nebrija (ca. 1444–1522; 2003, 635), and he indicates the modernity of his enterprise in offering a new type of erudition – criticizing his sources and thereby yielding new meanings to old texts. He invents neologisms and emphasizes, in his narratives, recent or contemporary items that he then relates to the present.

Mexía's interest in illustrating the pairing of curiosity and modernity also expresses itself in a fascination with technology. The technologies of language acquisition, of reading, and of writing occupy some of his most memorable pages. The technologies of writing spaces, of surfaces, for example, a technology that permits blind people to write, consume his attention and, not surprisingly, the technological advances constituted by the printing press. As noted above, this is the "modern" invention that Mexía singles out as "la mejor invención del mundo" (2003, 546) [the best invention in the world].

At the same time that he savours such modern innovation and progress, though, he clearly does not simply correct erroneous attitudes from the past. This too speaks to his attentiveness to the space of memory by correcting previous received ideas. He admits, for example, that according to many venerable sources, the age of sixty-three is to be dreaded since many illustrious men (including Aristotle) died at that age. Mexía does not respect such numerology, seizing on it instead to entertain the reader: "Esto que tengo dicho, más lo quise escribir por curiosidad y ejercicio que porque lo tenga por muy verdadero" (2003, 294) [what I have said I wrote more out of curiosity and as an exercise than because I believe it to be true]. Likewise, he notes that not only writers from antiquity but even Petrus Gyllius, the sixteenth-century French naturalist, recounts the existence of a Triton: "hombre marino [que] se ascondía en una Cueva, y desde allí estaba en asechanza hasta ver alguna moza sola" (2003, 174) [an aquatic man who would hide in a cave, and from there he would hide until de saw a solitary maiden. Rather than dispelling this myth, Mexía says instead that "cosa que tantos la escriben, y el pueblo la tiene por cierta, no hay por qué se deje de creer" (2003, 174) [a thing that so many writers affirm, and that people assume to be true, has no reason to be disbelieved].

His playful authorial stance persists to the very end of his long book, not with a perspective on modern technology or perception, but rather with an evocation of the normal dry pedantry readers had come to expect from encyclopedic ventures since antiquity (with the exception of the *Noctes*). Adopting the stance of a typical didactic narrator committed to the communication of informative details, the massive *Silva* (amounting to more than nine hundred pages in Isaías Lerner's admirable edition) ends with a discussion of the accurate number of winds that exist in the world (something that Aulus Gellius does in 2.2 of his *Noctes*). We are told that the narrator need not resort to the "fábulas e alegorías poeticas que les dan padres y madres a los vientos ... que Ovidio tracta en sus *Transformaciones*" (2003, 927) [fables and allegories that fathers and mothers give to the winds ... that Ovid treats in his *Metamorphoses*]. Taking into account the four corners of the earth in a very lengthy explanation, Mexía concludes that there exist a total of thirty-two winds – referring to a well-known engraving that was not reproduced in the *editio princeps* (whose production he oversaw) or in the successive ones either – "como se verá en la misma figura, porque la escriptura es plática más confusa" (2003, 928) [as will be noted in the image because writing is more confusing]. These final words of his text thus acknowledge and undercut the power of words compared to the power of images, which is mischievous indeed. Telling the reader to reference the absent "figura" instead is his final (proleptically Borgesian) farewell.

Torquemada's Expansion of the Space of Memory

Antonio de Torquemada (ca. 1507?–ca. 70?) is the renowned – though somewhat enigmatic – author of four very diverse books. The most well-known is the *Jardín de flores curiosas* (1568), a best-seller that was translated into every major European language. He also authored the *Coloquios satíricos* (Satirical colloquies) in 1553, a social commentary in colloquy form that ends, surprisingly, in a pastoral environment. Keenly aware of the power of the pen, he likewise published the *Manual de escribientes* (Writers' manual) in 1574. His meta-literary *Don Olivante*, however, was stolen from him and published anonymously without his authorization in 1564.

This text – its theft and its pirated circulation are less frequently invoked than its disparaging mention in the bookish inquisition of Don Quijote's library, where it is referred to as a "tonel a "brick" (either because of its size or disapproval of its contents) – by the bumpkin priest who passes judgment on it with his fellow inquisitor, the equally questionable barber. The comic relief (and institutional critique) generated by this scene is enhanced by an additional commentary the country cleric makes – one that publicly, albeit obliquely, identifies the text's author for the first time in history. He remarks that

> El autor de este libro – dijo el cura – fue el mesmo que compuso a *Jardín de flores*; y en verdad, que no sepa determiner cuál de los dos libros es más verdadero, o, por decir mejor, menos mentiroso; solo sé decir que éste [*Olivante*] irá al corral, por disparatado y arrogante. (Cervantes, 2015)

> ["Its author … also wrote *The Garden of Flowers*, and to be frank I couldn't say which of the two is more truthful – or rather, less mendacious. What I can say is that this one [*Olivante*] shall go out into the yard [to be burned] for its arrogant nonsense."] (Cervantes 2003)

With respect to Cervantes's unequivocal roast of Torquemada's chivalric *Olivante* as well as his encyclopaedic *Jardín*, several points should be made. Firstly, the act of entrusting the Inquisition to a pair of bumpkins (the village priest and the barber) is a deflationary gesture, to say the least. Moreover, when Cervantes's narrators or characters make categorical assessments regarding other texts or ideas – reader beware. As he dramatizes time and again in so many of his texts, Cervantes is very aware that no one can prescribe interpretation. So the priest's outspoken pronouncements are at least as much a critique of his own powers as a reader as they are of Torquemada's texts. Not to mention that Cervantes appreciated and made use of the *Jardín* in his monumental *Trabajos de Persiles y Sigismunda* and in his *Coloquio de los perros* as well as in the *Quijote*, as Américo Castro has noted: "Cervantes tenía muy en la memoria este libro de Torquemada" (1925, 377n3, 391).

In this context we also recall that Cervantes is notorious in railing against books and literary environments that he prizes more highly than those about which he offers no commentary. Witness, for example, the romances of chivalry, which he categorically vilifies in the prologue to part 1. In the beginning of his text he explains that the whole project of writing the *Quijote* is to definitively demolish any shred of legitimacy that these books may contain – his text is "una invectiva contra los libros de caballerías, de quien nunca se acordó Aristóteles" (2015,

13) [from beginning to the end an invective against books of chivalry – which Aristotle never dreamed of] (2003, 15–16), as we are categorically informed in the prologue.

Of course, this remark is calculated to make the reader laugh, since the genre did not exist at the time of Aristotle. It is also a jibe at the hidebound, conservative Neo-Aristotelian critics who short-sightedly rejected the chivalric romance as pernicious imaginative fiction. We recall that the canon of Toledo surprises his readers by offering a profound defence of imaginative fiction – particularly of chivalric romance – in what amounts to Cervantes's most extended discussion of literary theory. Romance "purified" of the excesses of style and unbelievability could be the most satisfying and responsible of forms (both ethically and artistically). The canon himself admits to having written more than two hundred pages of such a romance, though he ultimately gives up the project because of the small readership that was able to appreciate the purified romance form. Again, with a touch of eminently Cervantine irony we recall that while the canon gave up writing his "purified romance," his creator not only thought and wrote about its allure, but assumed that his lasting legacy would be not the *Quijote* but his purified romance, the posthumously published *Trabajos de Persiles y Sigismunda* (1616).

The same argument can, I think, be made in the case of Cervantes's motivation for his disparaging remarks regarding Torquemada's *Jardín* (1568). In spite of the tremendous popularity that his *Jardín* enjoyed both at home and abroad, it has received relatively little modern critical attention not only because of Cervantes's negative assessment delivered by Don Quijote's friend, the priest, but because it falls through the traditional disciplinary cracks: it is not literary or historical. It treats both of these discourses, however, – as well as scientific, ethnographic, and philosophical ones, in its articulation of progress.

Traditionally characterized as belonging to the "miscellany" genre, a continuation of an ancient and medieval form, the *Jardín de flores curiosas* offers its readers intellectual rather than natural *flora*. As he tells us explicitly, each flower represents "an idea."[5] While the medieval *florilegium* reflects the association of narratives with flowers, Torquemada's are carefully collected and presented in his compendium of ideas (the product of human artifice and design), not chaotically strewn, as in the case of his predecessor Pedro Mexía in his *Silva*.

In contrast to Mexía's unruly *Selva*, Torquemada's manicured *Jardín* is carefully cultivated, divided into six days of logically conceived discussions between three humanist friends in a literal garden setting. In their trialogue, Antonio, Luis, and Bernardo dwell on such topics as the natural world, the supernatural realm of ghosts and witches, the meaning of Fate and the regions of the Far North – the *Septentrionis*. Torquemada's text is centrally concerned with the modern desire to understand the phenomenal world scientifically from his "modern" sixteenth-century perspective as well as to question the problematic yet culturally powerful and enduring status of myth and its relationship to reality. He combines such authorities as Pliny and Olaus Magnus with autochthonous and timely, currently debated issues: narratives pertaining to contemporary witch trials and the cultural paranoia they reflect, to the social and political implications of Moors and Jews, to Spain's imperial ventures in the New World, and to uniquely Spanish monstrosities and events.

Torquemada's is a cognitive, analytical garden devoted to the thorny problem of objects and objective truth, of "Conceived" space. It offers the reader a thought-provoking meditation on progress, modern science, and the value of empirical (rather than bookish) experience for the detection of human error in the pursuit of truth.

Everyone from philosophers to fans of tabloid fiction who read in order to become invested in (consumed by) the desire to rethink old assumptions and beliefs in the wake of geographic and ethnographic discoveries and of technological advances can no longer be content to adopt the wisdom of ancient and medieval *auctores* at face value. In the literary domain, this exploration of truth and fiction, of truth *in* fiction, was evident in the hotly debated Neo-Aristotelian *romanzi* polemic waged between the so-called Ancients and Moderns that concerned such literary titans as Ariosto, Tasso, and Cervantes so centrally.[6]

The status of truth – the sorting out of the space between science, history, and fables – is the mission of the *Jardín*'s three interlocutors. And this desire for a direct and unmediated experience of the truth, rather than a reliance on venerable authorities, is a modern pursuit. The interest of Torquemada's text is readily apparent to the multitudes of its curious readers at a time when there existed an unprecedented proliferation of print, providing contemporary discussion (referencing contemporary events) with an interactive philosophical apparatus and commentary by which to process the information contained within data collected from around the world, not from the reading of ancient authorities, but from empirical eyewitness testimony designed to corroborate or correct such traditional forms of knowledge and belief. Not surprisingly, such modern periods, naturally consumed with the conquest of scientific and intellectual domains, tend also to be times of political conquest. As Michael Taussig remarks, "scientific curiosity and conquest existed side by side" (2006, 190).

On the road to accomplishing its surprisingly modern epistemological venture – the desire to rethink ancient, medieval, and modern sixteenth-century myths and ideas and phenomena from the informed perspective of the day – this book is calculatedly organized. It is an innovative encyclopedic dimension in the history of the encyclopedia as genre. I would call it a proto-encyclopedia rather than a miscellany because of its coherent overarching theme.

As Richard Yeo explains, the Enlightenment provided a revolution in the development of the encyclopedic genre. Both in the Middle Ages and in antiquity as well, the cyclopedia or encyclopedia involved the cycle (κύκλος) of the Εγκύκλιος παιδία, the "circle of subjects considered the basis of a liberal education" (Yeo 2007, 48). Latinizing the Greek term and concept, Quintilian speaks of "a round of learning." This circular (circumscribed) metaphor representing the body of knowledge that any educated man should possess came to be replaced by a different spatial metaphor – the field. This transformation is addressed and justified by Jeremy Bentham, who explains that "By the image of a circle is presented the idea of a limited extent, determined by the circumference. By the image of a field no limitation whatsoever is presented" (Yeo 2007, 57).

Yeo's illuminating essay points to two essential developments in the encyclopedia's evolution regarding its premodern as opposed to its modern nature. In this context he explains that "From the early 1700s, the 'modern' encyclopaedia was in the ascendant. During the next half century this term came to signify the total of all knowledge, encapsulated in summary form, rather than the prescribed learning of an educated individual" (2007, 50).

It is significant that the *Jardín* does not conform to either category. It is decidedly encyclopedic in its ambitions, exceeding the boundaries of knowledge that an educated individual should control, but, as Torquemada himself points out at several moments, his work is by no means offering "the total of all knowledge." His subject matter – though decidedly encyclopedic in its scope – is avowedly selective. He admits that logically one could never address all the wonders and timely topics of the universe. Nonetheless, he, like Mexía, does offer a transitional phase in two senses: on the one hand, between the limited curriculum of the cyclopedia and the pretence of offering the sum of all knowledge in encapsulated form, and, on other hand, an additional intermediate stage between the cosmological ordering of the premodern encyclopedia and the alphabetically ordered modern form to which we are accustomed.

Torquemada's scepticism is programmatic and – to give one example made famous by the *Persiles* – we can cite the example of the "bird-producing tree." This anomalous tree is instructive in signalling the distance separating Cervantes's arboreal *excursus* from that of his predecessor. Torquemada's eponymous character, Antonio, records this striking avian metamorphosis with an intensely analytical eye, indicating that according to one source – Alejandro in the *Días geniales* – on the western shores of England the debris from shipwrecks gives rise to mushrooms (*hongos*) that turn into birds. Citing a different source thereafter, Antonio recounts that Pope Pius II (Aeneas Silvio Piccolomini) offers an appreciably different explanation for the origin of these birds, i.e., in Scotland there are trees by the water's edge whose leaves wither, falling into the water, thereafter producing worms that become birds that take to the skies. A third explanation exists in Cassaeus's *Catalogus gloriae mundi*, which alleges that these birds, native to England, are the result of an *árbol milagroso* that grows next to the water's edge. The fruit it bears, if it falls to the ground, rots and wastes away, yet if it falls into the water, it turns into a bird that takes wing and flies away. Some sources claim that many such trees existed, resulting in numerous "wood birds" of this sort.

Torquemada does not stop his *excursus* here, however, with this catalogue of sources. Instead he adds one more detail, culled from a *mappa mundi* printed by the Venetian cartographer Andreas Valvasor, which claims that his neighbour Andreas Rofo had in his possession at the time during which the *mappa mundi* was produced not one but two of these birds: "tenía al presente dos de estos pájaros de tamaño de dos ánades pequeñas, y que se los había llevado de España" (1982, 205) [had, at that time, two of these birds of the size of small *ánades*, which had been brought to him from Spain].

Antonio takes issue with this account as a result of what he assumes to be a scribal error ("debe estar errada la letra"; 1982, 205). He assumes instead that the journal entry should have referred to England or Scotland rather than Spain, "pues no estaría tan encubierto este milagro, si en España estas aves se engendrasen o se criesen" (1982, 225) [It would not be such an unknown miracle if these birds were native to Spain]. Voicing scepticism concerning such differing accounts of this interspecies *rara avis*, his interlocutor Bernardo suggests that though it might be a miraculous phenomenon ("un milagro"), it may also be a fabrication ("cosa fingida") (1982, 205).

The space of memory is also challenged as Torquemada, early in the text, considers human reproduction. In the *Jardín*'s first book, Antonio, the author's eponymous narrator-protagonist, alludes to the celebrated case in chapter 12 of Augustine's *City of God* of a white couple that engendered a black child (1982, 123). Antonio accounts for the striking racial disparity by concluding that the woman, at the moment of conception, must have been thinking about or imagining the portrait of a Moor represented in a painting on the wall. Antonio explains that in addition to Augustine's attribution of this racial anomaly to the power of the imagination, other thinkers, ancient (e.g., Plutarch) as well as modern (Ambroise Paré), concur with this diagnosis. Yet he himself takes issue with them, saying that it is instead a question of genetics: "Eso no fue por esa vía, sino porque naturaleza hizo un salto del abuelo al nieto, que pareció haber sido la madre concebida de un etíope en adulterio, y lo que en ella encubrió por salir blanca, descubrió en el hijo, saliendo de ella negro" (1982, 123) [It did not occur in that way, but rather because Nature jumped from the grandfather to the grandson, whom the mother seemed to have conceived adulterously with an Ethiopian, and what she concealed by being white was revealed by her son who came out black].

This passage seems to be at least – if not more – interested in questioning cultural memory and genetics than it is in the ancestor's sinfulness. Torquemada's insight here is very progressive. Speaking primarily of eighteenth-century developments (but equally applicable, I think, in its implications for Torquemada), Thomas Laqueur explains that: "scientific race, for example – the notion that either by demonstrating the separate creation of various races or by simply documenting difference, biology could account for differential status in the face of 'natural equality' – developed at the same time and in response to the same sorts of pressures as scientific sex" (1990, 155).

This is a striking example of the scepticism that Torquemada occasionally stages for his reader. He is, moreover, acutely aware of encyclopedism in diachronic terms. He ends his monumental labour by acknowledging the relentless effects of progress – which, he notes, will before long make his work obsolete. Places will not be known by the same names, and even the Spanish language itself will change so markedly that its current way of expressing things will become virtually unrecognizable: "Los que vendrán después de nosotros algunos años hablarán [el castellano] tan diferente que lo que se hallare escrito de nuestros tiempos les parescerá a ellos tan bárbaro como a nosotros nos parece el romance de algunas historias antiguas que se hallan en España" (1982, 498) [Those who will come a few years after us will speak Spanish in such a different way that what is written in our time will seem to them as barbarous as ancient Spanish narratives seem to us].

Acutely aware of the effects of progress not only on human understanding but on human articulation as well, Torquemada acknowledges that words invented in his time will be effaced by others within thirty to forty years (1982, 498). In his encyclopedic enterprise he is cognizant of the relentless advance of progress and the anxieties of value – two eminently modern concerns. Thus, the *Jardín*'s innovative use of humanist learning, its generic sophistication and originality, its realism and meta-literary nature, make it easy to understand why Cervantes reacted so strongly to Torquemada.

Huarte de San Juan's Sceptical *Examen de ingenios para las ciencias*

Juan Huarte de San Juan's influential *Examen de ingenios* (*The Examination of Men's Wits*, 1575) is the third proto-encyclopedic work of the period that deserves consideration in terms of "Thirdspace" and the rewriting of the space of memory, that is, a serious questioning of authority based on empirical observation. This work is routinely invoked in the context of Don Quijote's madness, but its impact is felt far beyond the literary realm. Indeed, it is the reason why Huarte is considered to be the father of the discipline of psychology (Velarde Lombraña 1993). Huarte's widely known acceptance of the viability of Galen's humoral theory is immortalized at the beginning of the *Quijote*, in that the hero's dry, hot constitution leads to madness. In addition, as this essay seeks to demonstrate, Huarte's *Examen* involves much more than a positivistic transmission of Galen.

To make this point, I would like to focus on the encyclopedic nature of Huarte's enterprise. He ranges over so much territory (sometimes in contradictory ways) that he has been read by some as heterodox. This is the assessment of Marañón (the twentieth-century physician, scientist, historian, and philosopher) and Yriarte (the twentieth-century author who writes about Huarte's Catholic orthodoxy). Some see Huarte, because of his commitment to rationalism, as a healthy alternative to the mystical inclinations of many of his compatriots, while others view him as a utopist because he puts forth a method by which each citizen can realize his full potential in identifying the optimal form of employment given his aptitude, thus bringing him satisfaction while contributing to the good of the nation.

Though some readers assume that encyclopedias are collections of old facts, encyclopedism is a constant of any period that perceives itself as modern. And given that modernity involves exceeding what has come before, it is not surprising that modern encyclopedists document the breadth and newness of their thought experiments – of their new space of lived experience. Philosophers, scientists, and writers labour to determine what is true and what is false. Epistemology is the focus, and encyclopedic projects make the rethinking of ideas and institutions possible by documenting such progress in understanding. At such times, respected sources of authority are questioned, leading to the anxiety of values as well as to the exuberance of discovery.

The reason why Huarte as well as Torquemada and Mexía were bestsellers not only in Spain but throughout Europe, and not only in the 1500s but for centuries thereafter, is because they each interrogate the frontiers of knowledge and belief. Political, religious, and scientific upheavals and their documentation made compelling reading. Even today, these texts fascinate because they do much more than provide a compendium of narratives from which literary authors and sermon writers can cull inspiration. They do much more than merely record and transmit data – they stage the cultural controversies of their day.

Huarte's *Examen de ingenios* was published in eighty-four printings and in seven languages (1989, 108–9). Lessing translated it into German, and Herder was, likewise, captivated by Huarte's book. It is an ambitious philosophical-psychological enquiry into the possible humoral combinations, and a theoretical exposition of the resulting three wits: memory, understanding, and imagination. From these categories he advocates which attributes incline one to a particular vocation: theologian, jurist, soldier, monarch, etc. He also offers readers a treatise on eugenics, concerning the optimal choice of spouses to produce a (male) child of superior wits. (However, female children, we are told, lack the capacity for excellence in this cognitive category.)

Pondering the example of Don Quijote's melancholy, there is a case to be made even in his physiognomy. The *ingenio* of the *ingenioso* derives less from his memory, but from his understanding and imagination. There are, according to Huarte, three faculties of the soul: memory (*memoria*), imagination (*imaginación*), and understanding (*entendimiento*). And the expression for these three faculties depends on the configuration of heat or cold, dryness or moisture as they exist in an individual's brain. That is, a moist brain makes for an outstanding power of memory, whereas a dry one excels at a quick understanding and heat makes for a powerful imaginative faculty. A brain that is old, however, is not an advantage in any way.

From this blueprint Huarte arrives at the challenging – though debatable – conclusion regarding the antipathy of memory and understanding, because the faculty of memory requires a moist and soft environment and the understanding a hard, dry one, so that a given subject can possess one or the other, but not both:

Desta doctrina se infiere claramente que el entendimiento y la memoria
son potencias opuestas y contrarias; de tal manera, que el hombre que
tiene gran memoria ha de ser alto de entendimiento, y el que tuviere
mucho entendimiento no puede tener buena memoria, porque el cerebro
es imposible ser juntamente seco y húmedo a predominio. (1989, 494)

[From this doctrine it clearly follows that understanding and memory
are facilities opposed to each other and in such a way that a man who
has a powerful memory has to be lacking in understanding and that one
who has much understanding cannot have a good memory, for the brain
cannot be predominantly dry and predominantly moist at the same time.]
(2014, 57)

Harald Weinrich notes how Don Quijote conforms to the *ingenium*
derived "not from memory, but from an acute understanding and a fertile imagination" (2004, 46), adding that this humoral profile is at a high
risk for melancholy and madness. Sancho, by contrast, given his cold
and moist-phlegmatic profile, is a man of limited creative capacities, but
he is blessed with a highly developed memory as a result of his cold
humoral substratum. Indeed, we recall that he is a venerable memory
bank of proverbs and that he is, in addition, inextricably linked to his ass,
Rucio – an animal that is emblematic of memory. Since antiquity, this animal has been associated with "the smallest faculty of understanding, but
the greatest memory" (Weinrich 2004, 47). In a moment of frustration,
Don Quijote tells Sancho, "Asno eres, y asno has de ser, y en asno has de
parar cuando se te acabe el curso de la vida" (Cervantes 2015, 2.28.770)
["An ass you are, an ass you will remain and an ass you will still be when
you end your days on the earth" (Cervantes 2003a, 2.29.680)].
   This cognitive equivalence is clearly debatable, however. It was taken to
task by the Inquisition that deleted the passage on the enmity (*enemistad*)
at issue between memory and understanding. For us too, it is a problematic notion. Nonetheless, Huarte's model was widely disseminated. The
Inquisition was, in fact, disapproving of Huarte's entire enterprise since
it upholds biological determinism rather than free will, thereby seeming
to be too much like a scientific version of Luther's notion of predestina-
tion. For the same reason, the Inquisition frowned upon his linking of
physiognomy to humoral theory. That is why the *Examen* was placed on
the Index in 1583 and why a posthumous, expurgated edition appeared in
1594. Not only did Huarte react sceptically towards a belief in miracles, he
spoke rather provocatively against the notion that preachers have a superior ability for comprehending scriptural exegesis. Such attitudes have
contributed to the claim that he is a *converso*. And to these reactions can

be added the lengthy passage in which Huarte praises the superior skill of Jewish doctors, and, in general, of Jews by comparison with Gentiles:

> Ello verdad es que no son ahora tan agudos y solertes como mil años atrás; porque dende que dejaron de comer del mana lo han vendido perdiendo de sus descendiente poco a poco hasta ahora, por usar de contrarios manjares, y estar en región diferente de Egipto, y no beber aguas tan delicadas como en el desierto; y por haberse mezclado con los que descienden de la gentilidad, los cuales carecen de esta diligencia de ingenio. Pero lo que no se les puede negar es que aun no lo han acabado de perder. (1989, 251–2)

> [The fact is that they [the descendants of the people of Israel] are as quick-witted and intelligent now as they were a thousand years ago. It is true that they began to lose their distinctive wit as soon as they ceased to eat manna, and began to live off other foods, inhabit regions other than Egypt, and intermarry with Gentiles, who lack this wit. But it cannot be denied that they have not lost it entirely.] (2014, 221)

Huarte is committed to rationalism, but at numerous junctures in his text he must admit the unavoidable presence of scepticism. To give one example, four men are asked to identify the colour of a piece of cloth that is put before them, and they each see a different colour. This is inevitable because of humoral variation. Likewise, and even more incriminating, Huarte explains that

> Si juntamos cien hombres de letras y los proponemos alguna cuestión, cada uno hace juicio particular y razona de diferente manera ... Y no solo tiene verdad en diversos entendimientos, pero aun vemos por experiencia que una mesma razón concluye a un mesmo entendimiento en un tiempo, y en otro no. Y así, vemos cada día mudan los hombres el parecer: unos cobrando con el tiempo el mas delicado entendimiento, conocen la falta de la razón que antes los movio; y otros, perdiendo el buen temperamento del celebro, aborrecen la verdad y aprueban la mentira. (1989, 220)

> [If we gather together a hundred men of letters and put a particular problem to them, each one will come to his own conclusion, and reason in a different way ... And this is not true merely with respect to different intellects, for experience shows that the same proof will convince a man at one time but not at another. Thus we see men change their views every day. Some refine their intellect with the passing of time, and recognize the mistaken reasoning that moved them before whereas others, because the

temper of their brain is disturbed, come to hate the truth and accept what is false.] (2014, 39–40)

This admission clearly shakes the foundation of an epistemology based on rationalism.

Indeed, the notable uncertainty that results, the lack of consensus, leads Huarte to conclude – like Democritus – that the world is a virtual "madhouse": "este mundo no e[s] mas que una casa de locos, cuya vida e[s] una comedia graciosa representada para hacer reir a los hombres" (1989, 135) ["This world is nothing but a madhouse where life is an amusing play performed to make men laugh" (2014, 122)]. Huarte is intrigued by Democritus, the natural philosopher from the fifth century BCE known as the "laughing philosopher" because of his belief in the value of cheerfulness. Beyond his interest in Huarte as an advocate of positive thinking, Democritus was important to him because he was fascinated by the workings of the mind and thought, as was Huarte, believing that thought was caused by the physical motion of atoms and that thought as well as sensation or perception result from the stimulation of images external to the body.[7] Yet as we know, "the price of greatness is to be misunderstood." Democritus's neighbours thought that he was mentally ill, but Hippocratus, the famed doctor esteemed as "the father of medicine," after asking him various questions, "halló que era el hombre más sabio que había en el mundo" (1989, 434) [found that he was the wisest man in the world].

Additional case studies pertaining to madness are recorded by Huarte such as the following, which reminds us of the *Licenciado Vidriera* (*Man of Glass*), in whom Cervantes famously figures some of the paradoxes of madness. Huarte tells of a dull-witted page who, in his mad state, was transformed into a dazzlingly impressive commentator; however, once he was restored by a well-intentioned physician to his true, humble nature, he complained about his restored sanity:

Estando en mi locura vivía en las mas altas consideraciones del mundo y me fingía tan gran señor que no había Rey en la tierra que no fuse mi feudatorio. Y que fuse burla y mentira, ¿qué importaba, pues gustaba tanto de ello como si fuse verdad? ¡Harto peor es ahora, que me hallo de veras que soy un pobre paje y que mañana tengo que comenzar a servir a quien, estando en mi enfermedad, no le recibiera por mi lacayo! (1989, 109)

[When I was mad I had the most lofty thoughts and imagined myself to be so great a lord that there was no king who was not my liege. And if it was a joke and a lie, what did it matter since it gave me as much satisfaction as if it were true? It is much worse now that I see that I am in fact a poor page, and that tomorrow I must begin to serve someone who, while I was ill, I would not have accepted as my lacky!] (2014, 87)

The study of mental illness and various forms of madness was, of course, a topic of intense commentary in Huarte's time as much for scientists and philosophers as it was for social engineers.[8] This issue and its social ramifications was hotly debated. In terms of Cervantes, of course, we have a wealth of examples provided by the *Quijote*, the *Licenciado Vidriera*, the *Coloquio de los perros*, and the *Persiles* as well.

Huarte is of two minds about this type of creative expression. On the one hand, he denigrates those readers who steep themselves in this type of writing: "Estos se pierden por leer en libros de caballerías, en Orlando, en Boscán, en *Diana* de Montemayor y otros así; porque todas estas obras son de imaginativa" (1989, 70) ["They lose themselves in books of chivalry, in Orlando, in Boscán, in Montemayor's *Diana* and other similar books; because all of these works are of the imagination" (2014, 107)]. About the writers of fiction he says first, quite pointedly, that "el hombre cuerdo y que está en su libre juicio no puede ser poeta" (1594, 396) [the man who is in his right mind cannot be a poet], yet later in his treatise he praises the work of the responsible poet, siding with Aristotle, claiming that the poetic inspiration "dichos y sentencias tan elevados" (1989, 433) [capable of such lofty maxims and sententiae] comes from a particular humoral configuration – rather than from divine inspiration – as Plato would have it (1989, 433).

Huarte's view that natural ability rather than training is of paramount importance finds adherents in such theorists as Alonso López Pinciano and Baltasar Gracián, while Gracián perpetuates Huarte's false derivation of "ingenio" from "ingenerare," that is in-generare, i.e., "generative power," connecting genius with imagination vs. ingenium, "innate or natural quality," while following almost word for word Huarte's definition of the arts and sciences (1989, 109).

When it comes to Don Quijote, of course, Huarte's humoral theory accords with both the physiognomy and psychology of the hero – his lean, hirsute, and crazy nature – as well as the prominence of the concept of "ingenio" in the very title of the book: *El ingenioso hidalgo … The Imaginative, strange hidalgo*. This striking example of the book that Cervantes describes as "the child of his brain" can also be seen in Huarte, who explains that "el entendimiento tiene virtud y fuerzas naturales de producer y parir dentro de si un hijo" (1989, 427) [the faculty of understanding has the virtue and natural ability to produce and give birth to a child within itself]. Likewise, Huarte's reference to "cosas tan delicadas, tan verdaderas y prodigiosas que jamás se vieron ni oyeron ni escribieron" (Huarte 1575, 376) [things that are so subtle, truthful and prodigious that they have never been seen or heard or written] appears in the description of Quijote as a man "full of thoughts numerous and never before imagined."

Of course, one could argue, as some scholars have, that these similarities in ideas and phrasing are commonplaces for which Huarte cannot take credit. And while this is a valid point, and even though Huarte at times derails his rationalism with scepticism stemming from his complex appreciation of the perceiving subject (or precisely because of this derailing), his encyclopedism, like that of Mexía and Torquemada, stages many of the most important cultural controversies of his day. The spaces of perception, conception, and experience lead to an insatiable curiosity and a productive, forward-thinking questioning of previous authority, of memory.

With these few examples from Mexía, Torquemada, and Huarte, we glimpse the complexity of their understanding of the space of memory.

Notes

1 See Lefebvre 1991, Foucault 1971, and Soja 2008.
2 Jonathan Bradbury summarizes the characteristics of the miscellany genre as "unchecked variety of content; looseness of structure; an eschewal of traditional notions of literary decorum; an emphasis on the vulgarizing and democratizing of knowledge; the excerpting of more authoritative writers, from both classical and humanist traditions; a desire for novelty and a wish to provoke *admiración* in the vernacular reader; as well as the growing presence, as the tradition progresses, of contemporary information and anecdotes, and of fictional materials" (2010, 1053). See also Rossi 2006.
3 Unless otherwise indicated, all translations are my own.
4 See Alcalá Galán 1996; Bradbury 2010; and Bradbury 2017.
5 For a new interpretation of the *Jardín de flores*, see Wheeler (forthcoming).
6 See Forcione 1970.
7 See Bauer 2021.
8 See Cruz 1999.

4 Geographic Games: Cosmic Miniatures and Creative Play from Jewish Theology and Medieval Alexander Romances to Cervantes's Modern Fiction

KEITH BUDNER, UNIVERSITY OF ILLINOIS CHICAGO

Spheres and Seeds

Early modernity, according to some, began with a shape: the round ball. In his *Spatial Reformation: Euclid between Man, Cosmos, and God* (2018), Michael Sauter argues that around 1350 renaissance readers began to gravitate towards Euclid's discussion of spheres in the second half of his *Elements*. Euclid's presentation of idealized spherical space challenged the medieval separation of human and divine spheres, a cosmology that fused biblical creation with Aristotelian physics. Sauter may be correct to note "terrestrial globes' curious absence" when it comes to works of geometry proper during the Middle Ages (60). But literary texts reveal how the medieval spatial imagination was fascinated by both a spherical world and the round ball.

Among the most popular literary traditions of the Middle Ages are romances of Alexander the Great that appear in Latin, Hebrew, Arabic, Persian, Byzantine Greek, and a plethora of European vernaculars. The thirteenth-century Castilian *Libro de Alexandre* has been particularly analysed for its geographic imagery (Pinet 2016; Riva 2020). And yet, such studies overlook an exchange between Alexander and the Persian king Darius that enacts Sauter's notion of "space-making" through acts of play and the imagination. After Alexander crosses into Asia, Darius sends him a gift along with a personalized note: "Envióte … pello con que trebejes" [I send you … a ball you can play with] (st. 783).[1] Darius's insult is aimed at Alexander's youth; with this ball, the young Alexander can play with boys his own age. Alexander cleverly responds by imagining that this ball is not a toy but rather the round world:

> La pella, que es redonda todo'l mundo figura:
> –¡sepas que será mío, est' es cosa segura!–; (st. 801)

[This ball that's round, represents all the world.
You should know it will be mine; this is a sure thing!]

Alexander's retort demonstrates that spherical thinking was of such prevalence during the Middle Ages that even a simple round ball could become a terrestrial globe within one's imagination, or at least the imagination of one like Alexander the Great. Indeed, this scene of space-making is dually imaginative: an act of the imagination within a work of imaginative literature. In this way, Alexander's retort ironically confirms Darius's initial insult. Though he's not playing ball with other young men, when he imagines his ball to be the world – and conversely miniatures the world into a hand-held ball – Alexander uses his imagination to play.

The lens of imaginative play allows us to appreciate the role of spherical thinking within imaginative literature. In this essay, I take the *Libro de Alexandre* as a point of departure to tell a history that looks both backward and ahead. The Castilian poem is not the only Alexander romance with a connection to medieval Iberia. One Hebrew Alexander romance (London MS Jews' College, no. 145) is attributed to the Sephardic Jew Samuel Ibn Tibbon, best known as a translator of Arabic texts that transmitted Greek philosophy and physics into the Middle Ages. In this Hebrew romance, the slippage between geometry and play is underscored in language since the same Hebrew word "kadur" refers to both a recreational ball and the geographic globe: "You brought me good news sending me a ball [*kadur*] which signifies that I shall rule over the globe of the world [*kadur ha-olam*]" (Van Bekkum 1992, 69). To be sure, I am not proposing direct links between this Hebrew Alexander and the Castilian *Alexandre*. Rather, with a more capacious approach to these romances as Iberian "cousin" texts, I will present a long yet intertwined journey of spherical thinking and imaginative play that begins in premodern Jewish theology and concludes in modern literary fiction.

The Hebrew romance attributed to Ibn Tibbon invites us to plunge the historical depths of Jewish creation theologies. From the Hebrew Bible to medieval Sephardic Hebrew poetry, and from the ancient Mediterranean to medieval al-Andalus, Jewish theology regularly represents divine world-making as an act of imaginative play. At the same time, the Castilian *Alexandre* propels us forward within the history of Spanish literature towards a single work: Cervantes's *Don Quixote* as the first modern novel. Like Alexander with his ball-world, *Don Quixote* combines spherical thinking with playful miniaturization. Among the many games carried out by the Duke and the Duchess in the second 1615 volume is the episode of Clavileño: Quixote and Sancho are told they will ascend into the heavens upon the eponymous wooden horse, all the while blindfolded and of course remaining on the ground. In a surprise literary twist, Quixote is sceptical of this journey, but the Duke and Duchess's game absorbs Sancho, who "returns to earth' with a report. Sancho describes cosmic map of what he saw: "miré hacia la tierra, y pareciome que toda ella no era mayor que un grano de mostaza" ["I looked down at the earth, and it seemed to me that it was no larger than a mustard seed"] (2004, 1.61.1053; 2003b, 1053).[2] Even smaller than Alexander's hand-held ball, Sancho's cosmic map miniaturizes the world into a mustard seed.

As with the two Alexander romances, I am not proposing that Cervantes's Clavileño was directly influenced by the Jewish texts I discuss. I will, however, propose ways by which Jewish theologies of world-making were indirectly transmitted to Spanish readers. Hebraic conceptions of cosmic creation were filtered through the *Libro de Alexandre* as well as other Castilian texts that emerged out of medieval Iberia's multiconfessional world of Christians, Jews, and Muslims.

But like the Alexander romances themselves, our story begins further back in antiquity. In the ancient Mediterranean, and particularly places like Hellenistic Alexandria, Jewish thought negotiated contact with the dominant Graeço-Roman culture. In medieval al-Andalus, Judaism once again encountered Greek philosophy and science through Arabic transmission. The ancient Greek, medieval Hebrew, and even medieval Castilian Alexander romances mark historical moments when intercultural contact pushed Jewish thought to embrace literary form and express cosmic theology through narrative. In both eras, I will situate the Alexander romances within a network of Jewish texts that blur the boundary between theology and imaginative literature.

Shared imagery of playful world-making, as I show, reveals how intercultural negotiation transforms Jewish theologies of cosmic creation and divine play into literary fiction. This intercultural transformation of theology into fiction happens, we might say, first slowly and then all at once. After a longue durée of intercultural transformation spanning the Hellenistic Mediterranean to medieval Iberia, Cervantes completes the secularizing process. The Clavileño episode of *Don Quixote* substitutes theologies of creation with a theory of literary fictionality.

Both Alexander's ball and Sancho's mustard seed enact the imaginative creation of new and separate worlds through play, fiction, and miniaturization. As such, our pre- and early modern texts anticipate contemporary theories of fiction and aesthetics. Thomas Pavel discusses how literary texts create fictional worlds by encoding non-literary language, including spatial vocabularies of borders, distance, and size (1986, 73–113). Susan Stewart observes that there are "no miniatures in nature" (1993, 55) – that the very act of miniaturizing space belongs to the realm of culture and fiction. For Stewart, playing with miniatures like toys "initiates another world, the world of daydream … an entirely new temporal world, a fantasy world parallel to (and hence never intersecting) the world of everyday reality" (57). With her emphasis on daydream and fantasy, Stewart echoes aesthetic theories that comprehend artistic creation as a mode of playing. The philosopher Kendall Walton (1990) proposes that all mimetic representations are games of "make-believe" in which works of art function like toys or props that spur the viewer or reader to playfully imagine their own fictions. The ball that leads Alexander to imagine the world is one such example, but so too is the very premise of *Don Quixote* – the story of a man whose books of chivalry prompt him to imagine a chivalric world in which he quests, or plays, as a knight-errant by making use of other props such as a barber's basin for his helmet.[3]

Alongside such aesthetic and literary theories are frameworks that identify a playful component to religious practices and thus help us appreciate modern fiction's debt to premodern theology. In his seminal study *Man, Play and Games*, Roger Caillois proposes that playful costumed mimicry and games of exhilarating vertigo both descend from shamanistic ritual: "[The shaman] renews his travels … the feathers and head of the eagle or owl, in which he is dressed, enable him to fly magically up to the heavens. Next, despite a costume weighing more than thirty pounds because of the iron ornaments sewed into it, he leaps into the air to show that he is flying very high. He yells that he can see a large part of the earth" (2001, 90–1). Caillois's shaman resembles Sancho; both imaginatively return from the heavens to narrate their adventures seeing a small and distant world. With his cosmic visionary experience, Caillois's shaman is also ancestor to Jewish prophets I shall discuss who are divinely granted the privilege of seeing the cosmos God created.

But where prophecy perceives God's cosmic plan, idolatry challenges it. In an almost too perfect echo of Cervantes's Clavileño, art historian Ernst Gombrich grounds his aesthetic theory in the object of the hobby horse that for a child at play "becomes a horse in its own right" just as an "idol takes the place of the god … it is a man-made god in precisely the sense that the hobby-horse is a man-made horse" (1963, 2–3). Like Sancho atop Clavileño, we can ride Gombrich's hobby horse into the cosmos, or at least to cosmic mapping. If as Gombrich proposes art is less representation than substitution, then the map takes the place of God's created cosmos; mapping becomes a form of idolatry. On one side of creation theology's cosmic coin, we find the geographic prophet who perceives God's world; on the other side, we see the cartographic idol-maker who usurps the creator God by creating a man-made world.

Much recent scholarship in literature and the history of science emphasizes how the early modern era uniquely experienced terrestrial and celestial space. Disparate disciplines of cartography, poetry, philosophy, and science came together to constitute new endeavours of early modern "world-making" (Ramachandran 2015) and the "cosmic imagination" (Aït-Touati 2011). Similarly, Spanish literature was shaped by technological advances in optics and astronomy (García Santo-Tomás 2017) as well as by the imperial mapping of the Americas and Pacific (Padrón 2020). Sauter's Euclidean renaissance similarly proposes a "spatial secularization ... the continual distancing of the divine from both humanity and the cosmos" (2019, 31). I don't reject the historical realities of early modern rupture, but my vision of early modern secularization is closer to that of Amos Funkenstein (2018), who argues that early modern science simultaneously secularizes medieval theology while preserving its pre-secular origins.[4] I will similarly propose that modern literary fiction secularizes premodern Jewish theologies in ways that allow us to see traces of divine creation as playful world-making. Both Alexander's playful act of turning the world into a ball and Sancho's cosmic mustard seed secularize the visionary experience of the prophet as well as the transgressive creation of the idol-maker.

Cosmic Play from the Hebrew Bible to Alexandria and Al-Andalus

Playful creation of the cosmos begins with the wisdom literature of the Hebrew Bible. In the Book of Proverbs, Lady Wisdom (*hokmah*) narrates a verse cosmology in which she repeatedly describes herself as a companion in God's games: "His delight [*sha'ashuim*] day after day, / playing [*mesaheket*] before Him at all times / playing [*mesaheket*] in the world, His earth, / and my delight [*ve-sha'ashuai*] with mankind" (8:30–1). This playful God also resembles a cartographer drawing a map: "He engraved a circle on the face of the deep" (8:27).[5] In medieval Iberia, Proverbs' verse cosmology was rendered into Castilian within the *General Estoria* of Alfonso X el Sabio, where its representation of play and spherical space-making echoes the *Libro de Alexandre*. Mirroring Alexander's round ball, El Señor creates "los quiciales de la redondeza de la tierra" [the hinges of earth's roundness] (2009, 390; translation my own). And just as Darius tells Alexander that he should play ("trebejes"), Proverbs describes Sapiencia "trebejando en el cerco de las tierras" [playing in the circuit of the lands] (2009, 390; translation my own).

In the Hebrew original, Proverbs establishes a connection between creative play and craftsmanship. Words for "delight" (*sha'ashua*) and "play" (*sahaq*) are compounded when Lady Wisdom refers to herself as God's *amon* – an ambiguous term that Michael V. Fox describes as "one of the great puzzles of the Hebrew Bible" (2010, 285). Within a context of childhood, the *amon* is a friend, a "companion," "intimate," or fellow "nursling" (286). We might even say "playmate" given the surrounding terminology of play. The rabbinic commentary *Bereishit Rabbah* connects Proverbs to the creation story of Genesis within a framework of divine craftsmanship. According to the rabbis, there is actually a meaningful slippage between two *a-m-n* root words: *amon* (אָמוֹן) "playmate" and *umman* (אֻמָּן) "artisan" or "artisan's instrument" (1.1). Lady Wisdom the divine playmate is also God's artisan or instrument for creating the cosmos.

The rabbis' fusion of *amon*/playmate with *umman*/artisan draws, directly or indirectly, on the synthesis of Jewish theology with Greek philosophy in Hellenistic Alexandria. According to the first Jewish Neoplatonist Philo, God created the cosmos just as an architect sketches "the image of a city" on wax tablets the (1929, 18). Philo's architectural drawing is a metaphor for the mind imprinted with ideas; the architect's blueprint is the spatial imagination of a cosmic artisan. Philo's divine architect first imagines a "beautiful pattern" (*paradeigmatos*) and then creates a "beautiful copy" (*mimema*) that is the "visible world" (*cosmon*) (16). In Philo's Jewish Platonism, the map precedes the territory.

Jewish Neoplatonism re-emerged in medieval Iberia with the Arabic transmission of Greek philosophy. In eleventh-century al-Andalus, the Jewish Neoplatonist and poet Solomon Ibn Gabirol composed verse cosmologies that extend the slippage between the divine playmate and artisan. In his *Kingly Crown (Keter Malkhut)*, Ibn Gabirol articulates a Neoplatonic system where Wisdom is from the beginning of time God's *amon*/playmate but then subsequently generates a "creative desire" (*hefetz*) that functions as a "craftsman and artisan" (*ke-puehl ve-umman*) who assists God in the creation of the world (2003, 52–3). Also gesturing to Proverbs' engraved circles, Ibn Gabirol's God creates the cosmic order through "hewing and engraving" (*ve-hatzav ve-hakak*)" (2003, 52–3). Ibn Gabirol rearticulates this cosmology in a shorter poem where God turns to an *amon* to reveal the spheres and wheels of the cosmos (2001, 126). Within this medieval Andalusí Neoplatonism, Ibn Gabirol wholly collapses the *amon*'s role as personified playmate with the *umman*'s instrumental function as a spatial blueprint of the cosmos.

And indeed, after creation, Ibn Gabirol's God sits "High above all, and of all the strongest, / he sees the cosmos" (127). Having created the cosmos like a cartographer, Ibn Gabiro's God exercises the cartographic privilege of gazing upon the whole of creation.

The Jewish Neoplatonisms of Philo and Ibn Gabirol illustrate how Proverbs' biblical poetics of cosmic play was especially nurtured in an ongoing interaction of Hebraism and Hellenism. Within the cultural cross-pollination that spanned ancient Alexandria to medieval al-Andalus, mapping the cosmos was spatial and aesthetic. Classicist Tim Whitmarsh defines fiction as "the logic of the cosmos in narrative form" (2014, 14). Hellenistic literature, including that of the "Jewish Sophistic," reflects the "gradual mapping out of a wider *oikoumene*" (33). The post-classical period witnessed scientific advances in geography and astronomy as well as the cultural expansion of Greek thought and literature from Athens across the Mediterranean to places like Alexandria and Judea with established Jewish communities.

From Hellenistic antiquity to the Middle Ages, Alexander the Great held a distinct place in this literary mapping of the cosmos. Beyond the romances, a mysterious text, *On the Cosmos*, is addressed to an "Alexander" often read as the Macedonian king. The treatise opens by describing cosmology as the mind's eye leaving "the earth behind" to travel and explore the heavens (Thom 2014, 21).[6] Because *On the Cosmos* was long attributed to Alexander's tutor Aristotle, the text was of interest to Islamic Aristotelians, and as such accessible to medieval Jews through Arabic translation.[7] But according to one Jewish Aristotelian of fifteenth-century Spain, it was actually Alexander who proffered cosmic wisdom to his teacher Aristotle. Abraham Ben Shem Tov Bibago relates that when Alexander conquered Jerusalem and plundered the Temple, he came upon King Solomon's writings about the cosmos. Alexander gifted the Hebrew texts to Aristotle, who had them translated to Greek. Aristotle then destroyed the Hebrew originals and passed off the Greek translations as his own original cosmology (Stoneman 2008, 59).[8] Marina Brownlee (2010) has proposed that Castilian Christians saw Alexander as a "bivalent hero"; Shem Tov Bibago's story of Alexander and Aristotle steeling cosmic wisdom from the Jews reflects that such ambivalent attitudes crossed confessional lines in medieval Iberia.

MAKING A MAP, MAKING AN IDOL

As Alexander narratives and Greek cosmologies migrated from ancient Alexandria to medieval Iberia, cultural hybridity became theological tension. The Alexander who "pushes the boundaries of human knowledge" with his travels to marvellous lands may have been an "inventor and sage" for ancient Jews Hellenized into Greek cultural attitudes (Stoneman 2008, 111). But for medieval Christians and Jews alike, Alexander could also be a tyrant, at once imperial and empirical. This Alexander challenged God's cosmic authority by attempting to violate the ordered limits of space and earthly knowledge. Fernando Riva (2019) situates the *Libro de Alexandre* within the Christian cloister that distinguished between spiritual *sapientia* and earthly *scientia*, with Alexander embodying the latter's diabolical pride. When the poem submits that Alexander's desire "En las cosas secretas quiso él entender" [to know secret things] exceeds even Lucifer in its "mayor sobervia" [great hubris] (st. 2327), the condemnation comes after Alexander returns from exploring the depths of the sea in a giant glass diving bell. David Nirenberg similarly identifies a Christian anxiety surrounding the "dangers of knowledge" across a variety of medieval texts. His discussion allows us to connect a scene from the Castilian romance where a young Alexander studies the stars (st. 19–20) to a legend about Alfonso X el Sabio that recalls the playful cosmic creation of Proverbs. Supposedly, the "wise" king took his moniker a bit too seriously and imagined himself in the role of Lady Wisdom, boasting that the world would be better ordered had he accompanied God at the creation (Nirenberg 2014, 253 and 266). Nirenberg emphasizes how Christians labelled such learning "Jewish" (264–4). But medieval Jews were similarly anxious that cosmic knowledge was a challenge to God's authority and saw Alexander the Great as the embodiment of this overweening desire to know the world.

Like Alexander's aforementioned aquatic adventure, his ascent into the heavens in a flying machine powered by griffins comprises one of the romance's best-known episodes, present in Greek, Hebrew, and Castilian versions. Together the episodes track shifting attitudes towards Alexander as one who experiences and knows space. Alexander's journey into the heavens receives extended treatment in the Castilian romance, describing at length the lands he sees below: "Tanto pudo el rëy a las nuves pujar: veyé montes e valles ... Mesuró toda África" [So high could the king climb into the clouds, that he could see mountains and valleys ... he measured all of Africa] (st. 2504–6). Simone Pinet has situated the geographic information of the *Alexandre's* aerial adventure within a Christian context that spans the clerical curriculum of north Castilian monasteries to the medieval Hereford and Ebstorf *mappae mundi* of northern Europe (2016, 13–58). Medieval Christian cartography helps explain why Alexander explores the seas and the skies in various romance traditions, yet only in the Castilian *Alexandre* does he behold a physical map. In his battle tent, Alexander looks upon a "mapamundi esripta e notada" [a map of the world, inscribed and annotated] (st. 2576). And when bequeathing his empire, Alexander draws his own map: "Compassó todo'l mundo: cómo son tres quiño-nes, / cómo son cadaúno de diversas regiones" [He measured all the world with a compass, how it was of three parts, and how in each there were diverse regions] (st. 2459). The episodes that track Alexander's experiential mapping of oceanic, celestial, and terrestrial spaces also exemplify Witmarsh's thesis that fiction's *oikoumene* expands as spatial sciences advance and cultures come into contact. Indeed, despite the absence of explicitly Jewish themes, the episode of the diving bell likely originates from Jewish source material and suggests that Hellenistic Jews were familiar with experiments in hydraulics and air pressure undertaken by Alexandrian scientists (Stoneman 2008, 112). Both the sea and sky episodes, moreover, are retold by rabbis.

Long before the Castilian romance describes Alexander's desire to know nature's secrets as Luciferian, rabbis condemned Alexander's pursuit of celestial and terrestrial knowledge as a threat to the divine order. The *Chapters of Rabbi Eliezer* juxtaposed Alexander's global empire that spanned "from one end of the world to the other" with his desire to understand this world: "to ascend to heaven in order to know what is in heaven, and to descend into the depths in order to know what is in the depths" (Friedlander 1981, 82–3). Where the Castilian Alexander gazes upon maps, this Alexander arouses the rabbis' suspicion in his need to transcend material mediation and cartographic representation; he must know the world with his own eyes.

The Jerusalem Talmud, a rabbinic text composed in Roman Palestine where Jewish contact with Hellenism abounded, brings us full circle to Alexander's ball-world. Here rabbis debate what sorts of statues are idols prohibited by Jewish law: "The Sages say, prohibited are only those [statues] in whose had is a rod, or a bird, or a ball [*kadur*] … a ball, for the world is shaped like a ball … Rebbi Jonah said, when Alexander the Macedonian wanted to ascend, he rose, and rose, and rose, until he saw the world as a ball [*ha-olam ka-kadur*]" (AZ 3:1).[9] Unlike *Rabbi Eliezer*, the Talmud's rabbis are concerned with visual representation, indeed, representation within representation: the statue representing a human holds a ball that represents the world. The idolatrous statue that Rebbi Jonah likens to Alexander also resembles the romances' Alexander who holds a ball and imagines the world. And yet, once again, the rabbis' Alexander does not himself hold a ball-world. Instead, Alexander's aerial ascent creates the spatial experience and scalar perception of seeing the world as small as a ball. This perspectival miniaturization of terrestrial space is akin to representing the sphere of the world in the form of a geographic globe. But mapmaking is not exactly idol-making. Idolatry is instead relating to the world *as if* it were a cartographic object, or we might say, mistaking the map for the territory.

The entangling of idolatry with mapping takes us from ancient Alexandria and Palestine to medieval Al-Andalus and its most famous rabbi-philosopher, the Cordoban Moses Maimonides. Maimonides wrote his most important philosophical text, *The Guide for the Perplexed*, in Judaeo-Arabic, but the work was soon after translated into Hebrew by Samuel Ibn Tibbon – the same who supposedly authored the Hebrew Alexander romance.[10] Though Samuel ibn Tibbon lived in Provence, the colophon sephardizes him as the "son of Rabbi Judah Ibn Tibbon, of blessed memory, from Granada, Spain [*Sepharad*]" (Van Bekkum 1992, 205). The romance further inscribes itself into the intellectual landscape of Jewish Iberia when the colophon favourably compares Samuel Ibn Tibbon's translation of Maimonides to that of another Sephardic Jew: Judah Al-Harizi of Toledo (then in Christian Castile).[11] Regardless of its actual origins, the Hebrew Alexander attributed to Samuel Ibn Tibbon wants to be read as a Sephardic-Iberian text.

In his *Guide*, Maimonides expands Jewish definitions of idolatry to include any anthropomorphizing of God. Influenced by Islamic prohibitions on image-making and Aristotelian theories of a non-corporeal Primer Mover of the cosmos, Maimonides's expansive definition of idolatry departed from Jewish tradition. For example, a mysterious text known as the *Shi'ur Komah* (*The Measurement of the Stature*) lists numerical measurements for God's body. Maimonides dismissed the work as the writings of Christian priests. But a Catalan disciple of Maimonides, Moses Narboni, took a different approach. Narboni argued that the enormous measurements delineate not God's actual body but rather the cosmos. Where the Jerusalem Talmud articulated a dangerous slippage between mapping and idol-making, Narboni instead transformers the potential idolatry of *Shi'ur Komah* into a verbal map of the cosmos.

Inspired by the Hebrew romance's stated ties to Maimonidean theology, we can project Narboni's cosmological reinterpretation of *Shi'ur Komah* onto Alexander's ball-world. By playfully miniaturizing the world into a ball, Alexander's game conversely grants him the gigantic proportions of a divine body. Perhaps following the rabbis of the Jerusalem Talmud and Maimonides's expansive approach to idolatry, the Maimonidean Samuel Ibn Tibbon – or whoever wrote the Hebrew romance – condemns Alexander by presenting him as a living idol, as an earthly ruler who makes himself into cosmic giant. Or perhaps, paralleling Narboni's turn to cosmology, the Hebrew Romance seeks to inoculate the scene's potential idolatry by turning it into something else – not a cosmic map, but literary fiction, a scene not of idol-making but play.

(Con)fusions and Secular Rule, Games, and a Miniaturized World

The journey of Jewish idol-making to fictional world-making is one of secularization. The word "secular," from the Latin *saeculum*, indeed encompasses meanings of the worldly. For Ayesha Ramachandra, early modernity's cosmopoetic confidence results from new sciences and empires that transfer God's monopoly on "the world's creation and its domination … from divine to human hands" (2015, 15). William Eggington similarly discusses how Cervantes and Velázquez respectively used the printed word and painted image to explore a world that through these same media had become "uprooted, put into a box … made portable" (2016, 84).[12] But as we well know, well before either the printing press or the new sciences, Alexander was able to dominate the globe with his empire and even contain it as a hand-held ball. Modernity's secularization is thus a reconfiguration of premodernity's idolatry. According to both categories, human hands grasp the world from God's grip.

It is impossible to know what indirect cross-pollination could have occurred between the two Alexander romances separated by language but sharing, broadly understood, an Iberian provenance. Nonetheless, the Castilian *Alexandre* nods to a Jewish world view of artistic creation. The poem's master craftsman Apelles is described as "el ebreo" [the Hebrew] (st. 1239). This Hebraic-Jewish designation is a confusion of Alexander's court painter Apelles of Kos with "Apelles Hebreus," a figure from Horace's satires. Despite its error, the poem explicitly embraces Apelles's Jewishness with an ekphrasis of a tomb he sculpts for the Persian queen Stateira that is replete with imagery from the Hebrew Bible. Stateira's tomb includes a cartographic representation of the post-diluvian world where the earth's continents are divided between Noah's three sons (st. 1241), evoking the tradition of T-O *mappae mundi* that emerges from Isidore of Seville's reading of Genesis 11's Table of Nations. Apelles's map-making continues in a second tomb he later sculpts for Stateira's husband Darius, the very Persian emperor who gifted Alexander his ball-globe. On Darius's tomb, Apelles sculpts the circuit of the cosmos – "cúemo corre el Sol, la Luna e estrellas" [how the sun, moon, and stars course] – as well as the earth's lands and byways: "quáles tierras son buenas … de quál lugar a quál responden los caminos" [which lands are good … how the roads corresponded from this place and that] (st. 1792–93). Apelles's knowledge of the cosmos is further emphasized with an inscription that calculates creation: "el mundo quándo fue fecho, quántos años avié" [when the Earth was created and its age] (st. 1799). Unlike his patron Alexander who must see the world, Apelles knows it through artistic creation.

The *Alexandre*'s first ekphrasis, moreover, evokes Jewish perceptions of cosmography as idolatry. Extending a tradition from classical epic, Apelles crafts a shield for Alexander whose surface imagery is described: "debuxaba la tierra e el mar / los regnos e las villas, las aguas de prestar, / cascuno con sus títulos por mejor devisar" [he depicted the earth and the sea the kingdoms and villages, rivers of renown, each with its designation for better demarcation] (st. 96). But while the shield only depicts the earth, it rivals the heavens: "vençié a la Luna e al Sol refertava" [it outshined the moon and rivalled the sun] (st. 98). Though never explicitly accused of idol-making, the *Alexandre*'s "Jewish" Apelles makes a map that competes with God's creation.

Centuries after the Hellenistic painter Apelles was Judaized, the Renaissance painter Raphael committed his own (con)fusion of a cartographer's identity (see figure 4.1). In his *School of Athens*, which Frederick de Armas argues influenced (2006, 29–51), Raphael represents Ptolemy holding a terrestrial globe in his hand, yet also donning a crown and golden robe. Ptolemy's regal costume has long puzzled art historians.[13] But one possible explanation lies in the writings of the Spanish Jew who reintroduced Greek astronomy into Jewish thought.

The eleventh-century Tudelan Abraham Ibn Ezra mistakenly believed that Claudius Ptolemy, the astronomer and geographer, was one of the Ptolemaic rulers of Hellenistic Egypt. Specifically, Ibn Ezra believed that the geographer Ptolemy was Ptolemy II, who according to Jewish tradition oversaw the translation of the Hebrew Bible into Greek. Like the tale of Alexander and Aristotle stealing Hebrew cosmology, Jews accused Ptolemy of using translation as theft. Philo writes that Ptolemy commissioned this translation because of the Hebrew Bible's account of cosmic creation (1929, *Moses II*, 31 & 37). Thus, both Ibn Ezra and Raphael believed that the monarch and the geographer were one and the same Ptolemy. The orb in Ptolemy's hand is simultaneously the king's spherical symbol of worldly rule and the geographer's terrestrial globe for scientific study. Visually echoing the romances' Alexander, Raphael's Ptolemy is a portrait of knowledge and power who gestures with a hand-held world.

Indeed, Raphael's Ptolemy king-and-geographer is also Alexander the Great. With his back towards us, Ptolemy looks towards a figure, visible only in facial profile, who is none other than Apelles.[14] Ptolemy

Figure 4.1. Raphael's *School of Athens* (detail). This portion of the painting evokes the ties between geometry, geography, and astronomy as the three main figures likely represent Ptolemy, Zoroaster, and Euclid.

holding a globe of geographic study is thus not only king Ptolemy but also Alexander himself, posing with a ball-world before his court painter. The posture and props of this Alexander-Ptolemy take us back to a Greek recension of the romance. When Alexander enters Egypt, a statue of the last Pharoah Nectanebo mechanically comes to life. The automaton crowns Alexander and deposits in his hand a sphere that "portrayed the creation of the world" signifying how Alexander "will travel over the whole earth" (Stoneman 1991, 173). In many versions of the romance, Nectanebo is in fact Alexander's true father who deceptively seduced Alexander's mother Olympia. With its mechanical actions, the automaton thus recognizes Alexander as Nectanebo's true son and dynastic heir to the Pharaohs. The geographer-king is also a hybrid Greek-Egyptian.

Alexander's hybrid Egyptian heritage further connects play and miniaturization through magic. The Greek romance begins with Nectanebo receiving a prophecy of Persia's impending attack on Egypt, a warning enacted through game-like figurines. Nectanebo moulds "ships and men of wax," which he places in a bowl filled with water, and with a "spell the wax figures came to life" to enact a prophetic game of Egypt's ensuing defeat (Stoneman 1991, 35). In both Greek and Hebrew versions, Nectanebo flees to Macedonia, where he seduces Alexander's mother. To Macedonia, Nectanebo makes sure to bring his precious astrological tablet that Richard Stoneman fittingly likens to a "travelling chess set" (2008, 21). Like the cosmic globe held by the automaton version of himself, Nectanebo's tablet portrays in precious stones the planets and twelve signs of the zodiac, a "pictured miniature heaven" (Stoneman 1991, 31).

The Hebrew romance imagines Nectanebo's cosmic tablet as a cipher for its own textual wisdom. Just as the Egyptian tablet contains "secrets from the power of nature and creation" (Van Bekkum 1992,41), so is supposed author Samuel Ibn Tibbon described as a "true scholar and searcher of the secrets of existence and wisdom" (Van Bekkum 1992, 205). At its outset, the Hebrew romance presents itself as a pseudo-document, a "book written by king Ptolemy together with the sages of Egypt who study the formation everything and the creation of all living beings and plants as well as the images of the idols and visions and magic and sorcery" (Van Bekkum 1992, 37). Echoing Alexander's Greek- Egyptian hybridity, the Hebrew romance purports to be a work of collaborative authorship between an unspecified "Ptolemy" and Egyptian sages and idolaters – a group later said to include Nectanebo himself. Nectanebo and Ibn Tibbon thus become mirror images of one another. The Egyptian sage's idolatry with wax figurines stands opposite the Jew's pious search for the cosmological "secrets of existence." The romance's pseudo-author Ptolemy – the geographer? the king who stole Jewish wisdom? or both, as in Raphael? – hovers somewhere in between, bridging the Egyptian pharaoh-idolater with the Jewish philosopher-rabbi. The contradictions across these collaborative authors – attributed or wholly imagined – reveals tensions in Jewish theology and its attempt to differentiate between similar spatial acts. Seeing and creating the cosmos can be either idolatry or philosophy, divine transgression or pious wisdom.

Jewish theology also privileges prophets with visions of miniaturized space – raising the possibility that Alexander's hand-held world renders him not an idolator but a holy ruler. Another Hellenized Jew of Alexandria, the tragedian Ezekiel adapted the biblical Exodus story into Greek tragedy. But Ezekiel added one scene found nowhere in the Hebrew Bible. In a dream, Moses ascends mount Sinai. In the Hebrew

Bible, Sinai is where Moses receives the Ten Commandments, but atop Ezekiel's dream Sinai, Moses receives a world-vision. Upon a throne sits a "noble man" holding a sceptre and crown (Jacobson 1983, vv. 70–1). The royal figure is ostensibly God, who gifts the sceptre and crown to Moses, just as the Nectanebo automaton did to Alexander. Yet also like Alexander himself ascending into the heavens, Moses beholds "the whole earth all around and saw/beneath the earth and above the heavens" (vv. 77–8). Alexander's resemblance to this Hellenistic Moses presents an alternative to his world-vision as idolatry; perhaps instead, Alexander's ball game is a kind of prophetic vision of the cosmos that symbolizes divine sanction of his global empire.

The Jewish tragedian's namesake, the prophet Ezekiel, likewise connected prophecy to miniaturized space in a biblical scene that dramatizes mapping and playing. In the Book of Ezekiel, the eponymous prophet is commanded by God to perform what are often referred to as symbolic actions. Though typically such symbolic actions take penitential form, such as walking barefoot or donning sackcloth, Ezekiel's is a more complex act of map-making and gaming. God first commands him to take a brick and "engrave on it the city of Jerusalem" (4:2). Ezekiel's cartographic act closely resembles the earliest known city maps, those of the Babylonians who rendered their cities on brick-like clay tablets.[15] With his brick/tablet map of Jerusalem, Ezekiel is then instructed by God to enact a siege by building miniature bulwarks, towers, a mound, army camps, battering rams, and an enclosing wall with an iron pan (4:2). Even more than Nectanebo's "chessboard" tablet of a "miniature heaven," Ezekiel's interaction with his tablet map of a miniaturized Jerusalem mimics boardgames. Anticipating the comic store basement by several millennia, Ezekiel is thus our first tabletop, or brick-*tablet*-top, wargamer.

In medieval Castile, board games resembling the tablets of Nectanebo and Ezekiel similarly miniaturized terrestrial and cosmic space. Alfonso X el Sabio's *Libro de juegos* describes several games whose boards represent the cosmos, such as two "Juegos de Astronomía" that evoke the zodiac and the board game "a que dizen el mundo" [which is called "the world"] (2007, 340–1, 368–71). Like Alexander's ball, such games are themselves a form of play through miniaturization. Lavish illuminations present the players like cosmic giants surrounding their tablet-top miniaturized world (see figure 4.2). Other illuminations present Christians, Jews, and/or Muslim playing together. By seeing their board games as worlds, players of all three faiths could enjoy spatial experiences reserved for prophets like Ezekiel and Moses; even more, they could be like Proverbs' God and *amon* who create the world by playing and playful mapping.

Fig. 4.2. Alfonso X el Sabio, *Libro de juegos, o Libro del ajedrez, dados y tablas*, folio 89 V, 1283. Biblioteca del Monasterio de San Lorenzo del Escorial, Madrid, Spain. Album/Art Resource, NY. The manuscript page is illuminated with a painting of four male figures seated at a table gambling with dice.

Jewish theology attempted to contain experiences of a miniaturized cosmos – to contain the containers of terrestrial and cosmic space – by privileging such experience as prophecy or condemning them as idolatry. Because God created the world as a map and in play, prophets could similarly receive God's plan by gazing upon, even playing with, a miniaturized earth. But for the same reasons, any unsanctioned experience of miniaturized space was the idolatrous usurpation of God's spatial relationship to the cosmos. Fissures in this Jewish theology of space were produced, or revealed, through contact with Greek geography and cosmology, first in Hellenistic Alexandria and then in medieval al-Andalus. The Alexander romances mark these tensions across Greek, Hebrew, and Castilian versions. Likely influenced by similar narratives, Raphael represented the same tensions by visually collapsing Alexander's worldly rule with Ptolemy's geographic study. All these uncertainties pave the way for Cervantes to secularize the theological binary of prophetic vision versus idol-making into a theory of literary fictionality.

SANCHO'S COSMIC RULER

Like Alexander and Jewish prophets, Sancho returns from his cosmic journey atop Clavileño, having experienced the world in miniature, specifically as a mustard seed. But his game is not exactly theirs. Though Sancho's mustard seed echoes Alexander's ball, he does not physically hold his world in his hand; instead, his material object is Clavileño, the hobby horse that prompts him to imagine a cosmic map. I earlier likened Clavileño to Caillois's shaman who dons a mechanical bird costume to enact celestial flight and return with a report of the earth. Indeed, Clavileño is described as a "maquina" (Cervantes 2004, 1.61.1044) whose name evokes his very mechanical components and material hobby-horsiness: "cuyo nombre conviene con el ser de leño y con la clavija que trae en la frente" ["a good name for him because it shows that he's made of wood, and has a peg on his forehead"] (2004, 2.60.1040; 2003b, 716). For Giuseppe Mazzotta, such "overt artifice and an array of false elements" (2001, 80) grants the episode a "ludic perspective" within the literary tradition of Renaissance cosmopoiesis. Indeed, like the lance, barber's basin, and actual horse Rocinante within Quixote's game of chivalry, Clavileño is a prop within Sancho's cosmic game. But Sancho's game proves irreconcilable with the those played by the Duke and Duchess and even that of his master Quixote.

Like the world-grasping Alexander, Sancho's miniaturization of space is a game of power. As with the English "ruler," the Spanish "regla" connotes both measurement and authority, or even authority through measuring. With his vision of a mustard-seed world, Sancho has usurped the rules of the game set by the Duke and Duchess. Sancho elaborates that atop his mustard-seed earth walk humans "poco mayores que avellanas" ["not much bigger than hazel nuts"] (2004,1.61.1053; 2003b, 725). To this, the Duchess responds that Sancho's map makes no sense: "un hombre solo había de cubrir toda la tierra" ["only one man would have covered the entire earth"] (2004,1.61.1053; 2003b, 725). The Duchess is no doubt correct that Sancho's scalar inaccuracy is geospatially illogical, but her chastisement is also an attempt to regain control of her game with her rules – her rule. By drawing his own cosmic map to his desired scale, Sancho makes himself the ruler, and the Duchess knows it. Indeed, Sancho's scalar distortion violates the same theology of space that led the rabbis to equate mapping with idol-making: thou shall not represent the earth so much smaller than a human, or a human so much larger than the earth. And of course, larger yet than his hazel-nut-men is Sancho himself, who stands before his small world like a cosmic giant, like the rabbis' celestial ascendant Alexander or the players of the Alfonsine *juego mundo*. For the rabbis, distortions in cosmic scale violated the hierarchy between God and man, but the Duchess seeks to maintain a social hierarchy where both the earth's measurements and a game's rules are delineated by aristocrats like herself, not rustics like Sancho.

Composed of mustard seeds and hazelnuts, Sancho's cosmos is itself rustic. And such rusticity goes hand-in-hand with its playfulness as Sancho recounts a more embodied game:

> íbamos por parte donde están las cabrillas, y en Dios y en mi ánima que como yo en mi niñez fui en mi tierra cabrerizo, que así·como las vi, me dio una gana de entretenerme con ellas un rato ... bonita y pasitamente me apeé de Clavileño y me entretuve con las cabrillas, que son como unos alhelíes y como unas flores, casi tres cuartos de hora.

> [we were passing by the seven nanny goats [i.e., the Pleiades], and by God and my immortal soul, since I was a goatherd when I was a boy at home, as soon as I saw them I wanted to spend a little time with them ... very quietly and gently, I got down from Clavileño, and I played with the nanny goats, and they're as sweet as gilly flowers, for almost three-quarters of an hour.] (2004, 2.61.1054; 2003b, 726)

Here Sancho's game fully manifests as childlike play. Alban Forcione reads the moment as "a return to a condition of childhood innocence and irrepressible joy" (2004, 470). And yet, by conjuring the familiar rusticity of his childhood, Sancho is less imagining a nostalgic return home than imaginatively transforming the cosmos into his rustic childhood; he imposes his childhood world on the cosmic order. As Yi-Fu Tuan writes in his *Cosmos & Hearth*, the "small world of childhood" stands in contrast to the expansive cosmos that elites control through sacred rituals and secular world-making sciences (1996, 2–3). As a site of control, the cosmos is thus also an arena of conflict between elites and peasants, masters and servants. Indeed, Quixote joins the Duchess and protests that Sancho's cosmic game is "fuera del orden natural" ["outside the natural order"] (2003, 1.61.1054; 2003b, 726). That the delusional Quixote invokes a "natural order" betrays that this order is a system not of scientific truth but for social control. Quixote's "orden natural" is a secularization of Jewish theologies that condemn world-visions as idolatrous. Cosmic authority is transferred from God to social elites.

Sancho leaves the episode on a power "high." Both Mazzotta and Anthony Cascardi read the episode as a moral lesson where Sancho's small earth evokes the smallness of human ambition, as similar world-visions had articulated in Lucian, Cicero, and Macrobius. Cascardi writes, "pride is rooted in a distorted and exaggerated perspective of things ... In its extreme forms, pride leads mortals to adopt perspectives that out to belong to the gods" (2011, 124). But who learns this lesson? Despite the Duchess's attempts to corral Sancho's cosmic map-game, he dismounts Clavileño, dissatisfied with her husband's promise of earthly governorship: "desde su alta cumbre miré la tierra y la vi tan pequeña ... qué grandeza es mandar en un grano de mostaza ... darme una tantica parte del cielo" ["I looked at the earth from that great height and saw how small it was ... where's the greatness in ruling a mustard seed ... give me just a tiny part of the sky"] (2004, 2.62.1056; 2003b, 728). Having grasped a small earth, only cosmic rule will do.

THE MAP, THE COSMOS, AND MODERN FICTION
At several points along our journey, I have intimated a theory of fiction at the intersection of play and world-making. Recent debates over fictionality have, however, adopted a different set of terms. And by means of a conclusion, I want to square this discussion. In her article "Who Has Fiction?," Julie Orlemanski questions modernity's monopolization of fiction as overly reliant on a secularization thesis where premodern religious belief is overcome by a modern disbelief in fiction (2019, 150). Indeed, among the alternative paradigms Orlemanski suggests is "the framework of games, especially chess, whose avatars and rule-bound confines mirrored fictions' self-differentiation from their contexts" (159). Orlemanski's primary target is Catherine Gallagher, who differentiates between romances too implausible to warrant belief and novels that never happened yet credibly could. For Gallagher, modern fictionality begins with the eighteenth-century rise of the English novel. But Gallagher also acknowledges Cervantes as a precursor to fictionality; Quixote is novelistic "nobody" who clashes with the marvellous knights he reads and emulates (2006, 353). That Gallagher places Cervantes within fictionality yet before the novel's rise is an invitation for us to read the *Quixote* as a modern work that nonetheless retains Orlemanski's forms of premodern fiction.

For Quixote and the Duchess, the problem with Sancho's cosmic fiction is that it lacks believability; his map is spatially implausible and his cosmic game a fantastical violation of the "natural order." But by tracing the episode's genealogy back to the Alexander romances, and from there to Jewish theology, we have seen how Cervantes's fictionality involves a more complex negotiation of the religious and the secular. This secular is not a linear movement from premodern faith to modern science and literature but rather an ongoing cultural negotiation. From Hellenistic Alexandria to multiconfessional medieval Iberia,

Jewish theologies of spatial experience are repeatedly repackaged in the literary language of romance. This theological discourse provides fiction with far more than a counterpoint of naive faith in a divine supernatural. Instead, fiction is produced out of theological tensions in which world-making too easily becomes idol-making, prophetic vision crosses over into imaginative play.

Fiction thus requires not the overcoming of the religious by the secular but rather the secularization of theological vocabularies of cosmic. Here we can also turn to Cervantine scholars who look yet further ahead, from *Don Quixote* to modern theories of fiction and physics. In *The Subject of Modernity*, Anthony Cascardi responds to Georg Lukács's theory of the novel, which begins with Cervantes, as an aesthetic expression of not only modern disenchantment but also "the very disintegration ... of the world" (quoted in Cascardi 1992, 104). For Cascardi, *Don Quixote* instead illustrates how the novel enjoys "the special privilege of a mimetic activity seen as dangerous, illicit, or archaic" in part because its "techniques of representation" simultaneously "allow [readers] to 'naturalize' a world" and seek "other-worldly experiences" (1992, 104). Just as board games risk the illicit dangers of rabbinic idolatry by enabling players to play like galactic giants and the playmates of a creator God, the novel invites readers to share the cosmic experiences of Alexander and Sancho. Or the novel's readers can even experience more modern forms of physics. Chad Gasta emphasizes "the mutability and malleability of space, motion, and time" (2011, 55) in *Don Quixote* and situates the Clavileño adventure within a series of episodes that anticipate Einstein's theory of relativity. In Gasta's reading, the exchange that results from Sancho's cosmic mapping ends in a literary relativity, an epistemological "truce ... making the fictional real and the real fictional" (77).[16]

Helping us square modern physics with modern theories of the novel, and even relativity with Jewish theology, is Lukács's Spanish contemporary José Ortega y Gasset. Rachel Schmidt points out how both Einstein and Ortega were influenced by the French theoretical physicist and philosopher of science Henri Poincaré (2011, 230). Inspired by Poincaré's hypothesis of perspectival relativity across microcosms and macrocosms, Ortega defines the novelist as a miniaturizer who "must contract and confine" the vast horizons of the real world, then "imprison [the reader] in a small, hermetic, and imaginary horizon."[17] Ortega's inspiration to look to physics to theorize the novel may itself have Jewish origins. Schmidt also outlines how Ortega studied with, and was deeply influenced by, the German Jewish philosopher Hermann Cohen, who applied Kantian rationalism to his studies of both

Judaism and the aesthetics of the novel (120). Cohen also borrowed from Newtonian physics that theorized the most miniature of all miniatures: the infinitesimal, in which the Jewish neo-Kantian found "a kind of nothing" that paradoxically provided material for both the building blocks of the universe and the objects of rational ideas (128–9). Cohen's desire to rationalize Judaism through philosophy and physics presents a modern echo to the project of medieval Andalusí Aristotelians like Maimonides and Samuel Ibn Tibbon, but in his fascination with the infinitesimal, we also see a latter-day Alexander and Sancho building worlds from the smallest of things. Like Cohen with his infinitesimal and Poincaré and Ortega with their microcosmoses, Cervantes with his modern novel may follow Alexander into the heavens and disregard theology's concern with scalar idolatry. But with their playful imaginations, neither the physicist, nor the philosopher, nor the novelist can fully let go of the cosmic seeds and child's ball that create worlds.

Notes

Special thanks go to Raphael Magarik and Jeff Gore for reading an early draft of this essay. Preliminary material was also workshopped at the Newberry Library's NEH Summer Institute "Mapping the Early Modern World" – thanks go as well to my fellow participants and to directors Lia Markey and James Ackerman.

1 All references are to the edition of *Libro de Alexandre* edited by Juan Casas Rigall. All translations are my own unless otherwise indicated.

2 Here and following, the first citation is to Rico's edition of Cervantes and the second is to Grossman's translation.

3 Michael Scham (2014) focuses on reading as a leisurely activity that opens up a broader world of games within *Don Quixote* and the *Novelas ejemplares*. Scham relies largely on Caillois's categories of games and does not discuss make-believe vis-à-vis Walton, which is where our approaches fundamentally differ.

4 See especially pages 3–12 and for relevant discussion of divine corporeal world-making 42–57.

5 Robert Alter's translation with some modifications.

6 James Porter situates *On the Cosmos* within a sublime aesthetics of "cosmic mapping" and "flights of the mind" alongside Hellenistic texts like Longinus's *On the Sublime* and Lucian's *Icaromenippus* (2016, 25–6, 175–7, 473–83). Longinus indeed quotes Genesis's creation story, and Daniel Boyarin connects Lucian to rabbinic texts (2009, 193–242).

7 See the essays that accompany Thom's edition and translation by Hidemi Takahashi and Hans Daiber on, respectively, Arabic transmission (2014, 153–68) and echoes in Islamic, Christian and Jewish thought (169–80).

8 For the broader tradition of such Jewish legends, see Norman Roth's "The 'Theft of Philosophy' by the Greeks from the Jews" (1978).

9 Avodah Zarah is the tractate of the Talmud on idolatry or "foreign worship." I have slightly modified Guggenheimer's translation (2011, 362) to underscore the slippage between "globe" and "ball" within the Hebrew *kadur*.

10 Luis Girón Negrón has discussed the Christian reception of Maimonides's *Guide* through Spanish adaptions by Alfonso de la Torre and Pedro de Toledo (2001 and 2019).

11 Though the attribution to Ibn Tibbon is disputed, Colette Sirat, a historian of Jewish philosophy and Hebrew manuscripts, is less dismissive and notes how translating the originally Greek romance from an Arabic version would be linguistically in keeping with Ibn Tibbon's project as a translator (1996, 217). Shamma Boyarin (2016) charts a middle path by reading the attribution as a motivated invention that through Ibn Tibbon purposefully situates the Hebrew Alexander romance within disputes over astrology and Aristotelianism particularly prevalent among Jewish intellectuals of medieval Iberia and the western Mediterranean.

12 Both Ramachandran and Eggington refer to Heidegger's essay "The Age of the World-Picture."

13 Confusion over the three figures goes back to Vasari and Bellori who believed the geometer was not Euclid but Bramante. Bellori, moreover, explained the crown and royal robes by identifying the figure not as Ptolemy but Zoroaster, leaving the third figure not specifically identified (Rowland 1997, 156).

14 Adding another level of identity slippage, Raphael's Apelles is also a self-portrait.

15 For discussion of this moment in the history of ancient cartography, see Rochberg (2012).

16 Also elucidating is Gasta's reading of cartographic and astronomic terminology in the episode of the enchanted boat, which he connects to the early modern study of not only Ptolemy but also the *Tractatus de Sphaera* (The sphere of the cosmos) of the medieval astronomy Johannes de Sacrobosco (2011, 68–71).

17 Translation my own, selecting for clarity from a longer passage: "La táctica del autor ha de consistir en aislar al lector de su horizonte real y aprisionarlo en un pequeño horizonte hermético e imaginario que es el ámbito interior de la novela … en vez de querer agregar su horizonte – ¿qué horizonte o mundo de novela puede ser más vasto y rico que el más modesto de los efectivos? – ha de tender a contraerlo, a confinarlo" (2005, 44).

Unlike the spatial experiences of Alexander and Sancho, Ortega's ultimate point, and debt to Poincaré's physics, is that the novel's miniaturized worlds retain scalar power by leaving intact relative perception: "El microcosmos y el macrocosmos son igualmente cosmos;

sólo se diferencian en el tamaño del radio; mas para el que vive dentro de cada uno, tiene siempre el mismo tamaño absoluto. Recuérdese la hipótesis de Poincaré, que sirvió de incitación a Einstein: 'Si nuestro mundo se contrajese y menguase, todo en él nos parecería conservar las mismas dimensiones'" [The microcosm and macrocosm are equally a cosmos; the only difference is the size of the radius; but for the person living inside each, the absolute size always remains the same. Remember Poincaré's hypothesis, which served as inspiration for Einstein: "if our world is contracted and shrunk, everything in it will appear to us to preserve the same dimensions"] (2005, 44).

PART TWO

Spaces for the Performance
of Alternate Realities

5 Early Modern Geotagging in Cervantes's "El coloquio de los perros"[1]

CAROLYN A. NADEAU, ILLINOIS
WESLEYAN UNIVERSITY

As a travelling resident of the city of Seville between 1587 and 1600, employed as a commissary officer for the provisioning of the king's galleys, Cervantes came to know well the urban landscape that approximately 150,000 inhabitants claimed as their home. In several of his works of fiction the city itself functions as one of Cervantes's rich characters.[2] This is certainly true in "Rinconete y Cortadillo" when the two picaresque protagonists enter Seville for the first time. Their impressions fill the reader with awe: "Se fueron a ver la ciudad, y admiróles la grandeza y suntuosidad de su mayor iglesia, el gran concurso de gente del río en tiempo de cargazón de flota" (I.182) ["They went to have a look round the city. They were amazed by the size and magnificence of its cathedral, and by the vast crowds gathered at the river because the fleet was being loaded up"] (I.183).[3] Cervantes highlights the recently constructed Puerta de la Aduana (1587) and Puerta del Arenal (1566); he points out linguistic curiosities like calling a *tiesto* [pot] a *maceta*; and lures readers in with rich detail specific to this commercial hub. We see this same fondness for this gateway to the new world in "El celoso extremeño," where Cervantes's treatment of the May-December motif is grounded in the very materiality of the bustling city of Seville of the late sixteenth and early seventeenth centuries. Cervantes's careful attention to details of urban Spain, his use of popular cultural markers like saraband music, and his attention to material objects like clothing and food help to create a familiar atmosphere that both frames and advances the story.

The goal of this essay is to examine the role of the city of Seville in "El coloquio de los perros" as Berganza recounts the time he spent there. Different from "Rinconete and Cortadillo," where the city serves as a contact zone for economic trade between the New World and Old World or "El celoso extremeño," in which a Seville home transforms into a metaphor for repressed sexual desire, in "El coloquio de los perros," Cervantes's detailed portrayal of the city exposes food insecurity, corruption, and violence underlying heterogeneous social groups that define early modern Spain. My argument is that Cervantes's dynamic spatial frames and portrayal of the city play a crucial role in creating a familiar space in which he can then reveal social issues of the underbelly of Spain seen across distinct social groups.

Ever since critics, like Frederic Jameson (1991, 154) and others, have recognized the importance of space and place in their respective disciplines, literary scholars have brought space into the realm of narrative theory to examine what roles spatial frames and story spaces have on understanding social, political, economic, cultural, and historical references in literary texts.[4] Marie-Laure Ryan, in her definition of "space" in *The Living Handbook of Narratology*, reminds us that "Narratives are not only inscribed on spatial objects, they are also situated within real-world space, and their relations to their environment go far beyond mimetic representation" (2012, np).[5] She goes on to explain that describing landscapes builds a "spirit" of place and that pointing out certain objects and areas can allow readers to better imagine character movements. In fact, "GPS and wireless technology have made it possible to create stories on mobile phones, attach them to particular geographic locations, upload them on the Internet, and make them accessible only to people who happen to be in the right place" (2012, np).[6]

Of course, Cervantes did not have access to the most recent version of an iOS device, but his intentional details of the urban spaces that Berganza occupies brings the reader into the city in a similar way and for a similar purpose. His descriptions of specific physical environments create a sensual intimacy for the reader so that we can more deeply engage with the narrative structure, the social commentary, and the artistic concerns that fill the pages of the tale. Again, returning to the work of Marie-Laure Ryan, she reminds us that "The various techniques of space presentation ... give flesh and shape to the visualizations that immerse the reader in the narrative world" (2012, np). It is clear that Cervantes is keenly aware of the power of mental visualizations and that providing spatial frameworks of the slaughterhouse, the merchant's home and workspace, and City Hall plaza, the centre of law and justice, offers his readers a unique geographical depth to Berganza's tale.

PART I

Berganza begins his autobiography with a specific geographic location: the slaughterhouse beyond the Puerta de la Carne in Seville, named appropriately as this gate served as the entry point for meat from the slaughterhouse that was sold at the Plaza de la Alfalfa, where the royal butchers were located.[7] He goes on to describe the criminal activities of the slaughterhouse beginning with the portrayal of his first master, Nicolás el Romo, "mozo robusto, doblado y colérico" (IV.86) ["a strong lad, stocky and bad-tempered"] (IV.87)), and others who work there, "ancha de conciencia, desalmada, sin temer al Rey ni a su justicia" (IV.88) ["people with little conscious, without mercy, with no fear of the King nor of his justice"] (IV.89), who steal for their friends and lovers. Berganza is astonished at how little those who work there care about rules and basic respect. He is astonished by the level of violence seen on a daily level: "estos jiferos con la misma facilidad matan a un hombre que a una vaca" (IV.88) ["these knifemen could kill a man with the same ease as they kill a cow"] (IV.89).

Berganza goes on in detail about how in the early hours of a meat day, people came by and filled their bags with the best parts of stolen meat: "pedazos de carne, criadillas y lomos medio enteros. No hay res alguna que se mate de quien no lleve esta gente diezmos y primicias de lo más sabroso y bien parado" (IV.88) ["chunks of meat ... sweetbreads and almost complete shoulders of meat. No animal is killed without these people carrying off their tithes and the best and tastiest cuts"] (IV.89). The law specified that animals had to be slaughtered at the slaughter-house. Garrido Aranda explains that in this way, authorities could control "las condiciones del ganado, cantidad de carne, limpieza y hierros" [the conditions of the cattle, quantity of meat, cleanliness and irons] (1995, 206). Animals were first bled, skinned and then weighed for sale. The skins and animal fat were the property of the owner, though violations were frequent (Garrido Aranda 1995, 206). Mary Elizabeth Perry confirms that this type of corruption was rampant in part because the government oversight of food control was shoddy:

> The stability of any government depends to some degree on its ability to provide food for its people at a price they can afford. The city government had been charged with this responsibility since the eleventh century, although the Crown occasionally interfered. Millers, bakers, innkeepers, and food-retailers were required to post official prices, and they were prosecuted for charging more than these prices. (1980, 48–9)

Similarly, as Berganza continues to expose the corruption, he confirms that both workers and government officials are to blame: "Y como en Sevilla no hay obligado de la carne, cada uno puede traer la que quisiere" (IV.88) ["and as in Seville there is no official supplier of meat, everyone can bring what he likes"] (IV.89). The *obligado* is the city official who auctions off needed goods. Regarding meat, Garrido Aranda explains it in these terms:

> Para evitar problemas de carestía, el gobierno local recurre al *obligado* persona que, anualmente, asegura a la ciudad el avituallamiento de vaca, carnero, cerdo, y, a veces, tocino. Al inicio del concierto Ayuntamiento-Obligado, éste deposita una fianza con la cual, cuando falte género, se comprarán reses a los ganaderos del entorno.

> [To avoid shortage problems, the local government turns to the *guarantor*, the person who, annually, assures the city of supplies of cow, mutton, pork, and, sometimes, fatback. At the beginning of the agreement between City Council-Guarantor, the latter deposits a bond with which, when there is none at all, cattle will be bought from the surrounding ranchers.] (1995, 204)

This corruption manifests itself in the form of bribery when he describes magistrates who will overlook even a murder for the right amount of meat: "no hay ninguno que no tenga su ángel de guarda en la plaza de San Francisco, granjeado con lomos y lenguas de vaca" (IV.88) ["there isn't one of them without a guardian angel in the Plaza de San Francisco, bought with shoulders of meat and ox tongues"] (IV.89). Again, Cervantes use this geonarrative move of citing a location, Plaza de San Francisco (see figure 5.1), which was the seat of government, to generalize the rampant criminal behaviour located both within the industry and the very government that oversees it. In this way, he enriches the story space by referencing the spatial framing of one area of the city to reinforce the corruption happening throughout.

Within this opening of his tale, Berganza brings into sharp focus the issue of food insecurity, corruption, and violence that is not only associated with the slaughterhouse but will become a guiding theme as he travels from master to master across space and social class. Cipión as both "reader" and "critic" engages with his companion. He critiques the narrative process, thus bringing together the physical journey of the storyteller's life with his narrative journey as his friend recounts those trials and tribulations. Critic Steven Hutchinson articulates this very point in his study *Cervantine Journeys* when he notes, "Because the narrative is bound to the journey it recounts, and because the journey traveling keeps shifting ground, the telling is also bound somewhere with the traveling" (1992, 46). He continues, "Although narrative, owing to its intangibility, frequently imitates the space and movement of what it narrates, it has its own metaphorical space and movement

Fig. 5.1. Louis de Meunier's rendition of La plaza de San Francisco, 1668, copper and etching, in Albardonedo Freire (2002, 247).

independent in principle from those it represents" (1992, 48). This is the genius of Cervantes at play: Through the stories that Berganza shares with Cipion of his travels in and around Seville's urban and later rural workforce (slaughterhouse butcher, shepherds, and a rich merchant), the institution of education (school and teacher of merchant's children), and forces of law and order (constable and notary), and later across Spain – the military (drummer of a company of soldiers), marginalized groups of Roma and Moriscos, and intellectuals and artists (poet and a theatrical manager) – readers are introduced to these social institutions that are defined, in part, by the spaces where they are located and the material culture that surrounds them. These geographical touchpoints and the objects found within reinforce and at other times question certain social expectations.

Moreover, commentaries that Cipion interjects throughout Berganza's autobiography function on a parallel level and also either reinforce or critique attitudes regarding narrative strategies and social mores that Cervantes highlights. Cipion's first critique goes directly to both the content and style of storytelling. He suggests to Berganza that he speed up his pace and consider how he delivers his tale: "otros hay que es menester vestirlos de palabras, y con demostraciones del rostro y de las manos y con mudar la voz se hacen algo de nonada, y de flojos, y desmayados se vuelven agudos y gustosos" (IV.88) ["There are others which need to be dressed up in fine words, and accompanied by facial expressions and gestures of the hands and with changes in the tone of voice so that something is made out of very little, and from being weak and insipid they become witty and entertaining"] (IV.89). Cervantes establishes these parallel spaces at two different diegetic levels, the narrative space in the hospital in Valladolid and the descriptive, plot-driven space of Seville and later other parts of Spain. In both cases, the textualization of space enhances the readers' ability to open ourselves to the real-world messages that are presented within the framework of the fantastical story of two talking dogs.

The space that Berganza and Cipion inhabit, the Hospital of the Resurrection in Valladolid, is in no way randomly chosen. Well known to Cervantes, who lived in the city at the start of the seventeenth century, the hospital had been taking in patients since the middle of the sixteenth century. But, with the needs of the city expanding, in 1553 the city council hired noted architect Juan de la Vega to build a new hospital and consolidate resources of other local hospitals. Thus, the dogs are positioned in a curative space of renewal and renovation and from this position can critique and amend Berganza's tale. From the outset, this primary narrative space for "El coloquio de los perros" ["The dialogue of the dogs"] connects this exemplary tale with the proceeding one, "Novela del casamiento engañoso" ["The deceitful marriage"], whose protagonist, the ensign Campuzano, had recorded Berganza's tale and whose friend, the licentiate Peralta, reads aloud. This rich narrative structure in which writer and reader fully share in the tale is emulated by the two dogs as Berganza (the autobiographical "writer") and Cipion (the astute "reader") together participate in the storytelling.

From the opening words, Cervantes provides concrete mental visualization cues to enhance the real-world space in which a fantastical event is occurring. "Berganza amigo, dejemos esta noche el hospital en guarda de la confianza y retirémonos a esta soledad y entre estas esteras, donde podremos gozar sin ser sentidos de esta no vista merced que el cielo en un mismo punto a los dos nos ha hecho" (IV.84) ["Berganza, my friend, tonight let us leave the hospital to be guarded by trust and let us repair to peace and quiet between these mats where we can enjoy undisturbed this unique gift which heaven has bestowed upon both of us at one and the same time"] (IV.85). Moreover, the intentional shifting of spatial frames, from those in which Berganza's life unfolds to those in which the story is recast, critiqued, and amended, also contribute to the complex and dynamic story space. In his monograph *Story Logic: Problems and Possibilities of Narrative*, David Herman explains how these spatial objects help readers focus on narrative shifts. "By detaching specific incidents from the ongoing flux of experience and focusing narrators', listeners', and readers' attention on localized areas of concern, stories help humans structure the world into a foreground and a background to begin with, thereby making it cognizable, manipulable, liveable" (2002, 275). In this case, Cervantes moves readers in and out of these shifting urban spaces to focus the readers' attention on what is occurring in Berganza's tale (Seville) and what social and artistic critiques are brought forth from that tale (Valladolid).

Heeding his friend's advice, Berganza then returns to his tale and recalls his master Nicolás's violent attack that almost cost him his life when Nicolás, upon realizing the meat intended for his mistress had been stolen while Berganza was delivering it, throws a knife straight at him. Berganza escapes, "tomando el camino en las manos y en los pies, por detrás de San Bernardo me fui" (IV. 90) ["out to the street and taking to my heels as fast as I could behind San Bernardo I set off"] (IV.91). Through this effect of zooming in to a specific incident as he traverses the streets of Seville, Cervantes varies the distance between the observer's spatial situation and the narrated events, moving from foreground to background and in between. Through these shifts in focus, this zooming into the city streets, he moves objects of description, in this case, Berganza carrying meat being delivered in a basket to the butcher's lover, into the foreground. In this way, Cervantes exemplifies what will be the first in a series of experiences, the violence Berganza endures as he tries to faithfully serve his master. As he closes out this first episode, with the marker San Bernardo, a neighbourhood located precisely outside the walls of the city where the Puerta de la Carne was located, and known for its disreputable characters living there, Cervantes provides another geomarker that bestows additional authenticity to Berganza's tale.[8]

Once beyond the walls of the city, Berganza joins a group of shepherds and reflects on the difference between the fictional lives of characters in pastoral novels and the hard reality of his new shepherd masters. He also reflects on his life at the slaughterhouse and the external forces of love on his master: "la [vida] que tenía mi amo y todos los como él, que están sujetos a cumplir los gustos impertinentes de sus amigas. ¡Oh, qué cosas te pudiera decir ahora de las que aprendí en la escuela de aquella jifera dama de mi amo" (IV.92) ["the life my master and all those like him had, having to satisfy the whims of their mistresses. Oh how many things I could tell you now which I learned in the school of my master's lady at the slaughterhouse"] (IV.93). Berganza also introduces the story of Camacha de Montilla, arguably the most intriguing of Berganza's life episodes and certainly the one most critics have written about.[9] As Cervantes so deftly carries his readers from present to past into the future tales and back again, we find evidence of how the *telling* of the travels is bound with the spaces of those very travels. In the end, the shepherds, like those who worked in the slaughterhouse, gamed the system and took for themselves "lo más y lo mejor" (IV. 96) ["the biggest and best bits"] (IV.97). Cipion's response to Berganza's disillusionment, "no hay mayor ni más sutil ladrón que el doméstico" (IV.96) ["there is no greater or cleverer thief than the one which is from within the household itself"] (IV.97), acts as both a reader response and a foreshadowing of what is to come when Berganza decides to return to Seville and enters into the service of the rich merchant.

PART II

As Berganza returns to Seville after having spent time with disreputable members of the working class, first in the slaughterhouses on the edge of town and then with shepherds in the fields beyond the city, the narrator begins with a wide-angle description of the city as "amparo de pobres y refugio de desechados" (IV.98) ["shelter for the poor and refuge for the outcasts"] (IV.99) before zooming in to Berganza's entrance into the house of a wealthy merchant. Berganza explains that he quickly gained the run of the house "visitando los corrales, subiendo a los terrados, hecho universal centinela de la mía y de las casas ajenas" (IV.98) ["visiting the yards, going up to the terraces, having become the sentry of both my own and other people's houses"] (IV.99). As in the zoomed-in description of material objects at the slaughterhouse, once again Cervantes's focus on the concrete spaces of yards and terraces allows readers to fully enter into this elite, urban narrative space. For his work Berganza was duly rewarded with bread, bones from the table, and other kitchen leftovers.

For readers of Cervantes's day, the merchants of Seville would certainly bring to mind an international group from Amsterdam, Genoa, Florence, and Lisbon as well as others from throughout Andalucia and other parts of Spain.[10] Curiously, from the early sixteenth century onward, foreigners were prohibited to engage in commercial enterprise with the New World. However, Eufemio Lorenzo Sanz notes that concessions were granted to those who married a Spanish woman and resided in Spain for at least ten years as they were considered naturalized citizens and could petition the Crown to engage in business (1979, 53). In the application process, merchants were asked, among other things, about their children, the real estate they owned, and their residence (Lorenzo Sanz 1979, 54).

Apart from the house itself, the key geographical spot is the master's workplace: la Casa Lonja de Mercaderes (see figure 5.2). Berganza explains that this is where he carried out his business and that one black

Fig. 5.2. Louis de Meunier's rendition of La Lonja, "La Casa de Contratación y la catedral de Sevilla vista por detrás,"1668, copper and etching, in Albardonedo Freire (2002, 252). Courtesy of Biblioteca Nacional de España.

servant accompanied him. The Casa Lonja de mercaderes de Sevilla [Seville's Merchant Exchange] was an architectural wonder. Designed by the royal architect, Juan de Herrera, in the plateresque style, the project received official approval in 1582 and was built between 1584 y 1598 under the direction of Juan de Minjares and later Alonso de Vandelvira and then Miguel de Zumárraga.[11] It was constructed in response to merchants trading with the New World who had no single designated space to conduct business. New World commerce included food products such as wine, wheat and other grains, baked goods, sugar, and oil; cloth such as linen and silk; and dye bases such as indigo and cochineal. But among the biggest commerce for foreign merchants, particularly the Portuguese, was human trafficking of people from Africa (Lorenzo Sanz 1979, 93–102).

Returning momentarily to his master's residence and family, Berganza explains that the merchant's vanity and ambition were seen through his children, who attended school with the Jesuits. They arrived at school with an imposing manner, in sedan chairs or carriages, and had tutors and pages at their disposal.[12] Cipion affirms this portrayal:

es costumbre y condición de los mercaderes de Sevilla… mostrar su autoridad y riqueza, no es sus personas, sino en las de sus hijos; porque los mercaderes son mayores en su sombra que en sí mismos ... Como la ambición y la riqueza muere por manifestarse, revienta por sus hijos, y así los tratan y autorizan como si fuesen hijos de algún príncipe. (IV.100)

[that is the custom and practice of the merchants of Seville, and of other cities too, to show off their riches, not on themselves, but on their sons; because the merchants are greater by virtue of the shadow they cast than because of their own persons ... As ambition and riches long to be displayed, they burst forth in the children, and so they treat them and invest them with authority as if they were sons of some prince.] (IV.101)

While at school, Berganza is likewise treated like royalty and describes his relaxed lifestyle of playing fetch with the students and being fed nuts, salad, and buttered rolls. These bucolic foods, which are not found previously with the shepherds but here among children, bring him happiness, albeit short-lived. Because the teachers saw Berganza as a distraction to learning, he was returned to the merchant's house and was left in the care of an enslaved black woman: "volví a mi ración perruna y a los huesos que una negra de casa me arrojaba" (IV.104) ["I returned to my dog's rations and the bones which a Black woman in the house threw to me"] (IV.105).[13] Berganza continues explaining both the love relation between two enslaved household members and the layout of the house, which immediately reminds readers of the house in "El celoso extremeño," for the enslaved black males in both tales live in this in-between space, between the public and private realms:

la negra de casa estaba enamorada de un negro, asimismo esclavo de casa, el cual negro dormía en el zaguán, que es entre la Puerta de la calle y la de un medio, detrás de la cual yo estaba ... las más noches bajaba la negra, y, tapándome la boca con algún pedazo de carne o queso, abría al negro, con quien se daba buen tiempo, facilitándolo mi silencio, y a cosa de muchas cosas que la negra hurtaba. (IV.106)

[The Black woman in the house was in love with a Black man, also a slave in the house, who slept in the porch between the front door and the middle door, behind which I was, and they could only get together at night, and for this they had stolen or forged the keys; and so most nights the Black woman came down, and shutting my mouth with a piece of meat or cheese, let the Black man in and had a good time with him, helped by my silence and the many things that she had stolen.] (IV.107)

As Berganza and Cipion unpack this moment and discuss how people deceive others with false knowledge, Berganza interjects with examples that include false claims of those who know Latin and Greek, to which he adds, "como hacen los portugueses con los negros de Guinea" (IV.108) ["as Portuguese [do] with Black people in Guinea"] (IV.109). This side comment in the midst of Berganza's merchant tale brings to mind the tacit connection between who was at the forefront of the merchant class at the close of the sixteenth century in Seville, that is, the Portuguese, and what their primary goods were: enslaved humans.[14]

From 1441, when the Portuguese first brought enslaved Africans to Portugal, it signalled first a lucrative slave trade market within the Iberian Peninsula and later with the New World. Citing the work of Antonio Almeida, historians Manuel Francisco Fernández Chaves and Rafael M. Pérez García remind us that "hasta mediados del siglo XVI el destino principal de los esclavos rescatados por los portugueses en las zonas africanas de aprovisionamiento fue la Península Ibérica antes que América" [until the middle of the sixteenth century, the main destination of the slaves taken by the Portuguese in the African supply areas was the Iberian Peninsula before America] (2012, 203). At this time, Seville was the second major slave-trading city after Lisbon on the Iberian Peninsula (Ortiz Arza 2015, 149).

As Nicholas Jones has pointed out in his book *Staging Habla de negros: Radical Performances of the African Diaspora in Early Modern Spain*, "In the sixteenth century, slaves from Africa, Asia, the Americas, and the circum-Mediterranean world made up a sizeable constellation and conspicuous part of the population of Seville" (2019, 2). Jones continues, "The city of Seville and the kingdom at large has a voluminous black population that reached a height of 11 per cent. In a one-year period between 1569 and 1570, 1,100 slaves were sold annually, of whom more than 85 per cent were purchased by neighbouring cities across Andalusia" (2019, 2–3).

Fernández Chaves and Pérez García corroborate these data as they submit that the indisputable success of the Portuguese in Seville had been developing around a series of activities that they controlled, both the slave trade and the "pastel" [cake/pie] industry:

> Lucharon por conseguir un control de todos los elementos de estos negocios y así fueron desplazando a lo largo del siglo, y paulatinamente, a los grupos financieros y mercantiles no lusos (principalmente genoveses, florentinos, sevillanos y andaluces) de la participación o liderazgo en las mismas, hasta hacerse con el control de los distintos aspectos del negocio: la producción, la comercialización, la financiación y la especulación.

> [They fought to get control of all the elements of these businesses and thus gradually displaced non-Portuguese financial and mercantile groups (mainly Genoese, Florentines, Sevillians and Andalusians) from

participation or leadership in the same, until taking control of the different aspects of the business: production, marketing, financing and speculation.] (2012, 202)

Data taken from the *almojarifazgo* [customs] taxes between 1569 and 1579 indicate how many merchants dealt in human trafficking and to what extent:

18 comerciantes que llevan a América 150 o más esclavos, entre los cuales hay cinco portugueses que controlan un tercio de los envíos de esclavos. Quien lidera la lista de forma indiscutible es Simón de Tovar, que se introduce en el negocio en 1575 y en solo cinco años envía más de 2.000 esclavos negros, continuando su actividad negrera de forma frenética durante las dos décadas siguientes.

[18 merchants bringing 150 or more enslaved people to America, including five Portuguese who control a third of slave shipments. The one who is undoubtedly at the top of the list is Simón de Tovar, who entered the business in 1575 and in just five years sent more than 2,000 enslaved black people, continuing his slave activity at a frenzied pace over the next two decades.] (Fernández Chaves and Pérez García 2012, 219)

Records show that other well-known figures, like the naturalist Dr. Nicolás Monardes, also dealt directly with the slave economy. In reference to how the Portuguese grew their business, in particular one well-known merchant, Bento Vaez, Fernández Chaves and Pérez García explain:

No es casualidad que en 1561 lo encontremos trabajando para el doctor Nicolás Monardes, actuando como su fiador y pagador precisamente en la paga del precio de los derechos de las licencias para llevar a América 500 esclavos. Como se sabe, Monardes no fue solo uno de los grandes naturalistas y médicos del siglo, sino también un activo comerciante con las Indias y uno de los principales negreros de aquellos años.

[It is no coincidence that in 1561 we find him working for Dr. Nicolás Monardes, acting as his guarantor and paymaster precisely in paying the price of the licence rights to bring 500 slaves to America. As is known, Monardes was not only one of the great naturalists and doctors of the century, but also an active merchant with the Indies and one of the main slave traders of those years.] (Fernández Chaves and Pérez García 2012, 218)

Berganza's portrayal of the merchant reveals neither his nationality nor his specific trade but the insertion of the side comments regarding those in the household and the narrator's intradiegetic exchanges with Cipion offer points of reflection for the active reader. As he concludes the tale of his third master, Berganza underscores how he views enslaved black people: "habiendo visto la insolencia, ladrocinio y deshonestidad de los negros, determine estorbarlos, por los mejores remedios que pudiese" (IV.108) ["having seen the insolence, thieving and dishonesty of the two Black people, I resolved, as a good servant, to put an end to it by the best means at my disposal"] (IV.109). This denouncement of their behaviour as a tipping point for Berganza's own arouses ethical reflection on the part of the reader. Readers first note a shift because Berganza is responding to Cipion's challenge that insists if Berganza were human, he would be a hypocrite: "y todas las obras que hicieras fueran aparentes, fingidas y falsa, cubiertas con la capa de la virtud solo porque te alabaran, como todos los hipócritas hacen" (IV.108) ["and all the works you performed would merely be appearance, falsehoods and sham, covered with the cloak of virtue to attract the praise of others, as all hypocrites do"] (IV.109). The second shift happens when Berganza decides to act on the repeated offences he has witnessed throughout his life. Here, the behaviour of the two enslaved house servants is comparable to the dishonesty and thievery Berganza has experienced in every area of the workforce and will continue to experience throughout his life. In discussing the ending of "El celoso extremeño," Paul Johnson, in his work *Affective Geographies*, has noted that Cervantes often chooses "to seize suspension as an invitation to ethical reflection as well as action" (2020, 62) and that it occurs in many of the *Exemplary Novels*. I am arguing that this type of reflection is evident here as well as Berganza and Cipion discuss the ethical behaviour of laborers and enslaved people, and more generally, human beings.

In the end, Berganza decides to no longer accept the gift of food and attacks the unnamed enslaved woman on several occasions. She finally decides to poison Berganza, but he catches on and leaves before he ends up dead. On his own once again, he quickly finds another master to serve, this time entering into the world of law and justice.

PART III

Cervantes has often critiqued law enforcement agents as arrogant and insolent, men who abuse the system whenever they feel like it, as Cipion so shrewdly notes even while complimenting the exceptions to the rule as "buenos, fieles y legales" (IV.116) ["good, trustworthy and honest"] while listening to his friend's tale (IV.117).[15] Recalling his fourth master, Berganza begins without geographic specificities, as if to give his audience a sense of the ubiquitous nature and proliferation of corruption within the system. Together the sergeant, his lover, two police officers, and a law clerk collude to swindle a foreigner, who is literally fresh off the boat, this time from Brittany. After Berganza foils their scam, a "teniente de Asistente" ["magistrate's lieutenant"] gets involved and hauls off the Breton, the lover La Colindres, and the landlady of the inn where the action occurs. Even when justice is served, certain officials and eventually the landlady are not held accountable.

After this lengthy introduction, Berganza returns to specific geographical markers to paint a detailed picture of the true nature of his new master. This part of the story is framed by the city's two principal gates: Puerta de Jerez and Puerta de Macarena. In a letter to the City Council, Felipe II himself describes them in the following way: "para maior autoridad [...] y mas façilitar la entrada y salido dellas han hecho adreçar las [...] principales de la dicha ciudad que llama al macarena y el xerez" [for greater authority and to make it easier to enter and exit through them, they have adorned the main gates of said city which are called Macarena and Jerez] (cited in Albardonedo Friere 2002, 427). Cervantes uses the Puerta de Jerez along with the nearby Colegio de Maese Rodrigo, another well-known landmark that would later become part of the University of Seville (Cervantes, "The Dialogue of the Dogs" 1992b, 165n30), as markers to frame how the "alguacil" [sergeant] displayed his valour when singly taking down six armed men at once. Berganza even includes a historic figure, Sarmiento de Valladares, whom historians place as chief magistrate of Seville from 1588 to 1589, as someone impressed by his deeds. That evening Berganza specifies the Triana neighbourhood and particularly a street next to "el Molino de la Pólvora" [the gunpowder mill], as the place where he meets up with his six accomplices who all work for Monipodio, head of the Seville mafia and famous for his exploits in another of Cervantes' novels, "Rinconete y Cortadillo." Again, this series of sharp focuses into a specific part of the city, from overview to neighbourhood to a specific street, lends specificity and credibility to Berganza's tale.

At the same time, it deepens its connection to the pages of fiction as the character Monipodio ties this narrative to another picaresque tale that takes place in Seville. It is also worth noting that at that time Triana was experiencing massive growth and was home to both a colony of Portuguese emigrants and enslaved Black people from the Algarve.[16] In this way Berganza's episode as a police dog also ties into his time as a merchant's pet. Later, in the famed Plaza de San Francisco, where City Hall, the centre of law and order, is located, the sergeant is finally duped and his greed exposed as he prances around on a stolen horse that some tricksters had swindled him into buying. This section comes to a close in the evening when the chief magistrate, the sergeant, and others are making the rounds in the San Julian district (near the Macarena Gate). Here, Berganza turns on his master and attacks him, thereby exposing him as the thief that he is. As we have seen at other moments in the novel, Cervantes provides an early modern "geotag" that validates the space when the climactic action occurs.

In this way Cervantes creates a "feed-back loop effect," which Ryan explains is a mental model and is "built to a large extent on the basis of the movements of characters" that "enable readers to visualize these movements within a containing space. Mental maps, in other words, are both dynamically constructed in the course of reading and consulted by the reader to orient himself in the narrative world" (2012, np). Berganza then realizes it is time for him to depart his native city and slips away on his next adventure.

Geographic markers and material objects associated with those markers provide readers with much needed information to better understand character development and thematic expression in works of fiction. They serve as concrete markers in which Cervantes can place his fictitious tale narrated and commented on by two talking dogs. Cervantes early modern "geotags" act as spatial categorizations of experience and, in this way, add authenticity to the work of fiction and create a richer environment in which readers then and now can immerse ourselves. Urban landscapes in works by authors and later film-makers writing centuries after Cervantes, for example, James Joyce's use of Dublin in *Ulysses* (1918–20),[17] Manuel Vázquez Montalbán's portrayal of Barcelona in *Mares del sur* (1979),[18] or most recently Bong Joon-ho's characterization of Seoul in the Oscar-winning *Parasite* (2019), define with particular clarity the deep inequalities and injustices found within their respective urban landscapes. Cervantes's construction of Seville and his early modern geotagging of key sites orient readers so we can travel with Berganza through his woeful tale. This literary device also captures the allure of the city and all of its unsavoury flaws for readers who may never have the opportunity to experience its wonders in person.

Notes

1 This research was supported by an Illinois Wesleyan University "Artistic and Scholarly Development" grant.

2 In his biography of Cervantes, Richard Predmore reminds us that Seville figured at least fifty times in his writings (1973, 40) and Jean Canavaggio insists that "we owe to the author of the *Exemplary Novellas* the most

colorful picture of this Sevillian underworld that exists" (1990, 173). Scholars debate when Cervantes departed Seville for the last time. Canavaggio believes it was sometime in the latter part of 1600 when the Black Plague was decimating the city (1990, 190) but Francisco Navarro Ledesma contends that he left at the beginning of 1603 after having served a second prison term (1973, 237). For an overview of Cervantes's Seville, see Piñero Ramírez and Reyes Cano (2013) and Núñez Roldán (2005).

3 All translations from Cervantes's *Exemplary Tales* are from the Ife edition; all other translations are my own.

4 For studies on space in Cervantes's *Galatea*, *Don Quijote*, and *Persiles*, see de Armas (2022); on Lisbon as an urban setting in *Persiles*, see Fraticelli (2002); on interior space in "Rinconete y Cortadillo," see Candia Pérez (2020) and Stephen Boyd (2004); on domestic space in "El celoso extremeño," see Áviles (1998) and Cox Davis (1995); and on domestic space in both "El celoso extremeño" and *Don Quijote*, see Navarrete and Quinn (2016).

5 For more on the role of space in narrative, see Ryan, Foote and Azaryahu (2016).

6 Perhaps one of the most well-known examples of digitally formatted literature that incorporates geotagging is *The Silent History* by Eli Horowitz, Kevin Moffett, and Matthew Derby (2012–2013) and the adjacent "Field Reports." These latter texts are short, site-specific accounts that are only read via the app with an iOS device at a specific location. The Silent History website explains that the field reports "are deeply entwined with the particularities of their specific physical environments – the stains on the sidewalk, the view between the branches, a strangely ornate bannister, etc. – so that the text and the actual setting support and enhance each other" (Horowitz, Moffett, and Derby 2012–13).

7 Its name *Puerta de la carne* is first documented in 1425. Previously it was named *Puerta de la Judería* [Jewish gate] given its location next to the Jewish quarters and also *Minjoar*, from 1402 onward, but by the mid-sixteenth century, it was known as such. The gate, which served as the entry point for meat that was sold at the Plaza de la alfalfa where the royal butchers were located, never closed as the movement of animals for slaughter and slaughtered was ongoing. This differed from other city gates that had regular hours of controlled access in and out of the city. Historically, it was also an area of the city where *pícaros* gathered for entertainment related to the slaughter of animals. In the last quarter of the sixteenth century, the gate underwent a series of renovations (Albardonedo Freire 2002, 273–9).

8 For a description of San Bernardo in the late sixteenth century, see Albardonedo Freire (2002, 98).

9 For the role of Camacha and, more generally, witchcraft in "El coloquio de los perros," see Shuger (2011), Cárdenas-Rotunno (2008).

10 Eufemio Lorenzo Sanz reports that Italians, Portuguese, and Flemish made up the largest groups of international businessmen, followed by French, English, and German/Scandanavian (1979, 55–102).

11 For details on the construction of the Casa Lonja de mercaderes, see Cruz Isidoro (1997, 36–7) and Martínez Lara (2016).

12 Jean Canavaggio notes in his biography of Cervantes that "the same biographers who have made him a pupil of the Jesuits in Córdoba readily inscribe his name in the registers of their Seville school, established in the very center of the city, in the district of Don Pedro Ponce" (1990, 34). But rather than reading Berganza's praise of the Jesuit pedagogy, Canavaggio proposed that it is "an inverted image, a ferocious denunciation of the order's worldly involvements" (1990, 35).

13 As translations of the label *negro* have evolved with time, I have amended the translation of *negra* and related words to align with language used today, for example, from *negress* to *Black woman*.

14 For more on the slave trade in Sevilla, see Ortiz Arza (2015), who focuses on the slave trade of the Martínez de Jáuregui brothers and also mentions others who moved from Northern Spain to Seville and profited from the slave trade industry in the late sixteenth-century. See also Mira Caballos (1994). In this latter article, Mira Caballos includes an appendix with licences for trafficking enslaved people from 1544 to 1550. The list includes dates, contractors, shipmasters, number of enslaved people and their destination.

15 Don Quijote questions law enforcement standards when he comes across the *galeotes*; in the exemplary novel "Rinconete y Cortadillo," the narrator provides additional commentary on corrupt law officials. A similar portrayal is common in other works, for example, throughout Quevedo's *El buscón*.

16 For more on the history of Triana, see Albardonedo Freire 2002, 102–4.

17 In *The Book as World: James Joyce's "Ulysses,"* Marilyn French talks about Dublin as "the third character in the plot" (1976, 93).

18 Agustín Cuadrado (2010) address the use of space in Vázquez Montalbán's *Los mares del sur* to expose the social violence of the transition to democracy in the late 1970s.

6 Eluding Surveillance and Repression in Early Modern Madrid: Manufacturing Safety through Street Performances in Cervantes's *La gitanilla*

MATÍAS A. SPECTOR, UNIVERSITY OF CHICAGO

In the prologue to *Novelas ejemplares* (*Exemplary Novels*), Miguel de Cervantes visualizes his book as a gaming table located in the main square, one of the most crowded venues in a city in the 1600s: "Mi intento ha sido poner en la plaza de nuestra república una mesa de trucos, donde cada uno pueda llegar a entretenerse, sin daño de barras" ("My intention has been to bring out into the public square of our nation a gaming table where each person can be entertained, with no harm to anyone"; 2013, 18; 2016, 4).[1] The author assures the readers – the anonymous passersby – that his street game is legitimate, and even encourages them to engage in it. After all, the book had been granted authorization for publication by the pertinent censors – without fear, Cervantes advertises his literary work in the commercial and social heart of the Spanish kingdom, a place under strict surveillance. However, by the end of the prologue, Cervantes mentions in passing a revealing detail: "pues yo he tenido osadía de dirigir estas *Novelas* al gran Conde de Lemos, algún misterio tienen escondido que las levanta" ("Since I have had the courage to dedicate these *Novels* to the great Count of Lemos, they hide a mystery that elevates them"; 2013, 20; 2016, 5). At first glance, the author seems to be insisting on the legitimacy of his enterprise. However, he is also admitting that his book may strike some readers as frivolous, even detrimental, had it not been for such a mystery "que las levanta" ("that elevates them"). Even more interestingly, Cervantes confesses that his gaming table is not as uncomplicated as he has presented it: regardless of the trick and the purpose of it, the game is dubious, like the cards we find in *Rinconete y Cortadillo* (*Rinconete and Cortadillo*). In short, Cervantes prides himself all throughout the prologue for displaying rigged entertainment, even in the core of the kingdom and under the very gaze of the authorities.

In the following pages, I explain the pivotal role that street entertainment plays in Cervantes's *La gitanilla* (*The Little Gypsy*), included in *Exemplary Novels*, with regard to dominant social groups in emerging modern cities. In particular, I argue that Preciosa and her grandmother deploy street performances to avoid surveillance and repression from a predominantly anti-Roma society and to transform Madrid's hostile streets into a more secure location for their people. Moreover, I describe how Cervantes uses the story to contrast the Romani's fortunes in the court with the setbacks they endure in Murcia, where they are barred from artistic endeavours and where part of the community is even imprisoned. From a Cervantine perspective, then, the Gypsy people should be understood as more likely to thrive in European metropolises than in minor cities such as Murcia.[2] By portraying street entertainment as a source of empowerment for marginal communities in the Madrilenian milieu, *La gitanilla* ultimately presents nascent modern metropolises as sites of contention in which performative intervention constitutes a way of eluding danger and achieving security.

Following the court's establishment in 1561, Madrid began a process of continual and dramatic transformation. The city increased drastically in both size and diversity by attracting a variety of new residents, including peasants from all over Spain, merchants, artisans from other declining urban centres like Toledo and Burgos, former soldiers of the king's army, and both Spanish and foreign officials and bureaucrats. No longer a village, Madrid faced the underlying problems of a modern European capital such as food supply, public health, infrastructure, and public order. In this context, a new public space emerged, characterized by its anonymity, velocity, and confusion (García Santo-Tomás 2004, 131–86), a meeting and crossing point for an ever-changing crowd. At the same time, the city became a contested site where authorities struggled to control a fast-growing population and where marginal communities tried to thwart and/or resist such control.

In his fictional work, Cervantes demonstrates remarkable interest in marginalized characters who live in large urban spaces and who develop innovative tactics to evade the authorities and gain control of the street. *La gitanilla* provides a persuasive case. In this story, critics have usually disputed, among other issues, whether Cervantes grants us a truthful, plausible, or idealized portrait of the Romani community, and whether this portrait is morally positive, negative, or neutral.[3] In the following pages, I refocus this discussion on the interaction between the Gypsy people and the urban landscape in Madrid and Murcia. In these places, a group of Gypsy women not only resorts to street performances to earn money, but also to avoid diverse threats. By "street performances,"

I mean artistic manifestations (such as singing and dancing) that originate in the public thoroughfare (but sometimes carry on in domestic spaces) and that lack any sort of institutional regulation. In this sense, street performances are not a modern urban phenomenon. However, they do gain distinctive qualities when performed in a crowded city.[4] Indeed, in *La gitanilla*, Cervantes illustrates how street performances allow the Romani people to circumvent oppression and turn Madrid into a more favourable space for their community.

The story begins when a group of Gypsies returns to Madrid after fifteen years of absence. In the first paragraph, Cervantes points out a central hardship that the Gypsy community must face in the Court: for the mere fact of being Romani, they have to bear the suspicious eye of society:

> Parece que los gitanos y gitanas solamente nacieron en el mundo para ser ladrones: nacen de padres ladrones, críanse con ladrones, estudian para ladrones, y, finalmente, salen con ser ladrones corrientes y molientes a todo ruedo, y la gana del hurtar y el hurtar son en ellos como accidentes inseparables, que no se quitan sino con la muerte.

> (It seems that Gypsies were born into the world only to be thieves; they are born of thieving parents, grow up with thieves, study to be thieves, and finally, in the end, become very common thieves under any and all circumstances, and desiring to steal and stealing are, in them, like inseparable accidental qualities that cannot be shed except in death.) (2013, 27–8; 2016, 11)

Some critics have argued that, by starting the sentence with "Parece" ("It seems"), Cervantes confers a tone of doubt or unreality to the subsequent ideas, thereby preparing the ground to narrate imaginary events (Selig 1962, 274), introduce the virtuous and discreet Gypsy Preciosa (Presberg 1998, 69), or portray the Romani people in a non-stereotypical way as the story advances (Lerner 1980, 48–9). These readings are correct as far as they go, but we must not forget that "Parece," in seventeenth-century Spain, is also used to indicate conventional belief. Thus, rather than just interpreting this paragraph as additional proof that the Gypsy community was alienated and persecuted by Spanish society, we may instead read the first lines as foreshadowing the harsh conditions that Preciosa and her friends will have to endure throughout the story. By this reading, Cervantes shows from the onset of *La gitanilla* that the Romani people were forced to cope with the suspicion of society, since everything they said or did could be regarded as illegal. In this way, the author anticipates how Preciosa and her friends will be subjected to potential condemnation throughout the story, even by characters who do not explicitly express animosity against the Romani community. In other words, even though Cervantes will only occasionally mention the hostile eyes directed towards the Gypsy women in Madrid, he does not mean that such eyes were not upon them. In fact, the Gypsy women's decisions repeatedly help them avoid surveillance and other repressive measures.

Indeed, by the beginning of the seventeenth century, the situation of the Romani community in Madrid was extremely unfavourable. The authorities attempted to force the Roma to assimilate into Spanish society through highly restrictive ordinances, for which failure to comply would result in expulsion. In the 1600s, for example, legislation sought to destroy Romani community bonds by prohibiting them from walking together, living near each other, or even speaking their own language (San Román Espinosa 2010, 17–18). Such restrictions, however, were rarely successful: the authorities were forced to re-enact them several times throughout the sixteenth and seventeenth centuries, which suggests that Gypsy people repeatedly managed to outwit the laws. For instance, the Romani community was expelled from Madrid after the court's establishment in 1561. Nevertheless, we have evidence that the Roma were again residing on the outskirts of the city by 1600, just like the fictional Preciosa and her friends, who returned to Madrid by 1610.[5] Indeed, following the prominent xenophobic discourses of Sancho de Moncada (1619) and Salazar de Mendoza (1618), the authorities again renewed their efforts to expel the Romani community, to some extent in vain, as attested by ongoing Romani social and business relationships with other residents of Madrid throughout the seventeenth century (San Román Espinosa 2010, 28–9).[6]

Beyond repressive legislation, diverse social agents were in charge of surveilling the Romani people on the streets of Madrid. In the seventeenth century, for example, guards policed the city's entrances and patrolled its streets day and night, while a special body of officials monitored and pursued the Roma people along the kingdom's roads (San Roman Espinosa 2010, 22). At the same time, both professional and amateur informants infiltrated Romani communities in order to gather privileged information and transmit it to the authorities, sometimes in exchange for monetary rewards. For example, Sánchez Ortega has uncovered the case of a constable who commanded an ordinary Irishman, Juan de Falbco, to enter the house of a Romani woman and collect information about any illegal activity that she was involved in (1988, 307). In addition, the Romani people had to deal with members of the population eager to report them to the authorities, or even to verbally and/or physically assault them. As a matter of fact, many subjects of the kingdom held a close relationship with the inquisitors and actively collaborated with them to detect any transgression of Christian law (Pulido Serrano and Childers, 2020).[7]

Perhaps surprisingly, even though Cervantes's first paragraph anticipates the adversity with which the Gypsy women must cope in Madrid, the author ultimately describes few instances of hostility towards the community, instead preferring to focus on the women's fear of violence. For example, Preciosa's grandmother fears that someone could kidnap her granddaughter (2013, 33; 2016, 14). Likewise, the Gypsy women are wary of entering a house filled with men (2013, 41; 2016, 19). As Alloza explains, by the beginning of the seventeenth century, Madrid suffered from a very high crime rate (including homicides, robbery, assault, fraud, cohabitation, illegal markets, etc.), especially in comparison to other European cities (1998, 31–3). In this context, and given a xenophobic and patriarchal society, a group of young Romani women were no doubt doubly vulnerable.

Having said this, Preciosa and her friends nevertheless freely move throughout the city in the first part of the story, singing and dancing, even though the Gypsy community must have been exposed to various threats there. As we saw above, Cervantes does not simply portray Madrid as a sort of "safe place" for young Romani woman, so there must be another explanation for their behaviour. To resolve this apparent contradiction, I argue that the Gypsy women actually benefit from singing and dancing (and other related activities) to stay safe in the court, because doing so allows them to escape surveillance and avoid the menace of the authorities and other citizens.

In the first place, the Gypsy women display an exceptionally heightened use of their senses to protect themselves while they stage street performances in the crowded streets of Madrid. Most obviously, although not strictly speaking part of the performance, we must mention Preciosa's grandmother, who carefully watches over her granddaughter while the latter sings and dances before a crowd. The old Gypsy's main fear is that Spanish onlookers might "despabilasen y traspusiesen" ("steal away"; 2013, 33; 2016, 14) Preciosa. Later on, we learn that "Más de doscientas personas" ("More than two hundred people"; 2013, 39; 2016, 18) had gathered around the young Gypsy ("casi todos los que en la rueda estaban" ["Almost all those in the encircling crowd"]; 2013, 34; 2016, 14). In this story, the old Gypsy woman stands against the threat of the audience by metaphorically opposing their surveilling gazes with her own countersurveillance. Surrounded by a crowd of eyes, Preciosa's grandmother becomes Argus, the many-eyed shepherd: "Nunca se apartaba della la gitana vieja, hecha su Argos" ("Always with her was the old Gypsy woman, who watched over her like Argos"; 2013, 33; 2016, 14). Having metaphorically transformed into the mythical shepherd, Preciosa's grandmother thus manages to transform a hostile urban environment into a peaceful rural landscape through which the Gypsy girls can safely move. Once again, Cervantes identifies the old Gypsy with a shepherd, this time to allude to the calm with which she leads her protégés through the bustling city: "antecogió sus corderas y fuese en casa del señor teniente, quedando que otro día volvería con su manada a dar contento a aquellos tan liberales señores" ("She gathered together her lambs and moved them ahead of her and to the house of the Deputy Mayor, agreeing that on another day she would return with her flock to the delight of those generous gentlemen"; 2013, 44; 2016, 21). In this way, Preciosa's grandmother adapts to the harsh conditions of Madrid's streets by using her own visual perception to reflect back the possessive eyes of the crowd. With a heightened sense of sight, the old Gypsy manages to securely move throughout the public space.[8]

While performing, Preciosa too displays exceptional visual abilities through which she gains some control over the city. As she dances through the streets, she internalizes a map of Madrid, turning the chaotic and unfathomable urban landscape into a manageable and familiar space. Thus, on the few occasions when Preciosa visits the court, she attentively registers the layout of Madrid and therefore develops an extraordinary sense of direction. For example, the young Gypsy walks into the city to verify the information that an enamoured gentleman has given her about himself:

> Y como ella llevaba puesta la mira en buscar la casa del padre de Andrés, sin querer detenerse a bailar en ninguna parte, en poco espacio se puso en la calle do estaba, que ella muy bien sabía; y habiendo andado hasta la mitad, alzó los ojos a unos balcones de hierro dorados que le habían dado por señas.

> (And as she was determined to find the house of Andrés's father, and did not wish to stop and dance anywhere, she was soon on the street where the residence was located, a street she knew very well; and having walked half its length, she looked up at a gilded iron balcony that she had been told was a feature of the house.) (Cervantes, 2013, 61; 2016, 33)

In search of Andrés's father's house, Preciosa does not hesitate. "En poco espacio" ("Soon"), she finds the right street. Cervantes suggests that the young Gypsy is highly familiar with the urban topography. In fact, the author explicitly informs us that Preciosa "muy bien sabia" ("she knew very well") the street where the residence was located. Indeed, Preciosa shows an astonishing knowledge of Madrid's urban spaces, considering that this episode occurs on only her third visit to the city, and that in all previous visits she had been dancing and singing in festive procession. It is remarkable that Preciosa manages to apprehend a map of the court and learn the streets well, even while being so busy. We can conclude, then, that the young Gypsy must have attentively observed the urban landscape while dancing and singing. Strategically located "a la sombra" ("in the shade"; 2013, 33; 2016, 14), she avoids any visual impairment. On the other hand, "dando en redondo largas y ligerísimas vueltas" ("making long, light turns"; 2013, 31; 2016, 12), Preciosa symbolically gains a global perspective of her surroundings, as if she had eyes on both sides of her body, just like Argus. In this sense, Preciosa's choreography seems to be designed not only to captivate the audience, but also to assimilate the city's layout. As the old Gypsy spins around Preciosa collecting donations (Cervantes 2013, 33–4; 2016, 14), both grandmother and granddaughter work together to exert visual control over a threatening urban space.

Preciosa's heightened vision allows her to internalize a map of Madrid, a fast-growing urban space in which many people felt disoriented and confused. Since the establishment of the court in 1561, for example, home construction had increased dramatically and uncontrollably. In this context, the city landscape became messy and chaotic, even for long-term residents of Madrid, as expressed in a Calderón de la Barca's 1628 play *Hombre pobre todo es trazas* (*A poor man is all tricks*): "En Madrid, no es cosa llana, / señor, que de oy a mañana / suele perderse una calle; / porque segun cada dia / se hacen nuevas, imagino, / que desconoce un vezino / oy a donde ayer vivia" (Is it not evident, master, that in Madrid a street can disappear overnight? As every day new streets are made, I imagine that a resident does not know today where he used to live yesterday; 1641, 168; my translation). Moreover, thanks to the telling testimony from a town hall meeting at the end of the sixteenth century, we know that Madrid's streets were "muy pequeñas y angostas y torcidas y de mala gracia" (cited in Alvar Ezquerra 1989, 198; very small, narrow, twisted, and unpleasant) – all qualities that added to the general sense of disorder. In fact, the situation was even worse than that: numerous streets lacked names, a problem that Juan de Xerez and Lope de Deça attempted to resolve to help foreigners, letter carriers, and servants (ca. 1601; 2001, 216).

Even under these unfavourable circumstances, Preciosa manages to compose a private map of Madrid, which she uses to easily move from one point to another. In this way, the young Gypsy overcomes the challenges of an unfathomable urban space. Even more, through attentive visual perception and memorization of the streets, Preciosa becomes empowered in relation to the rest of society. If we understand that topography has historically been an instrument of power, given that it allows individuals to efficiently travel from one location to another, then Preciosa possesses powerful knowledge that she can use to quickly escape or hide from the authorities in the event of a conflict. In this way, while performing, the young Gypsy employs a heightened level of vision to steer clear of danger, making hospitable what was originally a confusing landscape.

On the other hand, the Gypsy women also benefit from the effect that their performances have on their spectators. In particular, by strongly appealing to spectators' senses, Preciosa neutralizes both surveillance and threats coming from other social agents, thereby granting herself protection in the space of the court. In early modern Spain, the Jesuit priest Juan de Mariana reported how musical performances could deprive the audience of their critical faculties and leave them defenseless and vulnerable to manipulation: "vence y se apodera de todas las partes y potencias del alma, resuelve el vigor de las virtudes, y el alcázar, puesto en lo alto, la razón y entendimiento le derriba y despeña en todo género de vicios" ([music] overcomes and takes hold of all parts and powers of the soul, reduces the vigour of virtues, and up high the fortress of reason and understanding crumbles and collapses under all manner of vices; 1854, II.418; my translation). In this respect, we should note that Cervantes employs the notions of *admiración* (admiration) and *suspensión* (suspense) to refer to how the Gypsies' songs and dances affect their audience (Cervantes 2013, 33, 42, 43, 44, 66; 2016, 14, 19, 21, 36). As B.W. Ife explains, by the seventeenth century, those terms referred to a psychological state in which an individual was intensely fixated on something or somebody else, to the point of being disconnected from their material reality. For instance, Ife states that the notion of suspense "express[es] the non-rational aspects of imaginative literature (…) conveying both the rapture which fiction inspires in its audience, and the willing or unwilling suspension of the rational and critical faculties which is what ultimately brings that rapture about" (1986, 58). Similarly, Ife points out that admiration entails a phenomenon in which, after a sudden distancing from a work of art, the audience is immediately immersed again into the enchantment of fiction (1986, 87–8). Through the notions of *admiración* and *suspensión*, then, Cervantes emphasizes the strong grasp that the Gypsy women hold over their spectators.[9]

In fact, in the first part of *La gitanilla*, Cervantes illustrates how the audience loses control of itself and remains at the mercy of the street artists. For instance, we read that Preciosa's fortune telling pushes her audience to put reason aside and give in to desire: "encendió el deseo de todas las circunstantes en querer saber la suya" ("and at the same time aroused the desire of all the other ladies to know their fortunes"; Cervantes 2013, 49; 2016, 25). On another occasion, Preciosa's songs and dances impel the audience to spend their money compulsively. Cervantes compares the spectator's coins to hail, expressing their giving to be as erratic and as rash as a weather phenomenon (2013, 34; 2016, 14). Thus, the Gypsy women suspend the onlookers' normal commercial activities, which are based on the calculated (rather than impetuous) exchange of goods and services in the court, a place where "todo se compra y todo se vende" ("where everything is bought and sold"; 2013, 30; 2016, 12).

Beyond earning profits, Preciosa and her friends also gain protection by suspending their audience. Of course, their songs and dances do not achieve the impossible goal of actually eradicating anti-Romani sentiment among the onlookers. However, their performances do have the peculiar effect of channelling feelings of hate into more profitable – although still violent – actions for the Gypsy community. For example, while Preciosa dances, we learn that "llovían en ella [la abuela] ochavos y cuartos como piedras a tablado" ("*ochavos* and *cuartos* rained down like stones against a wooden target"; 2013, 34; 2016, 14). The saying is also found in Fernando de Rojas's *La Celestina*, when Celestina regrets the passage of time: "Espesos como piedras a tablado entraban mochachos cargados de provisiones por mi puerta" ("As thick as a rain of stones on a target, youths laden with provisions poured through my door"; 2011, 217; 2009, 138). Gonzalo Correas sheds light on the saying: "Solían los caballeros levantar un tablado para ejercitarse en él en tirar bohordos, como se refiere en muchos romances viejos, y en aquellos de los siete Infantes de Lara, y otros del Rey D. Fernando de León" (Knights used to set up a target and practice by throwing short spears at it, as it is referred to in many old romances, and in those of the seven Infantes de Lara, and others about king D. Fernando de León; 1924, 362; my translation). Correas adds that, following such a chivalric tradition, people would raise targets and then compete to bring them down for the prize of a rooster (1924, 362). Just like Fernando de Rojas, Cervantes employs the saying "como piedras a tablado" to denote large quantities: just as men arrived at Celestina's house with copious provisions, so too did a considerable number of coins fall over the old Gypsy. Nevertheless, in the context of the scene, the saying not only indicates abundancy but also suggests violence: spectators threw coins at the Gypsy woman as if they were stones. If we consider the game evoked in the old saying, one might conclude that the spectators threw coins like they might have thrown stones or javelins: to bring down the target, the old grandmother, in order to win the prize, Preciosa. Strikingly, this image invokes the old woman's previously mentioned fear, that someone might kidnap her granddaughter.

Therefore, as should now be clear, street performances cannot override people's hatred, but they can at least channel those sentiments into behaviours that are beneficial for the Romani community. So, even though the spectators throw coins violently at the Gypsy artists, those artists also collect abundant profits. In doing so, they amass resources to help them evade a repressive legal regime: "Y si alguno de nuestros hijos, nietos o parientes cayere, por alguna desgracia, en manos de la justicia, ¿habrá favor tan bueno que llegue a la oreja del juez y del escribano como destos escudos, si llegan a sus bolsas?" ("And if through some misfortune one of our children, grandchildren, or kin fell into the hands of the law, would there be any help as good as the sound of these *escudos* reaching the ears of the judge and the court clerk and then their purses"; 2013, 57; 2016, 30). In other words, Gypsies' songs and dances are able to transform anti-Romani sentiment into assets that afford protection against the authorities.

Similarly, in another scene, Preciosa's performances manage to overcome (or at least ameliorate) repressive acts from law officials against the Romani community. At the time, one of the Spanish authorities' main tasks was to patrol the court. In Madrid in the 1600s, officers were obliged to ensure that all Gypsies had a legitimate occupation, as indicated in *Novísima recopilación* (1805, vol. V, book 7, tit. 16, l. 1–3). In *La gitanilla*, we read that the deputy mayor "acertó a pasar por allí" ("happened to pass by"; 2013, 39; 2016, 18), presumably on one of his patrols. At first glance, Cervantes offers us a humorous scene, highlighting law enforcement's negligence and inclination to leisure: "viendo tanta gente junta, preguntó qué era, y fuele respondido que estaban escuchando a la gitanilla hermosa, que cantaba" ("seeing so many gathered together he asked what was going on, and they replied that they were listening to the singing of the beautiful Gypsy girl"; 2013, 39; 2016, 18). We cannot assert that the officer was hypnotized ("suspendido") by Preciosa's songs, as he shows a certain degree of conscientiousness ("por no ir contra su gravedad, no escuchó el romance hasta la fin" ["to preserve his dignity, he did not listen to the ballad until the end"; 2013, 39; 2016, 18). Still, Preciosa's performance greatly affects the officer, who enjoys her show very much ("habiéndole parecido por todo extremo bien la gitanilla" [the Gypsy girl had seemed fine on all counts"; 2013, 39; 2016, 18).

In any case, through her street performances, Preciosa manages to assuage the authorities' repressive disposition. For instance, the deputy mayor "mandó a un paje suyo dijese a la gitana vieja que al anochecer fuese a su casa con las gitanillas, que quería que las oyese doña Clara, su mujer. Hízolo así el paje, y la vieja dijo que sí iría" ("sent one of his pages to tell the old Gypsy woman to come to his house at nightfall with the Gypsy girls, for he wanted his wife, Doña Clara, to hear them"; 2013, 39; 2016, 18). In the context of the Gypsy persecutions of the 1600s, the officer's invitation cannot be regarded as a kind gesture. On the contrary, it should be viewed more as a command, since Preciosa's grandmother had no other option than agreeing to it, when faced with the risk of attracting ill will from an authority figure. In other words, despite the humorous tone of the scene, we should not overlook how the deputy mayor exploits his power by requesting a private performance from a marginalized group of women. More importantly, for an early modern readership, the officer's request could have brought to mind the repressive procedures of the Madrilenian justice. For instance, the deputy mayor's official duty should have led him to detain the Gypsy performers and bring them before the judges of the Sala de Alcaldes. In *La gitanilla*, the officer partially fulfils such procedures by requesting that the Gypsy women visit his house. Yet, this is only partial fulfilment, because the officer does not expect that the Gypsy women will be subjected to a trial. However, they do have to exhibit themselves before the deputy mayor's wife and her friends, who conduct a careful scrutiny of the artists, especially Preciosa ("la señora su vecina la desmenuzaba toda, y hacía pepitoria de todos sus miembros y coyunturas" ["her neighbour analysed Preciosa minutely and made a jumble of all her"; 2013, 45; 2016, 22). In other words, Preciosa's street performance has not fully exempted the Roma from repression, but it has at least made such repression more tolerable: instead of appearing before a court of judges, the Gypsy women must perform for a court of ladies. The Gypsy artists' only reward is to be able to walk free from the house of a court authority in a time of strict anti-Gypsy policies.

Preciosa's performances in Madrid illustrate another way that street performances can keep the Roma safe from repressive authorities and strategically transform the public space. Counterintuitively, Preciosa and her friends distance themselves from justice officers by gathering a crowd around them. In a study of street performances in modern cities, Sally Harrison-Pepper claims that street artists may affect the public thoroughfare in terms of "density, accretion, durations, dispersal, and flow" (1990, 127, 131). In the story, the Gypsy women manage to interrupt the *flow* of people, attracting more than two hundred passersby

(2013, 39; 2016: 39). In doing so, they gain more visibility as they become the centre of attention, which leaves them more exposed to the authorities' gaze. On the other hand, however, they become more unreachable to the authorities. In fact, if they were to intervene in such a crowd, the authorities would run the risk of creating more turmoil (especially considering that a part of society would have ties with the Romani). Thus, the officer might have to wait for reinforcements before detaining the Gypsy women, or at least delay until the crowd dissipates.[10] In this sense, when Cervantes writes that Preciosa positions herself "a la sombra en la calle de Toledo" ("in the shade on Calle de Toledo"; 2013, 33; 2016, 14), we should understand that she is taking shelter from the sun by standing close to the walls. But she also benefits from the shade provided by the crowd, which separates the dancers from the authorities. From this perspective, Cervantes illustrates how Preciosa and her friends could benefit a great deal from the urban spaces of Madrid, which, given its substantial density, could easily guarantee the artists a crowd

In sum, the Gypsy women in the first part of *La gitanilla* employ street performances to evade danger and to transform a threatening city into a safer one. After they leave the court, we have to wait until the end of the story to see them in another city. At the end of the story, Cervantes contrasts the fortune that the Roma experienced in Madrid with the harsh setbacks that they endure in Murcia. There, Preciosa and her friends do not gain control over Murcian territory by performing songs and dances. On the contrary, the Gypsy community weakens and ultimately dissipates. In drawing this contrast, Cervantes not only emphasizes the relevance of street performances to prosperity in urban spaces but also suggests that the Gypsy community is more likely to blossom in large, modern European metropolises than in smaller peripheral cities.

After departing from the court, the Gypsy community passes through numerous small villages. When they arrive in Murcia, they experience events diametrically opposed to the ones they enjoyed in Madrid. Thus, the end of the story can be regarded as an inverted mirror of the beginning. On the one hand, "a tres leguas de la ciudad" ("three leagues from the city"; 2013, 94; 2016, 57), the Gypsy group no longer dances before a crowd of two hundred people, as they did in Madrid. In contrast, in a "mesón de una viuda rica" ("an inn owned by a wealthy widow"; 2013, 94; 2016, 57), they dance for a restricted audience in an intimate context. In such intimacy, Preciosa and her friends become more vulnerable to spectators' assaults. For instance, while dancing, Andrés suspends a young woman, who then falls in love with him as if "la tomó el diablo" ("[she] was seized by the devil"; 2013, 94–5; 2016, 57). Naively, Andrés neglects his belongings, so the young woman, resentful of her beloved's rejection, places a personal possession in Andrés's bags and later accuses him of theft (2013, 95–6; 2016, 57). As a consequence, the Roma people will be targeted by repressive authorities with strong anti-Gypsy beliefs. On the other hand, Preciosa and her friends are unable to execute street performances as they enter the city of Murcia. Previously, we saw that the Gypsy artists had burst into Madrid in powerful, festive processions that allowed them to assemble a suspended crowd. In Murcia, on the other hand, they take part in a very different procession, together with "el alcalde y sus ministros con otra mucha gente armada" ("the mayor and his ministers, with many other armed people"; 2013, 97–8; 2016, 59). Instead of dancing freely, they walk under force, wearily and at a monotonous pace, especially Andrés, "ceñido de cadenas, sobre un macho y con esposas y pie de amigo" ("wrapped in chains, with his hands manacled to his waist and unable to move his head"; 2013, 98; 2016, 59). As a result, the Roma are kept from the artistic expression through which they might otherwise control the situation.

Similarly, Cervantes illustrates how Preciosa, while in Murcia, symbolically gives up street performances by taking part in a sincere display of affection that differs substantially from the artificiality of her dances and songs in Madrid. Even though the Roma are unable to stage artistic performances after arriving in Murcia, Preciosa, because of her mere appearance, nevertheless becomes the centre of attention in the upper echelons of society. In particular, she meets the magistrate's wife, the Señora Corregidora, before she is sent to prison. The Señora is overcome with curiosity by the beauty of the Gypsy girl. Here, Preciosa begs for her lover:

> En todo el tiempo que esto decía, nunca la dejó las manos, ni apartó los ojos de mirarla atentísimamente, derramando amargas y piadosas lágrimas en mucha abundancia. Asimismo, la corregidora la tenía a ella asida de las suyas, mirándola ni más ni menos con no menor ahínco y con no más pocas lágrimas.

> (As she was saying this, she never let go of the Corregidora's hands or allowed her eyes to stop looking at her very attentively, shedding bitter and pious tears in great abundance. By the same token, the Corregidora clasped the girl's hands, looking at her as intently, with no less urgency and no fewer tears.) (2013, 99; 2016, 60)

Cervantes portrays a version of Preciosa quite different than the one we previously saw in Madrid. The young Gypsy no longer dances and spins in the middle of the crowd. On the contrary, she cries on her knees in a submissive position, while her hands are "encadenadas" ("clasped") with the Corregidora's. In this way, Cervantes stresses the purity of the scene by turning the notion of "chains," a few paragraphs above associated with the prison of the Gypsy people (2013, 98; 2016, 59), into a symbol of love. On the other hand, Preciosa's eyes, instead of serving as a valuable tool to apprehend her surroundings, become a conduit for "amargas y piadosas lágrimas" ("bitter and pious tears"), a flow of emotions that runs without restraint. We learn that the audience, in this case the magistrate, is in a state of suspension.[11] Such suspension, however, differs from the one that the crowd in Madrid experienced when they watched the Gypsy women's dance: in this case, instead of losing himself in impulsive acts and giving in to Preciosa's wishes, the magistrate assesses the current situation and asks for more information. In doing so, Cervantes illustrates how Preciosa symbolically quits her artificial street performances by taking part in a pure and lofty act of love with her real mother, the magistrate's wife.

At the same time, the old Gypsy quits her role as Preciosa's protector during this scene, which is perhaps the most decisive of the whole novel. In Madrid, Preciosa's grandmother had become a many-eyed shepherd who guards her granddaughter against the dangers of modern urban spaces, "temerosa no se la despabilasen y traspusiesen" ("afraid that someone would steal away the girl"; 2013, 33; 2016, 14). In the meeting with the magistrate's wife, however, the old Gypsy must face her worst nightmare: that Preciosa's true identity will be uncovered, which will allow her real parents to change her name and thus to take her away from the Roma community to which she belongs – in other words, to steal her away. Despite this, Preciosa's grandmother chooses to tell the truth (another symbolic means of leaving behind the artificiality of street performances) and to transfer authority over her granddaughter to the magistrate and his wife. As it turns out, the old Gypsy opts in the end to stay in the magistrate's house with Preciosa, which ultimately results in Preciosa holding unexpected power over her former grandmother.

By giving up street performances in Murcia, the Gypsy community remains defenceless against the authorities and other social actors. In this sense, it is not surprising that, at the culmination of the story, the band of Gypsies ends up dissolving. First, the group loses two renowned leaders, Preciosa and Andrés, as well as the old Gypsy, a guide and protector of the young Gypsy girls. Even worse, Preciosa and Andrés (now Juan and Constanza), both daughter and son of the highest urban authorities (from Murcia and Madrid, respectively), will potentially inform against the Romani to their parents, since they possess detailed and confidential information about the Gypsy community.[12] Finally, many of Preciosa's Gypsy fellows are freed from prison "en fiado" ("on bail"; 2013, 107; 2016, 67), that is to say, in a state of dependency on their releasers, presumably Constanza and Juan.[13]

In the end, then, Cervantes illustrates how a group of Gypsies can thrive in an early modern urban capital by employing street performances, but how such a group also withers, unable to dance and sing, in a peripheral city of the kingdom. In so doing, he suggests that street performances cannot be deployed with equal success in any place, but rather that these are especially effective in emerging European metropolises. Here, Gypsy women exercise heightened vigilance while they perform songs and dances, which allows them to defend themselves against the specific dangers of large, modern cities, including crowds and confusing urban layout. Similarly, Preciosa and her friends carry out musical spectacles to "suspend" people and take advantage of them, meaning that the success of their spectacles is dependent on the number of spectators they can affect. Hence, street performances yield good results only under the concrete circumstances of the bustling new metropolises.

In short, Cervantes shows us how the Gypsy community employs songs and dances to neutralize any potential risk, and thus to transform a dangerous Madrid into a safer space. In doing so, he presents street performances as empowering tools for marginalized individuals in burgeoning urban milieus. Through these pages, we can see a new notion of urban artistic manifestations in the seventeenth century, not necessarily as a means of entertainment, nor exclusively as a commercial activity, but as an embodied practice through which vulnerable social groups – as many still do today – can circumvent surveillance and repression from the authorities and gain temporary control over the public space. In the end, this allows us to grasp the distinctive Cervantine vision of an early modern city, as a site where safety may be secured through artistic performance.

Notes

1 I will be citing from Jorge García López's edition of *Novelas ejemplares* (Cervantes 2013) and Edith Grossman's translation (Cervantes 2016).

2 I am aware that today the word "Gypsy" (in Spanish, *gitano*) may be used pejoratively or have negative connotations. However, I use the term throughout this essay (rather than regularly recasting it as "Roma" or "Romani") because, for better or worse, it was the word employed by Cervantes.

3 For example, see Marie Laffranque (2016), Joseph Ricapito (1996), Isaías Lerner (1980), Carol Koch (2008), Francisco Márquez Villanueva (1985), and Ana Eva Guasch Melis (1999).

4 In the last decades, scholars in the field of performance studies and human geography have focused on how street performance artists interact with urban crowds and alter the social and political order of cities. For an overview of some of these approaches, see Simpson (2011).

5 In effect, Preciosa had been kidnapped in 1595 (2013, 100; 2016, 61). If Preciosa is fifteen years old in the story's "present," then the story must take place in 1610.

6 Having said this, we should not conclude that the Gypsies had a strained relationship with all members of Spanish society. As some scholars have shown, the Gypsy community held social and economic ties with the lower class as well with the upper class. See, for example, Teresa San Román Espinosa (2010, 32) and Manuel Martínez Martínez (2004, 427–9).

7 To all these concrete surveillance mechanisms, we should add Michel Foucault's influential hypothesis that spectacular public executions served mainly to inspire fear in the beholder and obedience to the sovereign figure (1979).

8 For other references to Mercury and Argus in Cervantes's novel, see de Armas (2013).

9 Juan José Pastor Comín also studies how, in Cervantes's *Novelas ejemplares*, music suspends the spectators (2017, 189–219). For her part, Ariadna García-Bryce points out the captivating power of cultural representation in Cervantes (2015, 88).

10 Repressive procedures in cases of massive attendance can be found in chapter 59 of the *Advertencias para el ejercicio de la plaza de Alcaldes de Casa y Corte* (Counsel for the fulfillment of the role of Alcaldes de Casa y Corte): "Alborotado el Pueblo no han de acudir los Alcaldes a sosegarle, ni prender ni castigar culpados, sino es con prevención vastante de Ministros y gente por que si una vez lo pierden el respeto (…) cobrado el Pueblo abilantez y atrevimientos no se le pueden poner ni obrar sin mano armada, cosa que debe procurar la Justicia escusar" (With the town in turmoil, the Alcaldes ought not to appease the people, nor capture nor punish the guilty, unless it is with great precaution by ministers and lackeys, for if the people lose respect once (…) the town imbued with brazenness cannot be put upon or managed without force, that which Justice should seek to avoid; 2015, 220–1; my translation).

11 "Estando en esto, entró el Corregidor, y hallando a su mujer y a Preciosa tan llorosas y tan encadenadas, quedó suspenso" ("Then the Corregidor came in, and finding his wife and Preciosa weeping so fervently and so closely joined, he was perplexed"; 2013, 99; 2016, 60). Later, we read that

"Con nueva suspensión quedó el Corregidor de oír las discretas razones de la gitanilla ("The Corregidor was again perplexed when he heard the discerning words of the Gypsy girl"; 2013, 99; 2016, 60).

12 For a study of Preciosa and Andrés as potential informants, see Spector (2024).

13 It is intriguing that Cervantes chose Murcia as the peripheral city in which the Gypsy group dissipates. One possible hint is that Murcia was known to be a particularly hostile place for Gypsies. In fact, Murcian authorities expelled the Gypsies several times in the last decades of the sixteenth century, including in 1581 and 1591 (Martínez Martínez 2004, 422).

7 Performance Space in Cervantes's
Pedro de Urdemalas

EDWARD H. FRIEDMAN, VANDERBILT UNIVERSITY

"I am out with lanterns, looking for myself."

Emily Dickinson

Pedro de Urdemalas, one of Miguel de Cervantes's eight *comedias* published with eight *entremeses* ("nunca representados" [never presented on stage; 1987, 3; my translation]) in 1615, reflects a structural plan that does not coincide with the model of the *arte nuevo* of Lope de Vega.[1] Lope's plays are based on adherence to the unity of action, whereas *Pedro de Urdemalas* is built around what could be called a unifying concept.[2] This essay will focus on the structure of *Pedro de Urdemalas* and on the ways in which Cervantes uses dramatic space. The title figure, based on a character from folklore,[3] has led a picaresque life, and he intervenes in assorted scenarios until he finds his niche in society, ironically that of actor and playwright. His narration of his adventures and his interaction with characters of a broad range of stripes help to determine the progression of the plot. Pedro de Urdemalas has a co-protagonist of sorts in the work: a young gypsy woman, Belica, who feels that her true lineage is far different than her current status would suggest. Her air of superiority defines her, and, in fact, she will be proven to possess noble blood. The dramatis personae of *Pedro de Urdemalas* include shepherds and shepherdesses, a rustic mayor, gypsies young and old, farmers, a miserly widow, musicians, dancers, a passionate king, a mistrustful queen, their servants, a troupe of actors, other theatre people, and more, in a variety of settings. Space is significant in the play because each site can be shown to be a type of performance space, in which the world becomes a stage, figuratively and literally. The locales are fundamental to the development of the dramatic storyline. As he explores questions of identity, Cervantes takes his characters (and the spectators that he would have wished to participate in the process) from place to place in order to emphasize that what we now label as *metatheatre* has far-reaching connotations. The fact that roles are unstable is a boon to drama, in general and in this case. The dialectics of identity and performance determines the course of Pedro de Urdemalas, Belica (subsequently Isabel), and the play as a whole. *Pedro de Urdemalas* bears the distinct signature of Cervantes, a highly inventive, if underappreciated and ultimately frustrated, playwright.

Pedro de Urdemalas can be seen as a play about variations on the theme of performance. It deals with the interplay of reality and fiction, within fiction. The portrayal and characterization of Pedro de Urdemalas is complex, flexible, and built around the motif of acting. Pedro's story is set against that of the gypsy Belica, who becomes the princess Isabel, with crucial intersections, parallels, and contrasts. Cervantes does not have a set formula for his dramatic compositions, and the structure of *Pedro de Urdemalas* is, in many ways, unique. One may use the play as a key to describing, or delineating, Cervantes's theatrical vision, with respect to language, plot, themes, and messages, and his particular treatment of space. It is possible to reflect on differences between a reading and analysis of the written text versus imagining a production (and staging) of the play, which could provide a clear challenge to a director. *Don Quijote* is inevitably a part of the equation, as is Cervantes's tendency to appropriate and modify existing literary forms in his writings. *Pedro de Urdemalas* exhibits self-consciousness on a number of levels. Pedro's backstory is picaresque to the core, but Cervantes's *pícaro* can move forward to find an outlet, and a vocation, that will satisfy his – and society's – needs. He seeks, and ultimately recognizes, his place in the scheme of things. The play's conclusion is no surprise, given that the protagonist's trajectory moves naturally from the past towards the present and towards a logical and reasonable future. By highlighting its conventions, *Pedro de Urdemalas* seems to encompass Cervantes's approach to drama: self-reflexive, paradoxical, and symbolic.[4] *Pedro de Urdemalas* is very much about space. Is there space for it on the stage? Can its content mark a path to clarify and justify its form, so as to accommodate and satisfy spectators?

Act 1 of *Pedro de Urdemalas* opens with a particular rendering of the countryside, with a mixture of the rustic, the literary, and the real. This is not the setting of pastoral romance, nor are the rustic figures buffoons. Cervantes creates his own space for the pastoral element in the play. Clemente, a young man of modest means, consults with Pedro de Urdemalas, dressed as a farmhand. Clemente wishes to pursue Clemencia, daughter of Martín Crespo, Pedro's employer, but his financial woes threaten to reduce the chance of success. Clemencia has other – wealthier – suitors, and she has not responded to Clemente's amorous gestures. Assuring Pedro that his intentions are pure and that he has treated Clemencia with respect, Clemente sees himself as a victim of love and begs for help. Pedro says that Clemente is in luck for having conferred with him; destiny is on his side. Convinced that Clemente is acting in earnest, Pedro will help him in the wooing of Clemencia. Clemencia and her friend Benita approach. Clemente talks with Clemencia. She has had to be careful, but she seems to be open to his advances. There is hope for Clemente. In his first scene, Pedro is an advisor, an arbitrator, a trusted friend, and a man of mystery. He demonstrates self-confidence and authority, but his identity is uncertain at this point. From the beginning, Cervantes brings the subject of negotiation into the frame. Pedro is ready to intervene on behalf of others, as long as they win his approval and consent. The title figure reveals himself little by little, piece by piece. He is a work in progress. The character and the play simultaneously acknowledge and stray from the intertext, pastoral and picaresque. Clemente and Clemencia are *zagales*, young people within the pastoral community. They are neither foolish nor sophisticated, inarticulate nor lofty. Economics, class, and courtship rituals factor into the scheme. Clemente asks for Pedro's guidance. This interaction sets up the shift to the court of the newly elected mayor, Martín Crespo, who is charged with making judgments and who likewise requests the aid of Pedro.

The judicial procedures reflect the rural ambience. Crespo is more a bumpkin than a sage, and he is coached by an upstart. The decisions are laced with farce, as Cervantes blends the courtly scenario with a comic rewriting of the rules of jurisprudence. The mayor discusses the upcoming cases with a scribe and council members who will attend the proceedings. Crespo depends on Pedro, who devises a strategy. He will write out verdicts on pieces of paper, and the decrees will be placed in the mayor's hood, to be pulled out on cue. Pedro can offer additional advice when necessary. The first case involves two farmers, and the litigants are satisfied with the ruling regarding a loan. Then Clemente and Clemencia, the mayor's daughter, appear, dressed as shepherds with their faces covered. Clemente defends his right to marry his beloved, despite his fiscal condition. He declares that love should conquer all. The veiled Clemencia communicates only through signs. Everyone is elated when the – predetermined – positive judgment is read aloud. Varied subgenres come together in this parody of judicial licence. Pedro extends his mediating role as Clemente triumphs and will become a member of the family of the judge. In Crespo's courtroom, Pedro's intervention is no longer behind the scenes, and the satire is linked to the exhibition of the protagonist's wit and wisdom. With Clemente's problem resolved, Pedro remains alone on stage for a moment. Cervantes introduces Pascual, a friend whom Pedro has promised to help, and a rival, a sacristan, who boasts that he is superior in ingenuity (*industria*) to both of them. Pascual and the sacristan exit. Their plot line will be delayed for a bit, as a major character, Maldonado, leader of the gypsies, appears.

Maldonado enquires if Pedro is ready to associate himself with the gypsies, and he describes gypsy life in some detail. He alludes to a special gypsy girl who has been "stolen," and he foresees a match between her and Pedro once he and Pedro have sealed their pact. Cervantes has the opportunity to expound on the habits and lifestyle of the gypsies and, moving from the general to the specific, to incorporate Belica into the story. This is a diverse and rather exotic realm, and Belica will have a substantial role in what follows. Like Pedro, the gypsies are outsiders. They relish their independence from the constraints of society. And, like Pedro, Belica wants to establish a place in the world that fits her individual feelings and impulses. Under the pretext of deciding whether he should join the company of gypsies, Pedro will narrate his story, a story with obvious picaresque overtones. He is of unknown parentage ("hijo de la piedra," v. 601),[5] with no memory of his first years. He does remember going hungry and being beaten. He learned to read and write and to recite prayers. His "education" includes stealing, lying, and begging for alms. From an early age, he has sought to better his lot. He takes a job as a cabin boy ("grumete," v. 620) on a ship going to and from the Indies, and he suffers on the seas. Back in Spain, he finds himself penniless in Seville, where he participates in activities of the city's underworld as a delivery boy and a thief. Danger lies all around him, with officers of justice and with his comrades in crime. Pedro loses masters when they are apprehended and punished. He serves a soldier who ends up as a galley slave. He is thwarted in job after job. He transfers to Córdoba, where he sells drinks ("aguardiente y naranjada," vv. 694–5) but fails to prosper. He has a series of masters, some of whom he chooses to leave and some of whom abandon him. He has no luck with a master from Asturias, but his service to a blind man yields rewards, educational if not pecuniary. When the blind man dies, Pedro is penniless, but far more alert: "sin blanca, pero discreto, / de ingenio claro y sotil" (with no money, but discreet / of clear and subtle wit; vv. 718–19). He has a brief career as a mule boy. The next master is a gambler, and Pedro prospers when he is successful, but left on his own when the gentleman is caught as a thief. This brings Pedro to the present and his service to Martín Crespo.

In his picaresque-inflected backstory, Pedro de Urdemalas makes reference to the prediction that a fortune teller named Malgesí has made: Pedro will have many positions and professions, from king to priest to pope to ruffian, but in the end he will have only one, which will integrate the others (see vv. 744–59). He will sit among monarchs and gypsies. Maldonado reiterates his welcome and once more brings up the beautiful and baffling gypsy girl. As Maldonado takes his leave, Pascual joins Pedro to resume the rivalry between Pascual and Roque the sacristan. It is St. John's Eve. Pascual wants to win the hand of Benita, but she insists that she is bound to accept a man named Roque. As she gives a ribbon to Roque, Pascual grabs it away from him. Pascual is furious but helpless in this predicament. Pedro intercedes, noting that Pascual can simply change his name to Roque. Benita and Pascual are satisfied with the results, and Roque the sacristan seems relieved. Pedro yet again has saved the day – or the night – as mediator and controlling agent. As a type of harmonious flourish, a group of musicians enters, along with Clemente and the freshly betrothed couple. They play instruments and sing. Their lyrics cite Benita, Pascual, and Clemencia. Benita praises "mi Roque" (v. 1020) as the procession moves offstage. The gypsies Inés and Belica enter. Inés scolds Belica for her haughtiness, her superior attitude, her dream that she is of noble lineage. Belica defends herself; she is certain that she is more – far more – than a gypsy. Inés sees delusions of grandeur. Belica is committed to proving the force of blood that motivates her. The musical interlude is a recapitulation of prior events and an overture to the entry of Belica, obsessed with her genuine identity, with Inés, who, in stark contrast, is proud of her gypsy ancestry. Pedro and Maldonado enter. Maldonado praises Belica's superhuman beauty, and Pedro says that he is disposed to do anything for her. Marina Sánchez, a well-to-do widow, enters, led by a farmhand who serves as her squire. Inés asks for alms, and the widow ignores them. Inés is disappointed. The independent Belica cries out that the widow can keep her money. Maldonado explains the widow's situation to Pedro, who vows to take a bit of revenge. He wants the name of every relative and contact of hers. Pedro and Belica converse. He is awed by her radiance. She has her aspirations. As act 1 concludes, he wishes her well.

The first act of *Pedro de Urdemalas* contains extensive stage business. Pedro conceives plans to win Clemencia for Clemente and Benita for Pascual. He supervises the judgments of the mayor. He embraces the gypsy community, and he is struck by the charms of Belica. The parsimonious widow Marina Sánchez rejects the gypsies; she will be a recurring character. To complement the action, Cervantes puts forth two expository accounts – Maldonado's commentary on the gypsies and Pedro's narrative of his background – and he adds musical accompaniment. Scenes take place in the countryside, the courtroom, the darkness of St. John's Eve, and the gypsy camp and its environs, all adjusted to the play's use of perspective. It would be difficult, if not impossible, to do more than suggest the settings. At the play's centre is, of course, Pedro de Urdemalas, a man in search of his destiny, that is, his genuine identity. This draws parallels with Belica, who wishes to renounce her ties with the gypsies in favour of a royal pedigree. The issue of performance looms large. Pedro crafts scripts for himself and others, and Belica adheres to an interior disposition that must be legitimized. The musicians underscore the performative aspects of the play. Pedro and Belica are incompletely drawn characters, linked by the notion of finding themselves. Shepherds, gypsies, farm people, and representatives of the clergy go in and out, but they are rarely, if ever, stereotypical. Maldonado and Inés, for example, have minds, functions, and idiosyncrasies of their own. Malgesí has forecast Pedro's coming into his own. Belica has forecast her imminent victory. The demands of the dramatic medium will defer the culmination of these revelations to act 3, so that tension and suspense can reach the audience or reader, who should be engaged and entertained by the interconnected themes and plot lines.

Act 2 expands the performance space. The mayor Martín Crespo, an alderman, and a constable discuss a program to be presented in honour of the king, who is nearby, partaking in a hunt. The mayor proposes a program with twenty-four male dancers. The alderman approves; the constable dissents. They will deliberate further. Two men enter: a blind man and Pedro posing as a blind man. They speak of prayers for the dead. The widow Marina Sánchez observes them from a window and wants to arrange prayers for her family members. The blind man accentuates the affluence and the frugality of the widow. Pedro has the blind man leave, and, with a trick in mind to relive the widow of her funds, he promises to send a venerable old man, who he says will resemble him, to aid her. Maldonado and Belica enter. Her air of superiority remains on full display. Maldonado disparages her fantasy and, decrying her behaviour, he counsels her to view the gypsies as her compeers. Pedro would be ideal match, he argues. She adamantly refuses. Pedro, who reappears dressed as a gypsy, is captivated by her allure and quick to defend her egocentric position. The king enters with his retinue. Belica dares to converse with the king, who seems enchanted by her. She calls herself a "gitana bien nacida" (a well-born gypsy girl; v. 1657). The king's servant Silerio reminds his master of the jealous temperament of the queen. Silerio is worried about the proximity, and the attitude, of Belica. The constable concurs. In a dialogue with Belica, Pedro notes that he will not pursue her, but that he will be mindful of her circumstances. He suggests that she will profit from his ruse against the widow. Preparations are made for the dance recital for the king and queen. In the face of harsh admonitions, Belica is fearless to the extreme. She knows what (and whom) she wants.

The king anxiously awaits the performance, with Belica in mind. He is nervous about the queen, who arrives and expresses her annoyance. The dance troupe starts the show. The mayor Martín Crespo is upset with the quality of the choreography, and he has the alderman escort the young men off. The queen asks to have them brought back. The alderman returns with Diego, the mayor's nephew, who falls and says that he has broken a toe. The king sends him away with the mayor and the alderman. A group of gypsies, including Maldonado and Pedro dressed as a gypsy, enter, along with Inés, Belica, and two other gypsy girls. They are all gifted, but Belica unmistakably outshines the rest. Belica – hardly accidentally – falls against the king. The king picks her up. The queen is outraged. The queen wants to incarcerate the gypsy girls. The king cannot believe that the queen is envious of a gypsy girl. Inés promises to explain the details to the queen in order to stay out of prison. Pedro and Maldonado are left on stage to discuss the entertainment gone awry. Maldonado is disappointed in Pedro, but Pedro promises to find a way out of this, with patience, as he deliberates a course of action. In the second act, Cervantes cleverly employs the motif of the hunt to further the plot. Belica takes advantage of the king's visit to insert herself into the picture, as part of a triangle of sorts with the infatuated king and the querulous queen. Belica's superior presentation stands out from the less-than-ideal performance of the male dancers. The royal figures bring a new realm into the dramatic setting, and their presence places Belica closer to her desired lot in life. The theatrical space widens, with the intermingling of gypsies, pastoral characters, rural officials, musicians and singers, other performers, and the regal pair. Pedro de Urdemalas continues to progress, but at the end of act 2 his fortune, like the play, is open-ended.

In act 3, Pedro appears as a hermit with the widow. He has instructed himself in theological concepts. He claims that he can rescue souls in purgatory, with contributions from her; this is an elaborate scheme involving a considerable amount of money. The widow is more than willing to pay for the pardoning of her kindred souls, and he will give the proceeds to Belica, even though he realizes that he is not a candidate for her affections. On his departure, he blesses the widow. In a royal setting, the queen, who carries a handkerchief filled with jewels, enters with Marcelo, an elderly gentleman. The queen asks Marcelo to explain the origin of the gems, which have been found in the possession of Belica. Marcelo confides that the owner is the queen's brother, Don Rosamiro, his master. Marcelo was waiting to see his fiancée when the duchess, Félix Alba, handed him a newborn baby and bid him to give her a name and to have her baptized. The baby was taken into the care of an old gypsy woman. There were jewels in the swaddling clothes. Don Rosamiro admitted that the baby was his and that she must have been born prematurely. The mother died unexpectedly, and the father left to battle the Muslim enemy, but he hoped that Marcelo would visit the child, who had been named Isabel. The queen feels that she now knows half of the story. She asks if Marcelo would recognize the girl, and he answers in the affirmative. The queen brings out Inés and Belica. Inés says that she has seen Marcelo converse with her mother. The queen is sure that Belica is her niece. The king enters and talks with the queen. Belica wonders if they are making fun of her. The queen will tell the king what she has ascertained. They and Marcelo exit. Inés and Belica remain behind. Inés advises Belica to remember her good moments with the gypsies, but Belica already seems to have adjusted to her new status. She has no sense of nostalgia for her time in the gypsy camp.

Pedro enters in an academic cap and gown. He compares himself to Proteus ("un Proteo fui segundo" [I was a second Proteus; v. 2675).[6] He says that he is fleeing the queen, allowing God to determine his path. A farmer passes by, with two hens that he could not sell. Two actors enter, and they will play along with Pedro. The farmer leaves without his hens. Pedro is delighted to have met up with the actors. He understands that through acting he can validate the prophecy of Malgesí. He will appropriate the name of Nicolás de los Ríos, an actor, playwright, and impresario.[7] He has found his niche. A new production is in rehearsal for a premiere before the king and queen and her new niece. Musicians, the king, the constable, and actors are onstage, joined by the queen, Belica (now Isabel), Maldonado, Martín Crespo, the producer, and Pedro himself. The king grants Pedro's wish to join the acting company. Belica approves. Pedro calls attention to the fact that Belica has found her authentic identity in fact, while he has done so in fiction, in the domain of the theatre. Maldonado attempts to speak with Isabel. She swiftly spurns him and Inés, who has called her a "sister." Inés feels insulted. Isabel is resolute. In accordance with the laws of mutability (*mudanza*), the former gypsy and the former *pícaro* will leave their pasts behind, she relocated to the royal household and he on and around the stage. Crespo lauds Pedro as a "great man" and reports that Clemente and Clemencia and Benita and Pascual are getting along well. Pedro closes the play with a commentary on the fickle nature of theatre. As for the work at hand, the showing of the play will be for the royal family alone; others can return the following day.

Pedro de Urdemalas covers a lot of ground and a broad assembly of characters and social ranks, from gypsies, rustic types, rural ministers of justice, and musicians to a king and queen, with settings to match and with significant others in between. The play is, in essence, about performance art and performance spaces. The protagonist is consumed with role playing until his connection with an acting ensemble defines his future. Cervantes juxtaposes Pedro's story with that of Belica, who discovers her selfhood when her bloodlines are made known. The theme of identity unites them. Pedro can satisfy his protean spirit through acting. Belica/Isabel can come into her own when society sustains her claim that she is of royal lineage. Pedro's new career confirms what the play has shown all along: that he is a consummate actor and dramatist. Isabel's acceptance into the regal family corroborates the elevated status that she has advocated for herself throughout the play. Pedro grows into his role. Isabel substantiates her sense of superiority. Cervantes has designed the play to show the parallel lives in multiple contexts. He intensifies the *theatrum mundi* metaphor, bringing characters on stage at the end for a curtain call as a new play is about to go on. The self-consciousness and self-referentiality of metatheatre combine with a depiction of "reality" that has as many points of contact as distinctions. *Pedro de Urdemalas* is ambitiously emplotted. Pedro's backstory merges with his present and future. The proficient and adroit actor becomes a professional actor. Belica's personal probing of her background leads to official recognition of her birthright through the unfolding of her secret. Each tale in the play is filled with countless ironies. There are many stories and stories within stories, and there are many backdrops. Clemente and Clemencia, the mayor Martín Crespo and his administration, Benita and Pascual, Maldonado, Inés, the widow Marina Sánchez, and the king and queen enter the frame repeatedly, as do musicians, singers, and dancers. The world is a stage, and the stage is a world.

Critics have looked at the relation between plot and subplot in Lope de Vega's *Fuenteovejuna* (1619) and Pedro Calderón de la Barca's *La vida es sueño* (1636).[8] The antagonist of *Fuenteovejuna* is Fernán Gómez de Guzmán, who holds the rank of commander (*comendador*). The commander abuses the inhabitants of the town of Fuenteovejuna and betrays his sovereigns, King Fernando and Queen Isabel. His treason towards the monarchs is pivotal. The townspeople kill the commander, who has exceeded the bounds of his authority, and they attribute the act to the town itself, to the citizens at large, conjointly. The king and queen condemn the act, but they ultimately choose not to punish the entire town. This is the exception, not the rule, and the double tyranny of the commander – the plot and the subplot – are coordinated to make a statement and to qualify it. In *La vida es sueño*, the fate of the protagonist Segismundo is intimately linked to that of the dishonoured Rosaura. She has an impact on him that helps to determine his decisions and his actions. Her influence turns him (in the three-act structure) from figurative monster to a man with feelings to "the perfect prince," with his eyes on heaven. What is a parallel structure in *Fuenteovejuna* becomes interrelated and interdependent plot lines in *La vida es sueño*. The connection between Pedro and Belica/Isabel in *Pedro de Urdemalas*, one might submit, is parallel and independent, while strikingly synchronized. Pedro's life is a training ground for his career as an actor and man of the stage. His affiliation with the theatre company is the logical conclusion to his personal development and the resolution of Malgesí's prophecy. Similarly, when Belica is recognized as a member of the royal family, she can assume a role commensurate with her royal lineage. Each character has a name change to mark the transition: Nicolás de los Ríos and Isabel. The motif of performance and the fusion – and confusion – of fact and fiction unite the two narratives. The dénouement completes both searches for identity, which take place on an array of "stages," real and figurative. Cervantes creates spectacles within spectacles to represent the itinerary of Pedro de Urdemalas and the world around him, with a cast that consists of extremes: social outcasts to a king and queen. Pedro takes the initiative in accommodating his neighbours and in planning his own adventures. The audience views his lessons, his exercises, and his trial runs. Belica becomes more than an unusually attractive diversion. She must promote her own cause, and her means is theatrical performance, which draws her to the king, and vice versa. Belica has a bond with Pedro – and he with her – even though she has no romantic interest in him. Her acceptance into royal society mirrors his into the theatrical mainstream. Her intervention and compelling personality broaden the scope and the consequences of the world-as-stage theme. The shifting vantage points heighten the messages of the play. Cervantes inundates the theatrical space with verbal, visual, auditory elements, and with constant changes of scene, to occupy the minds and the emotions of the spectator. Life and art are in dialogue, as are performance art and performance spaces.

Although *Pedro de Urdemalas* was not staged prior to its publication, Cervantes likely would have envisioned a staging of the play, and the text includes stage directions. Costume design could be vital. The shifts in setting would tend to gear a director towards signs or suggestions of places rather than any kind of elaborate set. Again, theatre and meta-theatre coalesce. The progression of scenes shows how Pedro becomes an artist and how Belica becomes a noblewoman. Pedro casts himself into increasingly intricate situations, and thus he gets closer and closer to the climax of his instruction. Correspondingly, Belica distances herself ever more emphatically from the gypsy tribe as she gets closer – physically and symbolically – to the king and queen. Music and dance provide extra fanfare. *Pedro de Urdemalas* is planted in reality but not in realism. Theatre is a metaphor, but hardly a pure abstraction. Cervantes focuses on the capacity of drama to reflect reality on its own terms. *Pedro de Urdemalas* treats self- fulfilment, education, social hierarchies, judgments, religion, the conventions of love, and so forth, all positioned under the rubric – implicit, at any rate – of role playing. The primary action of the play is the movement towards the discovery of Pedro de Urdemalas's true calling, his métier, a discovery that is ingeniously ironic and paradoxical. The boy of unknown background learns to adjust to circumstances and to win over – in contradictory ways – those around him. Like other *pícaros*, he is the product of his collective experiences, as revealed in his backstory and in his encounters within the play. The secondary action is Belica's conversion to Isabel: her resistance to the gypsy lifestyle, her dogged determination in the search for acknowledgment of her bloodlines – for her backstory – and her maneuverings with the king and queen. Individual episodes are not frivolous; they further the objectives of Pedro and Belica, with strong doses of humor, seriousness, and complementary music. If *Don Quijote* is a master class in metafiction, *Pedro de Urdemalas* examines the theory and practice of metatheatre. There is an underlying philosophy in the play, in which acting is a means and an end, and performance is a sine qua non of existence. Cervantes crowds the stage for a reason.

In 2018, I published an adaptation of *Pedro de Urdemalas* titled *Pedro the Schemer: A Work in Progress*. My wish was to capture the spirit of Cervantes's play and to avail myself of the poetic licence allotted to writers. For me, the principal features of *Pedro de Urdemalas* are the parallel stories of Pedro and Belica, unified by the concept of identity; the movement towards the culmination of their goals; examples of Pedro's growing expertise as a trickster and problem solver; a broad view of society, from the *pícaro* and the gypsies to the king and queen; Belica's adjustment to her new role; and Pedro's coming into his own as an actor. The stage directions (*acotaciones*) following v. 1053 note that Inés and Belica enter, and that they can be played by the same actors who play Benita and Clemencia. The content of the play lends itself to multiple casting. *Pedro the Schemer* has one actor in the role of Pedro and one

138   Edward H. Friedman

in the role of Belica/Isabel. Four men and three women would play the other twenty-two characters. My aims were to recreate the substance and tone of Cervantes's play, to make the dialogue witty and lively, and to add a new dimension to the motif of performance. *Pedro the Schemer* has two acts, with six scenes in the first and five in the second.

In act 1, scene 1, Pedro talks directly to the audience. He praises his talent as a performer on the stage of life. He helps himself as he helps others. He overhears Clemente and Clemencia, disturbed by their state of affairs. Clemente wants to marry her, but he has few prospects, and her father, the newly elected mayor Martín Crespo, wants to wed his daughter to a well-to-do suitor. The couple approaches Pedro for help. In scene 2, Pedro checks in with his employer, the mayor. He presents the idea of judgments written in advance, to be read as verdicts. In the first two cases, the issues are a loan versus a gift and a contract dispute. The papers note, respectively, that no one does something for nothing and that a contract demands a meeting of minds. Then Clemencia enters, veiled and disguising her voice. She pleads her case. The note says that virtue should be rewarded. Pedro interprets this to mean that the decision is in favour of her suitor, for whom the mayor should find a suitable position. The much-relieved Clemencia reveals her identity. In scene 3, Pedro speaks with Maldonado, who describes gypsy life and mentions the beautiful but unhappy Belica. Pedro narrates his back-story to Maldonado. I "rewrote" the autobiography in spots, in order to stress class differences. For example, I borrowed from Francisco de Quevedo's *Buscón* (1626) material related to Pablos's suffering at the hands of students when his master begins university life. This is followed by Pedro's resolution of the Benita, Pascual, and Roque dilemma. In scene 4, Crespo and Maldonado speak of the performance scheduled for the king and queen, in which Belica and Inés will perform. Inés advises Belica to give up her fantasies. Belica will not budge. Scene 5 has two parts. Pedro, as Brother Leandro, tricks a tight-fisted widow out of good sum of money, and the king, on the hunt, comes across Belica, who charms him. Scene 6 features the performance before the king and queen. A dancer and Inés as a singer have been on stage. Belica appears, performs provocatively, and falls into the lap of the king. The queen responds by having guards carry Belica off to prison.

In the first scene of act 2, Marcelo informs the queen and king of Belica's story. Belica herself adapts quickly to her new and destined role, for she already has a clear sense of superiority. In scene 2, Pedro tricks a farmer by offering him counterfeit money. An actor has observed the deceptive action and lauds Pedro's skill. The two discuss the ups and downs of the acting profession, and the actor agrees to set up an interview for Pedro with the manager of his company. In scene 3, Maldonado and Inés try to communicate with Isabel, but she shuns them; she wants no part of her former life. Scenes 4 and 5 are addenda, embellishments to *Pedro the Schemer*. The actor and the theatre manager will test Pedro. The first challenge is the reading of a script with the actor. The second is an extemporaneous dialogue with the leading lady of the company. Pedro wins high marks for his performances, but the actor makes a comment on decorum. He feels that Pedro's lofty language in the spontaneous dialogue was inconsistent with the background of the character. Pedro counters that educated citizens, and not only the élite, can have extensive and learned vocabularies. The actor notes that Pedro is a polished debater as well as an accomplished actor. The final challenge consists of two parts: five questions and a concluding synthesis:

THEATRE MANAGER: Name three indispensable qualities that an actor should possess.

PEDRO: Good diction … A good memory … Good feet.

ACTOR: Name three elemental challenges for an actor.

PEDRO: Staying in character … Keeping the sweat from showing through … Ignoring boos and hisses from the audience.

THEATRE MANAGER: Give three cautionary directives for an actor-to-be.

PEDRO: Balance art and reality on the stage and in life … Realize that less can be more … Do not use all your tricks in every scene.

ACTOR: Give three pieces of advice for acting in a comedy.

PEDRO: Do not just go for the easy laugh … Do not laugh at your own jokes … Give due credit to the straight man.

ACTOR: Give three pieces of advice for acting in a tragedy.

PEDRO: Let your suffering be more from the inside than from the outside … Let your voice be the primary vehicle of your emotions … Remember that it is only a play.

THEATRE MANAGER: Thank you, Pedro. This completes the first part of Phase 3 … Here is the question for Part 2, to be answered in less than a minute: Why are you, Pedro de Urdemalas, qualified to be an actor?

PEDRO: My dear sirs, I will start by saying that my life to this point has been a rehearsal for this audition. I have, in fact, played many roles, some of them scripted, most of them fabricated on the spot. I have learned the significance of timing, inflection, modulation, and – last, but hardly least – consciousness of one's interlocutors and of the spectators. I am less educated in taking direction, because hitherto I have been my own director. Nonetheless, I believe that I have the intellect, the perseverance, and the disposition to be an actor. To be frank, I would be so bold as to proclaim that I am already an actor … And that is my speech. [*He takes a modest bow.*] (2018, 96–8)

In the final scene, the king and queen are seated for the performance of a new work when Isabel arrives fashionably late. The theatre manager announces that the play, *The Secret Duchess*, is by Pedro de Urdemalas, who will also be one of the three actors. It is obvious that the play is based on Belica/Isabel's journey to nobility. The script has the female lead say, "I will be patient, for my story is by no means over" (101), the closing line of *Pedro the Schemer*. The king and queen look uncomfortably at Isabel, who looks uncomfortably at them. The author and the public are onstage. The play is unquestionably the thing, the subject of the enterprise and the common denominator between Pedro and Isabel.

In *Pedro de Urdemalas*, Cervantes looks at the many phases – and faces – of performance. The play records the trajectories of the two leading characters towards the realization of their dreams, with episodes that move them forward. Theatre becomes an emblem and a component of reality, an icon and a tangible presence. The play is an entertainment and a commentary, or metacommentary, on psychology, behaviour, customs, and growth, in stages and on stage. As in *Don Quijote*, the consumer is never separated from the artistic product, and that is, needless to say, a benefit to both.

Notes

1 For introductions to Cervantes's theatre, see Maestro (2000) and García
   Aguilar, Gómez Canseco, and Sáez (2016). See also Friedman (1998). In
   The Oxford Handbook of Cervantes, edited by Aaron M. Kahn and published
   in 2021, the section "Cervantes the Dramatist" (333–429) contains essays
   by David G. Burton, Melanie S. Henry, Carolyn Lukens Olson, Moisés R.
   Castillo, and Kathleen Jeffs.
2 I used this term to define my approach to Cervantes's *comedias* in my 1981
   book on the topic (and earlier, in my dissertation). The chapter on *Pedro
   de Urdemalas* (81–102) includes the analysis of a play of the same title by
   Lope de Vega, with a figurative – and female – version of the title character;
   the commentary appeared earlier in a 1977 article in *Hispania* ("Dramatic
   Structure"). For a discussion of Lope's play, see Rodríguez and Villa (1990).
3 On the folkloric figure of Pedro de Urdemalas, see, for example, Estévez
   Molinero (1995).
4 A select bibliography on Cervantes's *Pedro de Urdemalas* could include
   essays by Müller- Bochat (1984), Precht (1988), Canavaggio (1992),
   Spadaccini and Talens (1993), Smith (2005), Sáez (2014), and Campbell
   (2019), as well as a monograph by González Puche (2012). The essays cover
   social, political, historical, psychological, theoretical, and theatrical issues.
   Spadaccini and Talens (1993) reflect on Cervantes's theatrical vision and its

relation to contemporary theory though analyses of *El rufián dichoso* and *Pedro de Urdemalas*.

5 I have used the text of *Pedro de Urdemalas* in Cervantes, *Teatro completo*, edited by Florencio Sevilla Arroyo and Antonio Rey Hazas (1987). The quotations from the play refer to this edition. I will cite verse numbers. All translations are my own unless otherwise indicated.

6 Among other commentaries on the protean nature of Pedro de Urdemalas, see Forcione (1970), Surtz (1980), and Teixeira de Souza and de Pontes Rubira (2017).

7 On the Nicolás de los Ríos connection, see Morillo (2019).

8 Two classic starting points for an examination of this issue are Everett W. Hesse's introduction to his 1964 edition of *Fuenteovejuna* and a 1953 essay by Albert E. Sloman on the structure of *La vida es sueño*.

8 The Person of a King: Sovereignty, Performance, and Court Spaces in Three Royal Impostor Plays

CHRISTOPHER WEIMER,
OKLAHOMA STATE UNIVERSITY

What are thou / That counterfeit'st the person of a king?

1 Henry IV V.iv.27–8

Any survey of the theoretical enquiries into the nature and functions of "space" reveals a dizzying array of distinctions, definitions, and disputes, ranging from Michel de Certeau's post-structuralist linguistic parallels between place/space and *langue/parole*, leading to his oft-quoted maxim that "Space is a practiced place" (1984, 117), to Henri Lefebvre's Marxist/materialist analysis of space, according to which, Andrew Merrifield winkingly notes, "place can be taken as *practiced space*" (1993, 522; emphasis in original). However one might define space or place, they always ultimately seem, as Merrifield observes, to "melt into each other" (1993, 520). Curiously, and perhaps serendipitously, a similar observation might be made of theatres and royal courts in early modern Europe, a culture in which theatre was often political and politics were even more often theatrical. The following essay will consider courts and theatres as simultaneously political and theatrical spaces in a discussion of three *comedias*, all of them involving the impersonation of kings by commoners: *La ventura con el nombre* (Fortune is his name), *El rey por semejanza* (King by likeness), and *El rey muerto* (The dead king).

Royal courts in early modern Europe seem particularly apt for consideration in terms of place as well as space. In one sense, to think of the most storied courts of the era was to envision places – or, more specifically, palaces: the Buen Retiro, Hampton Court, Versailles. In another, more fundamental sense, however, a court was a conceptualized space that depended as a site of sovereign authority on the presence, or at least the imprimatur, of an individual rather than on its location. A court was a hierarchical political community consisting of a monarch and all the individuals orbiting around them – family members, lesser nobles, appointees, civil servants, petitioners, domestic servants and bodyguards, and so forth – whose identities, and whose relationships to one another, were defined by their respective relationships to that ruler whose person served, as Michel Foucault explains, "as the effective embodiment of sovereignty" (1980, 95). A palace was only a building, however opulent, until a monarch and their courtiers transformed it from a material place constructed of stone and wood into a dynamic space animated by the circulation, the exercise, and above all the performance of power.

Perhaps inevitably, one metaphor repeatedly employed by commentators describing early modern European courts is that of the theatre. We would do well to note that we might likewise consider that era's theatres as places that become spaces only when a company of actors performed there for paying audiences. A monarch's sovereignty in this era had to be performed, as Stephen Greenblatt observed of Elizabethan England: "Royal power is manifested to its subjects as in a theater" (1988, 65). Jonathan Brown and J.H. Elliott employ precisely this metaphor for the Habsburg Spanish court, identifying the monarch as its leading performer and describing the Buen Retiro palace as the stage on which he acted out his role: "The court of the King of Spain resembled a magnificent theatre in which the principal actor was permanently onstage. The stage instructions were meticulously detailed; the scenery was imposing, if a little antiquated; and the supporting cast was impressively large" (1980, 31). At the same time, during this era of insatiable demand for theatrical performances, places such as public and even palace stages often represented royal courts, thus becoming spaces in which audiences watched sovereignty asserted and contested, usurped and defended, affirmed and criticized in a plethora of plays concerned, obliquely or explicitly, with the political preoccupations and debates of the day. The result could be considered a *mise en abyme*, a specular relationship between two spaces: the court, where monarchs asserted the authority intrinsic to their identities as a kingdom's political foundation, and the theatre, where evanescent artifice and impersonation – including that of kings and emperors – reigned supreme. Rarely could *lo verdadero* and *lo fingido* have appeared so intrinsically opposed yet so provocatively indistinguishable.

Fully aware of this paradox and its theatrical potential, Spanish playwrights of the sixteenth and seventeenth centuries deployed courts as the settings for *comedias* in a range of genres, from comedies of romantic confusions to bloody struggles for political survival. One small but particularly fascinating group of plays offers instances of impostors who assume royal identities by virtue of an apparently fortuitous resemblance to real monarchs. The trope of the *rey sustituido* has of course proven for centuries to be a remarkably durable one, as popular culture's seemingly inexhaustible variations on Alexandre Dumas's *Le Vicomte de Bragelonne* (better known in English as *The Man in the Iron Mask*), Mark Twain's *The Prince and the Pauper*, and Anthony Hope's *The Prisoner of Zenda* demonstrate. For Spanish playwrights and audiences in the late sixteenth and early seventeenth centuries, moreover, this plot device had a uniquely contemporary resonance and relevance. As Yves-Marie Bercé has argued, these decades in Europe were an unexpected era of what he elegantly terms *les rois revenants* (the reborn kings), impostors and pretenders who embodied "l'image du roi caché, d'un gran monarque ou d'un sauveur en qui les peuples espèrent" (the image of a king hidden from sight, of a great monarch or a saviour in whom the people placed their hopes; 1990, 14).[1] Following the death of Felipe II's nephew Sebastián I of Portugal in the Battle of Alcazarquivir, in 1578, no fewer than four successive impostors were hailed as the true Sebastián by credulous followers eager to accept any account of his miraculous survival, often with the encouragement of those who opposed Spanish hegemony in the Iberian peninsula; in 1595 in France, François de La Ramée claimed to be an unknown son, kidnapped at birth, of Charles IX and Felipe II's niece and sister-in-law Isabel of Austria; similarly, during the years after the 1598 death of the Russian czar Feodor I, at least three pretenders declared themselves his brother Dmitry Ivanovich, Ivan the Terrible's youngest son, who had died in 1591. Though only one of these impostors – the first False Dmitry – succeeded even briefly in occupying any of the thrones to which they laid claim, the collapse of their deceptions paradoxically emphasized the performative, theatrical nature of these attempted impostures: the pretenders were ultimately judged to be nothing more than presumptuous actors whose efforts to imitate legitimate monarchs and to usurp their sovereignty had, perhaps inevitably, failed.[2]

Within these contexts, not only did *comedias* of royal impersonation such as *La ventura con el nombre*, *El rey por semejanza*, and *El rey muerto* provide the metatheatrical spectacle of actors impersonating impostors impersonating kings, but also, by presenting impostors indistinguishable from true monarchs, they staged questions about the stability of court spaces that depend on the person of a sovereign as the political centre of gravity. These plays represented royal courts as spaces in which sovereign identities were literally performed even as the action simultaneously transformed the stages representing those courts into spaces in which performances of royal identity were metatheatrically doubled: the actual stage as fictitious court as figurative stage. As we shall see, the Spanish playwrights could exploit this potentially dizzying infinite recurrence of reflections between the two spaces, one immediately present and one represented, to foreground the theatricality of court life and to simultaneously raise and contain, though usually not in equal parts, the subversive suggestion that royal identity, and the stability of political spaces reliant upon it, might depend at least as much on effective performance as on any intrinsic sovereign essence.[3]

Perhaps the most conventional of the three plays is Tirso de Molina's *La ventura con el nombre*, which Ruth Lee Kennedy dates to 1620–1 (Kennedy 1969). Set in Bohemia, it depicts the unlikely path to the throne travelled by the eponymous protagonist, the shepherd Ventura. The *comedia*'s action begins after the funeral of King Primislao, secretly murdered in his sleep by his traitorous brother Adolfo. The Claudius-like Adolfo assumes his childless brother's throne, but his true object is Primislao's widow, Sibila. Seeking to bring about this end and to divert any suspicion away from himself, Adolfo immediately arrests the nobles Lotario and Uberto for the assassination and accuses his own wife Basilisa of having conspired in the crime so that she might become queen. The courtier Otón soon learns the truth of Adolfo's machinations, including his plan to poison Basilisa, and takes it upon himself to avenge Primislao, save Basilisa, and deliver the court from Adolfo's tyranny by killing the usurper in the countryside and concealing his corpse in a lake. By fortuitous coincidence, Ventura overhears the lengthy exculpatory explanation Otón offers to his fellow courtier Matías; by even more fortuitous coincidence, he subsequently encounters the fleeing Basilisa and the Bohemian nobles, all of whom initially take the shepherd for Adolfo, whose double Ventura thus discovers himself to be. Unable to escape and unwilling to discard such a stroke of luck, Ventura assumes the dead tyrant's identity, though once in the space of the Bohemian court, he proves reluctant to wield Adolfo's authority in any but the most nominal ways. The ensuing complications multiply until Sibila's brother, the Duque de Sajonia, leads an army against the kingdom and Ventura-as-Adolfo commands the Bohemian forces on the battlefield. He returns victorious but confesses his true identity to everyone, having come to prefer, like Sancho Panza, his prior rustic life to the burdens of kingship. To his shock, he learns from Otón that he is in fact the half-brother of both Primislao and Adolfo, the son of their father Segismundo and an inevitably beautiful, conveniently dead *serrana*, and that he is thus the rightful heir to Bohemia's vacant throne after all.

Even before Ventura first appears, the Bohemian court is presented from the outset of the *comedia* as a politically unstable space in which the villainous Adolfo, fresh from his murder of his own brother, performs his newly acquired sovereignty in an unexpected fashion for a court audience whose bewilderment makes it immediately clear that something is indeed rotten in Prague. As Isabel Ibáñez observes, the opening scene "montre un tyran au paroxysme de son activité criminelle, comme si la representation commençait à la fin de la pièce" (shows a tyrant at the climax of his criminal acts, as though the performance began at the end of the play; Ibáñez 2005, 371). Rather than allow the court to believe that Primislao, whom Adolfo smothered in his sleep, died a natural death, the usurper declares it an assassination that he vows to avenge:

> los dos ángeles que un rey
> tiene por divina ley,
> me advierten que vive oculto
> algún aleve tirano,
> de tal delito agresor.
> Heredero y vengador
> tengo de ser de mi hermano.

> (the two guardian angels that a king has by divine law warn me that some treacherous brute, author of such a crime, conceals himself. Heir and avenger of my brother I must be.) (Tirso de Molina 1958, 958a)[4]

As noted above, Adolfo feigns this righteous determination to avenge Primislao's death so that he can lay siege to Sibila, his brother's widow, which in turn requires that he remove his own wife as an obstacle from his path by implicating her in the assassination as well. If any spectators remain more persuaded by this performance than by Basilisa's protestations of innocence, not to mention those of Lotario and Uberto, they will soon be undeceived by the vigour with which Adolfo presses his amorous attentions on Sibila, who reproves him in vain: "El reino se hereda, / señor, mas no el matrimonio" (The kingdom is inherited, my lord, but not the marriage; 1958, 960a). A few scenes later, Otón (overheard by Ventura) will leave no doubt of Adolfo's deceit as well as his guilt when he justifies taking the fratricide's life:

> Adolfo, de Primislao
> Caín hermano, el Infante
> que agora rey, disimula
> traiciones entre piedades;
> [...] esclavo de su apetito,
> consintió precipitarse

hasta el más horrendo insulto
que dio al escarmiento anales.
Mató a su hermano, a su rey.

(Adolfo, Primislao's Cain, the prince who is now king, cloaks betrayals with pieties; … slave of his desire, he hurled himself into the most dreadful offence that history preserves. He killed his brother, his king.) (1958, 965b)

It was Adolfo who disrupted the stability of the Bohemian court, first by murdering the rightful sovereign and subsequently by justifying his tyrannical abuse of his usurped authority with his performance of feigned outrage and his false accusations; what results is the "caos y desorden moral del reino" (chaos and moral disorder of the kingdom; Oteiza 2020, 23).

Despite Ventura's physical likeness to Adolfo, however, the shepherd's assumption of the dead regicide's identity in the Bohemian court proves to be a politically ineffective and precarious masquerade, and not only because of Adolfo's tyrannical behaviour before meeting his own demise at Otón's hands. Domínguez-Hermida points out that Ventura does not act decisively as king until he takes command of the Bohemian army on the battlefield near the end of the *comedia*: "Hasta este momento, el pastor ocupaba el lugar real pero no ejercía de rey. Hay que recordar que prometer mercedes al pretendiente y proponer un amor cortés a la reina son estrategias evasivas ante sus nuevas responsabilidades" (Until this moment, the shepherd occupied the throne but did not govern as king. It must be remembered that promising favours to the petitioner and declaring a chaste love to the queen are evasive strategies in the face of his new responsibilities; 2009, 144). Moreover, Ventura's "spectators" in the court repeatedly receive his performance with suspicion. Not surprisingly, Otón remains sceptical of Ventura's claim, knowing perfectly well that he himself killed Adolfo and disposed of his corpse, no matter what tales of divine intercession Ventura might improvise. Indeed, Otón and Matías consider the possibility that "Adolfo" may be a lookalike, pointing out that nature offers "[m]il ejemplos" of such uncanny resemblances (a thousand examples; 1958, 974b).[5] Ventura's display of knowledge that only Adolfo could possess (in fact acquired by Ventura's initial eavesdropping on the two courtiers) confuses but nevertheless fails to entirely convince them: "¿cómo puede/haber engaño bastante / para adivinar secretos / que entre el rey y yo pasaron, / y agora me ha dicho?" (how can there be a deception great enough to guess the secrets that passed between the king and me that he now tells me?; 1958, 974b). They even wonder if this "Adolfo" might be an angel taking the dead monarch's form, considering this hypothesis a plausible alternative to the possibility that Ventura is truly Adolfo (1958, 977).

Ventura is no less aware of the vulnerability of his deception, leaping to the mistaken conclusion in act 2 that Otón seeks to test him by bringing him face to face with Sibila, who had left the court before Ventura's arrival there, to see if he would recognize her (1958, 982b). After this encounter with Primislao's widow results in disaster, Ventura abandons the court's "confusos engaños, lisonjas y cortesías" (perplexing deceptions, flatteries, and courtesies; 1958, 984a) and returns to his village. Basilisa – who had been more willing to accept his imposture, despite her doubts, due to the tender feelings that his likeness to Adolfo and his unexpectedly loving behaviour provoked in her – finds him there, dressed again as Ventura, and angrily accuses him of the fraud that he did in fact commit: "Di, traidor: / ¿qué desatino, qué error / darte atrevimiento pudo/siendo un mísero vasallo / a engañar mi corte ansí?" (Speak, traitor: what madness, what error could make you, only a lowly vassal, dare to thus deceive my court?; 1958, 993). Despite the pivotal importance of Ventura's impersonation of Adolfo to the plot, it is ultimately nothing more than a fragile artifice. This false sovereign's presence and performance in the space of the Bohemian court cannot provide a firm foundation for the political stability that the court or the kingdom needs.

As the *comedia*'s action reaches its climax in the third act with the approach of the Saxon army, Basilisa's inability to resolve the conundrum created by Ventura's two names and two selves leads to an exchange between the impostor and the queen in which both ultimately abandon any attempt to define his identity as something "esencial y divina" (essential and divine; Domínguez-Hermida 2009, 146). Instead, when Basilisa asks plainly, "¿Eres Adolfo o Ventura?," the shepherd-turned-king replies that he is both at once: "Uno y otro soy, señora" (Are you Adolfo or Ventura?; I am the one and the other, my lady; 1958, 995b). Pressed to explain himself, Ventura assures Basilisa that he can be whichever of the men she chooses:

Uno de los dos está
en ese templo enterrado,
o es Ventura transformado
en Rey, o Adolfo será:
al otro tienes presente;
tu confusión le amenaza,
o Adolfo en mi se disfraza
con este traje indecente,

o Ventura en mi es pastor;
determínate a escoger,
que yo a aquel sólo he de ser
que te estuviere mejor.

(One of the two is buried in this temple; it is either Ventura transformed into
the king, or it may be Adolfo; the other stands before you. Your confusion
threatens him: either Adolfo has disguised himself as me in this lowly garb,
or else Ventura the shepherd conceals himself in me. Make your choice, and I
will be he alone whom you prefer.) (1958, 995b–996a)

Ventura rejects the basic premise of Basilisa's question, boldly defining both "Ventura" and "Adolfo" as roles that he could perform in
the space of the Bohemian court at the queen's pleasure; the role she
chooses will become his identity. Basilisa accepts this notion, perhaps
realizing that neither she nor her kingdom can afford the luxury of
essentialist certainty at this critical moment: "Pues tu ser, ¿está en mi
mano? / ¿Dependes tú de mi idea?" (Who you are is in my hands,
then? You depend on my thought?; 1958, 996b). She exhorts him to lead
Bohemia's soldiers into battle and to win a permanent royal identity for
himself on the battlefield: "Ya pastor seas, / ya rey, la ocasión te llama /
para ennoblecer tu fama: / vence, si el reino deseas" (Whether you be
shepherd or king, opportunity calls you to ennoble your fame: triumph,
if you desire the kingdom; 1958, 996b). Ventura agrees: "Adolfo soy, si
al sajón / venzo ..." (I am Adolfo, if I vanquish the Saxon ...; 1958, 997a).
   Ventura, of course, does triumph in battle: "Si consiste en mi victoria /
ser yo Adolfo, prenda cara, / victorioso Adolfo vuelve / del Sajón, por
vuestra causa" (If my being Adolfo lies in my victory, beloved one,
Adolfo returns victorious from fighting the Saxon for your cause; 1958,
1000a). Nevertheless, the subversive terms of his secret pact with Basilisa are never put to the test, thanks not only to his public confession of
his true identity but also to the timely discovery of his paternity among
the documents left by Otón's late father, King Segismundo's *privado*.
The play's treatment of sovereign legitimacy and of royal identity –
and of Bohemia's court as a space in which both questions must be
resolved – thus ultimately depends on this final revelation that Ventura
is the only surviving son of Segismundo and the half-brother of Primislao and Adolfo. As Wido Hempel notes, most *comedias* depicting a
commoner's unexpected ascension to a throne sooner or later resort to
just such a plot device, with the result that "en ellas no se quebranta la
jerarquía social sino que por el contrario ésta se ratifica con insistencia"
(in them the social hierarchy is not shattered, but on the contrary, it is

insistently ratified; 1986, 124). In the final scene of *La ventura con el nombre*, Ventura's ultimately successful performance on the battlefield of an appropriated royal identity is discovered to be evidence of his unrecognized noble blood. The play thereby contains the subversive potential of Ventura's imposture, implicitly ruling out the possibility of any such successful simulacrum of royalty by a true commoner. This denouement de-theatricalizes the Bohemian court, banishing the dangers of mimesis from a space imperiled by performative artifice since Primislao's murder and Adolfo's ascension to the throne, and the coronation of Segismundo's remaining heir restores the court's political stability; Ventura will reign authentically in his own name and by virtue of his own birthright.

As we shall see, *El rey por semejanza* addresses these concerns very differently, despite the plot parallels it shares with *La ventura con el nombre* – so many parallels, in fact, that Ruth Lee Kennedy proposes *El rey por semejanza* as Tirso's source (1969, 35). The authorship of this *comedia* remains unresolved: Kennedy echoes S. Griswold Morley and Courtney Bruerton's doubts about Lope's paternity (his name appears only on the first page of act 2 of the sole surviving contemporary manuscript), but Melveena McKendrick argues persuasively "that Act I might well not be Lope's but that Acts II and III are more convincingly his" (Kennedy 1969, 43n5; Morley and Bruerton 1940, 336; McKendrick 2000, 87). Whatever its authorship, Morley and Bruerton date the play to 1597?–1603, about two decades before *La ventura* (1940, 336). The events of *El rey por semejanza* nominally take place in the court of "Asiria," an exoticized spelling of "Siria," and this setting, along with the names of the monarch Antíoco and his double Altemio, suggests that the playwright found the germ of his plot in a historically questionable anecdote about the death of the Seleucid emperor Antiochus II (286–246 BCE) (Hempel 1986, 129). As recounted by Pliny and subsequently by Valerius Maximus, the emperor's wife Laodice murdered her husband but concealed his death long enough to stage-manage the lookalike Artemo's impersonation of Antiochus on the latter's supposed deathbed, from which the impostor named Laodice and her children as the heirs to the throne (Pliny 1855, VII.10, 146–7; Valerius Maximus 2000, IX.14, 388–9). However, no such fraud appears in *El rey por semejanza*, while the playwright displays total disregard for any consistent historical grounding for the play (including sending his explicitly Christian protagonist into battle against a Muslim sultan's fleet) and confronts Altemio-as-Antíoco instead with those problems familiar to any reader of Spanish political *comedias*, among them a *privado* accustomed to ruling in the king's name, greedy and selfish nobles, and a steady stream of *memoriales* demanding favours and gifts, in addition to the aforementioned menacing Moorish foe. Like *La ventura con el nombre*, *El rey por semejanza* begins with the abuse of royal status by Antíoco (this time the legitimate king rather than a usurper, and shamelessly rather than secretly tyrannical), whom we see brazenly forcing his attentions on his wife's maid Julia and striking the queen in front of their courtiers when she protests his lack of respect. Outraged, she promises her hand to her cousin Roberto if he will kill the king, a task that Roberto carries out with alacrity on a hunting trip in the countryside. The queen and Roberto soon find themselves under suspicion for Antíoco's disappearance and assumed murder, a justifiable deed that she nevertheless regrets having so impulsively commanded. They escape arrest only thanks to the fortuitous appearance of Altemio, a peasant who has come to seek his fortune at court but discovers to his – and the queen's – shock that he is Antíoco's lookalike. The queen wins Altemio's promise to help her, and she coaches him in his impersonation of the king, while he in turn quickly falls in love with her. Unlike *Ventura*, Altemio immediately proves himself to be an exemplary monarch, the very opposite of the man whose name and title he has assumed, and his imposture leaves the courtiers marvelling at what they believe to be Antíoco's sudden transformation: "Ayer un Sardanapalo, / pródigo, injusto y vicioso, / hoy Trajano virtuoso" (Yesterday a Sardanapalus, prodigal, unjust, and vicious, today a virtuous Trajan; Vega 1916, 956–8).[6] The queen herself wonders if he might be Antíoco in disguise, but after seeking out Altemio's father, the peasant Riseo, to confirm his identity, she eventually decides (perhaps similarly to Martin Guerre's wife Bertrande de Rols) that the husband she now has is vastly superior, both as a man and a monarch, to the one she had killed and whose name and throne he has now taken for his own with her active encouragement. After Altemio undoes or makes amends for Antíoco's most grievous and corrupt acts as king, he leads his Christian troops to victory over an attacking Muslim force, wielding "un tronco de un árbol" (a tree trunk; 1916, 2593 s.d.) in the manner of Don Quijote's much-admired Diego Pérez de Vargas y Machuca. Upon Altemio's return, the queen declares her devotion: "Muy bien sé que Altemio sois/pero [a] Altemio es [a] quien quiero" (I know very well that you are Altemio, but it is Altemio whom I love; 1916, 2602–3). The play ends with Altemio granting the betrothal of Julia and Roberto, thus rewarding rather than punishing Antíoco's assassin, and with the promise of Altemio's continued reign at the queen's side. Like *La ventura con el nombre*, then, *El rey por semejanza* ends with the impostor's permanent accession to the throne, but with an essential difference: *El rey por semejanza* does not attribute Altemio's talent for government to, nor justify his future rule with, any revelation of royal lineage. Altemio is instead a rare instance in the *comedia* of "el labrador hecho rey" (the peasant become king), a trope of which Hempel declares, "Nada más inversosímil e inimaginable que este hecho, pues no se conciben más distantes extremos en el escalofón clasista" (Nothing could be more unrealistic and unimaginable than this event, since more distant extremes on the ladder of social class cannot be imagined; 1986, 123–4). Although Kennedy proposes that the final lines of the play – "Los demás de sus sucesos / no se refieren aquí / por no dar lugar el tiempo" (The rest of [Altemio's] deeds are not recounted here for lack of time; 1916, 2621–3) – may suggest a sequel in which the dramatist might have thus explained the protagonist's unexpected aptitude for the responsibilities of monarchy, the fact remains that this play concludes with no textual indication of any blood kinship between the slain ruler Antíoco and his double (Kennedy 1969, 35). Indeed, Altemio's father Riseo appears onstage to affirm his paternity, and one test of Altemio's character is whether or not he will acknowledge himself the rustic villager's son: at first, he refuses to do so for fear of ejection from his new life at court, but then, ashamed of his own denial, he embraces Riseo: "¡Padre de mi corazón!" (My beloved father!; 1916, 1945). The *comedia* thus severs fitness for the throne (and for the royal bedchamber) from lineage, following the queen's own conclusion about the man who has assumed her husband's identity with her connivance: "que mejor es, caso llano, / un villano, si es de ley, / con pensamientos de rey, / que un rey con los de villano" (better a peasant, provided he be legitimate, with the mind of a king, than a king with the mind of a peasant; 1916, 2533–6). In Tirso's play, however convenient or contrived the discovery of Ventura's birthright might seem, it ultimately permits him to don Segismundo and Primislao's crown as the foundation of Bohemia's political order and wed Basilisa (pending the necessary dispensation) and it retroactively justifies Ventura's imposture. In sharp contrast, *El rey por semejanza* indicates not even the slightest ambivalence about the morality of Altemio's assumption of Antíoco's identity with the active collusion of Antíoco's widow or the still thornier question of Altemio's supplantation of Antíoco's son as the latter's successor.

To justify this provocative ending, *El rey por semejanza* devotes much of the action to Altemio's exemplary performance wielding Antíoco's authority within the space of the Syrian court. Indeed, this *comedia*'s focus is primarily political: McKendrick argues that "the fairy-tale nonsense of the plot is in effect an unconcealed frontal attack on bad government" (2000, 87), while Kennedy describes the play as "essentially a mirror for princes, one of uncommonly strong didactic tendency" and declares that it is "the political material that gives its very *raison d'être* to *El rey por semejanza*" (1969, 40). It is the absence of such content in *La ventura con el nombre*, Kennedy asserts, that makes Tirso's *comedia* "little more than a romantic love-story" (1969, 40). In contrast to the events of that play, Altemio is presented with a lengthy series of *memoriales* to which he responds very differently than was Antíoco's custom: according to Kennedy's summary, "he shows himself to be generous to the church, appreciative of his soldiers' services, wise in not giving too much favour to his *privado* nor to his buffoon, prudent in refusing to put his signature on the blank piece of paper which his *valido* presents him" (1969, 37). Altemio subsequently teaches the nobles that they should treat their own vassals how they would want their king to treat them, repudiates a ludicrous treaty with the Sultan of Egypt to which Antíoco had agreed, makes amends to a woman whom Antíoco raped, restores to the Church tithes that Antíoco seized for the royal treasury, and even arrests the crown prince for carrying out an illicit love affair within the palace, all before he leads the country to war and returns victorious. In short, Altemio's improvised, unscripted performance as king repeatedly demonstrates an innate moral compass and an instinctive command of statecraft both so vastly superior to those of the depraved, tyrannical, and entirely unlamented Antíoco that the commoner proves himself on the strength of his own merits to be a formidable political centre of gravity around which the court, and by extension the kingdom, can orbit securely. Altemio in effect rewrites the "role" of Antíoco so radically, remaking the dead man in his own virtuous image for the common good, that mimetic artifice becomes transformative and this *comedia* presents a striking contrast to *La ventura con el nombre* with its embrace of the performative theatricality of court spaces.

Finally, Damián Salucio del Poyo's *El rey muerto* presents a counterpoint to *La ventura con el nombre* and *El rey por semejanza* with a different kind of royal imposture: a king who is forced by circumstances to impersonate a lookalike peasant rather than a peasant, like Ventura or Altemio, who stumbles onto an opportunity to impersonate a lookalike king.[7] However, the playwright also invents an additional metatheatrical parallel to those plays' action: this king, Anteo of Epirus, will feign his alleged peasant double's impersonation of Anteo himself, thus pretending to be his own impostor. *El rey muerto* depicts the desperate stratagems employed by Anteo and his faithful courtier Artandro after the young ruler's impulsive, ill-advised naval assault on Macedonia results in disaster and leaves him shipwrecked there. Artandro counterfeits Anteo's death by substituting another cadaver for the alleged royal corpse, then devises an elaborate deception in which Anteo will play the role of "Alejo," a Macedonian peasant who happens to be the reportedly drowned king's double. Artandro deceives the Macedonian king Eleusipo into believing that he can execute a bloodless coup and seize the throne of Epirus for himself by having "Alejo" impersonate Anteo in the Epirote court. Anteo and Artandro eventually turn the tables on Eleusipo when the latter attempts to claim the crown in Epirus, and all ends happily after the Macedonian king consents to his daughter's marriage to Anteo and ensures permanent peace between the two realms. *El rey muerto* thus reverses the usual dynamics of lookalike plays, a theatrical tradition going back to Plautus's *Menaechmi* and including *La ventura con el nombre* and *El rey por semejanza*, in which two separate but identical characters are thought to be the same person, either by accident or by design; in this *comedia*, a single character instead deceives others into believing that he is two distinct individuals. Not only does the *comedia* multiply the protagonist's impostures, since Anteo must impersonate his own double and perform that double's impersonation of him, but it also multiplies the political spaces depicted onstage: this is a tale of two royal courts, Macedonia and Epirus, rather than one.

In the first of these spaces, the text does not problematize Eleusipo's position at the heart of his own court's political order. Indeed, the king is presented as a competent, fundamentally honourable ruler who agrees to Artandro's duplicitous scheme with initial reluctance and only because he believes Anteo dead and the Epirote throne, to which he has a legitimate claim in the absence of any direct successors, vacant. The Macedonian court is of primary interest instead as a theatricalized rather than a political space in which two different but overlapping and interwoven performances are played simultaneously. Artandro tricks Eleusipo by proposing that they conspire together to stage a peasant's impersonation of a (reportedly) dead king: he suggests, in other words, that they imitate the plots of plays such as *La ventura con el nombre* and *El rey por semejanza*. What Eleusipo does not know is that this metatheatrical conspiracy to mount a royal imposture for political gain is a play inscribed within yet another script, one devised to gull him just as he thinks he will gull the Epirotes: with Artandro's encouragement, Eleusipo imagines that Anteo's subjects can be easily convinced that the lookalike peasant Alejo is truly their king, but it never occurs to him how easily Artandro convinced him that such an unlikely double not only might exist, but might also dwell so fortuitously only a short distance from his own palace. The result is a sequence of scenes in which Eleusipo believes that he is watching the spectacle of Alejo playing the role of Anteo, while Antandro and the audience simultaneously witness the actual scenario of Anteo playing the role of "Alejo" playing the role of Anteo. What Eleusipo fails to realize is that he is the true principal spectator rather than Artandro's dramaturgical collaborator.

The most complex of these scenes is Anteo's interview with Eleusipo's daughter Laodicea, for whose hand Anteo had once proposed himself, only to have his offer rejected by Eleusipo because the latter had already arranged her betrothal to another kingdom's prince. Although the two young people never met, Laodicea fell in love with Anteo's portrait; she subsequently mourned his reported death and ironically insists that Anteo/"Alejo" is an impostor. Now that Eleusipo intends to convince the Epirotes that the alleged impostor is their king, however, he realizes that his daughter must also be persuaded of "Alejo's" identity if the plan is to succeed. Towards that end, he instructs Anteo to employ both lies and "mil palabras amorosas" (a thousand loving words; 2023, 1419) to soften her resistance and conquer her heart.[8] In the dialogue that follows, secretly observed and commented on by both Eleusipo and Artandro, Anteo discards his layers of feigned imposture to woo Laodicea sincerely. He even truthfully narrates how he survived the shipwreck without her father ever realizing that his narrative is not an invented tale taught to the rustic impostor by Artandro; the latter notes the Macedonian king's credulity with ironic amusement:

> REY: ¿Hay más galán invención?
>   ¡Embuste ha sido estremado!
> ARTANDRO: Quizá de aquesta manera,
>   vendrá por fuerza a querello.
> REY: No pongo duda en ello.
>   Creeralo aunque no quiera.
>   ¡Qué mentira singular!
> ARTANDRO: Muy buen trabajo me cuesta.
>
> (KING: Could there exist a bolder lie? What a tall tale!
> ARTANDRO: Perhaps she will be unable to resist falling in love with him.
> KING: I don't doubt it. She'll believe him against her will. What an
>   exceptional lie!
> ARTANDRO: It cost me enough work.) (2023, 1539–46)

By the end of the scene, the princess is contented and utterly convinced by her unexpected suitor's earnestness and ardour; equally contented and convinced by Anteo's performance is her father, who does not recognize the truth even when it is uttered in front of him.

The second royal court depicted in *El rey muerto* is of course Anteo's in Epirus, a court space that Eleusipo intends to reconstitute with himself as its sovereign centre once "Alejo"'s impersonation of its ruler gives him access to the royal palace. The *comedia* consistently represents this court, whatever its impulsive young monarch's flaws, as a political space largely inimical to intrigues and deceptions. When the false news of Anteo's death first arrives there, the Epirote general Filipo displays a noteworthy lack of ambition and agrees to ascend the throne only in order to preserve the kingdom from the danger of foreign rule; as soon as word of Anteo's survival reaches the court, Filipo is glad to renounce his newly acquired power. Eleusipo's efforts to theatricalize the court for his own political gain are doomed to fail. When Anteo at last returns to his homeland with Eleusipo and Laodicea in the play's final scenes, a series of court ceremonies follows: the Epirote king officially announces his betrothal to the Macedonian princess and the peace treaty between the two realms, after which Laodicea is crowned queen of Epirus and the courtiers all swear their loyalty to her as Anteo's consort. Eleusipo, of course, still believes that Anteo is the peasant Alejo, and he considers these rituals nothing more than a final fraudulent performance that sets the seal on his triumph. Once it is concluded, he loses no time in gloating over what he believes to be the success of his stratagem:

> Estos actos acabados,
> resta ahora que salgáis
> del labirinto en que estáis,
> Senadores, enredados,
> pues el que delante tenéis
> por el rey, vuestro señor,
> no es rey, sino un labrador,
> como agora lo veréis.

(These ceremonies concluded, all that remains now, Senators, is for you to emerge from the labyrinth in which you wander deceived, since he that you believe to be the king, your lord, is not a king but only a peasant, as you will now see.) (2023, 2376–83)

Eleusipo commands "Alejo" to strip himself of his borrowed royal garments, to which Anteo responds with metatheatrical mockery: "¿Tenéis algún interés / en hacerme a mí entremés / de esta representación?" (Do you wish to make me the intermission comedy of this performance?; 2023, 2397–9). Only when Anteo emphatically asserts his sovereignty in this political space by commanding Eleusipo, "Rey me llamad" (Call me "King"; 2023, 2438), does the Macedonian monarch realize how thoroughly he has been duped and understand that what he believed to be a staged simulacrum of the restoration of a king to his court was in reality exactly what it appeared to be – precisely like Anteo's account of the shipwreck. In this *comedia*, lies are at their most deceptive, and their most effective, when they are true. This certainly includes royal impersonation: *El rey muerto*, for all its metatheatricality, is ultimately the most conservative of the three *comedias* with regard to this question. In Salucio del Poyo's play, only a king can play the role of a king on a court stage; Eleusipo's greatest mistake may be that of accepting Artandro's assurance that a peasant might successfully impersonate royalty.

In conclusion, then, these *comedias* provide three distinct, contrasting portraits of theatrical royal impostures within theatricalized court spaces facing political crises. In *La ventura con el nombre*, Ventura's precarious masquerade as the usurper Adolfo fails to restore stability to the troubled Bohemian court until it is ultimately revealed that he is the kingdom's rightful ruler, a discovery that provides the court with the political centre of gravity that Ventura failed to provide in his initially deficient performance as Adolfo. The reverse is true in *El rey por semejanza*, where Altemio's exemplary performance as Antíoco offers such a potent remedy for the court's and the realm's political ills that a commoner who proves himself a better ruler and a better man than the tyrant he impersonates permanently assumes that king's throne. And in *El rey muerto*, Anteo regains his throne and saves his court from foreign takeover by successfully masquerading as a lookalike impostor capable of convincingly impersonating the king. Despite their very different plot arcs, all three *comedias* depict royal courts as spaces every bit as intrinsically theatrical as the spaces in which the plays themselves were presented – and every bit as dependent on accomplished performers.

Notes

1 All translations are my own unless otherwise indicated.
2 Bercé's monograph offers a rewarding study of all these cases (1990). On the history of Sebastián and his posthumous impostors, see also Brooks (1964), MacKay (2012), and Olsen (2003); see Brody (1972), Dunning (2001), and Morris (2018) on the false Dmitrys.
3 Categorizing and cataloguing the various metatheatrical techniques deployed in these plays lies beyond the scope of this essay, as does any

attempt at a comprehensive bibliography of the lengthy scholarly debates concerning metatheatre and its applicability to the early modern Spanish *comedia*. See, however, the fundamental book-length studies by Abel (1963), Hornby (1986), and Orozco Díaz (1969) as well as, more recently, Thacker (2002) and the edited collection by Andres-Suárez et al. (1997).

4 All quotations from *La ventura con el nombre* will cite Blanca de los Ríos's 1958 edition by page and column.

5 Classical catalogues of such wonders include those compiled by Pliny the Elder in his *Natural History* (1855) and Valerius Maximus in his *Memorable Doings and Sayings* (2000).

6 All references to *El rey por semejanza* will cite verse numbers from Martínez Fernández's digital transcription for Artelope of Cotarelo y Mori's 1916 edition.

7 The sole surviving seventeenth-century manuscript of *El rey muerto*, in the Biblioteca Nacional de España, attributes the *comedia* to Luis Vélez de Guevara, but a recent stylometric analysis contradicts this. Working from that analysis, C. George Peale credits the play to Salucio del Poyo in his edition. Unsurprisingly, the previously unpublished play has received very little critical attention, but see Zugasti's remarks in his study of Vélez de Guevara's palace plays (2017) as well as my own introductory essay to Peale's edition.

8 All references to *El rey muerto* will cite C. George Peale's edition.

PART THREE

Sacred Spaces

9 Poeticizing Spaces in Seventeenth-Century Religious Poetry

MARÍA CRISTINA QUINTERO, BRYN MAWR COLLEGE

The convent of early modern Spain was a paradoxical space. On the one hand, it represented a place of confinement and isolation, a structure whose architecture – itself regulated and repeated in various places in the Peninsula and the New World – clearly restricted movement and limited the spaces its inhabitants could occupy: the choir, the cloister, the refectory, the cell. In contrast with the male clergy who had the freedom to leave the monastery and circulate in secular spaces, Spanish nuns were expected to keep strict enclosure, a *voto de clausura*, with heavy penalties imposed if the stricture was violated. After the Council of Trent (1545–63), when convent rules became even more rigidly enforced, the emphasis on the supreme inviolability of the convent walls was meant to parallel the inviolability of the nuns' bodies inside. Within the convent, furthermore, the categories of private and public become singularly complicated. For one thing, a cloistered nun's life was constantly surveilled and determined by the rules and regulations of the convent; she was constantly seen by other members of the community and overseen by church authorities. Many of her daily activities took place in communitarian spaces shared with other women, where the nun's secular individuality was attenuated if not effaced.[1] And yet, the convent cell itself could become a privileged place that offered the possibility of solitude and the space to develop a semblance of subjectivity. Indeed, as numerous scholars have demonstrated, despite the multiple restrictions and subordination to a male clerical hierarchy, the convent became for women a site that permitted a measure of intellectual and creative freedom, a place where they could cultivate the arts: music, theatre, and literature.[2] The same limited and limiting space that regulated their daily lives provided an ideal setting for the development of an expansive interior life. The very discipline required of the cloistered body – with its emphasis on demanding spiritual exercises – encouraged intellectual and imaginative movement.

This article is limited to the consideration of a handful of poems by three nuns – María de San Alberto (1568–1640), Cecilia de Nacimiento (1570–1646), and Marcela de San Félix (1605–87) – that reveal a preoccupation with places and spaces, both real (the cell, the convent, shrines, and natural landscapes) and symbolic (the interior castle, the city of God). These writers manipulate the concepts of space and place to explore religious, psychological, and aesthetic realms. In particular, these women wrote allegorical poetry that often described a mystical union in specifically spatial terms. Claustration thus paradoxically facilitated spiritual journey and escape, and in many cases, contributed to the construction of a literary feminine subjectivity.

The connection of place and space with gender is a topic that has received steady critical attention in recent decades in diverse disciplines: philosophy, sociology, anthropology, and literary criticism.[3] This trend is part of a broader and sustained interest in what Henri Lefebvre (1991) called the production of space: how human beings use, occupy, and manipulate different spaces and how these spaces influence and determine all social interactions and even affect the construction of identity and subjectivity. Lefebvre has argued that space, moulded as it is by historical circumstances, is a social product with strong ideological connotations (1991). The convent, a product of the early modern imaginary, is no exception. In addition to Lefebvre, other theorists such as Michel Foucault and Michel de Certeau have formulated categories that help elucidate the function of space in our lives.[4] More recently, feminist critics such as Doreen Massey (1994) and Gillian Rose (1993), among others, have explored more specifically the role of gender in the social production of space. The categories of place and space suggested by these critics have been elaborated mostly within modern and postmodern contexts, but their theories can provide at the very least a useful lexicon in approaching women's engagement with space during the early modern age.

Michel Foucault famously established three spatial categories: real space, utopia, and a third space he called heterotopia (1986, 24). A heterotopia may be seen at its most basic as a type of *counter* social space where other official and hegemonic spaces may be questioned, and one in which certain subjectivities in crisis can be accommodated and protected (1986, 24). During the early modern period, feminine subjectivity with relationship to both public and private spaces was precarious; and any study of spatial practices with relationship to women must take into account the politics and ideology of enclosure that dominated the era. Religious tracts, sermons, and conduct manuals were concerned with controlling the space inhabited by women and restricting their access to public sites. Female mobility was perceived as a threat, and the need to restrain a woman's nature by fixing her to a stable place was deemed paramount. Women who managed to wander freely – that is, to traverse and appropriate public spaces unencumbered – were subjected to deep suspicion and surveillance. We know through the work of feminist historians that despite these restrictions, women exercised numerous crucial functions inside and outside their places of enclosure. Nevertheless, that desire to control the movements of women necessarily frames an understanding of early modern women's relation to space. Within the context of the ideology of enclosure and vigilance that limited women's public role, the convent may indeed be seen as a counterspace, a heterotopia, one that reproduced societal technologies of control – through the power wielded by male ecclesiastical authorities, for example – but also one that allowed for a subtle critique of hierarchies and the development of subjectivity.

The preoccupation with space on the part of the three nuns considered here may also be said to correspond to Michel de Certeau's binary theory of place (*lieu*) and space (*espace*); the first category represents univocal or stable sites, and the second denotes what he calls "practiced sites" where there is movement, fluidity, encounters, and change (1984, 117). These are useful categories for our analysis, although de Certeau, a deeply religious writer and an ordained Jesuit himself, would in later writings attenuate the strict binary definition of these concepts as applied to religious experience. Indeed, in texts such as "L'Éxperience spirituelle," the term *lieu* acquires what Paola di Cori calls "resonancias bastante especiales puesto que es la propia experiencia espiritual la que se constituye como 'lugar de la diferencia'" (2015, 89) (Special connotations since it is the spiritual experience itself that is constituted as that "place of difference"; my translation). Adapting these concepts to the life and work of the women in this study, we can often identify the transmutation of a specific place such as a conventual cell into that space of difference that accommodated solitude, meditation, and, in many instances, a mystical journey.

The three writers considered in this essay engaged with the fixed place or *lieu* of the convent in specific manners. Indeed, these women were often directly involved in the planification, construction, and renovation of their monasteries. That is, they were concerned with creating and fortifying the conditions of their literal enclosure, one regulated by a patriarchal hierarchy. We can take as a first example María de San Alberto, who, as Mother Superior of the Discalced Carmelites in Valladolid, personally supervised the renovation of the Convento de la Concepcion; and, in fact, took charge of the construction of certain shrines or rural hermitages (*ermitas*), places separated from the rest of the convent and specifically designated to facilitate private prayer and contemplation (Arenal and Schlau 2010, 132). Architectural historians have told us that the desire for solitude in remote places led to "ongoing experimentation with buildings and spaces that allowed for the desire for seclusion, withdrawal, and privacy and even reinforce it" (Göttler 2018, 24). These architectural, delimited locations would provide María and her religious sisters with the indispensable physical conditions that allowed for interiority and spiritual movement. She herself would document this interiority in mystico-allegorical poetry such as "Lira a la soledad" (Stanzas to solitude) where *soledad*, or solitude – a word that appears frequently in religious poetry – acquires connotations related to location and space. In this poem, the union with the divine husband is expressed through symbolic topographies that connote intimate spaces. María's model was Teresa of Ávila, who herself had an intimate acquaintance of both literal and symbolic notions of place and space. The tireless reformer and founder of numerous convents drew upon her lived experience overseeing the construction of actual edifices to fashion an architecture that she would describe in spiritual tracts such as *Las moradas: El castillo interior del alma*, wherein she describes her mystical journey and union with God through spatial metaphors.

María de San Alberto would also turn to spatial categories in her religious poetry. In the first stanzas of "Lira a la soledad," she not only personifies solitude, a psychological state depicted as a friend and companion, but also construes it as a specific place:

> O soledad amiga
> que de todo te muestras ser señora
> no sé de ti qué diga
> sino que él que en ti mora
> goza del paraíso desde ahora.
> Que tú eres compañía
> al alma que de amor está sedienta
> y su perfecta guía
> porque si en ti aposenta
> no dejará de estar en Dios contenta. (Arenal and Schlau 2010, 160–1)

(Oh, Solitude, my friend, / you prove yourself to be the mistress of all, / what shall I say about you / except that whoever dwells in you / enjoys paradise from that moment on. / For you are the companion to the soul who is thirsty for love / and you are her perfect guide / because if she resides within you / she will no doubt rest happily in God.)[5]

Through the use of phrases such as "él que en ti *mora*" and "en ti *aposenta*," solitude becomes a site of emplacement for the soul. As stated earlier, the word *soledad* itself is polysemic, connoting at one level an actual physical place, usually one secluded in nature – the Latin *solitudine* was used synonymously with words such as *desertum* or the Greek *(h)eremus* (Göttler 2018, 7). Solitude denotes, as well, the physical and emotional state of isolation and contemplation. María's poem comprises the multiple meanings of *soledad*: an actual place – the monastic cell or an exterior site such as one of the *ermitas* that she was involved in constructing – that, through spiritual practice, is transformed into a symbolic space signalling a union with the divinity. The vagueness of phrases such as "no sé de ti qué diga" in the first stanza emphasizes the ineffability of solitude that the mystical state can induce; and yet, the next line expresses certainty with the affirmation that "el que en ti mora / goza del paraíso desde ahora." Solitude, then becomes a u-topic space: a place out of place or, in de Certeau's terms, a place of difference. The last two stanzas of the *lira* reinforce this sentiment through the use of the preposition "en," meaning "within," and the repetition of terms that connote *places* of repose:

> *En* ti deseo verme
> para vivir en Cristo *reposando*
> por que si el cuerpo duerme
> el alma esté velando
> pues tengo de morir y no sé cuando
> Aqueste es buen *reposo*
> velar continuamente en tu *posada*
> por venir al esposo
> dándole tal *morada*
> que con la eterna gloria sea pagada. (Schlau 1998, 225–6)

(I wish to see myself within you / so that I may live resting in Christ / because even if my body sleeps / the soul will keep its vigil / and although I don't know when, I will die. / This is a good repose, keeping constant vigil within your abode, because by giving him such a home, I will reach my (divine) husband and be paid with eternal glory.) (my translation)

The use of phrases like "velar continuamente en tu posada" and "dándole tal morada" emphasize again the spiritual emplacement that parallels the nun's physical isolated location. Mystical experience itself is also often described as a displacement from one place, often described as *stasis*, to another animated space, in the spiritual connotation of the word *anima*. Pedro Ruiz Pérez has stated that "apoyada en la alegoría, la escritura desdobla los significados de los espacios reales" (sustained by allegory, writing unfolds the meaning of real spaces; 1996, 107); and this is an apt description of how "aposento" and "morada" are unfolded and transformed into sites that are, to borrow de Certeau's terminology, *different* or *animated* spaces, the locations of the soul.

Maria de San Alberto's younger sister, Cecilia de Nacimiento, was also a singularly accomplished poet; and we repeatedly find in her verse evocations of symbolic landscapes. Like Maria, Cecilia became personally involved in the planification and construction of a monastery; and, in fact, she wrote a history of the founding of the Convento de Calahorra (Arenal and Schlau 2010, 176–8). In this document, she records the mundane details of choosing a site for the convent, securing financial backing, and the travails of construction:

> También me dio Nuestro Señor por aquel tiempo deseo de que hiciésemos casa para nosotras en forma de Religión, y aunque me contradecían, en especial la Madre Magdalena de Jesús, diciéndome que con qué caudal quería edificarla, yo respondía que no con el mío, sino con el de Dios, y así fue, que siempre su Divina Majestad favorece las cosas de su servicio. También pedí licencia al mismo prelado y me la dio; traté de comprar sitio, que fue una heredad de Diego Roldán, que él no tenía gana de venderla, y era de mayorazgo, y así costó harto sacar la Provisión Real; era grande que tenía mucho campo, y así le hubo para huerta, porque era menester, adonde el trazador de la Orden puso la planta del edificio de la casa. (Arenal and Schlau 2010, 172)

> (At that time, Our Lord also gave me the desire that we should create a house for ourselves according to the [Teresian] Rule, although they opposed me, especially Mother Magdalena de Jesus, asking me with whose fortune did I intend to build it? I replied, not with my own, but with God's; and so it happened, for His Divine Majesty always favors those things that are to His service. I also asked license of the Prelate himself, and he granted it; I tried to buy a site, which was the property of Diego Roldán, which he had no desire to sell, and it was an entailed estate so that it cost a great deal to get the King's writ. The place was large, for it had much land, and thus there was enough for a garden; and too, because it was necessary, where the architect of the Order placed the site for the construction of the house.) (Arenal and Schlau 2010, 173)

The quote evokes the mundane details of dealing with prelates and other church authorities and the bureaucracy involved in choosing, buying, and getting permits. At the same time, her poetry and autobiographical writings transcend these pragmatic preoccupations and engage with imagined topographies. Lefebvre makes a distinction between *representations* of space – how space is conceived by planners and architects – and *representational* spaces – those spaces that the imagination seeks to change and appropriate (1991, 33). Cecilia's religious experience, like that of her sister, would seem to comprise both representations of and representational spaces.

Cecilia's allegorical poetry abounds with sensual descriptions of imaginary excursions through places and spaces in search of the Beloved. The sensuality and movement in her poetry contrasts with the regulated static space of the convent and its stated purpose of maintaining the nun's body inviolable. After all, the metaphors used in numerous treatises to describe virginity were often architectural, designating sealed spaces: *porta clausa*, *claustra*, or *hortus conclusus* (Hills 2004, 167). The poetry of Cecilia de Nacimiento inverts these male-imposed architectural categories of control in her lyrical accounts; and in the following sonnet, it is solitude again that provides respite for the anxious longing for a union with God:

Solitaria quietud a do se anida
el alma con inmensa sed sedienta,
que no cabe en el mundo ni se asienta
sino de estar de todo despedida.
Tú eres mi refugio, mi manida;
en ti me asconde adonde no me sienta,
¡oh soledad amiga! y tu me alienta,
que vivo ausente de mi propia vida.
Pues sabes bien mis ansias y fatigas
favoréceme en mal tan fuerte y grave,
mostrándote propicia y amorosa,
para que de mi parte a Dios le digas
que cesen sus enojos o me acabe,
que no puedo vivir en otra cosa. (Cecilia de Nacimiento 2012, 258)

(Solitary stillness that shelters / the soul with immense, unquenched thirst, / that has no place at all in the world / unless everything else is dismissed. / You will be my refuge, my haven; in you I lose myself where I have no place. / O solitude, my friend! And *you keep me going*, / for I live absent from my own life. / Indeed you know well my fears and fatigue, / *favor me* in such grievous misfortune, / showing yourself favorable and loving, / so that you request of God *on my behalf* / that either my life or his anger might cease, / for I cannot live in another mode.) (Cecilia de Nacimiento, 2012, 259)[6]

From the very first verse, she invokes *soledad* as a place the soul can call its home, while at the same time describing it as a space outside space:

"que no cabe en el mundo ni se asienta." In the second quatrain, after emphasizing the sheltering quality of *soledad* by calling it a "refugio" and "manida," the poetic voice situates itself in that place of difference, repeating almost the same words previously applied to *soledad*: "en ti me asconde adonde no me sienta." The poem ends requesting that the personified *soledad* tell the divine spouse that she "no puede *vivir en* otra cosa," again portraying the mystic union in sensual, spatial terms.[7]

Another sonnet by Cecilia begins by alluding to landscapes that seem contradictory: cities and extensive shores, images that seem removed from the restricted place that is the convent where these lines were written:

> Por ciudades y playas anchurosas,
> con desmedido paso, a mi albedrío,
> así anduve sin dar vado a mi albedrío
> por los campos y breñas más fragosas. (Cecilia de Nacimiento 2012, 260)

> (Through spacious cities and seashores, / with boundless pace, at my pleasure, / thus I went with no thought of my pleasure / through fields and densest thickets.) (Cecilia de Nacimiento 2012, 261)

This oneiric landscape that the "I" of the poem invokes seeks to communicate the ineffable experience of searching anxiously ("con desmedido paso") for the Beloved. The reference to "ciudades" brings to mind the mystical or allegorical spaces invoked by other writers, for example, the title of María de Ágreda's *Ciudad mística de Dios*, which in turn echoes the more distant model of St. Augustine's *De civitate Dei*. The etymology of *civitate* comes from the word *civis*, meaning citizen, and referred originally to a person who resides in a specific place, as opposed to a pilgrim or stranger who is someone out of place, without a fixed abode. In Cecilia's poem, the journey across cities (places with people in them) to presumably desolate beaches, fields, and rough terrain describes the trajectory of the soul and its constant displacement in the search for God, who represents her ultimate spiritual home. Cecilia's mystical trek through inhabited, urban places and, simultaneously, unoccupied spaces contain echoes of the poetry written by her spiritual father, Juan de la Cruz. The saint's *Cántico spiritual* describes such a sustained journey through space by the soul in search of her Beloved. The second quatrain of Cecilia's sonnet could be read as a retort or gloss to the saint's famous spatial question in the *Cantico*, "¿A dónde te escondiste amado y me dejaste con gemido?" ("Where have you hidden, Beloved, and left me moaning?"). Cecilia's poetic voice responds:

No te hallé entre las flores olorosas,
ni a do sueles dormir en el estío;
desfalleció mi amor en su desvío,
y halléle entre mis quejas amorosas. (Cecilia de Nacimiento 2012, 260)

(I found you not in the fragrant flowers, / or fast asleep in the summer ground; / my love faltered in its deviation, / and found you among my loving laments.) (Cecilia de Nacimiento 2012, 261)

The last lines of this stanza echoes Juan de la Cruz's "Noche oscura": "cesó todo, y dejéme, / dejando mi cuidado / entre las azucenas olvidado" (Everything ceased, and I abandoned myself / leaving my cares / Forgotten among the lilies; my translation). Verses like these explain why for a time, two of Cecilia's poems were attributed to the Saint (Arenal and Schlau 2010, 141).[8]

After describing, in the following first tercet, the *dolendi voluptuas* that the soul experiences when at last she encounters her divine lover – "¡Oh penas para mí las más sabrosas / que cuanto gusto todo el mundo alcanza!" (Oh agony, for me more delicious / than any pleasure the whole world can reach; my translation) – the poem summarizes the need for the soul to suffer repeated displacements through the symbolic topography previously described: "Para sufrir su gloria el alma sale / a las celestes playas espaciosas" (Cecilia de Nacimiento 2012, 260) ("To feel his glory, the soul saunters / along the spacious celestial shores"; Cecilia de Nacimiento 2012, 261). The poetic voice seems to be breaking the restraints of her confined space in order to achieve a place of rapture. In the changing language that de Certeau uses to describe spiritual experiences, the term *lieu*, which as we have seen had variously meant a stable place or a place of difference, acquires the meaning of a type of event:

brusque intuition qui déplace (sans que l'on sache encore trop comment) l'organisation d'une vie et le type de relations qu'on a avec les autres. Une trouée se produit. Une irruption ouvre une brèche. Le paysage, tout á coup, change, à notre étonnement. Ceci, c'est un lieu. Dans l'expérience individuelle comme dans l'histoire, il y a des "moments " qui font dire: Dieu est là. (de Certeau 1970, 491)

(brusque intuition that displaces (without our knowing how) the organization of a life and the type of relationship one has with others.

A gap is produced. An irruption opens an abyss. The landscape, all of a sudden, changes, to our surprise. *This, this is a place*. In individual experience as in history, there are moments when one has to say: God is there.) (my translation and emphasis)

When Cecilia describes the unfettered joy of the soul upon entering "las celestes playas anchurosas," we hear echoes of the experience de Certeau describes.

Cecilia also wrote a long poem (twenty-five stanzas) about another specific place, this one located in nature. In the final decade of the sixteenth century, the male Discalced Carmelites established several enclosed wilderness spaces called "desiertos." The Desierto of Batuecas was one of three established in Spain and provided the setting for a monastery founded in 1599 by Father Tomás de Jesús, who happened to be Cecilia de Nacimiento's confessor and confidant.[9] Arenal and Schlau tell us that "she based the detailed description on information provided by her botanist brother, Diego de San José, and Tomás de Jesús" (2006, 134). Although she herself probably never visited this wild nature reserve, the twenty-five stanzas she dedicated to its description suggest an intimate knowledge of the natural world, as we see in the following stanza:

> Hacen con esto el sitio muy vistoso
> los acebos, madroños, los sanguinos,
> los salces, el durillo, los lentiscos,
> cedros, tara, cerezos, bledos, pinos,
> el arrayán, la higuera, el espinoso
> polipodio, helechos, tamariscos ... (Cecilia de Nacimiento 2012, 286)

> (With this you have a most scenic sight: / the holly trees, strawberry trees, blood oranges, / the willows, laurustinus, blue-flowered vetch, / cedars, vetch, cherry trees, amaranth, pines, / myrtle, fig trees, the spiny / polypody ferns, bracken, tamarisk ...) (Cecilia de Nacimiento 2012, 287)

At one point, Cecilia borrows vocabulary taken from architecture to describe how nature's bounty and exuberance surpasses manmade constructions:

> Mostró también aquí naturaleza
> de su saber gran parte, fabricando
> del río en torno cuevas naturales,
> y porque a trechos vaya descansando
> sus estanques labrados de una pieza,

de los puros y líquidos cristales
del sitio reconozcan los raudales
labró sin instrumentos
en los riscos sus casas y aposentos,
bóvedas, puertas, pirámides, cornisas
paredes lagartadas, torres fijas
con sus medias naranjas,
sin echar cartabón ni abrir zanjas. (Cecilia de Nacimiento 2012, 288)

(Here, too, nature revealed / a large part of its wit, inventing / natural caves from the river's bend, / and because of the way it rests at times, / its pools are of one piece, / of crystals, pure and liquid, / acknowledged by the torrents, / carved without tools, in the cliffs, its houses and rooms, / domes, doors, pyramids, cornices, / wide walls, solid towers, / made by natural methods, without a T-square or foundation.) (Cecilia de Nacimiento 2012, 289)

In addition to this evocation of natural spaces, the poet turns halfway through the poem to an account of the various hermitages and shrines that were built within this wilderness:

Esto del sitio; que pasar ya quiero
mi descripción al templo y las ermitas
desta nueva Tebaida o Palestina,
a donde primitivos Carmelitas
del instituto rígido y austero
resucitan la antigua disciplina. (Cecilia de Nacimiento 2012, 290)

(Enough about the setting; now I wish to continue, / with my description of the temple and hermitages / of this new Thebaid or Palestine, / where primitive Carmelites / in a strict and austere institution / resuscitate the ancient discipline.) (Cecilia de Nacimiento 2012, 291)

As with the *ermitas* associated with her sister, María de San Alberto, these were small structures designed to facilitate spiritual practices. By invoking the ancient sites of hermitages associated with famous saints and anchorites – Saints Anthony, Onofrius, and others – she establishes a continuation between ancient ascetic religious practices and those of discalced Carmelites like Father Tomás de Jesús.[10] The shrines, she tells us, are integrated seamlessly into nature:

(se levanta) otra ermita pequeña dedicada
del Verbo de Dios a la Encarnación santa;
es de sus vistas la hermosura tanta,

> que de valles y cuestas,
> conventos, ermitas, fuentes y florestas
> es un vistoso puesto y atalaya. (Cecilia de Nacimiento 2012, 296)

> ([there appears] another small hermitage dedicated / to the Holy Incarnation of the Word of God; / its vistas are very beautiful, / that of valleys and hills, / convent, hermitages, springs, and groves, / a scenic place and overlook.) (Cecilia de Nacimiento 2012, 297)

It is important to note that this edenic *desierto* was conceived as a masculine space meant for Discalced Carmelite monks. In fact, in 1622, a papal bull was issued that stipulated that all women, including nuns, be prohibited from entering these wilderness sites owned by the order, on pain of excommunication (Hegstrom 2017, 148). As stated earlier, it is unlikely that Cecilia visited Batuecas given this interdiction; and yet towards the end of the poem, in the penultimate stanza, she communicates the sense that she understands herself to be an interloper in this masculine space, as she abruptly and self-consciously alludes to her pen:

> Restaba agora, puesto que el discurso
> tan cerca nos ha echado del convento,
> pues la ley del buen orden lo pedía
> y aun de nuestro deseo el cumplimiento,
> que de mi pluma la corriente y curso,
> cuando tal la materia le ofrecía,
> dejando por un rato de ser mía,
> segunda vez cortada,
> en aqueste palenque y estacada
> sus pies pusiera y nueva diligencia
> en deciros la rara penitencia
> pobrezas y rigores
> que practican aquí sus profesores. (Cecilia de Nacimiento 2012, 298)

> (let me stop now, because my train of thought has thrown us so close to the convent, that the law of good order plus our desire to fulfil it, demands that my quill pen – when presented with this material – temporarily stop being mine, and sharpened for a second time on this palisade and stockade, so that it could take on a new task of describing for you the unique penitence, poverty, and rigours that those who profess [the monks] practice here)[11]

The use of hyperbaton makes it difficult to fully interpret these lines, but Cecilia seems to be saying that after the depiction of natural beauty, she has strayed back towards the convent and that it is now time for her pen to describe the spiritual practices of the monks. Here, she neatly dramatizes the coexistence, both in the wilderness setting and in her poetry, of concrete places or *lieux* – the actual convent and its surrounding hermitages – and of practised spaces or *espaces* wherein to practise penitence, poverty, and religious discipline. These rigorous practices, she tells, will lead to what she will call in the next and last stanza "secretos son muy altos" (exalted secrets), only to then tell us that, in fact her pen is unable to capture those experiences:

Mas no lo sepa el mundo, aguarda, espera;
coge las alas, tente, no lo digas,
secretos son muy altos, no lo alcanza,
por demás es que la canción prosigas.
No es aqueste lenguaje de su esfera,
ni con su estilo tiene semejanza,
nunca su ciencia tal alto abalanza,
cuánto más si te pones
a contalle los raptos y visiones,
éxtasis, vuelos místicos, conceptos,
conocimientos altos y secretos
que de su Dios reciben
estos varones santos que aquí viven. (Cecilia de Nacimiento 2012, 298–300)

(But the world shouldn't know of this, pause and wait, / take flight, stop, and do not speak / these are exalted secrets, that cannot be reached / so there is no point in continuing your song. / This is not language of our sphere, /nor is there any resemblance with our style / never can our knowledge venture so high, especially when you set out / to recount the raptures and visions, / ecstasy, mystical flights, conceits / lofty and secret knowledge / that the holy men who dwell here / receive from God.) (my translation)

She openly praises masculine piety, and simultaneously uses the humility trope to claim she is incapable of describing mystical experiences. At the same time, we can identify in this stanza a playful if subtle subversion of male superiority. Even as she claims her purported inability to describe the spiritual experiences of the Discalced brothers, the self-referential allusion to her pen and the fact that she has completed twenty-five stanzas – not to mention the fact that she too is a practitioner of ascetic discipline – are a testament to both her authorship and religious authority.[12]

The last poet to be briefly considered is Sor Marcela de San Félix, the illegitimate daughter of Lope de Vega. Her biographers have conjectured that Marcela entered the famous Convent of San Ildefonso (also known as the Convent of the Trinitarias Descalzas) in Madrid at age sixteen in part because she wanted to escape the chaotic milieu of her famous father's home:

> [S]he was more hindered physically, emotionally, spiritually, and intellectually at home than in the cloister ... Physically, she had inhabited cramped as well as tumultuous quarters at home. She had shared an upstairs bedroom with a half-sister and a servant ... By contrast, in the convent ... large, high-ceilinged communal rooms were furnished with chairs for the nuns to sit on as they prayed, ate, sang and sewed ... Most important, each nun lived in a cell of her own. (Arenal and Schlau 2010, 229)

Furthermore, Marcela has been credited with saying, "Pobre de mí, que he venido a hacer más papel que hacía en el mundo, donde era una desvalida, que no merecía que me mirasen a la cara!" ("Poor me! I have come to play a greater role [here] than out in the world where I was destitute and unworthy even of being noticed!"; Arenal and Schlau 2010, 228).[13] Like María de San Alberto and Cecilia del Nacimiento, she wrote poems about different places and spaces, also often praising solitude. One of her most remarkable poems, "Loa a la soledad de la celda," (In praise of the solitude of the cell), was written after the convent underwent extensive renovations that had forced Sor Marcela and her religious sisters to be displaced.

Beginning with its title, an association is established between an actual place – the convent cell – and the symbolic space of solitude. The poetic voice welcomes ("mil norabuenas") her fellow sisters and invites them to enter the renovated edifice:

> A daros mil norabuenas
> de dicha tan deseada,
> vengo, santísimas madres,
> con mucho gozo en el alma.
> Y este gozo se origina
> de ver que ya vuestras ansias
> y deseo de retiro
> el piadoso dueño paga. (Sor Marcela, "Otra")

> (I come with great happiness in my soul to congratulate you, holy mothers, for the much longed-for happiness. And my joy arises when I see how our merciful Master now repays your longings and desire for seclusion.)[14]

The cell is identified as a place that provides shelter for the body but also permits access to that privileged realm of *soledad*. In a self-conscious *captatio benvolentiae*, Marcela claims that she does not have the adequate eloquence to describe the importance of *soledad*:

> Si yo espíritu tuviera
> y elocuencia soberana,
> de la amable soledad
> dijera las alabanzas,
> pero soy muy ignorante
> y en el espíritu zafia
> y pudiendo decir tanto
> u diré muy poco u nada. (Sor Marcela, "Otra")

> (If I possessed ingenuity and supreme eloquence, I would sing the praises of benevolent solitude, but I am very ignorant and have a boorish spirit, and although I have to say so much, I will say little or nothing.) (my translation)

She describes this presumed lack of ability in spatial terms in the next lines: "Como estoy tan exterior ... ignoro excelencias tantas" (Since I am on the outside ... I am ignorant of such great wealth [of knowledge]).[15] Her supposed lack of eloquence, however, does not prevent her from celebrating the importance of the cell and the convent by extension, where access to that privileged place of difference is achieved. Solitude in fact becomes, in her description, a place of exchange – de Certaeu's practised space – where

> La estrecha conversación
> que tienen con Dios las almas
> ... las hace humildes y sabias. (Sor Marcela, "Otra")

> (The intimate conversation that God has with our souls ... makes them humble and wise.) (my translation)

Through the use of anaphora, beginning with stanza 11 until 18, the poet repeats the preposition "en" to signal a triumphant entrance that is both physical and spiritual:

> Entrad, pues, madres gozosas,
> fervorosas y animadas,
> que el Señor que dio las celdas
> también dará lo que falta. (Sor Marcela, "Otra")

(Enter, then, Mothers, rejoicing, / fervent, and inspired; / for the Lord who has given these cells / will give whatever is lacking.) (Arenal and Schlau 2010, 232)

These verses once again invoke the concrete space of the cell, while at the same time proclaiming the emotional or psychological state of its inhabitants (gozosas, fervorosas y animadas), once again giving this place a symbolic transcendence. In stanza 20, the cell itself is personified as a "celda descalza" (barefoot cell), metonymically identifying the place with its occupants. We may say that here the cell itself acquires an anima or soul:

Lo que falta es el adorno,
que en una celda descalza,
no ha de faltar lo curioso
de muy vistosas alhajas:
desnudez, pobreza, olvido
de toda cosa criada
y un incesable deseo
de ser más pura y más santa. (Sor Marcela "Otra")

(What is lacking is adornment, because a barefoot cell should not lack the novelty of splendid jewels: nakedness, poverty, the forgetting of every created thing, and the unrelenting desire to be purer and more saintly.) (my translation)

The cell, a limited univocal place, comes to personify the qualities and virtues of the religious order: it lacks adornment because its authentic jewels are, as stanza 21 tells us, "la desnudez, la pobreza," and "el olvido de toda cosa criada." The next stanza brings together the duality of a heterotopia, combining the physical and material reality with the interiority of the practiced space that is mystical experience:

que la celda material
ha de servir como caja
que guarda la interior celda
donde el esposo descansa. (Sor Marcela, "Otra")

(The material cell / is like a box / that contains an interior cell / where the divine husband rests.) (my translation)

Sor Marcela simultaneously depicts both the interior and exterior cells. The use of "la interior celda" echoes Teresa of Ávila, who famously also described the soul in spatial terms:

> nuestra alma [es] como un castillo todo de diamante o muy claro cristal, adonde hay muchos aposentos, así como en el cielo hay muchas moradas … y en el centro y mitad de todas éstas tiene la más principal, que es adonde pasan las cosas de mucho secreto entre Dios y el alma. (Teresa de Jesús 2019, 15–16)

> (our soul [is like] a castle, made up entirely of diamonds or very clear crystal, in which there are many rooms, just as in heaven there are many mansions … and in the centre and middle of all of these, there is the most important room, which is where very secret things transpire between God and the soul.) (my translation).

While the architectural complexity of the seven *moradas* of Teresa's interior castle are not reproduced here, Marcela conflates in two lines the heterotopian duality of the cell. What's more, she explicitly states that while the cell itself is a place of vigilance, and enclosure, the cell as the space of spiritual practice allows the nuns to escape the physical limitations of the cell:

> Que si faltase el espíritu
> y la oración en el alma,
> más que santa religiosa,
> será mujer encerrada. (Sor Marcela "Otra")

> (For if spirit and prayer / are missing from the soul, / [a nun] would be nothing / but a woman confined.) (my translation)

Paradoxically, then, an enclosed woman ("mujer encerrada") is the opposite of a religious saint, thus affirming that she and her sisters are not subject to physical limitations: their religiosity and mystical experiences allow them to transcend claustration.

If we return to Foucault's idea that heterotopias represent social spaces within which the fundamentals of social order are interrogated, we see that for Marcela as for the other two writers here considered, the convent and its interior cells became spaces that could accommodate and protect vulnerable subjectivities in crisis. In poems like these, the writers emphatically surpass the limitations of the cell through imaginative displacements and through another space that can be called heterotopian: the space of poetry.

Notes

1 The following scholars have written specifically about the spatial and architectural configuration of the convent: Els De Paermentier (2008), Valerie Flint (2000), C. Flores Marini (1966), and Kim Knott (2005), among others.

2 Numerous scholars have contributed in recent decades to our knowledge of life in the convent for women religious in Spain including Electa Arenal and Stacey Schlau (2006, 2010), Nieves Baranda Leturio and María Carmen Marín Pina (2014), Nieves Baranda (2018), Elizabeth Lehfeldt (2005), and Alison Weber (2009). Arenal's and Schlau's pioneering book *Untold Sisters* (with translations by Amanda Powell), which first came out in 1989 and was revised in 2010, provided the first comprehensive introduction to and study of the three writers I engage with in this article.

3 See Doreen Massey (1994), Gillian Rose (1993), Daphne Spain (1992), among others.

4 See de Certeau's *The Practice of Everyday Life* (1984) and Michel Foucault's "Of Other Spaces" (1986).

5 I have used the version of the poem found in Arenal and Schlaum (2010). Amanda Powell provides in this book a fine translation of the poem, but to better illustrate my interpretation, I have provided my own alternative translation.

6 For Cecilia del Nacimiento's poetry, I have for the most part used the translations provided by Sandra Siser in *Journeys of a Mystic Soul in Poetry and Prose*, the bilingual edition of Cecilia's works by Kevin Donnelly. I have occasionally modified the translation and signalled the changes in italics. In one instance, as noted below, I have substituted my own translation entirely.

7 Cecilia described her mystical experiences in poems such as "Canciones de la unión y transformación del alma con Dios," reproduced in Arenal and Schlau (2010, 178–80).

8 See also Alison Weber's "Could Women Write Mystical Poetry?" (2009) for a study of Maria and Cecilia's poetic relationship to Juan de la Cruz.

9 Hegstrom (2017) mentions Batuecas, but her article deals with a remarkable poem by Bernarda Ferreira de Lacerda evoking another such *desierto* in Portugal, the Soledades de Buçaco.

10 According to Weber, Tomás de la Cruz would run afoul of the Church hierarchy and, as a result, Cecilia was closely watched although she was never charged with any misdeed (Weber 2009, 198).

11 I am providing my own translation of this difficult stanza, as Sider's seems somewhat off the mark.

12 In their brief discussion of this poem, Arenal and Schlau present it as an example of how Cecilia "projects herself beyond the female cloister and participates in the larger Carmelite realm" (2006, 134).

13 For further analysis of Sor Marcela's poetry, see also Sabat de Rivers (1986, 1993) and Arenal (2009).

14 I cite from the complete version of this poem edited online by Luis López Nieves in *Ciudad Selva*. Arenal and Schlau in *Untold Sisters* quote and Powell translates only a few of the stanzas of this long "Loa" by Sor Marcela. The translations I present here are mostly my own, except where noted. In these verses, for example, I translate the first four lines, but the next four are Powell's, slightly modified (Arenal and Schlau 2010, 230).

15 Georgina Sabat de Rivers (1993) comments on Marcela's "formulas de 'falsa modestia'" and the importance of *soledad* in her poetry: "la idea de que así como la libertad interior se encuentra en la soledad, también se encuentra en ella la inspiración para poder escribir" (30; the idea that just as interior freedom can be found in solitude, so too can the inspiration and the ability to write be centered there; my translation).

10 Mirrors, Self-Portraits, and Visionary Exemplarity: An Analysis of the Guadalupe Chapel, Royal Discalced Convent, Madrid

ROSILIE HERNÁNDEZ,
UNIVERSITY OF ILLINOIS CHICAGO

The study of women religious and convent culture in late medieval and early modern Spain provides fertile ground for examining the relationship between the spatial strictures imposed by convent walls and the imaginary life nurtured by the religious art and objects that populated those same walls and filled its chapels. Didactic in nature, religious art provided cloistered nuns with a visual key to the rituals, sermons, prayers, and texts that occupied their daily routines, fed their minds, calmed their spirits, and provided referents for their identifications and selfhood. Founded by Juana de Austria – Princess of Portugal, sister of Charles V, and queen regent for her brother Philip II during his prolonged absences from the Spanish seat – the Royal Discalced Convent, or Descalzas Reales, in Madrid is a fascinating example of this apparent contradictory dynamic, especially given the robust resources and complex political, familial, and social relationships of its inhabitants.[1] Welcoming widows, spinsters, and orphans of the high nobility, the monastery was home to powerful women, including many of the Habsburg family whose personal dowries and family wealth, added to the protections offered by the Crown, allowed for elaborate projects and lavish commissions. One such inhabitant was Sor Ana Dorotea de la Concepción, Marquise of Austria and illegitimate daughter of Rudolph II and Catalina Strada, who arrived at the Descalzas Reales in 1624 at age twelve, professed in 1628 at the age of sixteen, and remained interned until her death at the age of eighty-two in 1694. Rudolph II's family connection to the Spanish Habsburgs was pivotal to his daughter's eventual sojourn in Madrid. Not only was he the son of the Spanish princess María, daughter of Charles V and Isabella of Portugal, but he resided in the Spanish court of his uncle Philip II for more than eight years (1563–71). In fact, from that period spent in Spain, we have the first known portraits of the young future emperor at age sixteen, painted by Alonso Sánchez Coello and likely commissioned by Phillip II (1567, King's Closet, Windsor Castle, Royal Collection Trust). Therefore, his daughter's influence at the Descalzas Reales was not solely derived from her title and blood ties but was equally strengthened by the memories and personal relations that endured from her father's time at the Spanish court. As explained by María Leticia Hernández Sánchez,

> Fue Dorotea una de las monjas más influyentes de las Descalzas [...] Dorotea no vivió exclusivamente por y para el claustro, sino que desde su posición de profesa procedente de la familia real estableció una vasta red de contactos con miembros de la realeza, de la aristocracia, del mundo diplomático y de la Iglesia [...] Su labor *ad intra* del monasterio se plasmó en su mecenazgo artístico, fruto del cual se construyó esta capilla de Guadalupe, y se llevó a cabo la restauración de la escalera principal en la que se puede observar el óvalo de santa Dorotea con un rostro muy similar al del retrato que le hiciera Rubens en 1628 con motivo de su profesión solemne, y ubicado en el Salón de Reyes. (2014, 304)

> (Dorotea was one of the most influential nuns at the Descalzas [...] Dorotea did not live exclusively by and for the convent, but from her position as a nun with royal lineage she established a vast network of contacts with members of the royal family, the aristocracy, the diplomatic core, and the Church [...] Her work from inside the monastery was characterized by her art patronage, from which the Guadalupe Chapel was constructed, as well as the restoration of the main stairwell where we can observe an oval with the portrait of Saint Dorotea with very similar features to the portrait [of Dorotea] painted by Rubens in 1628 in commemoration of her professing her faith and found in the Salon of the Kings.)[2]

Ana Dorotea lived interned for most of her long life. Still, she used her position, money, power, and social relations to construct a physical space and a subjective place for herself within the convent's walls, which in turn allowed her to exert her influence far beyond its limits. Two major artistic undertakings in the convent resulted from her patronage and participatory design: the restoration of the murals in the main staircase and the Guadalupe Chapel.

The Guadalupe Chapel has been studied by art historians and historians who have identified Sebastián Herrera Barnuevo as the painter and commented upon Ana Dorotea's influence on the pictorial program and configuration of the paintings. Harold E. Wethey and Alice Sunderland Wethey were the first to compile a complete catalogue of the paintings and iconography of Guadalupe Chapel, noting how it "combines the artist's skill as painter, sculptor, and architect in a manner not often met in Spanish Baroque art" (1966 19). Signalling the aesthetic uniqueness and conceptual sophistication of the pictorial program – which we can largely attribute to Ana Dorotea's theological commitments in defence of the doctrine of immaculacy and the Habsburg *Pietas Austriaca* – the art historians state, "Nowhere can one point to another cycle of Old Testament heroines as extensive as this, and the small symbolic scenes (signalling the attributes of the Virgin of the Immaculate Conception), likewise, have almost no exact counterparts elsewhere" (Wethey and Sunderland Wethey 1966, 20).[3] Sánchez Hernández expands the analysis by focusing on the instructional nature of the project in the context of the Counter-Reformation: "La capilla de Guadalupe [...] fue un ejemplo de la utilización pedagógica de la Escritura a través de las imágenes [...] [E]l texto se transforma en imagen para ser contemplado de manera pedagógica por una comunidad de monjas" (The Guadalupe Chapel [...] was an example of the pedagogical utility of the Scriptures through images [...] [The] text is transformed into a pedagogical image to be contemplated by a community of nuns; 2014a, 498–9). The text referred to is Martín Carrillo's *Elogios de mujeres insignes del viejo testamento* (1627), a collection of *exempla* dedicated to Ana Dorotea's aunt Margarita de la Cruz, niece of Phillip II, who brought the young girl as an orphan to the Descalzas Reales and educated her. In her excellent article "El monasterio de las Descalzas Reales: Arte y espiritualidad en el Madrid de los Austrias" (The Descalzas Reales monastery: Art and Spirituality in Hapsburg Madrid), Ana García Sanz also highlights the tight didactic and intellectual bond between aunt and niece and text and paintings, resulting in the masterful execution of the Guadalupe Chapel:

> Esta capilla es un buen ejemplo de la estrecha relación entre manifestación artística y literatura pues la fuente de inspiración del programa iconográfico se encuentra en la obra de Martín Carillo [...] conservada en la biblioteca del propio monasterio y que fue dedicada por el autor a la infanta Sor Margarita de la Cruz.
>
> (This chapel is a good example of the close relationship between artistic design and literatura since the source of inspiration for the iconographic program is found in Martín Carrillo [...] kept at the monastery's library and dedicated by the author to Sor Margarita de la Cruz.) (2010, 20)[4]

As Sánchez Hernández and García Sanz noted, the chapel's visual program presents a catalogue of twenty-one Old Testament heroines leading to Marian privilege. The altar is framed by an additional fifty-two panels that represent the life and virtues of the Virgin, with an emphasis on the symbols of immaculacy. Conceptually tying together and positing a sanctified triumph for the pictorial program, the front of the altar features a large painting of the Virgin of the Immaculate Conception: "La imagen de la Virgen descansa sobre el globo terráqueo y la media luna rodeada de ángeles y nubes [...] detrás de ella, un gran espejo adornado con un sol naciente y seis ángeles portando palmas, rosas, y azucenas" (The image of the Virgin rests on the globe and the crescent moon surrounded by angels and clouds [...] behind her, a grand mirror adorned by the rising sun and six angles carrying palm branches, roses, and lilies; Sánchez Hernández 2014a, 501).[5] Together, the Old Testament exemplars and the Virgin Mary offer an unbroken lineage of heroism, activism, and purity to be emulated and embodied by the community of women that inhabited the Descalzas Reales.

In what follows, I hope to offer a new approach to studying the Guadalupe Chapel. In a previous publication, I noted how the chapel, with its Old Testament heroines, was designed to reinforce how the nuns at the Descalzas Reales positioned their identity as social and political agents.[6] In this chapter, I would like to return to this analysis but focus in much greater detail on the medium upon which these paintings are executed: mirrors. As noted by Wethey and others, this is one of the most notable aspects of the chapel.[7] The effect is that the cloistered nun kneeling at the altar in prayer would see her reflection on the paintings that fill the chapel walls and the façade of the altar, thus becoming a part of the images themselves. I argue that the spatial replication of the nun's reflection upon the mirrored paintings blurs the limit between the self, her spiritual foremothers, and the eternal Mother whose immaculate existence made possible and secured the promise of redemption. Following this proposition, I focus on how the experience of seeing the paintings that comprise the Guadalupe Chapel can be contextualized within the cultural parameters of the technical and symbolic use of the mirror, its relationship to portraiture and self-portraiture, and the religious visionary imagination of the early modern period.

It is often the case that religious images that depict an encounter with the sacred split the pictorial plane into halves. While the top segment is assigned to the transcendent – and is thus populated by the Holy Trinity, angels, and the souls who have ascended to the heavens – the bottom segment is dedicated to the immanent human realm. This is a conceptual arrangement best theorized by Victor Stoichita in his *Visionary Experience in the Golden Age of Spanish Art*: "The problem of unifying immanence and transcendence was taken up by Counter-Reformation Art precisely in [a] spirit of the dramatic verticalization of the visionary experience" (1995, 28).[8] Paintings such as El Greco's *The Assumption of the Virgin* (1577–9, Art Institute of Chicago, Chicago) and Francisco de Zurbarán's *Battle between Christians and Moors at El Sotillo* (1637–9, Metropolitan Museum of Art, New York) perfectly demonstrate this distinction visually representing biblical and historical events, respectively, in which the divine transcendental makes itself present above the earthly realm in the form of an opening or apparition in the heavens. Stoichita's study further reflects on the pictorial narrativization of visionary experiences where the mystical apparition, which takes place within the purified soul, is projected outside the body in an upper visual plane. These images simultaneously establish a link and spatial separation between the earthbound body and the spiritual realm, which is, in turn, ordered and contained within the strictures of the frame. As a result, Stoichita argues, "Far from inspiring uncontrollably mystical activities, the contemplation of the vision-painting is equivalent to 'taming' the visionary experience" (1995, 26). An excellent example of this type of painting is Bartolomé Esteban Murillo's *The Vision of Saint Anthony of Padua* (1656, Cathedral of Seville, Seville), where, following Stoichita's interpretation, the spectator is allowed to meditate upon the visionary in a sanctioned sacred space without the possibility for abandonment or excessive identification.[9]

Concurrent with this visual-spatial configuration, the late-medieval and early modern religious imagination also produced a plethora of exemplary religious narratives that called upon the readers or listeners to conceive of themselves as tangentially inhabiting the shoes, so to speak, of the holy or saintly figure whose physical and spiritual life was textually represented. In Spanish religious circles, for example, Thomas à Kempis's *Imitatione Christi* (1441 autograph manuscript) and the *speculum vita Christi* genre to which it belonged were highly influential and imitated widely throughout the fifteenth, sixteenth, and seventeenth centuries. Texts such as Isabel de Villena's *Vita Christi* (1490) extended the instructional intentionality of the genre into a *vitae mariae*, which was later reproduced and developed further in the writings of Valentina Pinelo and Sor María de Ágreda among many other women religious thinkers and writers.[10] As such, the exemplary model allowed for an alternative relationship with the sacred, in which the pious figured themselves alongside, in community with, or closely resembling the holy Other.

Within this interpretative framework, María Morrás asks us to account for the complex intersection of interests and historical specificity in which exemplary texts are produced alongside the potentiality for a "surplus of meaning [...] provided by the readers' imagination" (2020, 12). Focusing on the gender implications of the genre, Morrás further emphasizes that we as critics should engage with exemplarity, imagined commonality, and imitability as a continuum through which women – as readers and authors – were able to claim authority and create unexpected positions and voices vis-à-vis the power structures that often sought to delimit and prescribe their aspirations, actions, movements, thoughts, and voices.[11] This parallel schema – one that focuses on visual separation and experiential containment and the other on identification and assimilation – provides a productive framework for studying the Guadalupe Chapel's mirrored paintings. The history of mirrors and their pivotal role in the development of perspective in art in the early modern period has been widely documented.[12] By way of anecdote, and as noted by Yvonne Yiu, "the first passage linking the mirror with the self-portrait is found in Giovanni Boccaccio's *De mulieribus claris* (1361–62)," where the Roman painter Martia is exalted for painting her masterful self-portrait by using a mirror (2005, 189). In the early modern period, mirrors provided a medium that mediated the chasm between physical sight (the way light enters the eye and is interpreted by the brain) and the blank, flat canvas. As documented by Alan Macfarlane and Gerry Martin, in the early modern period mirrors – two-dimensional surfaces that reflect the world in reverse and three-dimensionally – were regularly analogized with painting and became a source of both inspiration and rivalry for artists who wished to reproduce the natural world faithfully. Leonardo called mirrors "the master of painters" and recommended to painters the following: "You should take the mirror as your master, that is a flat mirror, because on its surface things in many ways bear a resemblance to a painting. That is to say, you see a picture which is painted on a flat surface showing things as in relief: the mirror on a flat surface does the same" (cited in Macfarlane and Martin 2002, 64). Self-portraiture was likewise transformed in the sixteenth century by the advent of quality mirrors: "Although the genre of the self-portrait is reasonably well established in the fifteenth century, none of the texts examined refer to the mirror's function in this context. It is only from the sixteenth century onwards that references to concrete self-portraits with the adjunct 'fatto/ritrato allo specchio' become commonplace in art theoretical writing" (Yiu 2005, 189). As explained by Yiu, for artists and treatise writers such as Leonardo, Filarete, and Alberti, the mirror intensified and clarified certain aspects, qualities, and contours of the objects reflected, providing novel and unforeseen perspectival coordinates for visual artists across Europe (2005, 192):

> [T]he mirror was an object that unleashed the creative potential so characteristic of the period. Indeed, in the eyes of contemporary observers, the mirror was intimately associated with major innovations such as naturalistic representation, for which the realistic self-portrait served as exemplum […] Thus, the mirror's role in the production of the artist's self-portrait is embedded in a discussion of life-like depiction. (Yiu 2005, 209)

The history of self-portraiture is thus intimately linked to the development of higher-quality mirrors in the early modern period. Commonly coined as *ritratto allo specchio*, artists were trained to paint their self-images using a reflection in a mirror throughout the sixteenth century. The mirror provided a "third eye" that allowed the artist to observe him or herself as they had before observed nature (Macfarlane and Martin 2002, 64).

On the other hand, mirrors also deepened and problematized the visual experience by defamiliarizing the physical perception of reality, prompting the viewer to see the world and him or herself from skewed alternative perspectives. Regarding this technical aspect, mirrors have been identified as pivotal to the rise of the concept of the individual. Congruent with Eric Schatzberg's "cultural approach to technology," historians offer mirrors as participating in "the spirit of an age" (2018, 3) in which humanism, Ockham's nominalist legacy, the Protestant Reformation's emphasis on interiority, Catholic confessional introspection, and emergent pre-capitalist socio-economic structures make possible the imaginary of a unique self apart from a broad collective; or, as Ian Mortimer spells out in his examination of the effect of mirrors on identity, "What happened in the fifteenth century was not so much that […] community identity broke down, but rather that people started to become aware of their unique qualities irrespective of their loyalty to their community. That old sense of collective identity was overlain with a new sense of personal self-worth" (2016, 120). Arguing in favour of mirrors as a catalyst for this shift between the thirteenth and sixteenth centuries, Macfarlane and Martin clarify:

> The timing of the causal link is right; good mirrors developed at almost exact pace with the development of a new individualism between the thirteenth and sixteenth centuries. The geography is right; the epicenters of Renaissance individualism in painting and other art forms were Italy and the Netherlands, two of the most advanced areas of mirror making and

their use. The psychological link is plausible; people saw themselves in a new way that detached them from the crowd and allowed them to inspect themselves more carefully. (2002, 72)

To see the image in the mirror as a singular three-dimensional object, to look oneself in the eye, provides for psychological introspection and the terrain – spatial and conceptual – for an ideology of selfhood relative to other selfhoods and how others saw oneself that was not possible in the same manner before the advent of high-quality mirrors. The rise of self-portraits and paintings that included the self-image in a mirror demonstrates the richness of the interaction between the reflected I and the construction of the self in the early modern period. Murillo's late *Self-Portrait* perfectly exemplifies this relationship between the mirror, the self-portrait, and the ascendancy of the individual, where, in a masterful example of *trompe l'oeil*, the self-image emerges out of the represented mirror (ca. 1670, National Gallery).

Mirrors in sixteenth-century art were additionally linked to the topoi of *vanitas*. The symbol was often depicted as a single convex mirror in still lives thematized as *memento mori* and frequently included in female portraits. *Vanitas* portraits typically ask the viewer to reflect on physical beauty as an empty vessel that will be destroyed by time and dissolved by death. Moreover, as noted by Anthony F. Janson, the convex mirror's capacity for "extreme distortions, which heighten the viewer's ambivalence towards visual – and visionary – reality" further bolster the transitory and uncertain nature of the reflected image and the vanity it profiles (1985, 51). The genre offers sublime images (doubled by a reflection on a mirror) that often rely on an ideological reductionism of women as sexualized bodies whose ephemeral beauty diverts from what is true and lasting: the intellect, the purity of the soul, and charity. Representations of Venus contemplating her fleeting splendour best captured the *vanitas* ethos, with Velázquez's *The Toilet of Venus* (1644, National Gallery) – which was painted for Philip IV's private quarter and placed in the company of two similar paintings by Rubens and Titian – being one of the most exquisite examples.[13]

And yet, even if a *vanitas* conceptual framework offered the subject's look into a mirror as denoting the vacuity of physical life, Christian theology provided an alternative theological register. Humans, created in the image of God, reflect as mirrors the qualities and divine design of the supreme being. As stated by Saint Paul in 1 Corinthians 13:12, sin has made that mirror darken: "For now we see in a mirror, dimly, but then face to face. Now I know in part, but then I shall know just as I also am known" (New King James Version). If sin has made the image darken, salvation makes the reflection clear once again, illustrating the transformative power of God in and upon human beings: "But we all, with open face beholding as in a glass the glory of the Lord, are changed into the same image from glory to glory, even as by the Spirit of the Lord" (2 Corinthians 3:18, New King James Version). Following this theological premise, Teresa of Ávila made use of the mirror in *The Life of Saint Teresa of Avila by Herself*, or *Vida*, to relate a mystical encounter with Christ:

> Once when I was reciting the Office with the community, my soul suddenly became recollected, and seemed to me like a clear mirror; there was no part of it – back, sides, top, or bottom – that was not completely bright; and in the middle was a picture of Christ our Lord as I usually see Him. I seemed to see Him in every part of my soul as clearly as in a mirror, and this mirror – I cannot explain how – was entirely shaped to this same Lord, by a most loving communication which I cannot describe [...] It was explained to me that when a soul is in mortal sin this mirror is covered with a thick mist and remains so dark that the Lord cannot be reflected or seen in it, even though He is always present and gives us our being [...] Let us say that the Divinity is like a very clear diamond, much larger than the whole world, or a mirror, according to my description of the soul in my former vision, except that it is of so sublime a kind that I cannot find words to express it. Then let us suppose that all we do is seen in this diamond, which is so formed as to contain everything within itself, for there is nothing that can lie outside of its greatness. (1988, chapter 40, 308 and 310)

The purified soul turned into a clear reflective surface is thus the proper medium to see oneself in the image of and as intricately linked to the divine other. As indicated above, the *speculum vitae* genre speaks to this aspiration: a portrait of Christ or Mary's life conceived as a narrative reflective mirror for the reader. The power of the divine reflection was likewise closely associated with the Virgin Mary as *speculum justitiae* (mirror of justice). Featured in the Litany of Loreto, the mirror of justice indicates the relationship between the Virgin and God, who shines directly on her as the Sun of Justice, thereby reflecting his divine nature and the redemptive justice brought to the world by Christ Incarnate. Just as importantly, the symbolic association with the *speculum sine macula*, theologically bound to the Virgin's eternal immaculacy, recalls Mary's purity but also, as noted by Helena Goscilo, the "mirror of human conscience": "Insofar as it enjoins an introspection that can lead to self-improvement, the mirror possesses a moral function. In that sense, far from catering to vanity, it presumably catalyses laudable aspirations"

(2010, 296). In other words, to look in the mirror of the Immaculate Virgin is to look at oneself introspectively through her, to see oneself as an individual fashioned in and through her perfect image.

It is precisely this purifying reflective mechanism that leads us back to Ana Dorotea and the mirrored paintings of the Guadalupe Chapel. I have previously established the functional and social politics of exemplarity that the chapel afforded the nuns at the Descalzas (Reales): "[W]hen Ana Dorotea and her fellow cloistered nuns and royal women companions saw themselves reflected in these paintings, they looked upon a feminine biblical history that traces the Virgin's past, but which symbolically also deliberately reflects the strength, prudence, valor, courage, astuteness, and piety that their own "mothers" – and for Ana Dorotea more specifically, Margaret of the Cross – embodied and practiced" (2011, 237). Keeping these exemplary coordinates in mind, I would like to reflect on how the mirror as a canvas and the religious paintings that comprise the Guadalupe Chapel together function as a medium for a religious imaginary where the self is literally reflected upon and consequently superimposed upon the image of the saintly and divine Other. Given this spatial visual dynamic, the mirrored paintings of the Guadalupe Chapel can be understood to dissolve the divide between the transcendent and the immanent, allowing the worshipper to envisage a visionary self-portrait made possible through the mechanism of reflection and replication (both physical and contemplative). Worthy of the fervour that drove the defence of Marian privilege during this period in Spain and that consumed much of the religious and political activity of the nuns at the convent, the visual experience is punctuated in the mirrored painting of the Virgin of the Immaculate Conception situated at eye level at the centre of the altar, offering a visionary passage for the nuns that knelt to worship their divine mother.

I believe that the inventiveness of this visual experience can be primarily attributed to Ana Dorotea, who not only conceived of the iconographic program (as noted by Wethey and Sánchez) but who possessed the necessary background and theological knowledge that would lead to the concept of executing religious paintings on mirrors. As an illegitimate daughter of Rudolf II and Catalina Strada, Ana Dorotea lived up to the age of about ten at the Austrian Hapsburg court in Prague, surrounded by the immense art and curiosity collection her father famously gathered. The collection included many pieces by the most influential artists of the period and a vast assortment of decorative arts, mechanical devices, and scientific paraphernalia.[14] For example, in her dissertation *Alchemy of the Gift: Things and Material Transformations at the Court of Rudolf II*, Ivana Horacek documents the

1619 inventory that included, for example, valuable artefacts such as mirrors (2015, 84–5).

Although she could not have had any substantive memory of her father – he died about a year after her birth – her progenitor's legacy indelibly marked Ana Dorotea's life. As noted by García Sanz, "La figura de Ana Dorotea es un claro ejemplo de mecenazgo conventual, función en la cual se puso de manifiesto su refinado gusto artístico, condición que había heredado de su padre, gran coleccionista y declarado protector de las artes" (Ana Dorotea is a clear example of conventual patronage, a role through which her refined artistic taste was clearly manifested, a characteristic she had inherited from her father who himself was a renowned collector and self-proclaimed protector of the arts; 2010, 20). Ana Dorotea's provenance is, in fact, one of the key visual features of the chapel represented by the two eagles of the Hapsburg house placed atop the arched entryway. Majestic and proud, the eagles guard an inscription that names Ana Dorotea and her father as the conceptual, artistic, and religious keepers of the chapel (abridged translation): "The altar that you see, ceremoniously erected (an honour to the mind, confirming the devotion of the soul, a labour of love) […] is dedicated by Ana Dorotea, *versed in art*, daughter of Rudolf II, distinguished in his piety and in war in service of Christ" (emphasis mine). Declaring the individual faculties – intellectual, artistic, and religious – possessed by Ana Dorotea, the inscription traces a direct line to an elevated imperial heritage in her father's Prague court. Although we cannot venture a specific source in Rudolf II's collection and cabinet of curiosities for the mirrored paintings of the Guadalupe Chapel, it is hard to imagine that Ana Dorotea's unique childhood would not have shaped her capacity for invention and profoundly informed her vision, artistic and religious. A space composed of mirrors, images, and icons, the Guadalupe Chapel makes possible a spiritual experience where the devout nun can place her individual self at the intersection of the exemplary Old Testament heroines represented on the wall panels, the eternal purity of the divine Virgin mother placed at the centre of the altar, and the sacred visionary present afforded by Ana Dorotea's artistic, conceptual, and theological design. Contrary to the supposed function of Mary in the early modern period as a remote ideal, Ana Dorotea presents the nuns at the Descalzas Reales with a spatial and mediological configuration that facilitates a self-image both unified with and participatory of the lineage of power, sanctity, and redemption displayed and reflected on the walls and altar.

By the early 1650s, when Ana Dorotea planned and commissioned the chapel, religious self-portraits had enjoyed an illustrious history that could not have been unknown to her. Several examples come to mind. Sofonisba Anguisola's *Self-Portrai at an Easel* features her as a *pintora-divina*, usurping the narrative and visually familiar place of Saint Luke painting the Virgin (1556, Museum Castle in Łańcut). Zurbarán's *Saint Luke Painting the Crucifixion* offers an equally fascinating case, mapping his likeness onto the symbolic register of the evangelist at the very moment when religious devotion, the visionary experience, theological exegesis, and artistic execution are encapsulated in the self-portrait of the painter-prophet (1650, Prado Museum). Albrecht Dürer's 1500 *Self-Portrait at Twenty-Eight* is likewise a fascinating example, providing a pictorial *imitatio Christi* that conceptually offers perhaps the closest parallel to the visual effect of the mirror paintings of the Guadalupe Chapel with the rendered semblance of the painter perfectly superimposed upon the figure of Christ (1500, Alte Pinakothek, Munich). In fact, Dürer was one of the first artists to document and promote the practice of painting on a canvas by copying an object or subject's reflection on a mirror, an exercise that thereafter became customary in the production of self-portraits. As explained by Macfarlane and Martin, "[The mirror] gave the [early modern] artist a third eye [...] so that he could see himself. Without a mirror, the great autobiographical portraits [...] could not have been painted" (2002, 64). The artist, in other words, paints his image, replicating a reflection in a mirror. Similar to the visual experience of the Guadalupe Chapel, the canvas upon which the *Self-Portrait at Twenty-Eight* is painted perceptually reads as a mirror insofar as the subject seems to be looking straight at a mirror and simultaneously at us; Durer looks at himself, superimposes his likeness on the figure of Christ, and paints himself as Christ looking at us. Of equal importance, Rudolf II was Europe's most prominent collector of Dürer paintings and woodcuts (generally, of what has been called the "Dürer Renaissance"). Ana Dorotea's appreciation of the functional, conceptual, and religious relationships of mirrors to self-portraits could have been informed by her individual experience of the German master's works.[15]

Remarking on the use of the mirrors in the Guadalupe Chapel, Wethey notes, "Even the fact that the panels are actually painted mirrors points directly to the doctrine, for the mirror is one of the fifteen usual symbols of the Immaculate Conception" (1966, 24). Ángel Aterido Fernández likewise remarks on the chapel's conceptual connection to the Virgin as *speculum justitiae*, noting how the specific mirror symbol itself is not found in any of the panels with the entire chapel being transposed to perform this reflective, exemplary moral quality (2019, 142). The paintings of the Old Testament heroines, the small panels that represent the attributes of the Virgin, and the larger altar painting of the Virgin of the Immaculate Conception that anchors the pictorial program together offer the cloistered nuns at the Descalzas Reales a place upon which to see their reflections superimposed on the exemplarity represented. The play of reflections across the Guadalupe Chapel and downwards to the kneeling supplicant spatially make it possible for the viewer to see her image appear indistinguishable, much as in Dürer's *Self-Portrait at Twenty-Eight*, from the religious figures painted on the mirrored walls. Dissolving the division in the visual plane between the holy and the human or between the viewer and the divine vision, the nuns saw their reflections become one in an imaginary union with their biblical mothers and their venerated Virgin Mother. As such, this is a spatial and spiritual effect that works in the theological register of the visionary experience described by Teresa of Ávila: the purified soul/self as a mirror of the holy.

As stated above, the Guadalupe Chapel's pictorial program has as its referent Carrillo's *Elogios de mujeres insignes*. Speaking to the central role played by religious exemplary literature in the early modern period, Morrás notes the interplay between "gender, sanctity, and exemplarity," which provides an imitable pathway to authority, authorship, and early modern female selfhood: "[T]he way they (gender, sanctity, and exemplarity) intertwined was crucial not only for the evolution of spirituality and social values in the medieval and early modern period, but also for the construction of the female subject and a distinct women's literary tradition. From Hildegard of Bingen (1098–1179) right up to the seventeenth century, these three vectors upheld a model of *auctoritas* and authorship that in large measure shaped the role and aspirations of both religious and lay women across Europe" (2020, 1). Expanding on Morrás's point, I would argue that the exemplary authority of the *Elogios de mujeres insignes* is transferred from Carrillo's text via its dedication to Margarita de la Cruz to Ana Dorotea as a privileged reader and architect of the chapel. The visual experience made possible by Ana Dorotea's design expands the textual pedagogical potentiality of Carrillo's Old Testament heroines into a visual and spatial vehicle for direct identification and transformation. The image of the individual supplicant is superimposed on the mirrored paintings, making possible a performative act that metamorphoses a reflection into a visionary self-portrait. The authority symbolized by the heroines and the Marian attributes that populate the chapel is transferred through the nun's physical subjection to the divine order at the altar of the Guadalupe Chapel. In other words, the subject position of the kneeling supplicants is reconfigured in the experience of sanctity afforded by the blurring of the division between the sacred image and the self. As previously mentioned, the examples of the Old Testament heroines culminate in the holiness of the Immaculate Virgin represented in the mirrored painting placed at the centre of the altar. When the prayerful approach the altar of the Guadalupe Chapel, Mary's image presents itself as the perfect immaculate mirror. As I have argued concerning Sor María de Ágreda's *Mística ciudad de Dios*, the immaculist imaginary postulates two doctrinal tenets that drive much of the Spanish religious fervour during this period:

> Mary is the eternal Apocalyptic Woman miraculously conceived and birthed in order to fulfill her mission as the Mother of God; she is also, and no less, the original and unspoiled (either by the knowledge of evil or by disobedience) human being, a second unblemished Adam, who consequently contains in her the promise [...] of our own restitution to an originary prelapsarian shared immaculacy [...] [T]he nuns at the convent in Ágreda (and any reader for that matter) could hope for the day when they could also return to their originary created nature, aided by the Virgin of the Immaculate Conception's redemptive intervention. (2019, 194–5)

I propose we find this same aspirational reciprocity visually actualized through Ana Dorotea's design. The promise of redemptive restitution is heightened via a mimetic performative space where the prayerful nun sees her face reflected superimposed on the figure of the Old Testament mothers that lead to the always immaculate Mary centred at the altar. Returning to Morrás's argument, the pictorial program of the Guadalupe Chapel thus offers a unique conduit for the exalted connection of gender, sanctity, and exemplarity through the imaginary self-portraits that are created on the mirrored paintings, and most especially in the union of self and the divine other that the altar painting of the Virgin of the Immaculate Conception makes possible.

As such, Stoichita's critical position on the taming of the visionary experience through the split of the visual plane would seem to be refuted by the visual/visionary dynamic that I have argued is central to the experience of the Guadalupe Chapel. And yet, the critic's examination of portraiture and the use and effect of mirrors in his book *The Self-Aware Image* offers an additional important insight that can better inform our interpretation. For example, Stoichita's focus on the positionality of the object vis-à-vis the mirror and how it correlates to the distinction between image and sign is especially productive: "The copresence of the represented and the representing produces the specificity of the image in the mirror. For there to be an image, there must be someone or something in front of the mirror. If this person or thing moves away, the image in the mirror disappears. If I can see *an image* in the mirror without being able to see the represented in front of it, then and only then is the image I see also a *sign: aliquid pro aliquo*" (1997, 185). Following this logic, the mirrored paintings at the Guadalupe Chapel provide a double possibility. If viewed from an angle, the paintings function as signs ripe with connotations aligned with the cloistered community's social, religious, and political positionality and the individual selfhoods within it. To be precise, the paintings are visual representations of biblical narratives and liturgical symbols that invite Ana Dorotea and her fellow nuns to identify with the values represented and authorize them to initiate or participate in social, religious, and political projects tied to the complex web of influence that saw as its epicentre the Descalzas Reales monastery. On the other hand, when these same mirrored canvases capture the reflection of the supplicant, they make possible a "copresence," the narrative signified transformed into the reflected self-aware image represented on its surface. In fact, following Stoichita, what is enacted is a double representation: the figure of the supplicant reflected as a "natural sign" (the mirror "represents" by reflecting the natural figure) *and* the figure of the supplicant superimposed and unified with the biblical figure painted on the mirrored canvas (1997, 184). As also noted by Stoichita, "In the culture of 'resemblance,' all paintings, one way or another, lend themselves as 'mirrors of reality,' which is why the key metaphor of the European pictorial image was, from the time of the Renaissance, the specular metaphor" (1997, 185). In this sense, the cloistered nuns kneeling at the chapel's altar simultaneously subjected to and willed themselves into a spiritual reality; their physical reflections turned into idealized visionary self-portraits in a seamless specular resemblance.

Thomas DaCosta Kaufman – who has extensively catalogued and commented on Rudolph II's art inventory, including the many portraits that populated the Habsburg emperor's court – offers a complementary reading of early modern portraiture as a genre conceptually straddled between representation and ideality, or otherwise between the mimetic and the symbolic:

To follow the reasoning of Vincenzo Danti [...] a portrait might have been regarded as a form of imitation of reality that could be called an example of *ritrarre*, an exact (or scrupulously accurate) depiction of reality. But as such, it could not have been a form of "ideal imitation," that is, imitation that idealized the sitter's features or social or political status [...] For this end, another conception, that of the portrait as an ideal image (in fifteenth-century writing, an *imago*), was demanded [...] The painting of a court portrait would thus have presented late sixteenth-century artists with the problem of reconciling what may be called realistic with idealistic imagery, that is, the demands of portraiture as an objective rendering, with the notion that the portrait image was also a representation of ideal [...] values. (1988, 67)

Falling on the side of *imago*, the specular spiritual self-portraits of the Guadalupe Chapel transform the penitent sinful self into an idealized visionary revelation (again, let us think of Saint Teresa of Ávila) of the divine other upon the mirror canvas. Along these same lines, another interpretative possibility is to focus on the distinction between an existential reception of the biblical narrative versus an essential visionary experience of unity with the divine Other/order. On the one hand, the temporal existential experience inserts the viewer in a temporal narrative that originates with Eve (in Carrillo's text) and the Old Testament heroines, sees its pinnacle in the Virgin Mary's co-redemptive stature, and extends to the nun's piety and positionality within the cloistered community at the Descalzas Reales. On the other hand, the essential transformation of the self sanctioned by the specular experience negates time and resides on the side of the visionary and the eternal (outside of earthly time).

Theologically conceived and artistically designed by Ana Dorotea, the Guadalupe Chapel thus offers a profoundly innovative and unique visual space. The scriptural knowledge of Old Testament women's history, the revelation of the Virgin of the Immaculate Conception, and the forging of an early modern spiritual female selfhood authorized by a divine order populated exclusively by women exemplars are enacted all at once through the medium of the mirror canvas. One last thought regarding pictorial and spiritual permanence can be added. Paintings with mirrors included in the frame perform a function that is impossible in the real-world experience of specularity: the incorporated mirror permanently captures the reflection of the objects and/or subjects represented within the frame. For Ana Dorotea and her cloistered community, the mirrored canvases of the Guadalupe Chapel offer instead the permanence of spiritual transformation and authority conveyed by the visionary union with the divine exemplary Other.

Notes

1 Magdalena Sánchez (1998) offers a detailed account of the complex political and diplomatic life of the Descalzas Reales in her excellent book. For a detailed account of the Descalzas Reales inhabitants and their family connections see Karen María Vilacoba Ramos and Teresa Muñoz Serrulla's

"Las religiousas de las Descalzas Reales de Madrid en los Siglos XVI-XX: Fuentes Archivísticas" (2010).

2 All translations are my own.

3 For a detailed account of the Spanish early modern and Habsburg engagement with and defense of the doctrine of immaculacy, see my book *Immaculate Conceptions: The Power of the Religious Imagination in Early Modern Spain* (2019).

4 For a study on Margarita de la Cruz's own art patronage, see Tanya Tiffany's "The Infant Christ at the Spanish Court: Sor Margarita de la Cruz (1567–1633) and Sacred Material Culture" (2019).

5 For another complementary and excellent account of Ana Dorotea's life and the importance – biographical and artistic – of the Guadalupe Chapel see Cipriano García Hidalgo Villena's "Sor Ana Dorotea de Austria (1612–1694) y la exaltación de las mujeres fuertes" (2021).

6 See my article, "The Politics of Exemplarity: Biblical Women and the Education of the Spanish Lady in Martín Carrillo, Sebastián de Herrera Barnuevo, and María de Guevara" (2011).

7 Thus far I have not been able to identify another example at this scale of early modern paintings executed on mirrors.

8 See Stoichita (1995, 27–44).

9 In my book *Immaculate Conceptions* I engage in a debate with Stoichita's position on the pictorial taming of the visionary experience. See specifically Chapter 4: "*Visiones Imaginarias*: Pacheco, Velázquez, Zurbarán, and Murillo" (2019, 109–51).

10 See *Immaculate Conceptions*, Chapter 5 "*Concepción Maravillosa*: Theological Discourse and Religious Women Writers" (2019, 152–204).

11 See Morrás's introduction, "Saints Textual: Embodying Female Exemplarity in Spanish Literature" (2020, 1–39).

12 In his book *Mirror Mirror: A History of the Human Love Affair with Reflection* (2003), Mark Pendergast traces a different aspect of the medium in the late medieval and early modern periods: its role in alchemy, the occult, and science.

13 For further analysis on this type of representation, see Daniela Hammer-Tugendhat's "Mirror, Mirror on the Wall: Woman before the Mirror by Frans van Mieris" (2015).

14 For a comprehensive catalogue of Rudolf II's possessions and artefacts, see Eliska Fucikova, James M. Bradburne, and Beket Bukovinska, eds., *Rudolf II and Prague: The Court and the City* (1997). See also Thomas DaCosta Kaufman's *The School of Prague: Painting at the Court of Rudolph II* (1985), which includes reproductions of a large selection of religious paintings, including numerous portraits of female saints.

15 See Andrea Bubenik's "The Art of Albrecht Dürer in the Context of the Court of Rudolf II" (2005).

11 The Spatial Display of Poetry in the *Recibimiento al obispo Pimentel* (1629)

VÍCTOR SIERRA MATUTE, BARUCH COLLEGE,
THE CITY UNIVERSITY OF NEW YORK

Enrique Pimentel (1574–1649) paid a visit to Huete on 5 May 1629.[1] He was the son of Juan Alonso Pimentel de Herrera, the eighth Count of Benavente, and at that time, he held the esteemed position of the current bishop of Cuenca. His journey to this position was marked by a distinguished career across military, political, and ecclesiastical realms.[2] The celebrations organized to commemorate the bishop's visit to Huete, while humble, aimed to befit his revered figure (Martín Benito 2017, 72). Notably, his stay included a visit to the College of the Society of Jesus. This visit to the college, acknowledged as one of the most influential religious institutions of the time within the diocese, is documented in Manuscript 1895 of the Historical General Library at the University of Salamanca.[3]

When first encountering Ms. 1895, a reader without prior context might initially perceive it as a conventional *cancionero*. The title "Poesías" (Poems) on the spine, coupled with the content featuring writings in Spanish and Latin dedicated to Enrique Pimentel, could lead them to believe it is one of the many handwritten poetic compilations common in early modern Spain.

However, upon delving into the collection's first poem – a ballad in praise of the bishop – a distinct desire to vividly envision the spaces of the Jesuit college emerges for several reasons. First, its title mentions that a young boy recited the ballad aloud as Enrique Pimentel entered the building. Second, the poem is enriched with annotations and contextual references, as the young boy describes both the path the honouree took upon entering the cloister and the accompanying sounds – music, applauses, cheers, choruses – that resonated during the ballad's recitation. Lastly, the poem concludes with a statement that sheds light on how the remaining poems of the collection were spatially arranged: "Estava el claustro colgado y adornado de las poesías latinas y españolas que aqui van escritas" (The cloister was hung and adorned with the Latin and Spanish poems that are written here; 6r).[4]

Certainly, the decorative elements adorning the texts of this manuscript, including emblems, coats of arms, and coloured borders, strongly imply that every poem was inscribed on posters that adorned the walls of the college during this commemorative event.[5] The bishop would pause before each of these poems, taking a moment to observe the posters and read them attentively. This encourages us to perceive the words and verses not merely as written text, but as tangible components – pictorial decorations and images sketched onto the paper. Additionally, serving as the culmination of this collection of "visual poems" – if we may use that term – is a final panegyric.[6] This composition alternates between verses in Latin and Spanish and, much like the poem recited by the young boy, was delivered out loud by the Jesuits during the banquet that signified the conclusion of the celebration. Essentially, at its core, the *cancionero* rejects the notion of linear reading and guides us towards an interpretative approach that involves engaging with these material texts in their temporal and spatial context. By doing so, this collection aims to recreate the very experience the bishop himself had with the poems.

The primary objective of this chapter is to analyse the *Recibimiento al obispo Pimentel* (1629) not merely as a collection of poems but as a meticulously crafted artefact designed to outline and evoke a historical three-dimensional space (see figure 11.1). To achieve this goal, I will examine both the visual layout of the poems on the page and the sensory elements that arise from the verses, whether experienced through silent or oral readings, in contemporary or historical contexts. By delving into these aspects, encompassing both visual and auditory descriptions within the texts and indications that denote the spatial placement of the poems within the physical confines of the college, I argue that the *Recibimiento al obispo Pimentel* presents a "socially produced space," one that embodies discursive and sociopolitical relationships shaped by power dynamics (Lefebvre 1991). The collection aims to recreate the immersive experience that Pimentel encountered when confronted with these poems and the accompanying soundscape.[7] Within this spatial framework, each word and verse undergoes a transformation, becoming windows into the reverence that the Jesuit community of Huete aimed to convey to the bishop. Ultimately, the *Recibimiento al obispo Pimentel* transforms into a tangible testament, representing an event in which material words, spatial arrangement, and physical presence seamlessly merged, generating a unique experience that transcends the confines of the handwritten page.

Fig. 11.1. Cover of the *Recibimiento al obispo Pimentel*, ms. 1895. Biblioteca General Histórica, Universidad de Salamanca.

A Feast for the Bishop

In the dedication preceding the *Recibimiento al obispo Pimentel*, the Jesuits of Huete expressed that the bishop, in a kind gesture of humanity towards them, requested a copy of the poems to be able to reread them meticulously in private and thus recreate the memory of his visit (1v).[8] Considering that Enrique Pimentel left his extensive library of over 7,500 volumes to the Colegio del Arzobispo Fonseca at the University of Salamanca, we can infer that the manuscript we are examining here, Ms. 1895 of the Historical Library, is precisely that copy which the Jesuits prepared affectionately for Pimentel.[9] In essence, the manuscript compiles a series of poems not intended for a wide and undefined readership, but rather as a memento for the bishop and a personal commemoration of the event.[10] The fact that we, as readers, are now engaging with the *Recibimiento* is purely coincidental.

As we delve into the study of this collection, it is crucial to recognize that our engagement involves exploring a historical artefact. However, in order to comprehensively consider spatiality, it is imperative to reject the conventional historicist approach when examining the *Recibimiento*, as many historicist approaches "treat spatiality as a simple given, i.e., as an inert, frozen set of relations devoid of social origins and social implications" (Arias 2010, 31). The *Recibimiento*, while not initially intended for a broad audience, possesses the potential to unveil the intricate layers of a past event, enabling us to grasp the "complexities, silences, and problematic relationship between interpreters (i.e., readers, artists, viewers), texts, and the world they represent" (Arias 2010, 30), a potential that can only be fully revealed by taking spatiality into account.

In contrast to these historicist approaches, my analysis of the *Recibimiento* aligns with a materialist perspective.[11] Conventional historicist approaches often highly value print culture, to the extent that certain studies attribute the concept of modernity to the invention of the printing press and even suggest that printed texts significantly transformed the fundamental nature of humanity.[12] This reverence for print culture is driven by two primary biases: the belief in *permanence*, which centres on the notion that printed materials have lasting endurance; and the idea of *transcendence*, implying that print signifies a conclusive and definitive work that faithfully encapsulates the original intentions of its author.[13] As extensively demonstrated by Fernando Bouza (2001), these biases concerning print culture are erroneous and misrepresent our comprehension of the historical era. It is essential to perceive print, manuscript, and oral cultures as components of the same phenomenon, with each representing a distinct pole on the spectrum and specializing in different textual practices (Bouza 2001, 17).

When considering the circulation of poems in the early modern period, texts described by Dadson as "poesía que vive en variantes" (poetry that lives in variants; 2012, 73), it becomes evident that both oral and manuscript cultures played considerably more crucial roles than the dissemination of printed poems (Jauralde Pou 1982; Carreira 2004). The *Recibimiento al obispo Pimentel* further exemplifies the intricate interplay between various textual practices. The act of crafting a personalized handwritten and decorated book falls within the realm of manuscript culture, while the celebration of the event itself reflects the dynamic interaction between oral and manuscript practices.[14] This web of interactions – encompassing text and its material embodiment, oral and visual elements, spatial displays and performative aspects – attains even deeper significance when we recognize that the *Recibimiento* intentionally presents itself as a "feast of the senses" tailored exclusively for the bishop.

The Renaissance convention of the "feast" or "banquet for the senses," a trope originating from the Graeco-Latin tradition and extending its influence into the baroque, revolves around the idea of creating an event, whether artistic or otherwise, that actively engages and captivates all of the bodily senses (Wagschal 2012, 125). The dedication and epilogue of the *Recibimiento* explicitly frame the collection within this *topos*.[15] On the one hand, a literal banquet is described in the dedication, an event that is inferred to have historically taken place while also assuming strongly symbolic connotations.[16] The dedication states that while in the dining hall of the Jesuit College, the bishop was not merely a guest enjoying the served food, but rather a shepherd nourishing the attendees – referred to as "agnellos nostros" (our lambs), "Domini gregis" (Our Lord's flock) – with his presence and conversation, which they characterize as "caelestis panis" (celestial bread; 2r). On the other hand, the annotated panegyric, functioning as an epilogue, reinforces the concept of this metaphorical and actual banquet, and its title accurately reflects its content: "Ingentis laetitia panegyrica ostentatio in adventu illustrissimi episcopi eidem dicata et dicta dum in nostro triclino non tam cibis ipse parescetur quam incredibili humanitate nos omnes pasceret et recrearet" (An eloquent expression of immense joy greets the arrival of our distinguished bishop, honouring him during our gathering in the dining room. Here, he not only partakes in nourishment but graciously nurtures and rejuvenates us through his extraordinary humanity; 33r). A Jesuit brother recited the poem aloud during the banquet. The poem alternates between lines in Latin and Spanish, using deictics that draw attention to their auditory and spatial characteristics. The panegyric consistently underscores Pimentel's physical presence within the confines of the Jesuit College:

Ergo cum modo velis hic adstare
(que todos como es justo lo estimamos)
ostende nobis studium singulare
qual dese noble pecho lo esperamos
regere velis nos, et ordinare,
porque en nuestro Orden con mal orden vamos,
et interim hanc domum aude et vide
que con estas razones se despide. (37r)

(Therefore, when you wish to stand here for a moment
(which we all rightly value)
show us your exceptional zeal,
which we await from this noble heart of yours,
desire to guide and arrange us,

> for in our Order we proceed disorderly,
> and meanwhile, dare and see this house
> which with these words it bids farewell.)

Recognizing the necessity for guidance, the Jesuits urge the bishop to exhibit his exceptional leadership and build upon the metaphor of reciprocal nurturing.[17] With the poignant inclusion of the Latin word "hic" (here), the verses evoke a palpable sense of physical presence, inviting the bishop to embody his remarkable zeal within the confines of this space. Furthermore, the call to "hanc domum aude et vide" (dare and see this house) implies not only observing but actively engaging with the environment, emphasizing Pimentel's role in the dynamic interplay between space and celebration. The final verse, which bids farewell with the phrase "que con estas razones se despide," underscores the power of language itself as a conduit of reverence. The use of "estas" (these) intensifies the mutual interplay between Pimentel's palpable presence and the poem's recitation within a specific space. In its closure, this poem serves as the final note of the ceremony, concluding the intricate orchestration of sensory experiences and marking the culmination of both the material and metaphorical "banquet of the senses." This encapsulates the interplay of physical and symbolic nourishment, ultimately highlighting the role of space as an array of negotiated practices that shaped the collective memory of the event.

Soundscapes of Welcome

Having explored the organizational framework of the book, including its dedication and epilogue emphasizing the "banquet" motif, I will now shift focus to delve into the chronological progression of the celebration. Within the narrative presented by the *Recibimiento*, a pivotal moment emerges at the onset of the festivities: as previously mentioned, a young boy takes centre stage, reciting a ballad in honour of the bishop, thus becoming the catalyst for the unfolding spectacle. This ballad, titled "Reçebimiento que hizo a su Illustrísima un niño como Paranimpho a la entrada de el claustro" (Reception that a child performed for His Illustrious Grace as a Paranimph at the entrance of the cloister; 3r), holds a significant role in conveying the spatial significance. The word "Paranimpho," in its etymological sense, means "beside" (παρά-) and "the wife" (-νύμφη), as it referred to the child who accompanied the bride to her husband's house before the celebration of marriage in Ancient Rome, and over time the term came to signify the person who delivered an inaugural speech or prayer (Fernández Cuesta 1872, 757). Within the broader context of the *Recibimiento*, the metaphorical use of the word "Paranimpho" underscores the boy's dual role as both a ballad performer and a symbolic youthful figure who guided Pimentel into the transformative experience of the celebration. This auditory initiation not only sets the tone but also intricately intertwines the power of sound with the creation of an immersive spatial experience.

As the ballad unfolds, recited by the child, or "paranimph," it not only conveys semantic content but also provides directions that guide the bishop's movement within his entrance and establish the rhythm of the event:

Espera, escúchame, aguarda
ilustrísimo prelado, consagren
mi umbral tus pies,
detén (si puedes) el paso. (3r)

(Wait, listen to me, await,
illustrious prelate,
let your feet consecrate my threshold,
pause (if you can) your step.)

Intricately woven into the fabric of the celebration, the verses of the ballad serve as both linguistic and spatial signposts. By reciting his poem aloud from a situated location, the young boy not only appropriates a place for his expression but also engages in what Michel de Certeau termed a "residing rhetoric": "In the framework of enunciation, [he] constitutes, in relation to his position, both a near and a far, a *here* and a *there*. To the fact that the adverbs *here* and *there* are the indicators of the locutionary seat in verbal communication … this location (*here – there*) … also has the function of introducing an other in relation to this "I" and of thus establishing a conjunctive and disjunctive articulation of places" (1984, 99) The act of reciting the poem audibly within a specific spatial context goes beyond mere utterance. It transforms the recitation into a strategic utilization of language that intricately interlaces the speaker's presence and the surrounding environment into a cohesive discourse. Engaging with the spatial aspects of communication provides a lens through which we can understand the young boy's reading – and thus the poem – as a dynamic interaction involving his vocal performance, the attendees of the celebration, and the specific physical setting of the cloister.

The voice of the child is far from being the sole sound accompanying Pimentel's entry into the cloister. The poem itself elucidates the elements that will contribute to the soundscape of the celebration:

> Vátanse a tus pies vanderas
> suenen clarines templados,
> y al son de sonoros parches
> vomite el cañón sus rayos.
> (*Aquí se tocan cajas y clarines, y se despiden algunos tiros. Y prosigue.*)
> Salve, salve adalid fuerte,
> que a título de soldado,
> de Jesús la Compañíate hace la salva en llegando. (3v)

> (Let flags be beaten at your feet,
> let tempered bugles sound,
> and to the beat of resounding drums,
> let cannons spew their rays.
> (*Here drums and bugles are played, and some shots are fired. And it continues.*)
> Hail, hail mighty leader,
> who with the title of a soldier,
> the Society of Jesus
> greets you as you enter.)

These verses serve as a representative passage of the ballad, which, as can be observed, includes theatrical notations of performative actions that complement what the child expresses within the body of the poem. Scattered throughout the ballad, among the included notations are "Aquí se repican las campanas y las chirimías todo junto, y prosigue" (Here the bells and the shawms all play together, and it continues; 4r), "Aquí los estudiantes aclaman Víctor" (Here the students cheer; 4r), and "Tornan a decir Víctor, y dar palmadas" (They turn around to cheer and applaud; 4v). During the historical reading of the poem, several sounds emerge to enliven the atmosphere and signify the dynamic celebration within the cloister. The verses themselves evoke a symphony of sounds, from the beating of flags at the feet of the illustrious bishop to the explosive discharge of cannons. The musical interlude indicated by the notes features the ringing of bells and the harmonious blend of shawms, enhancing the soundscape, while the cheers capture the exuberant responses of the Jesuit students, effectively creating a sonic environment that reverberates with joyful acclamation.

As the historical reading of the poem unfolds, the "Paranimpho" continues to vocalize guiding instructions that articulate the bishop's progression and actively engage Jesuits and their pupils in bringing the event to life. Within this intricate choreography of words, actions, and space, one particularly notable gesture involves the incorporation of flowers into the celebration:

> En la tierra pingue y fértil
> de aquesta ciudad plantado,
> de quien Jesús es el riego
> y el jardinero es Ignacio,
> vos havéis oy este officio,
> estas plantas mutilando,
> y con la diestra tixera
> sacras coronas labrando.
> (*Ordenó los de cofia de corona.*)
> De aqueste jardín hermoso vengo
> de flores cargado:
> que de su planta a las vuestras
> he querido trasplantarlos,
> que siendo de vuestros pies
> illustre señor, hollados,
> se estenderá su fragancia
> a más estendido espacio. (4v–5r)

> (In the fertile and lush land
> of this city planted,
> where Jesus is the waterer
> and Ignatius the gardener,
> today you have this duty,
> mutilating these plants,
> and with the skilled shears
> crafting sacred crowns.
> (*He ordered to bring the coif for the crown.*)
> From this beautiful garden
> I come laden with flowers:
> for I wanted to transplant
> from its plants to yours,
> so that from being trampled
> by your illustrious feet, Lord,
> its fragrance will spread
> to a wider space.)

In this vivid passage, the poem employs a garden allegory to symbolize the spiritual growth nurtured by the Jesuit order in Huete. The bishop's role as a spiritual guide parallels Ignatius of Loyola cultivating the allegorical garden, while Christ, just like Pimentel, is depicted as a nurturing source. Furthermore, the instruction to bring a crown made of flowers emphasizes the ritualistic nature of the celebration. The young boy's dual actions – cutting and preserving some flowers – mirror an offering, shaping both flora and devotion. Most significantly, the poem evokes the fragrance of trampled flowers extending through the cloister and thus defining the performative space. Sound and scent intertwine to delineate the spatial dimension of the event, engaging Pimentel in a multisensory journey that has just begun.

Rhymes on the Wall

Once the reading that articulates the initial performance was over, the bishop received instructions to proceed to the cloister. The manuscript explicitly reveals the spatial arrangement of poetry: "Estava el claustro colgado y adornado de las poesías latinas y españolas que aqui van escritas" (The cloister was hung and adorned with the Latin and Spanish poems that are written here; 6r), where "aquí" (here) is a reference to the manuscript itself. Progressing further, the book unveils an array of poetic forms, encompassing sonnets, *décimas*, *octavas*, and *liras* (7r–12v), in addition to a "romance que se cantó a su Ilustrísima en la misa de la congregación" (ballad that was sung to His Excellency during the congregation's mass; 13r–14v). Following this collection of eleven Spanish compositions, a series of seventeen Latin poems unfolds, predominantly comprising odes and epigrams (15r–23v). Finally, the manuscript includes seven full-page emblems, illustrated across the subsequent seven folios of the collection (25r–31r). These drawings likely are the sketches of the emblems that adorned the walls of the cloister.

The specific sequence that Pimentel followed when observing the posters will always remain unknown. It is uncertain whether he read the emblems, the Spanish poems, or the Latin compositions first, or perhaps a combination of these. We cannot even confirm whether he engaged with all the poems or only a select few during the event. Nevertheless, it is clear that he must have dedicated time to traverse from one poster to another, thereby mapping a spatial trajectory between each composition. What we do know is that the act of navigating the cloister while contemplating each piece would have formed an integral part of the bishop's experience. Therefore, the purpose of this section is to illuminate how these poems and emblems were deliberately constructed to cultivate a deep spatial immersion within the confines of the cloister. In addition to their physical arrangement on the cloister walls, these poems further reinforce their engagement with spatiality through two additional aspects: their formal presentation and their thematic content.

The opening poem in the sequence is a sonnet that serves a metaliterary purpose by connecting the flowers used during the entrance to the Jesuits' written collection, which is characterized as a "Ramillete de flores olorosas" (Bouquet of fragrant flowers; 7r). However, while the poem recited aloud by the "Paranimpho" emphasized the auditory aspects of the celebration and introduced the sense of smell, which is also mirrored in the opening sonnet, the subsequent poems displayed on the walls clearly revolve around the theme of vision. Among these poems, we find a song that portrays Icarus being momentarily blinded by the sunlight (12r), a sonnet dedicated to Argus and his hundred eyes (11v), and a series of *liras* celebrating the vibrant green shade of the Cross of Alcántara that graces the bishop's chest (10v–11r).

The catalyst for this thematic preoccupation with vision seems to stem from the allegory of Enrique Pimentel as both an illuminating sun and a complementary celestial partner to the moon – an emblematic symbol of Huete.[18] This is clearly shown in a beautiful *décima* titled "Hermosea el Sol de Enrique la Luna de Huete" (Enrique's Sun beautifies Huete's Moon):

De Huete a la luna hermosa
se opone de Enrique el Sol,
cuio dorado arrebol
brillantes luçes rebosa.
Ella en esto vergonzosa
le salieron de turbada
los colores a la cara,
con que su plata esmaltó;
y en esta ocasión quedó
más resplandeciente y clara. (8v)

(From Huete to the beautiful moon,
Enrique's Sun stands in opposition,
its golden blush overflowing
with brilliant lights.
In this moment of shame,
the colours from her face faded,
with which she adorned her silver;
and in this instance she remained,
more radiant and clear.)

Fig. 11.2. Sketch of the third emblem, ms. 1895. Biblioteca General Histórica, Universidad de Salamanca, 27r.

The content of this poem is clearly replicated in the sketch of one of the emblems that were hanging in the cloister. This emblem depicted the sun facing a moon over a field of flowers, with a motto that reads "Oy Huete estará tu luna / en su creçiente, y pujante / pues se pone el Sol delante" (Huete, today your moon will be in its crescent and powerful, for the Sun sets in front of it; see figure 11.2). When considering this emblem within its spatial context, it is more than likely that the bishop stood right in front of the poster, his gaze fixed on its image while reading the words "se pone el Sol delante" (the Sun sets in front). This deliberate setup seemingly aimed to enhance the identification between the bishop and the Sun. By visually immersing himself in the emblem, he would have been prompted to resonate with the symbolism of the Sun's dominance. In other words, the intentional placement of the emblem encouraged the bishop to personally connect with the imagery, effectively reinforcing his sense of power through the manipulation of space. This interaction wasn't merely textual or visual; it was spatial, designed to engage Pimentel's physical presence and his perceptual experience. The alignment of the bishop with the Sun, both figuratively and bodily, symbolically underscored his significance and authority.

An additional example of this spatial interaction between text and image can be found in two acrostic poems, composed in both Spanish and Latin. In the Latin piece, the initial letters of each verse spell out the name "Henrico Pimentel" (23r), while the Spanish poem takes the form of an acrostic sonnet:

P retende Phebo hazer de su grandeza
A larde en un retrato dibujado:
S ale oy a la luz, y luce en el traslado,
T omando mayor lustre, su belleza.
O stentan de su lumbre la entereza
R ayos de vigilancia, y de cuydado,
V elas de Enrique sobre su ganado,
I resplandores de su gran nobleza.
G uarda es, que auyenta robadoras fieras,
I Sol, que aun en la noche mas obscura
L uz da al rebaño, que le glorifica.
A cuia claridad (si la confieras)
N o llega de el primero la hermosura:
S i aquel cuerpos, éste almas clarifica. (12v)

(Phebo aims to portray his grandeur, / boasting in a portrait so well traced. / He today emerges, shining in its [human] version, / taking his beauty greater brilliance. / His steadfast light is showcased / in rays of vigilance and carefulness, / veils of Enrique, watching over his flock, / and shinings of his great nobility. / He is a guardian, fending off voracious beasts, / and a Sun, who even in the darkest night, / illuminates the flock that glorifies him, / whose radiance, if you compare, / none surpasses in beauty. / If the former [Phebo] enlightens bodies, this one illumines souls.)

Similar to any acrostic, this poem enables two reading directions: the first, following the conventional structure of a sonnet; the second, by taking the initial letter of each line, forming the motto "Pastor Vigilans" (Vigilant shepherd; see figure 11.3). The allegory of a watchful shepherd is effectively conveyed in both thematic and structural aspects. Furthermore, when considered within its spatial context, it becomes clear that the power of the sense of sight is reinforced through a poem centred around the theme of vision as well as through the very act of

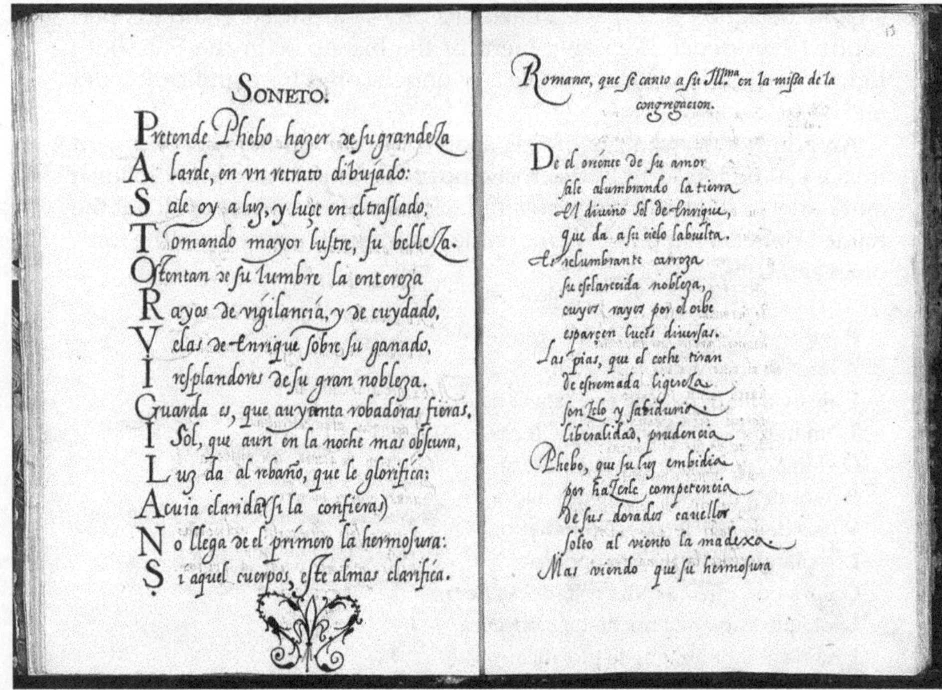

Fig. 11.3. Acrostic sonnet that displays the motto "Pastor Vigilans," ms. 1895. Biblioteca General Histórica, Universidad de Salamanca, 12v.

visual engagement undertaken by Pimentel. Once again, the spatial positioning of the bishop proves to be of radical importance, while the fusion of textual and visual elements aimed to create a multilayered and immersive encounter that resonated deeply with the bishop's role and the overarching themes of the ceremony.

Conclusion: The *Recibimiento* within the Spatial Turn

What does the *Recibimiento* achieve as a written artefact? Months or even years after the event, Pimentel could recall a unique experience through solitary reading. When delving into the opening ballad, the poetic verses would bring to light the words vocalized by the child. The theatrical notations would evoke lights, aromas, and sounds that synergistically combined to resurrect an almost synaesthetic encounter. During the reading of the subsequent poems, both the emblems and auditory textual cues would invigorate vivid mental imagery, intensifying the sensation of being wholly immersed within the remembered spatial context. Even the act of physically touching the book, feeling its pages beneath his fingers, could serve as a trigger for Pimentel to vividly recollect the sensory richness of the original celebration.

In the present day, as contemporary readers engage with the *Recibimiento*, it encourages them to imagine a space they haven't directly experienced, yet it enables them to immerse themselves in the sensory and spatial coordinates of a past event. However, it is important to be aware that this historical event took place within a relatively preserved architectural setting – the Colegio de Jesuitas in Huete. The building has now been renovated and divided into two distinct sections: the temple, currently housing the Church of San Nicolás el Real de Medina, and the conventual house, featuring a square layout and inner courtyard, now transformed into the Centro de Interpretación de las Fiestas de San Juan Evangelista (Interpretation centre for the festivities of John the Evangelist), the patron saint of the Barrio de Atienza, where the building is located. The architectural structure has undergone significant alterations over time. Its original construction traces back to 1570 when Esteban Ortiz, a clergyman from Huete, established the Jesuit College. The conventual house was erected in the first third of the seventeenth century, while the church was built between 1700 and 1703.[19] Delving into the *Recibimiento* offers a unique opportunity to bridge the historical uses of the Colegio de Jesuitas with its contemporary architectural form. By engaging with the text and its immersive qualities, we can navigate the shifts in the building's purpose and layout, tracing the echoes of its past functions. As a material artefact that triggers spatial awareness, the *Recibimiento* serves as a gateway to unlock a dialogue between the historical events it narrates and the evolving physicality of the space, creating a dynamic interplay that enriches our understanding of both the text and the architectural heritage it is embedded within.

Finally, the *Recibimiento al obispo Pimentel* serves as an illuminating example of how early modern texts must be interpreted within the framework of their spatial dimensions. Too often, the texts of the period are approached with a narrow focus on their textual content, detached from the physical and sensual environments they were meant to inhabit. This tendency overlooks a crucial aspect of these texts – their inherent connection to the spaces they were performed or read in. The *Recibimiento*, through its meticulous integration of poetic language, spatial arrangements, and performative cues, prompts us to shift our perspective and contemplate how the architecture of a space can shape the interpretation of a text.[20] It engages in a "socio-spatial dialectic," meaning it is deeply embedded within the coordinates of a space that represented "a social product rooted in practices, disciplinary power, and ideology" (Soja in Arias 2010, 30). The physical presence of individuals, the acoustics of the surroundings, and the interplay of images, tastes, and smells all contribute to the immersive experience of encountering an early modern written work.

The material exploration of the *Recibimiento al obispo Pimentel* has illuminated a remarkable facet of its significance – a profound engagement with spatial dimensions that invites us to reconsider early modern texts within the context of the spatial turn.[21] This approach not only enriches our understanding of historical events but also highlights the enduring power of the spatial dimension in shaping interpretation. Just as Pimentel stood at the centre of the event, we also find ourselves at the intersection of spatial, visual, and textual exploration – an experience that traverses the realms of the past and the present. In this context, the *Recibimiento* serves as a compelling illustration to the inherent interplay between space, images, and texts, or, more broadly, between materiality and human perception. It transcends time, inviting us to engage with early modern artefacts through the perspective of transhistorical experiences.

Notes

1 On Enrique Pimentel, see Williams (2014) and Martín Benito (2017).

2 Indeed, his impressive trajectory was shaped with the support of his father, a prominent figure during the early years of Philip IV's reign (Martín Benito 2017, 64). Before this date, Enrique Pimentel had taken on diverse roles, including serving as the rector of the University of Salamanca, a knight of the Order of Alcántara, and a counsellor of the Military Orders. Additionally, he had held the positions of archdeacon of the Cathedral of Jaén, a member of the Supreme Council of the Inquisition, and the president of the Council of Aragón. Furthermore, he had previously served as the bishop of Valladolid, a post he relinquished in 1622 to fully dedicate himself to the pastoral care of the parishioners in Cuenca. This devoted service garnered him deep admiration for his unwavering commitment to the diocese (Williams 2014).

3 The manuscript comprises thirty-eight folios written by two hands and bound in *pasta española* (Lilao Franca and Castrillo González 2002, 226). I extend my gratitude to the Biblioteca Histórica de Salamanca for granting the rights to reproduce the images included in this chapter. I am also thankful to the editors of the collection and the anonymous reviewers for their insightful comments. Special thanks to Mary E. Barnard for organizing the panel "Exploring Spaces in the Literature of Imperial

Spain" at the Renaissance Society of America annual meeting, where I
presented an earlier version of this chapter; and to Cristina Pardo Porto for
her unwavering support.

4 All translations are my own, unless otherwise noted.

5 The manuscript's cover is adorned with the bishop's coat of arms and
a decorative frame featuring ornate borders. In the centre, prominent
letters indicate both the collective authorship and the recipient, namely,
the "Collegium Optense Societatis Iesu munificentissimis illustrissimi ac
excellentissimi domini D. Henrici Pimentelii" (the College of the Society
of Jesus in Huete, to the most generous, illustrious, and excellent lord,
Enrique Pimentel; see ig. 11.1). As previously mentioned, the label on the
spine simply reads "Poesías" (Poems). In other words, we can infer that
the collection lacks an explicit title. However, in the *Catálogo de Manuscritos
de la Biblioteca de la Universidad de Salamanca*, the extended title, "Poesías
dedicadas a D. Enrique Pimentel, obispo de Cuenca, por el Colegio de la
Compañía de Jesús de Huete (Cuenca)" (Poems dedicated to D. Enrique
Pimentel, bishop of Cuenca, by the College of the Society of Jesus in Huete,
Cuenca), is suggested (Lilao Franca and Castrillo González 2002, 226). With
the aim of simplification and taking into account the evocative notion of
"recibimiento" (reception) that is conveyed in the title of the initial ballad
and resonates throughout the entire collection, I have chosen to utilize the
apt title *Recibimiento al obispo Pimentel* (Reception for Bishop Pimentel).

6 The term "visual poem" is used here anachronistically and intentionally
avant la lettre. However, poetry and visuality intersected in some contexts, as I
will show in this chapter. For an exploration of the visual dimension of early
modern poetry, particularly the interplay between sonnets and epigrams and
the visual effects created by their shapes, see Middlebrook (2009, 6–7).

7 For a definition and genealogy of the concept of "soundscape," as well as
illustrative examples of early modern and colonial soundscapes, see Sierra
Matute (2025).

8 Specifically, the dedication, written in Latin, says the following: "sed illud
et addidisti munificentiae, ut tibi velles exemplaria reservari; quasi sub
ea conditione spectasses, atque legisses, ut tibi postea describerentur, et
traderentur; quo ea posses deinde per otium lectitare, et eis animum (que
tua humanitas est) non perfunctorie pascens" (you further demonstrated
your generosity by requesting that copies of the poems be set aside for
you, as if under that condition you were looking at them, so that they
could later be transcribed and delivered to you; in order that you might
then leisurely read them, and with your characteristic kindness, not merely
skim through them; Colegio de la Compañía de Jesús de Huete 1629, 1v).

9 The *signatura antigua* "Arz. 52" confirms that the manuscript belonged
to the Colegio del Arzobispo (Lilao Franca and Castrillo González 2002,

226). Enrique Pimentel held a particular affection for this institution, to which he belonged around 1601 while studying theology and law at the University of Salamanca.

10 While the rhetoric of patronage relationships often employs hyperbolic expressions, the connection between the bishop and his diocese seems genuinely close and sincere (Williams 2014). Within the community of Cuenca, the acknowledgment of the bishop's achievements is prominent. An example arises in the work of historian Mártir Rizo, whose *Historia de la muy noble y leal ciudad de Cuenca* (History of the very noble and loyal city of Cuenca), published in the same year (1629), lauds Bishop Pimentel's accomplishments during his initial seven years in authority. Rizo described Pimentel as embodying "la idea de un príncipe perfeto, de un prelado santo, de un pastor vigilante, de un maestro docto y de un padre de los pobres" (the idea of a perfect prince, a holy prelate, a vigilant shepherd, a learned teacher, and a father to the poor; 206).

11 Adopting materialist approaches to analyse such artefacts is essential for reshaping our field of study. Examples of materialist practice in the study of early modern texts can be found in Barnard (2014, 2021) as well as the edited collection by Barnard and de Armas (2013). For an approach that utilizes early modern material theory in analysing texts of the period, see Sierra Matute (2023).

12 Take, for example, the title of *Gutenberg's Europe: The Book and the Invention of Western Modernity*, by historian Frédéric Barbier, wherein he presents a teleological perspective that regards "the printed word as taking the human race to a new stage in its history" (2016, 2).

13 This is what Bernard Cerquiglini referred to as the "religion of the text," a complete trust in the fixed text and the need to stabilize it through the illusion of an authentic and final version provided by the printing press (2004, 1). However, as Cerquiglini himself demonstrates, the early printing presses are less reliable than the medieval *scriptorium*, and even during the early modern period, the numerous errors of typesetters and the indiscriminate intervention of printers prevent us from speaking of a completely reliable text (2014, 2–7).

14 Furthermore, even when this is pure speculation, we should not completely discard the potential influence of minor printings for posters or ephemeral materials associated with the event, adding another layer to the complex web of textual production and circulation.

15 For a deep exploration of the *topos* of "the banquet for the senses" in early modern theatre, see de Armas (2022, 139–43).

16 For a comprehensive exploration of the banquet as both metaphorical and material representation of social relationships, see Nadeau (2013).

17 A subtle narrative that seeks the bishop's assistance due to some form
of discomfort or disorder within the college seems to underlie the entire
collection, although it is not explicitly stated, and no historical records
confirming this have been found. Interestingly, this theme only emerges
in the poems and texts written in Latin. For example, one of those poems
is titled "Sordentem, ac ruentem domum nostram clarissimus Episcopus
ingressu suo illustrat, ac fulcit" (The illustrious Bishop illuminates and
supports our house, which is squalid and crumbling, with his entrance;
15r). This aspect of the *Recibimiento* would require further research.

18 Since medieval times, Huete has been known as "Ciudad de Luna" (City
of the Moon) as indicated by its coat of arms featuring a prominent moon
guarded by a lion. The city's most significant building, the "Castillo de ·
Luna" (Castle of the Moon), further solidifies its connection to this lunar
symbolism. While there are several theories regarding the association
between Huete and the moon, the connection with its castle, whose
battlement has a lunar shape, appears to be the most widely accepted.
Another theory suggests that the city was captured during a moonlit night
in the twelfth century, symbolically overcoming the Muslims, who were
also linked with the moon (Amor Calzas 1904, 17–18).

19 A detailed analysis of the architectural spaces in Huete, including the
Jesuit College, can be found in García Martínez (2015).

20 A foundational work that explores the connections between poetry
and performance, thus showing us the path to follow, is *Poetry as Play:
"Gongorismo" and the "Comedia."* See Quintero (1999).

21 For insights into the impact of the "spatial turn" on cultural and literary
studies as well as its broader implications for the humanities, see Warf and
Arias (2009).

12 Spaces of Death: The Virgin of the Arch and the Cult of the Dead in María de Zayas's *La fuerza del amor*

RYAN D. GILES, INDIANA UNIVERSITY

One of the most well-known tales of the Golden Age writer María de Zayas takes place in and around the city of Naples. *La fuerza del amor* (*The Power of Love*) recounts how Laura, a beautiful maiden, is seduced by and marries a nobleman named Diego who at first neglects and then physical abuses her, while carrying out an adulterous affair with another woman. Desperate to win back her husband, Laura seeks help from a local witch, whose spell will require hair and teeth from a hanged man. In hopes of finding these objects, Laura disguises herself in a cloak and makes her way outside the city carrying a lantern. She arrives at a small chapel, on a road that leads to a famous shrine dedicated to Nuestra Señora del Arca (Our Lady of the Arch) (2000, 365).[1] Inside this *humilladero*, or roadside chapel, is a crypt and an unidentified image painted on the wall behind the altar (2000, 365). The narrator describes the iconic fresco of Nuestra Señora del Arca housed at the shrine further down the road as an "imagen muy devota de aquel reino" (2000, 365). We are told that executed criminals were left hanging on public display inside the roadside chapel, so that their decomposing remains could fall through an opening in the floor, down to a lower level, and be entombed on holy ground. Arriving at night, she enters the macabre chapel and finds herself in the company of the six corpses, the victims of a public hanging. Unable to bring herself to collect the body parts, the horrified young wife fears that she will fall into the crypt and be left for dead.

That same night her younger brother, Carlos, wakes up from a portentous dream and realizes that his sister is in peril. His horse miraculously refuses to proceed further down the highway to the city and stops at the chapel, where he rescues Laura and brings her safely to their father's country estate. This aspect of the story echoes age-old folk motifs, in which a horse refuses to move past a certain point (ej. Thompson B151.1.1.0.2), but – as will be shown – it might also relate to the legendary origins of the Virgin of the Arch's shrine. Reunited with her family, Laura recounts her ordeal, and her father orders the abusive husband to be brought before the viceroy, Pedro Fernández de Castro, the Count of Lemos. Although a remorseful Diego pleads for Laura to return to him, she decides instead to enter a convent. In a state of desperation, Diego takes his valuables and flees the city. He later joins Felipe III's army and ends up getting blown up by a mine.

A number of critics have studied this tale, which was collected in Zayas's 1637 *Novelas amorosas y ejemplares* (*Amorous and Exemplary Novels*). Some have found that it responds to elements from Miguel Cervantes's *Fuerza de la sangre* (*Power of Blood*), providing a feminist perspective on the problem of abused women and their marriages (Hernández 2002). The story has also been analysed from the standpoint of sermons directed at long-suffering wives (Salstad 1998). Studies of Zayas's *novelas* have also found that her baroque narratives draw on and rework conventions from the legends of female martyrs and their victimized bodies. Patricia Grieve (1991) has found that Zayas's gendered use of hagiography is subversive, while Mariana Brownlee observes that it "evokes the blood and gore characteristic of hagiography ... without devaluing it" (2000, 127). Elizabeth Rhodes points out that "Zayas's first public would have registered the presence of hagiography ... with an ease ... all but inaccessible to readers today" (2011, 34). At the same time, critics continue to shed light on how Zayas draws on models of Marian devotion, but the particular significance of the Virgin of the Arch cult has yet to be considered. Eavan O'Brien observes that Mary tends to serve as a surrogate mother for female protagonists who suffer abuse in a "patriarchal age" (2010, 215).[2] While this critic does not cite *La fuerza del amor* as one of the *novelas* that exemplify this tendency, her approach seems applicable since the narrator specifically states that Laura's mother died giving birth to her – and, as I will argue, the Virgin is implicated in the story. Scholars have also uncovered some limited biographical information about the author that can provide further insight into the *novela*. Baptized in 1590, she was the daughter of the aristocratic infantry captain Fernando de Zayas y Sotomayor. Most critics agree that she probably lived in Naples during her twenties, when her father was serving the viceroy, Pedro Fernández de Castro, from 1610 to 1616.[3] This experience would have informed her descriptions of Naples, together with indirect knowledge and written sources. My purpose in this essay is to show how *La fuerza del amor* relates to legendary and spatial aspects of the Neapolitan cult of Nuestra Señora del Arca and also evokes traditions surrounding executed criminals and meanings attached to their bodily remains in early modern Italy.

Contemporary visitors to Naples will have no difficulty finding the image of Nuestra Señora del Arca evoked by Zayas. It is still housed at the same sanctuary of Madonna dell'Arco a few miles from the city centre near Mount Vesuvius. Work on the current structure began in 1593, in response to a popular cult that had developed around a fresco dating from the fifteenth century and thought to be miraculous. The original image had been anonymously painted on an archway, giving rise to the name "dell'Arco." The most striking thing about what is an otherwise conventional depiction of the Blessed Mother and Child is that her mouth and cheek are stained dark red, with what appears to be a disfiguring wound on the left side of her face (see figure 12.1).

The icon was credited with healing and protecting devotees and pilgrims from all manner of ailments and dangers – including innocent devotees being subjected to violence – as can be seen in collections of miracles recorded at the shrine, and the many ex-votos left there over the centuries, including sixteenth- and seventeenth-century votive paintings illustrating these miracles (Miele 1995). More than 750 ex-votos, in the form of images painted on small wooden panels, were probably on display during the first part of the seventeenth century when Zayas is believed to have been in Naples (Jacobs 2008, 100).

According to legend, the cult began in 1450 after a man lost his temper during a game and threw his ball at this image of the Virgin. Blood marvellously flowed from her face, and the astonished and fearful ballplayer found himself unable to flee the scene. In spite of his attempts to escape, he could only circle around the frescoed archway, and was soon after hanged by order of the Count of Sarno, according to a 1608 account:

> Prese la palla et con gran furore et forza la tirò in faccia (il temerario) alla Madre Santissima percotendola ne la mascella sinistra dove subito apparve il sangue vivo, come al presente ancora si vide. Ma ecco incontinente l'ira dell Signore sopra il sacrilego et temerario che, vedendo i compagni il sangue et comminiciando ad alta voce a gridare: miracolo, miracolo! Volendosi fuggire il misero, no fu possibile, ma girava intorno intorno alla cappella come insensato senza potere partire punto da quella. (Miele 1995, 63).

> (He took the ball, and with great fury and force, (the reckless man) threw it at the most Blessed Mother's face, striking her left cheek, where suddenly flowing blood appeared, as it is now presently seen. But here is the Lord's unstoppable anger over the sacrilege and recklessness of this man, whose companions were seeing the blood and starting to cry out in loud voices: "miracle, miracle!" Wanting to flee, this was not possible for the wretch, as he circled round and round the chapel like a fool, unable to leave of that spot.)[4]

Fig. 12.1. Fifteenth-century painting of Virgin with Child, Santuario Madonna dell'Arco (public domain).

Pilgrims to the site have long been known as *fujenti* (those who flee) and *batenti* (scourgers), a tradition that has been studied by the anthropologist Tullio Tentori. Although the origin of these designations is unclear, both seem to be associated with the foundational legend. Unlike the man who tried and failed to run away from his crime, the *fujenti* "flee" the city of Naples, to arrive at the sanctuary and venerate the Virgin. The *batenti* traditionally mortified themselves as they approached the shrine, in tribute to the wounded Madonna. It seems highly likely that, if María de Zayas resided in Naples, she would have become aware of this extremely popular cult. In another story in *Novelas amorosas y ejemplares*, entitled *Aventurarse perdiendo* (*Taking a Chance on Losing*), she describes the setting of the famous Catalan shrine of Montserrat with its miraculous image of the Virgin, showing her interest in Marian pilgrimage sites. Adoration of the Neapolitan image had become so popular that Pope Gregory XIV received a 1591 report stating that "infinite numbers," to include "the major part of the nobility," were venerating Madonna dell'Arco "every hour" (Jacobs 2008, 106). Another account, written the year before Zayas's father arrived in the city, attests to the centrality of this pilgrimage in Neapolitan religious life: "so great was the multitude of nobility and commoners, of carriages, coaches, and horses that left from Naples that for many … days, from the Carmine gate up to Madonna Santissima dell'Arco, for four miles or more, it was difficult to be able to pass and walk forward or back" (Marino 2010, 112).

Whether or not Zayas saw the original fresco inside the sanctuary or viewed one of many reproductions, the legend of the bleeding image of Madonna dell'Arco – with its thematic connections to the gendered construction and reception of hagiography during the period – could very well have impacted her portrayal of the abuse suffered by Laura, and in particular the wounding of her "divine" face by Diego:

> Empezó a maltratar a Laura de palabra, diciéndolas tales y tan pesadas que la obligó a que, vertiendo cristalinas corrientes por su divino rostro … y encendido en una infernal cólera, le empezó a maltratar de manos, tanto que las perlas de sus dientes presto tomaron forma de corales, bañados en la sangre que empezó a sacar en las crueles manos. (2000, 360–1)

> (He began to abuse Laura verbally, saying such things and so harshly, causing her to spill crystalline tears that came pouring down her divine face … and overcome with an infernal rage, he began to abuse her physically, so badly that her pearl-like teeth suddenly looked like red coral, bathed in the blood that was shed by his cruel hands).

The poetically described face of Laura parallels the damage to Mary's portrait, as her angry husband plays the part of the enraged man bloodying the face of a saintly woman.[5] Importantly, the portrait evoked in the *novela* is, in the words of the art historian Frederika Jacobs, a physical object that has its own "identity" and is in this respect 'alive'" (2008, 107). Such devotional paintings "are valued for what they do; the miracles they perform and the prayers they answer" (Jacobs 2008, 107). It is the blood stain on the Madonna dell'Arco portrait that makes the Virgin materially, corporally present. This allowed viewers and devotees to overcome what Vibeke Olson has called the "challenge of veneration *'in absentia,'*" since Mary's body was believed to have been assumed into heaven, and, unlike other saints, could only leave behind relics like bodily fluids – or superficial fragments (2017, 12). Made present through Zayas's evocation of the "imagen muy devota," the bloodied, living Virgin of the Arch is identified with Laura and the battering she has suffered. Another possible connection between the Marian legend and the *novela* comes when Laura's brother is unable to ride past the roadside chapel, enabling him to rescue her, "teniendo por milagrosa su venida" (taking his arrival to be miraculous) (2000, 368). This miracle can be contrasted with the immobility of the ballplayer who was unable to leave the wounded image of Madonna dell'Arco. The implication of the Neapolitan Virgin in the story would seem to correlate with other *novelas* by Zayas, in which the Blessed Mother serves as a maternal surrogate for heroines (O'Brien 2010). Not only does the sacrilegious crime correlate with the violent outburst of Diego in *La fuerza del amor*, so does the fate of the ballplayer: both are punished with untimely deaths as a consequence of angrily striking an innocent woman. Unable to escape, the man who assaulted the Madonna is hung from a nearby tree, while the abusive husband in the *novela* flees the scene of his crime only to face a deservedly gruesome death in battle. In a final potential link with the cult of the Virgin of the Arch, comparable to the itinerary of a *fujenti* pilgrim, Laura leaves the city of the Naples on the same road that leads to this Marian sanctuary – but, as we have seen, her destination is a roadside chapel along the way that was being used as a crypt, where she intends to collect body parts for a witch.

The narrator of the tale comments on the prevalence of such superstitions in Naples, and characterizes the witch as a charlatan, who characteristically asks for gifts and hopes to create a profitable delay in casting her spell:

Oyendo decir que en aquella tierra había mujeres que obligaban con fuerzas de hechizos a que hubiese amor … pensando remediarse por este

camino, encargó que le trajesen una ... Hay en Nápoles, en estos enredos
y supersticiones, tanta libertad que públicamente usan sus invenciones ...
como no hay el freno de la Inquisición y los demás castigos ... la embustera ...
asegurando a Laura de su saber, contando milagros en sucesos ajenos ...
dijo que había menester para ciertas cosas que había de aderezar, para
traer consigo en una bolsilla, barbas, cabellos y dientes de un ahorcado,
las cuales reliquias, con las demás cosas, harían que don Diego mudase.
(2000, 361–2)

(Hearing it said that in that land there were women that could provoke love
through the power of sorcery ... hoping to receive a remedy by this route,
she ordered that such a woman be summoned ... With these intrigues and
superstitions there is so much liberty taken publicly in Naples ... as there
is no Inquisition or other punishments to quell them ... the trickster ...
assuring Laura of her wisdom, and recounting miracles with other cases ...
said that it was necessary that certain things be made ready to prepare, to
bring with her a bag of whiskers, hair and teeth from a hanged man, so
that such relics, with other things, would make Diego change.)

As critics have pointed out, depictions of old women using body parts
for witchcraft can be found in well-known Spanish works, such as *La
Celestina* by Fernando de Rojas (1499) and Lope de Vega's sixteenth-
century *El caballero de Olmedo* (*The Knight of Olmedo*). In both of these
works, witches involved in love magic are said to extract teeth from
a hanged man.[6] Another comparable example of ghoulish sorcery can
be found in Quevedo's *El Buscón* (*The Swindler*, published in 1626),
in which the mother of the picaresque title character is described as
a witch who collects skulls and dead men's teeth – while his uncle is
characterized as an executioner who eats meat pies made from human
flesh salvaged at the gallows. The characterization of witches as grave
robbers was not only a commonplace in late medieval and early modern literature, but also believed to have some basis in reality. As Julio
Caro Baroja observed, descriptions of witches using fat from cadavers
and the corpses of children coincides with lists of ingredients compiled
by Inquisitors in early modern Castile (1979, 101–2). The most notorious outbreak of witch burning on the Iberian Peninsula took place in
the Basque country between 1609 and 1614, around the time Zayas is
thought to have been visiting Naples. An Inquisitorial record from 1610
reports how witches from the area were said to carry away corpses to
make potions (Henningsen 2004, 141).

Although some ecclesiastical authorities took a sceptical approach
to evaluating such lurid stories, the basic practice of harvesting body
parts for magical cures and as superstitious amulets seems to have been

widespread. Across Europe, executioners sought to profit from the selling of corporal fragments. In recent years, Francesca Matteoni has studied intersections between medical and magical powers attributed to body parts in early modern Europe. Citing a seventeenth-century doctor, Matteoni finds that in both folk magic and early modern medicine the bodies of hanged and decapitated criminals were thought to provide greater potency than other corpses since their "untimely death" preserved a "life-force" or "obscure vitality surviving in bodies extinct by violence" (2016, 198). In order for this force to be implemented, some believed that it "had to be administered by peculiar witchy figures who knew its intrinsic magico-medical power" (Matteoni 2016, 203). Matteoni finds that pieces of executed men were employed in love spells or for other forms of magic, such as divination. A stilted lover could either consume parts of dead criminals in a potion or wear them as an amulet, which seems to be the case in the attempted gathering of "barbas, cabellos y dientes de un ahorcado," to be placed in a "bolsillo" in *La fuerza del amor*. In his study of the history of burial and cemeteries in the Castilian city of Cuenca, Diego Gómez Sánchez cites sixteenth-century examples of the teeth of hanged men being allegedly stolen from the grave by a notorious witch named Juana García de Santa Fimia, who was accused of trying to cause a priest and an adulterous nobleman to fall in love with her clients (1998, 93).

Zayas was no doubt most familiar with Spanish traditions surrounding the condemned love magic of witches in literature and lore, based in part on real Celestinesque figures like Juana García. However, in keeping with her probable knowledge of the legend and cult of the Virgin of the Arch, the Golden Age writer might have also been aware of the popular cult of the dead in Naples, as practised in the early seventeenth century, when she is thought to have accompanied her father to the Italian city. This context sheds further light on why the body parts she seeks are described by the witch as "relics" as well as the image of hanged men's bones falling into a "holy space," exposed beneath the ground level of the roadside chapel:

Hay puestos por las paredes garfios de hierro, en las cuales después de haber ahorcado en la plaza los hombres que mueren por justicia, los llevan allá y cuelgan en aquellos garfios; y como los tales se van deshaciendo, caen los huesos en aquel hoyo que, como está sagrado, les sirve de sepultura. (2000, 366)

(There are hooks attached to the walls, in which, having hung in the square men sentenced to death by the law, they are brought there and hung from these hooks; and as the bodies proceed to decompose, the bones fall into that pit which, being holy ground, serves them as a burial).

In early modern Italy, confraternities devoted themselves to comforting executed criminals and to the care of their bodies. In Naples, the brotherhood who carried out this mission was known as the Compagnia dei Bianchi dello Spirito Santo, a company of confraternity who wore all white (symbolizing the Holy Spirit) and were led by clergymen, as opposed to laymen, as part of a reform initiated by Spanish authorities (Black 1989, 3; Terpstra 2015, 22). In this way, members of the brotherhood could benefit spiritually from carrying out acts of mercy, and criminals sentenced to death – unlike the unrepentant ballplayer of the Marian legend – could hope to avoid damnation by relying on these brothers to help them repent and rededicate themselves to faith in Christ, prior to mounting the scaffold. To ensure that repentant sinners could maintain their status as unwavering converts, and redeem themselves by accepting death in imitation of the saints, brothers were assigned to carry out a number duties: they prayed with the convicts all night before the day of their execution, and distracted them from jeering crowds on the way to the gallows.[7] Making their way through the streets and outside the city walls, these newly reformed criminals were enclosed in a "sensory cocoon" of hymns, often to the Virgin Mary, long considered to be the Queen of Martyrs, and sheltered by a *tavollette*, or screen, of sacred images held in front of their faces featuring scenes of martyrdom and souls being saved (Terpstra 2015, 13).

I would suggest that the hanged men in *La fuerza del amor* can be understood as having undergone this process prior to their execution – a process which contributes to the significance of the bodies displayed in the roadside chapel. In the words of the historian Nicholas Terpstra, the prisoner was in this way transformed into a "new man," in the Pauline sense; brought into the confraternity as a spiritual brother; and seen as a "convert" and "martyr" closely identified with "the good thief Dismas crucified next to Christ" who "could enter directly in paradise" (2015, 7, 12). As elsewhere in Europe, the criminals' bodies were in many cases condemned to be gruesomely displayed and/or mutilated by executioners, as what Zoe Dyndor has called the typical "post-mortem punishment" (2015, 106). For example, Terpstra has brought to light a crude drawing of a hanged man from the second half of the sixteenth century, who was decapitated and quartered in Bologna as a warning to others, with his limbs left hanging from the scaffold (2015, 18).

Due in part to "the desire of many laypeople to grab bits of ... the prisoner's body after execution ... for popular magic," Italian authorities relied on the confraternities to ensure its "safe disposal" – in addition to helping convince prisoners to accept their fate peacefully (Terpstra 2015, 21). The corpses of criminals who had been assisted by the brothers were then deposited "in consecrated ground," like the final entombment described in *La fuerza del amor* (Terpstra 2015, 12). Their remains were often treated as "sacramental," "liturgical," and "iconic objects," comparable to what the witch in Zayas's novel refers to as "reliquias" (Terpstra 2015, 7, 17, 20). The connection between criminal and saintly bodies in this early modern cult of the dead drew on special powers attributed to their material remains – due not just to the vitality preserved by an untimely death – but to having been exposed, dismembered, and fragmented through what was viewed as a kind of quasi-martyrdom. Confraternities not only assisted in the salvation of sinners facing execution but continued to pray for them after their deaths as souls that could be trapped in Purgatory. Apart from this orthodox practice, there arose a superstitious tradition of praying to these souls and communing in different ways with their bodily remains in hopes that they might mediate on behalf of the living. This cult was particularly strong in Naples, known for its publicly accessible crypts, charnel houses, and ossuaries located beneath the ground floor of churches.[8] For example, a church founded in the 1630s by a charitable brotherhood dedicated to the poor and destitute is known as Santa Maria delle Anime del Purgatorio. It still contains an ossuary full of venerated skulls and bones, many of which belonged to victims of a seventeenth-century plague. The facade is also decorated with representations of skulls and bones, and the building as a whole exemplifies the early modern Neapolitan cult of the dead that seems to inform Zayas's *novela*. Visitors to the church will be aware that a baroque masterpiece by Massimo Stanzione hangs over the altar (see figure 12.2). Executed during the first half of the seventeenth century, it features the Virgin Mary coming to the aid of souls in purgatory, who are depicted as unclothed bodies rising and reaching upward, with the help of angels, from a tomb-like darkness at the bottom of the canvas.

The painting thus mirrors the spatial relationship in the church itself between the salvific centre of the altar and the crypt full of bodily remains in the space of death that lies below. Mary hovers as patron saint of the dead who remain unknown, unnamed, and abandoned in Purgatory. A spatial transition is made from the abject terror of death and the disgusting reality of decomposition exhibited beneath the floor, to the scene of redemption being represented above the altar. *La fuerza del amor*, like other *novelas* by Zayas, such as *La inocencia castigada* (*Innocence Punished*), draws on what Patricia Grieve has called the "secular martyrdom" of emotionally and physically abused wives – in addition to the surrogate motherhood of Mary in narratives studied by O'Brien, especially in *La perseguida triumphante* (*The Persecuted, Triumphant*)

Fig. 12.2. *Madonna delle Anime Purganti* (1638–42), altarpiece by Massimo Santzione, Santa Maria delle Anime del Purgatorio, Naples (public domain).

(2010, 214–41).[9] More specifically, Laura's story evokes the Neapolitan death cult together with popular devotion to the wounded Virgin of the Arch as Queen of Martyrs and patron saint of victims, rescued from a liminal space between life and death. The roadside chapel is, of course, a product of Zayas's rich, macabre imagination, but it can be seen as having been inspired in part by underground crypts or hypogea that were (and are) typical of Naples. While the above-ground space with its visual and symbolic triumph over death characterizes religious structures like Santa Maria delle Anime del Purgatorio, the morbid spectre of rotting human flesh decorates the walls above ground in the *humilladero* of *La fuerza del amor*. In place of the bloodied image of the Virgin of the Arch, the narrative fixes our gaze first on the injured face of Laura, and later on the horror of bodies subjected to judicial violence that recalls the trials of martyrs, and this wife's victimization at the hands of her husband.[10]

Notes

1 Translations of Zayas are my own. I am grateful for the assistance of Ali Alsmadi in gathering secondary sources to research this essay. The estate belonging to Laura's family is identified as Piedra Blanca (2000, 365), a translation of the Italian Pietra Bianca, located in what is now part of the town of Portici in the province of Naples. It was built in the sixteenth century by the secretary of Carlos V, the poet Bernardino Martirano, who named it after a nymph by the same name (in Greek), Leucopetra (Di Cristi). Zayas identifies Laura as part of the "Garrafa" family, Dukes of "Nochera" (Italian, Nocera), which refers apparently to House of Carafa, a family that produced several cardinals and one pope, Paul IV.

2 Religious and social contexts surrounding violence and the female body during the period have also been explored in Lisa Vollendorf study of Zayas (2001).

3 María de Zayas probably never married and lived most of her life in Madrid, where she earned fame as a writer of poetry as well as *novelas*. A number of references to Naples can be found in her works, seeming to be based on direct knowledge of the city rather than solely the conventional (see Gamboa and Marin 2007).

4 The translation of the legend is mine.

5 This visual imagery might be understood as an example of what Frederick de Armas has called "dramatic ekphrasis," insofar as it could be "using an art object to construct a developing action" – but would at the same time be "transformative" (2005, 22–3).

6 In *La Celestina*, the practice is attributed to Claudina, Pármeno's mother, who extracts seven teeth from a hanged man (act 7, lines 23–4). In the *Caballero de Olmedo*, it is the witch Fabia who is involved in pulling out a "muela" (molar) (act 2, vv. 960–4).

7 John Marino describes the practice of executing criminals in Naples during the seventeenth century: "the rite of capital punishment was a spectacle with a cortege that passed from the place of the condemned's incarceration (typically the Vicaria jail) through the *dense popolo* quarter on 'the way of the cross' to the place of execution in Piazza del Mercato, where the gallows were permanently erected and prominently displayed in most city maps" (2010, 111). As this piazza is adjacent to the Carmine Gate leading to the road to the Marian sanctuary (Marino 2010, 12), Zayas's geography of the city is not inaccurate.

8 The most famous example is the Fontanelle crypt, which was being filled with bodily remains long before Zayas's presumed arrival in Naples. Photographs of existing sites with brief studies of the phenomenon of the cult of death in the Italian city can be found in the work of Italo Pardo (1994), in addition to that of Paul Koudounaris (2011). Such ossuaries are less common in Spain. Koudounaris studies two medieval examples in Roncesvalles (Silo de Carlomagno) and another near Valladolid (the Mozarabic Church of Santa María de Wamba) (2011, 136, 152, 154, 188, 201). As he shows, later structures with ossuaries are more common in Portugal.

9 *La inocencia castigada* was published in Zayas's 1647 *Desengaños amorosos*, whereas *La perseguida triumphante* formed part of the same collection that includes *La fuerza del amor*.

10 As Steven Wagschal has shown, Zayas confronts us with disgusting sensory images that create a "moral disgust" concerning societal ills in *La fuerza del amor* as well as *La inocencia castigada* (2018, 113).

Works Cited

Abel, Lionel. 1963. *Metatheatre: A New View of Dramatic Form*. New York: Hill and Wang.

Andres-Suárez, Irene, José Manuel López de Abiada, and Pedro Ramírez Molas, eds. 1997. *El teatro dentro del teatro: Cervantes, Lope, Tirso y Calderón*. Madrid: Verbum.

Advertencias para el ejercicio de la Plaza de Alcalde de Casa y Corte, según están en un libro antigüo de la Sala que es el que cita el Señor Matheu por anotaciones del Señor Elaza-rraga, con las notas marginales con que se halla hasta el presente año de 1749. 2015. Edited by Francisco Javier Cubo Machado. Master's thesis. Universidad Autónoma de Ma- drid.

Agamben, Giorgio. 1993. *Stanze: Word and Phantasm in Western Culture*. Translated by Roland L. Martínez. Minneapolis: University of Minnesota Press.

Aït-Touati, Frédérique. 2011. *Fictions of the Cosmos: Science and Literature in the Seventeenth Century*. Chicago: University of Chicago Press.

Albardonedo Freire, Antonio José. 2002. *El urbanismo de Sevilla durante el reinado de Felipe II*. Seville: Guadalquivir Ediciones.

Alcalá Galán, Mercedes. 1996. "Las misceláneas españolas del siglo XVI y su entorno cultural." *Dicenda. Cuadernos de Filología Hispánica* 14:11–19.

– 2017. "Performing the Museum." Paper, Renaissance Society of America Conference, Chicago, 31 March 2017.

Alcalde, Pilar. 1997. "El poder de la palabra y el dinero en *La gitanilla*." *Cervantes* 17 (2): 122–32.

Alfonso X el Sabio. 2007. *Libro de los juegos: acedrex, dados e tablas; Ordenamiennto de las tafurerías*. Edited by Raúl Orellana Calderón. Madrid: Fundación José Antonio de Castro.

– 2009. *General Estoria. Tercera Parte, Tomo I*. Edited by Pedro Sánchez- Prieto Borja. Madrid: Fundación José Antonio de Castro.

Alloza Aparicio, Ángel. 1998. "El orden público en la corte de Felipe II." In *Congreso Internacional "Felipe II (1527–1598): Europa dividida, la monarquía*

católica de Felipe II (Universidad Autónoma de Madrid, 20–23 abril 1998),"
edited by José Martínez Millán, vol. 2., 29–51. Madrid: Parteluz.

Alter, Robert, trans. 2019. *The Hebrew Bible: A Translation and Commentary*. New York: W.W. Norton & Company.

Alvar Ezquerra, Alfredo. 1989. *El nacimiento de una capital europea: Madrid entre 1561 y 1601*. Madrid: Turner y Ayuntamiento de Madrid.

Álvarez Márquez, C. 2017. "Mujeres lectoras en el siglo XVI en Sevilla." *Historia. Instituciones. Documentos* 31:19–40.

Amann, Elizabeth. 2013. "'Ave (aunque muda yo)': The Image of the Nightingale in Góngora's Love Sonnets." *Symposium* 87 (2): 63–74.

Amor Calzas, Juan Julio. 1904. *Curiosidades históricas de la Ciudad de Huete (Cuenca)*. Madrid: Primitivo Fernández Impresor.

Anderson, Benedict. 2006. *Imagined Communities*. London: Verso.

Anderson, Graham. 2004. "Aulus Gellius as Storyteller." In *The World of Aulus Gellius*, edited by Leofranc Holford-Strevens and Amiel Vardi, 109–47. Oxford: Oxford University Press.

Arenal, Electa. 2009. "Sex and Class in the Seventeenth-Century Cloister: Sor Marcela de San Félix's Love Poems to God." In *Studies on Women's Poetry of the Golden Age: "Tras el espejo la musa escribe,"* edited by Julián Olivares, 233–54. London: Tamesis.

Arenal, Electa, and Stacey Schlau. 2006. "'Leyendo yo y escribiendo ella': The Convent as Intellectual Community." *Letras femeninas* 32 (1): 129–47.

– 2010. *Untold Sisters. Hispanic Nuns in Their Own Works*, translated by Amanda Power. Albuquerque: University of New Mexico Press.

Arias, Santa. 2010. "Rethinking Space: An Outsider's View of the Spatial Turn." *GeoJournal* 75 (1): 29–41.

Aronoff, Joel. 1962. "Freud's Conception of the Origin of Curiosity." *Journal of Psychiatry* 54 (1): 39–45.

Asher, Kenneth. 2017. *Literature, Ethics and the Emotions*. Cambridge: Cambridge University Press.

Aterido Fernández, Angel. 2019. "Capilla de Nuestra Señora de Guadalupe en el Monasterio de las Descalzas Reales," in *La otra Corte. Mujeres de la Casa de Austria en los Monasterios Reales de las Descalzas y la Encarnación*, edited by F. Checa, 138–42. Madrid: Patrimonio Nacional.

Ávila, Teresa. 1988. *The Life of Saint Teresa of Avila by Herself*. Translated by J.M. Cohen. New York: Penguin Classics.

Avilés, Luis F. 1998. "Fortaleza tan guardada: Casa, alegoría y melancolía en *El celoso extremeño*." *Cervantes: Bulletin of the Cervantes Society of America* 18 (1): 71–95.

Bachelard, Gaston. 1994. *The Poetics of Space*. Translated by Maria Jolas. Introduction by John R. Stilgoe. Boston: Beacon Press.

Barbier, Frédéric. 2016. *Gutenberg's Europe: The Book and the Invention of Western Modernity*. Translated by Jean Birrell. Cambridge: Polity Press.

Barkan, Leonard. 1986. *The Gods Made Flesh: Metamorphosis and the Pursuit of Paganism*. New Haven, CT: Yale University Press.

Barnard, Mary E. 2014. *Garcilaso de la Vega and the Material Culture of Renaissance Europe*. Toronto: University of Toronto Press.

– 2022. *A Poetry of Things: The Material Lyric in Habsburg Spain*. Toronto: University of Toronto Press.

Barnard, Mary E., and Frederick A. de Armas. 2013. *Objects of Culture in the Literature of Imperial Spain*. Toronto: University of Toronto Press.

Barthes, Roland. 1977. "The Grain of the Voice." In *Image. Music. Text*, translated by Stephen Heath, 179–89. New York: Hill and Wang.

– 1979. "From Work to Text." In *Textual Strategies: Perspectives in Post-Structuralist Criticism*, edited by Josué V Harari, 73–81. Ithaca, NY: Cornell University Press.

Bass, Laura R. 2008. "The Treasury of the Language: Literary Invention in Philip III's Spain." In *El Greco to Velázquez: Art during the Reign of Philip III*, edited by Sarah Schroth and Ronnie Baer, 147–81. Boston: Museum of Fine Arts.

Bataillon, Marcel. 1986. *Erasmo y España*. Mexico: Fondo de Cultura Económica.

Bauer, Rachel N. 2021. "Cervantes and Madness." In *The Handbook of Cervantes*, edited by Aaron Kahn, 297–314. Oxford: Oxford University Press.

Benedict, Barbara M. 2001. *Curiosity. A Cultural History of Modern Inquiry*. Chicago: University of Chicago Press.

Bercé, Yves-Marie. 1990. *Le roi caché: Sauveurs et imposteurs. Mythes politiques populaires dans l'Europe moderne*. Paris, Fayard.

Bhagavad Gita. 1967. Translated with commentary by Maharishi Mahesh Yogi. London: Penguin.

Black, Christopher F. 1989. *Italian Confraternities in the Sixteenth Century*. Cambridge: Cambridge University Press.

Blair, Ann M. *Too Much to Know: Managing Scholarly Information Before the Modern Age*. New Haven, CT: Yale University Press, 2010.

Blumenberg, Hans. 1983. *The Legitimacy of the Modern Age*. Translated by Robert M. Wallace. Boston: MIT Press.

Bouza, Fernando. 2001. *Corre manuscrito: Una historia cultural del Siglo de Oro*. Madrid: Marcial Pons.

– 2004. *Communication, Knowledge, and Memory in Early Modern Spain*. Translated by Sonia López and Michael Agnew. Philadelphia: University of Pennsylvania Press.

Boyarin, Daniel. 2009. *Socrates and the Fat Rabbis*. Chicago: University of Chicago Press.

Boyarin, Shamma. 2016. "Hebrew Alexander Romances and Astrological Questions: Alexander, Aristotle, and the Medieval Jewish Audience." In *Alexander the Great in the Middle Ages: Transcultural Perspectives*, 88–103. Toronto: University of Toronto Press.

Boyd, Stephen. 2004. "Un espacio ejemplar cervantino: El patio de Monipodio en *Rinconete y Cortadillo*." In *Memoria de la palabra: Actas del VI Congreso de la Asociación Internacional Siglo de Oro, I*, edited by María Luisa Lobato López and Francisco Domínguez Matito, 353–63. Madrid/Frankfurt: Iberoamericana/Vervuert.

Bradbury, Jonathan. 2010. "The *Miscelánea* of the Spanish Golden Age: An Unstable Label." *Modern Language Review* 105 (4): 1053–71.

– 2017. *The Miscellany of the Spanish Golden Age. A Literature of Fragments*. London: Routledge.

Brody, Ervin C. 1972. *The Demetrius Legend and Its Literary Treatment in the Age of the Baroque*. Rutherford, NJ: Farleigh Dickinson University Press.

Brooks, Mary Elizabeth. 1964. *A King for Portugal: The Madrigal Conspiracy, 1594–95*. Madison: University of Wisconsin Press.

Brown, Jonathan, and J.H. Elliott. 1980. *A Palace for a King: The Buen Retiro and the Court of Phillip IV*. New Haven, CT: Yale University Press.

Brownlee, Marina S. 2000. *The Cultural Labyrinth of María de Zayas*. Philadelphia: University of Pennsylvania Press.

– 2010. "Pagan and Christian: The Bivalent Hero of the *Libro de Alexandre*." *Kentucky Romance Quarterly* 30 (3): 263–70.

_ 2016. "Torquemada's *Olivante* and Cervantes' Anxiety of Influence." In *Studies in Honor of Ronald E. Surtz*, edited by Christina Lee and José Luis Gastañaga, 50–75. Newark, DE: Juan de la Cuesta.

Bubenik, Andrea. 2005. "The Art of Albrecht Dürer in the Context of the Court of Rudolf II." In *Studia Rudolphina: Bulleting of the Research Center for Visual Arts and Culture in the Age of Rudolf II*, 17–27. Prague: Artefactum.

Burke, Edmund. 1998. *A Philosophical Enquiry into the Origin of our Ideas of the Sublime and Beautiful*. Edited by David Womersley. London: Penguin.

Caillois, Roger. 2001. *Man, Play and Games*. Translated by Meyer Barash. Urbana: University of Illinois Press.

Calderón de la Barca, Pedro. 1641. *Segunda parte de las comedias de don Pedro Calderón de la Barca*. Madrid: En la imprenta de Carlos Sánchez.

– 1873. *Life Is a Dream*. Translated by Denise Florence MacCarthy. In *Calderon's Dramas. The Wonder-Working Magician: Life Is a Dream: tThe Purgatory of Saint Patrick. Now First Translated Fully from the Spanish in the Metre of the Original*. London: Henry S. King & Co.

– 1994. *La vida es sueño*. Edited by José Ruano de la Haza. Madrid: Castalia.

Campbell, Ysla. 2019. "*Pedro de Urdemalas*: Burla carnavalesca y crítica social en Cervantes." *Hipogrifo: Revista de Literatura y Cultura del Siglo de Oro* 7 (2): 11–24.

Canavaggio, Jean. 1990. *Cervantes*. Translated by J.R. Jones. New York: Norton.

– 1992. "*Pedro de Urdemalas*." In *Los baños de Argel. Pedro de Urdemalas*, by Miguel de Cervantes, edited by Jean Canavaggio, 43–68. Madrid: Taurus.

Candia Pérez, Eva. 2020. "El patio de Monipodio y la casa de la Maldegollada: Pícaros entre cuatro paredes." *eHumanista* 44:253–64.

Cárdenas-Rotunno, Anthony J. 2008. "Bestialidad y la palabra: El parto perruno en el 'Coloquio de los perros.'" *Hispania: A Journal Devoted to the Teaching of Spanish and Portuguese* 91 (2): 301–9.

Caro Baroja, Julio. 1979. *Las brujas y su mundo*. Madrid: Alianza.

Carreira, Antonio. 2004. "El manuscrito como transmisor de humanidades en la España del Barroco." In *Barroco*, edited by Pedro Aullón de Haro, 597–618. Madrid: Verbum.

Carrera, Elena. 2010. "Madness and Melancholy in Sixteenth- and Seventeenth-Century Spain: New Evidence, New Approaches." *Bulletin of Spanish Studies* 87 (8): 1–15.

Caruth, Cathy, ed. 1995. *Trauma: Explorations in Memory*. Baltimore: Johns Hopkins University Press.

– 1996. *Unclaimed Experience: Trauma, Narrative, and History*. Baltimore: Johns Hopkins University Press.

Carruthers, Mary. 2008. *The Book of Memory: A Study of Memory in Medieval Culture*. Cambridge: Cambridge University Press.

Casas Rigall, Juan, ed. 2014. *Libro de Alexandre*. Madrid: Real Academia Española.

Cascardi, Anthony. 1992. *The Subject of Modernity*. Cambridge: Cambridge University Press.

– 2011. *Cervantes, Literature and the Discourse of Politics*. Toronto: University of Toronto Press.

Castro, Américo. 1925. *El pensamiento de Cervantes*. Madrid: Anejos de la Revista de Filología Española.

Cátedra, Pedro M., and Anastasio Rojo Vega. 2004. *Biblioteca y lectura de mujeres (siglo XVI)*. Salamanca: Instituto de Historia del Libro y de la Lectura.

Cavarero, Adriana. 2005. *For More than One Voice: Toward a Philosophy of Vocal Expression*. Translated by Paul A. Kottman. Stanford, CA: Stanford University Press.

Cecilia de Nacimiento. 1971. *Obras completas*. Edited by J.M. Díaz Cerón. Madrid: Editorial de la Espiritualidad.

– 2012. *Journeys of a Mystic Soul in Poetry and Prose*. Edited by Kevin Donnelly and Sandra Sider. Toronto: Iter Inc. Center for Renaissance Studies.

Cerquiglini, Bernard. 2004. *In Praise of the Variant: A Critical History of Philology*. Baltimore: Johns Hopkins University Press.

Cervantes, Miguel de. 1987. *Pedro de Urdemalas*. In *Teatro completo*. Edited by Florencio Sevilla Arroyo and Antonio Rey Hazas, 632–720. Barcelona: Planeta.

– 1992a. "Rinconete and Cortadillo. *Rinconete y Cortadillo*." In *Exemplary Novels Novelas ejemplares* I, edited by B.W. Ife, translated by Richard Hitchcock, 171–229. Warminster, UK: Aris & Phillips.

– 1992b. "The Dialogue of the Dogs. *El coloquio de los perros*." In *Exemplary Novels Novelas ejemplares* IV, edited by B.W. Ife, translated by John Jones and John Macklin, 84–157. Warminster, UK: Aris & Phillips.

– 2003a. *Don Quixote de la Mancha*. Translated by John Rutherford. New York: Penguin Books.

– 2003b. *Don Quixote*. Translated by Edith Grossman. New York: Ecco.

– 2004. *Don Quijote de La Mancha*. Edited by Francisco Rico. Barcelona: Galaxia Gutenberg.

– 2013. *Novelas ejemplares*. Edited by Jorge García López. Madrid: Real Academia Española.

– 2015. *Don Quijote de la Mancha*. Edited by Francisco Rico. Madrid: Alfaguara.

– 2016. *Exemplary Novels*. Translated by Edith Grossman. Edited by Roberto González Echevarría. New Haven, CT: Yale University Press.

Chandler, Arthur R. 1934. "The Nightingale in Greek and Latin Poetry." *Classical Journal* 30 (2): 78–84.

Chartier, Roger. 2007. *Inscription and Erasure: Literature and Written Culture from the Eleventh to the Eighteenth Century*. Translated by Arthur Goldhammer. Philadelphia: University of Pennsylvania Press.

Cheney, Patrick. 2018. *English Authorship and the Early Modern Sublime: Spenser, Marlowe, Shakespeare, Jonson*. Cambridge: Cambridge University Press.

Colegio de la Compañía de Jesús de Huete. 1629. *Recibimiento al obispo Pimentel*. Ms. 1895. Biblioteca General Histórica de la Universidad de Salamanca.

Correas, Gonzalo. 1924. *Vocabulario de refranes y frases proverbiales y otras fórmulas comunes de la lengua castellana*. Madrid: Tip. de la Rev. de Archivos, Bibliotecas y Museos.

Costa, Gustavo. 1985. "The Latin Translations of Longinus' *Peri Ypsous* in Renaissance Italy." In *Acta Conventus Neo-Latini Bononiensis. Proceedings of the Fourth International Congress of Neo-Latin Studies, Bologna, 26 August to 1 September 1979*, edited by R.J. Schoeck, 224–38. Binghamton: Center for Medieval and Early Renaissance Studies.

Covarrubias y Horozco, Sebastián. 1611. *Tesoro de la lengua castellana o española*. Madrid: Luis Sánchez.

– 2006. *Tesoro de la lengua castellana o española*. Edited by Ignacio Arellano and Rafael Zafra. Madrid: Iberoamericana.

Cowell, Edward Byles. 1851. "Spanish Literature." *Westminster and Foreign Quarterly Review* 54:281–323.

Cox Davis, Nina. 1995. "Marriage and Investment in *El celoso extremeño*." *Romanic Review* 86 (4): 639–55.

Cresswell, Tim. 2015. *Place: An Introduction*. Chichester, West Sussex: Wiley Blackwell.

Cruz, Anne J. 1999. *Discourses of Poverty: Social Reform in the Spanish Picaresque Novel*. Toronto: University of Toronto Press.

– 2011. "Reading over Men's Shoulders: Noblewomen's Libraries and Reading Practices." In *Women's Literacy in Early Modern Spain and the New World*, edited by Anne J. Cruz and Rosilie Hernández, 41–58. Burlington, VT: Ashgate.

Cruz, Anne J., and Rosilie Hernández, eds. 2011. *Women's Literacy in Early Modern Spain and the New World*. Burlington, VT: Ashgate.

Cruz Isidoro, Fernando. 1997. *Arquitectura sevillana del siglo XVII. Maestros mayores de la Catedral y del Concejo Hispalense*. Seville: Universidad de Sevilla.

Cuadrado, Agustín. 2010. *La novela negra como vehículo de crítica social: Una lectura espacial de "Los mares del sur," de Manuel Vázquez Montalbán. Letras hispanas: revista de literatura y cultura* 7:199–217.

Curtius, Ernst Robert. 1973. *European Literature and the Latin Middle Ages*. Translated by Willard R. Trask. New York: Harper & Row.

Dadson, Trevor J. 2012. "'Poesía que vive en variantes': retorno a Antonio Rodríguez-Moñino de mano del conde de Salinas." In *De re typographica. Nueve estudios en homenaje a Jaime Moll*, edited by Víctor Infantes and Julián Martín Abad, 73–93. Madrid: Calambur.

Dante Alighieri. 1970–5. *Comedy*. Edited and translated by Charles S. Singleton. Chicago: University of Chicago Press.

– 2014. *Dante's Lyric Poetry: Poems of Youth and the Vita Nuova (1283–1292)*. Edited by Teodolinda Barolini, Richard S. Lansing et al. Toronto: University of Toronto Press.

de Armas, Frederick A. 1986. *The Return of Astraea: An Astral-Imperial Myth in Calderon*. Lexington: University of Kentucky Press.

– 1987. "Rosaura Subdued: Victorian Readings of Calderón's *La vida es sueño*." *South Central Review* 4:43–62.

– 1993. "The Critical Tower." In *The Prince in the Tower: Perceptions of "La vida es sueño,"* edited by Frederick A. de Armas, 3–14. Lewisburg, PA: Bucknell University Press.

– 2005. "Simple Magic: Ekphrasis from Antiquity to the Age of Cervantes." In *Ekphrasis in the Age of Cervantes*, edited by Frederick A. de Armas, 13–31. Lewisburg, PA: Bucknell University Press.

– 2006. *Quixotic Frescoes: Cervantes and Italian Renaissance Art*. Toronto: University of Toronto Press.

– 2013. "Los misterios de Mercurio: Viajes, mitos y latrocinios en *La gitanilla*." In *Viaje, ciudades y espacio*, edited by Luis Alburquerque y Oana Andreia Sambrian. *Hispania Felix* 4:58–75.

– 2019. "Chained by Her Words: Calderón's *La gran Cenobia* and the Perils of the Sublime." In *Women Warriors in Early Modern Spain*, edited by Susan L. Fischer and Frederick A. de Armas, 50–65. Newark: University of Delaware Press.

– 2022a. "Celestial and Transgressive Banquets in the Theatre of the Spanish Golden Age." In *The Gastronomical Arts in Spain: Food and Etiquette*, edited by Frederick A. de Armas and James Mandrell, 139–73. Toronto: University of Toronto Press.

– 2022b. *Cervantes' Architectures; The Dangers Outside*. Toronto: University of Toronto Press.

de Certeau, Michel. 1970. "L'Expérience spirituelle." *Christus* 68:488–98.

– 1984. *The Practice of Everyday Life*. Translated by Steven Rendall. Berkeley: University of California Press.

de la Flor, Fernando R. 2007. *Era melancólica. Figuras del imaginario barroco*. Palma de Mallorca: José J. de Olañeta/Edicions Univ. de les Illes Balears.

De Paermentier, Els. 2008. "Experiencing Space Through Women's Convent Rules: The Rich Clares in Medieval Ghent (Thirteenth to Fourteenth Centuries)." *Medieval Feminist Forum* 44 (1): 53–68.

Dent-Young, John. 2009. *Selected Poems of Garcilaso de la Vega: A Bilingual Edition*. Chicago: University of Chicago Press.

Di Cori, Paola. 2015. "¿Qué es un lugar? La topología espiritual de Michel de Certeau." *La torre del virrey. Revista de Estudios culturales* 17 (1):86–100.

Domínguez, Julia. 2022. *Quixotic Memories: Cervantes and Memory in Early Modern Spain*. Toronto: University of Toronto Press.

Domínguez-Hermida, Beatriz. 2009. "Sociedad decapitada en el teatro del Siglo de Oro: *El villano en su rincón* de Lope de Vega, *La ventura con el nombre* de Tirso de Molina y *El amor constante* de Guillén de Castro." PhD diss., University of Colorado at Boulder.

Dunn, Leslie C., and Nancy A. Jones. 1994. *Embodied Voices: Representing Female Vocality in Western Culture*. Cambridge: Cambridge University Press.

Dunning, Chester. 2001. "Who Was Tsar Dmitrii?" *Slavic Review* 60 (4): 705–29.

Dyndor, Zoe. 2015. "The Gibbet in the Landscape: Locating the Criminal Corpse in Mid-Eighteenth-Century England." In *A Global History of Execution and the Criminal Corpse*, edited by Richard Ward, 102–25. New York: Palgrave.

Eggington, William. 2016. *The Man Who Invented Fiction: How Cervantes Ushered in the Modern World*. New York: Bloomsbury.

Eisenstein, Elizabeth. 1968. "Some Conjectures about the Impact of Printing on Western Society and Thought: A Preliminary Report." *Journal of Modern History* 40 (1): 1–56.

Enterline, Lynn. 2000. *The Rhetoric of the Body from Ovid to Shakespeare*. Cambridge: Cambridge University Press.

Estévez Molinero, Ángel. 1995. "La (re)escritura cervantina de Pedro de Urdemalas." *Cervantes: Bulletin of the Cervantes Society of America* 15 (1): 82–93.

Etlin, Richard A. 2012. "Architecture and the Sublime." In *The Sublime from Antiquity to the Present*, edited by Timothy M. Costelloe, 230–74. Cambridge: Cambridge University Press.

Fenno, Jonathan. 2008. "The Mist Shed by Zeus in *Iliad* XVII." *Classical Journal* 104 (1): 1–9.

Fernández Chaves, Manuel F., and Rafael M. Pérez García. 2012. "La penetración económica portuguesa en la Sevilla del siglo XVI." *Espacio, tiempo y forma serie IV, Historia moderna* 25:199–222.

Fernández Cuesta, Nemesio. 1872. *Diccionario enciclopédico de la lengua española con todas las vozes, frazes, refranes y locuciones usadas en España y las Américas españolas, Tomo II*. Madrid: Imprenta y Librería de Gaspar y Roig.

Feros, Antonio. 2008. "Art and Spanish Society: The Historical Context, 1577–1623." In *El Greco to Velázquez: Art during the Reign of Philip III*, edited by Sarah Schroth and Ronnie Baer, 15–39. Boston: Museum of Fine Arts.

Ferri Coll, José María. 2006. *Los tumultos del alma: de la expresión melancólica en la poesía española del Siglo de Oro*. Valencia: Institució Alfons el Magnànim.

Ficino, Marsilio. 1985. *The Letters of Marsilio Ficino*. Translated by the Language Department of the School of Economic Science, London. New York: Gingko.

Findlen, Paula. 2006. "Anatomy Theaters, Botanical Gardens, and Natural History Collections." In *The Cambridge History of Science*, edited by Lorraine Daston and Katharine Park, 272–89. Cambridge: Cambridge University Press.

Flint, Valerie. 2000. "Space and Discipline in Early Medieval Europe." *Medieval Practices of Space*. Edited by Barbara A. Hanawalt and Michal Kobialka, 149–66. Minneapolis: University of Minnesota Press.

Flores Marini, C. 1966. "La arquitectura de los conventos en el Siglo XVI." *Artes de México* nos. 86/87, 5–10.

Font-Paz, Carme. 2022. "A Resounding God: Acoustic Representations of the Divine in Early Modern Women's Spiritual Writing." *Early Modern Women: An Interdisciplinary Journal*. 17 (1): 139–47.

Forcione, Alban K. 1970. *Cervantes, Aristotle and the "Persiles."* Princeton, NJ: Princeton University Press.

– 2004. "Cervantes' Night-Errantry: The Deliverance of the Imagination." *Bulletin of Spanish Studies* 81 (4–5): 451–73.

Foucault, Michel. 1971. *The Order of Things. An Archeology of the Human Sciences*. New York: Vintage Books.

– 1979. *Discipline and Punish: The Birth of the Prison*. Translated by Alan Sheridan. New York: Vintage.

– 1980. *Power/Knowledge: Selected Interviews and Other Writings, 1972–79*. Edited by Colin Gordon. New York: Pantheon.

– 1986. "Of Other Spaces." *Diacritics* 16 (Spring): 22–7.

Fox, Michael V. 2010. *Proverbs 1–8: A New Translation with Introduction and Commentary*. Anchor Yale Bible. New Haven, CT: Yale University Press.

Fraticelli, Bárbara. 2002. "La creación de un espacio imaginario: Los españoles y Lisboa." In *Historia y poética de la ciudad: Estudios sobre las ciudades de la Península*, edited by Eugenia Popeanga and Bárbara Fraticelli, 317–26. Madrid: Universidad Complutense de Madrid, Editorial Complutense.

French, Marilyn. 1976. *The Book as World: James Joyce's "Ulysses."* Cambridge: Harvard University Press.

Freud, Sigmund. 1978. "Mourning and Melancholia." In *The Standard Edition of the Complete Psychological Works of Sigmund Freud*, translated by James Strachey, 14:243–58. London: Hogarth.

Friedlander, Gerald, trans. 1981. *Pirk̤ê de Rabbi Eliezer (The Chapters of Rabbi Eliezer the Great)*. New York: Sepher-Hermon Press.

Friedman, Edward H. 1977. "Dramatic Structure in Cervantes and Lope: The Two *Pedro de Urdemalas* Plays." *Hispania* 60 (3): 486–97.

– 1981. *The Unifying Concept: Approaches to Cervantes' "Comedias."* York, SC: Spanish Literature Publications.

– 1998. "Miguel de Cervantes Saavedra (1547–1616)." In *Spanish Dramatists of the Golden Age: A Bio-Bibliographical Sourcebook*, edited by Mary Parker, 63–74. Westport, CT: Greenwood Press.

– 2018. *Pedro the Schemer: A Work in Progress. An Adaptation of Miguel de Cervantes's "Pedro de Urdemalas."* Newark, DE: Juan de la Cuesta.

Fucikova, Eliska, James M. Bradburne, and Beket Bukovinska, eds. 1997. *Rudolf II and Prague: The Court and the City*. London: Thames & Hudson.

Funkenstein, Amos. 2018. *Theology and the Scientific Imagination from the Middle Ages to the Seventeenth Century*. 2nd ed., with new forward by Jonathan Sheehan. Princeton, NJ: Princeton University Press.

Gallagher, Catherine. 2006. "The Rise of Fictionality." In *The Novel, Volume 1: History, Geography, and Culture*, edited by Franco Moretti, 336–63. Princeton, NJ: Princeton University Press.

Gamboa, Yolanda, and Noemi Marin. 2007. "Colonizing Naples: Rhetoric of Allure and the 17th Century Imaginary." *Journal of Electronic Antiquity* 11 (1): 125–38.

García Aguilar, Ignacio, Luis Gómez Canseco, and Adrián J. Sáez. 2016. *El teatro de Miguel de Cervantes*. Madrid: Visor Libros.

García Hidalgo Villena, Cipriano. 2021. "Sor Ana Dorotea de Austria (1612–1694) y la exaltación de las mujeres fuertes." In *Las mujeres y las artes: Mecenas, artistas, emprendedoras, coleccionistas*, edited by Beatriz Blasco Esquivias, Jonatan Jair López Muñoz, and Sergio Ramiro Ramírez, 115–33. Madrid: Abada Editores.

García Martínez, José Luis. 2015. *Arquitectura barroca en la ciudad de Huete. Un enclave arquitectónico en el obispado de Cuenca*. Cuenca: Diputación Provincial de Cuenca.

García Santo-Tomas, Enrique. 2004. *Espacio urbano y creación literaria en el Madrid de Felipe IV*. Pamplona/Madrid/Frankfurt: Universidad de Navarra/Iberoamericana/Vervuert.

– 2017. *The Refracted Muse: Literature and Optics in Early Modern Spain.* Translated by Vincent Barletta. Chicago: University of Chicago Press.

García Sanz, Ana. 2010. "El monasterio de las Descalzas Reales: Arte y espiritualidad en el Madrid de los Austrias." In *Obras Maestras Restauradas,* 11–38. Madrid: Patrimonio Nacional.

García-Arenal, Mercedes. 2020. "Introduction: Facing Uncertainty in Early Modern Iberia." In *The Quest for Certainty in Early Modern Europe: From Inquisition to Inquiry 1550–1700,* edited by Barbara Fuchs and Mercedes García-Arenal, 3–24. Toronto: University of Toronto Press.

García-Bryce, Ariadna. 2015. "*Caveat Lector*: A Female Public in 'El celoso extremeño.'" *Hispanófila* 173:79–95.

Garcilaso de la Vega. 2020. *Poesía.* Edited by Ignacio García Aguilar. Madrid: Cátedra.

Garoian, Charles R. 2001. "Performing the Museum." *Studies in Art Education* 42 (3): 234–48.

Garrido Aranda, Antonio. 1995. *Cultura alimentaria de España y América.* Huesca: Val de Onsera.

Gasta, Chad. 2011. "Cervantes's Theory of Relativity in *Don Quixote.*" *Cervantes: Bulletin of the Cervantes Society of America* 31 (1): 51–82.

Gilchrist, Roberta. 1994. *Gender and Material Culture: The Archaeology of Religious Women.* London: Routledge, 150–1.

Gillies, John. 2023. "Towards a Phenomenology of Shakespeare's Sky." *Linguaculture* 14 (1): 69–81.

Girón Negrón, Luis M. 2001. *Alfonso de La Torré's "Visión Deleytable": Philosophical Rationalism and the Religious Imagination in 15th Century Spain.* Leiden: Brill.

– 2019. "Pedro de Toledo's *Mostrador e enseñador de los turbados*: The Christian Reception of Maimonides' *Guide* in Fifteenth-Century Spain." In *Maimonides' "Guide of the Perplexed" in Translation: A History from the Thirteenth Century to the Twentieth,* edited by Josef Stern, James T. Robinson, and Yonatan Shemesh, 141–79. Chicago: University of Chicago Press.

Gombrich, Ernst H. 1963. *Meditations on a Hobby Horse, and Other Essays on the Theory of Art.* London: Phaidon Press.

Gómez Alfaro, Antonio. 2014. "La verdadera historia de los gitanos de Madrid." *O Tchatchipen* no. 88, 18–30.

Gómez Sánchez, Diego. 1998. *La muerte edificada: El impulso centrífugo de los cementerios de la ciudad de Cuenca (siglos XI–XX).* Cuenca: Universidad de Castilla-La Mancha; Diputación Provincial de Cuenca.

González Puche, Alejandro. 2012. *"Pedro de Urdemalas," la aventura experimental del teatro cervantino.* Vigo: Academia del Hispanismo.

Goscilo, Helena. 2010. "The Mirror in Art: Vanitas, Veritas, and Vision." *Studies in 20th & 21st Century Literature* 34 (2): 282–319.

Göttler, Christine. 2018. "Realms of Solitude in Late Medieval and Early Modern European Cultures: An Introduction." In *Solitudo: Spaces, Places, and Times of Solitude in Late Medieval and Early Modern Cultures*, edited by Karl. A.E, Enenkel and Christine Göttler, 1–28. Leiden: Brill. https://brill.com/view/book/edcoll/9789004367432/BP000010.xml

Grafton, Anthony. 2004. "Conflict and Harmony in the *Collegium Gellanium*." In *The World of Aulus Gellius*, edited by Leofranc Holford-Strevens and Amiel Vardi, 318–43. Oxford: Oxford University Press.

Greenblatt, Stephen. 1988. *Shakespearean Negotiations: The Circulation of Social Energy in Renaissance England*. Berkeley: University of California Press.

Grieve, Patricia. 1991. "Embroidering with Saintly Threads: María de Zayas Challenges Cervantes and the Church." *Renaissance Quarterly* 44 (1): 86–106.

Guasch Melis, Ana Eva. 1999. "Gitanos viejos y gitanos nuevos." In *Actas del VIII Coloquio Internacional de la Asociación de Cervantistas*: *El Toboso, 23–26 de abril de 1998*, edited by José Ramón Fernández de Cano y Martín, 327–40. Toledo: Exmo. Ayuntamiento de El Toboso.

Guggenheimer, Heinrich, trans. 2011. *The Jerusalem Talmud: Edition, Translation, and Commentary*. Vol. 13. Berlin: De Gruyter.

Guntert, Georges. 2002. "*La vida es sueño*: Algo más sobre el hipogrifo violento." In *Calderón 2000: homenaje a Kurt Reichenberger en su 80 cumpleanos*, edited by Ignacio Arellano, 495–507. Kassel: Reichenberger.

Hammer-Tugendhat, Daniela. 2015. "Mirror, Mirror on the Wall: Woman before the Mirror by Frans van Mieris." In *The Visible and the Invisible: On Seventeenth- Century Dutch Painting*, translated by Margarethe Clausen, 175–92. Berlin: De Gruyter.

Harrison, Robert. 1987. *Darkness at Night: A Riddle of the Universe*. Cambridge, MA: Harvard University Press.

Harrison-Pepper, Sally. 1990. *Drawing a Circle in the Square: Street Performing in New York's Washington Square Park*. Jackson: University Press of Mississippi.

Hegstrom, Valerie. 2017. "'La décima musa portuguesa' and Her *Soledades de Buçaco*: Gendered Landscape Poetry Dedicated to the Nuns of Santo Alberto." *Calíope* 22 (2): 145–64.

Heisenberg, Werner. 1972. *Physics and Beyond: Encounters and Conversations*. Translated by Arnold J. Pomerans. New York: Harper & Row.

Hempel, Wido. 1986. "El labrador hecho rey: Un tema con variaciones en la literatura del Siglo de Oro." *Ibero-Amerikanisches Archiv* 12 (2): 123–39.

Henningsen, Gustav, ed. 2004. *The Salazar Documents: Inquistor Alonso de Salazar Frías and Others on the Basque Witch Persecution*. Leiden: Brill.

Herman, David. 2002. *Story Logic: Problems and Possibilities of Narrative*. Lincoln: University of Nebraska Press.

Hernández, Rosilie. 2002. "*La fuerza del amor* or *The Power of Self-Love*: Zayas's response to Cervantes's *La fuerza de la sangre*." *Hispanic Review* 70 (1): 39–57.

– 2011. "The Politics of Exemplarity: Biblical Women and the Education of the Spanish Lady in Martín Carrillo, Sebastián de Herrera Barnuevo, and María de Guevara." In *Women's Literacy in Early Modern Spain and the New World*, edited by Anne J. Cruz and Rosilie Hernández, 225–41. Burlington, VT: Ashgate.

– 2019. *Immaculate Conceptions: The Power of the Religious Imagination in Early Modern Spain*. Toronto: University of Toronto Press.

Herrera, Fernando de. 1985. *Poesía castellana original completa*. Edited by Cristóbal Cuevas. Madrid: Cátedra.

Hesse, Everett W. 1964. "Introduction." In *Fuente ovejuna and La dama boba*, by Lope de Vega, edited by Everett W. Hesse, 9–21. New York: Dell.

Hills, Helen. 2004. *Invisible City. The Architecture of Devotion in Seventeenth Century Neapolitan Convents*. Oxford: Oxford University Press.

Hiniesta, R.M. 2007. *La antigua bóveda astrológica de Fernando Gallego: Nuevas aportaciones y evaluación de su estado de conservación*. Salamanca: Centro de Estudios Salmantinos.

Homer. *Odyssey*. 1995. Translated by A.T. Murray. Revised by George E. Dimock. 2 vols. Cambridge, MA: Harvard University Press.

Horacek, Ivana. 2015. *Alchemy of the Gift: Things and Material Tranformations at the Court of Rudolf II*. Vancouver: University of British Columbia.

Hornby, Richard. 1986. *Drama, Metadrama and Perception*. Lewisburg, PA: Bucknell University Press.

Horowitz, Eli, Kevin Moffett, and Matthew Derby. 2012–13. "FAQ." *The Silent History*. www.thesilenthistory.com/faq. Accessed 7 Oct. 2022.

Huarte de San Juan, Juan. 1989. *Examen de ingenios para las ciencias*. Edited by Guillermo Serés. Madrid: Cátedra.

– 2014. *The Examination of Men's Wits*. Translated by Richard Carew. Edited by Rocío G. Sumillera. London: MHRA.

Hutchinson, Steven. 1992. *Cervantine Journeys*. Madison: University of Wisconsin Press.

Ibáñez, Isabel. 2005. "Inversion et spécularité dans les 'comédies de tyrans' de Tirso de Molina." *Bulletin Hispanique* 107 (2): 347–432.

Ibn Gabirol, Solomon. 2001. *Selected Poems*. Translated by Peter Cole. Princeton, NJ: Princeton University Press.

– 2003. *The Kingly Crown/Keter Malkhut*. Translated by Barnard Lewis. Notre Dame, IN: University of Notre Dame Press.

Ife, B.W. 1986. *Reading and Fiction in Golden-Age Spain*. Cambridge: Cambridge UP.

Jackson, S.W. 1986. *Melancholia and Depression: From Hippocratic Times to Modern Times*. New Haven, CT: Yale University Press.

Jacobs, Frederika. 2008. "Rethinking the Divide: Cult Images and the Cult of Images." In *Renaissance Theory*, edited by James Elkins and Robert Williams, 95–113. New York: Routledge.

Jacobson, Howard, trans. 1983. *The Exagoge of Ezekiel*. Cambridge: Cambridge University Press.

Jameson, Frederic. 1991. *Postmodernism, or, The Cultural Logic of Late Capitalism*. Durham, NC: Duke University Press.

Janson, Anthony F. 1985. "The Convex Mirror as a Vanitas Symbol." *Notes in the History of Art* 4 (2–3): 51–4.

Jauralde Pou, Pablo. 1982. "El público y la realidad histórica de la literatura española de los siglos XVI y XVII." *Edad de Oro* 1:55–64.

Johnson, Mark. 1978. "La retórica del saber en el Jardín de flores curiosas de Antonio de Torquemada." *Journal of Hispanic Philology* 3:69–83.

Johnson, Paul. 2020. *Affective Geographies: Cervantes, Emotion, and the Literary Mediterranean*. Toronto: University of Toronto Press.

Johnson, William. 2010. *Readers and Reading Culture in the High Roman Empire: A Study of Elite Communities*. Oxford: Oxford University Press.

Jones, Nicholas. 2019. *Staging Habla de negros: Radical Performances of the African Diaspora in Early Modern Spain*. University Park: Pennsylvania State University Press.

Kagan, Richard. 1989. *Spanish Cities of the Golden Age: The Views of Anton van den Wyngaerde*. Berkeley: University of California Press.

– 2000. *Urban Images of the Hispanic World, 1493–1793*. New Haven, CT: Yale University Press.

Kahn, Aaron M., ed. 2021. *The Oxford Handbook of Cervantes*. Oxford: Oxford University Press.

Kaufman, Thomas DaCosta. 1988. *The School of Prague: Painting at the Court of Rudolph II*. Chicago: University of Chicago Press.

Kearney, Richard. 1999. *Poetics of Modernity*. Amherst, NY: Promethius Books.

Kennedy, Ruth Lee. 1969. "Tirso's *La ventura con el nombre*: Its Source and Date of Composition." *Bulletin of the Comediantes* 21 (2): 35–45.

Klestinec, Cynthia. 2011. *Theaters of Anatomy: Students, Teachers, and Traditions of Dissection in Renaissance Venice*. Baltimore: Johns Hopkins University Press.

Klibanski, Raymond, Erwin Panofsky, and Fritz Saxl. 1964. *Saturn and Melancholy: Studies in the History of Natural Philosophy, Religion, and Art*. New York: Basic Books.

Knott, Kim. 2005. *The Location of Religion: A Spatial Analysis*. London: Equinox.

Koch, Carol. 2008. "El silencio de Preciosa: El centro y el margen de *La gitanilla*." In *Novelas ejemplares: Las grietas de la ejemplaridad*, edited by Julio Baena, 79–90. Newark, DE: Juan de la Cuesta.

Koudounaris, Paul. 2011. *The Empire of Death: A Cultural History of Ossuaries and Charnel Houses*. New York: Thames & Hudson.

Laffranque, Marie. 2016. "Encuentro y coexistencia de dos sociedades en el Siglo de Oro. *La gitanilla* de Miguel de Cervantes." In *Actas del Quinto*

Congreso de la Asociación Internacional de Hispanistas: Celebrado en Bordeaux del 2 al 8 de septiembre de 1974, edited by Maxime Chevalier, François Lopez, Joseph Perez, and Noël Salomon, 549–61. Burdeos: Instituto de Estudios Ibéricos e Iberoamericanos, Université de Bordeaux III.

Laqueur, Thomas. 1990. *Making Sex*. Cambridge, MA: Harvard University Press.

Lara Alberola, Eva. 2011. *Hechiceras y brujas en la literatura española de los Siglos de Oro*. Valencia: Universidad de Valencia.

Lefebvre, Henri. 1991. *The Production of Space*. Translated by Donald Nicholson-Smith. Oxford: Blackwell. https://iberian-connections.yale.edu /wp-content/uploads/2020/04/The-production-of-space-by-Henri -Lefebvre-translated-by-Donald-Nicholson-Smith.pdf.

Lehfeldt, Elizabeth. 2005. *Religious Women in Golden Age Spain: The Permeable Cloister*. Farnham, UK: Ashgate.

Lehtonen, Kelly. 2016. "*Peri Hypsous* in Translation: The Sublime in Sixteenth-Century Epic Poetry." *Philological Quarterly* 95 (3–4): 449–65.

Lerner, Isaías. 1980. "Marginalidad en las novelas ejemplares. *La gitanilla*." *Lexis* 4 (1): 47–59.

– 1998. "Misceláneas y polianteas del siglo de oro español." *Actas del Congreso Internacional sobre Humanismo y Renacimiento*, edited by Maurilio Pérez González, vol. 2, 71–82. León: Universidad de León.

Levi-Strauss, Claude. 1979. *Tristes tropiques*. Translated by John and Doreen Weightman. New York: Atheneum.

Lida de Malkiel, María Rosa. 1975. "El ruiseñor de las *Geórgicas* y su influencia en la lírica española de la Edad de Oro." In *La tradición clásica en España*, 100–17. Barcelona: Ariel.

Lilao Franca, Óscar, and Carmen Castrillo Gónzález. 2002. *Catálogo de manuscritos de la Biblioteca Universitaria de Salamanca. II. Manuscritos 1680–2777*. Salamanca: Universidad de Salamanca.

Longinus, 1964. *On the Sublime*. Edited by Donald A. Russell. Oxford: Clarendon Press.

– 1991. *On Great Writing (On the Sublime)*. Edited and translated by G.M.A. Grube. Indianapolis: Hackett Publishing Company.

– 1995. *On the Sublime*. Translated by W.H. Fyfe and Donald Russell. In *Aristotle: The Poetics; Longinus: On the Sublime; Demetrius: On Style*, 182–5. Cambridge, MA: Harvard University Press.

Lope de Vega, Félix [attributed]. 1916. *El rey por semejanza*. In *Obras de…, Ac.N.*, 2, edited by Emilio Cotarelo y Mori, 494–523. Madrid: "Revista de Archivos, Bibliotecas y Museos." Digital edition by Ángela Martínez Fernández. *ARTELOPE: Base de datos y argumentos del teatro de Lope de Vega*. https:// artelope.uv.es/biblioteca/textosAL/AL0850_ElReyPorSuSemejanza.php

López Bueno, Begoña, ed. 1997. *Las "Anotaciones" de Fernando de Herrera: Doce estudios*. Seville: Universidad de Sevilla.

López Poza, Sagrario. 1990. "Florilegios, poliantheas, repertorios de sentencias y lugares comunes. Aproximación bibliográfica." *Criticón* no. 49, 61–76.

Lorenzo Sanz, Eufemio. 1979. *Comercio de España con América en la época de Felipe II*. Vol. 1. Valladolid: Servicio de Publicaciones de la Diputación Provincial.

Macfarlane, Alan, and Gerry Martin. 2002. *Glass: A World History*. Chicago: University of Chicago Press.

MacKay, Ruth. 2012. *The Baker Who Pretended to Be King of Portugal*. Chicago: University of Chicago Press.

Macrí, Oreste. 1959. *Fernando de Herrera*. Madrid: Gredos.

Maestro, Jesús G. 2000. *La escena imaginaria: Póetica del teatro de Miguel de Cervantes*. Madrid: Iberoamericana Vervuert.

Marcela de San Félix. 2016, 9 April. "Otra a la soledad de las celdas." *Ciudad Selva*. Edited by Luis López Nieves. https://ciudadseva.com/texto/otra -a-la-soledad-de-las-celdas

Mariana, Juan de. 1854. *Obras*. Edited by M. Rivadeneyra. Vol. 2. Madrid: M. Rivadeneyra.

Marino, John A. 2010. *Becoming Neapolitan: Citizen Culture in Baroque Naples*. Baltimore: Johns Hopkins University Press.

Martín Benito, José Ignacio. 2017. "El 'cursus honorum' de Enrique Pimentel (1574–1653), obispo de Valladolid y Cuenca." *Brigecio* 27:59–82.

Martínez, Miguel. 2006. "Quien me entendiere me declare": España, Holanda y los indios de América en *La hora de todos*." *Voz y Letra* 17:93–120.

Martínez Lara, Pedro M. 2016. "Casa Lonja de mercaderes de Sevilla." *Identidad e imagen de Andalucía en la Edad Moderna*. Dir. Francisco Andújar Castillo. http://www2.ual.es/ideimand/casa-lonja-de-mercaderes-de -sevilla/. Accessed 7 Oct. 2022.

Martínez Martínez, Manuel. 2004. "Los gitanos en el reinado de Felipe II (1556–1598). El fracaso de una integración." *Chronica Nova* no. 30, 401–30.

Martínez-Vidal, Álvar, and José Pardo-Tomás. 2005. "Anatomical Theaters and the Teaching of Anatomy in Early Modern Spain." *Medical History* 49 (3): 251–80.

Mártir Rizo, Juan Pablo. 1629. *Historia de la muy noble y leal ciudad de Cuenca…* Madrid: Herederos de la viuda de Pedro de Madrigal.

Márquez Villanueva, Francisco. 1985. "La buenaventura de Preciosa." *Nueva Revista de Filología Hispánica* 34 (2): 741–68.

Massey, Doreen. 1994. *Space, Place, and Gender*. Oxford: Polity Press.

Matteoni, Francesca. 2016. "The Criminal Corpse in Pieces." *Mortality* 21 (3): 198–209.

Mattioli, Emilio. 1988. "Gli studi di Gustavo Costa sul Sublime in Italia." *Studi e problemi di critica testuale* no. 36, 139–55.

Mazzotta, Giuseppe. 2001. *Cosmopoiesis: The Renaissance Experiment*. Toronto: University of Toronto Press.

McKendrick, Melveena. 2000. *Playing the King: Lope de Vega and the Limits of Conformity*. London: Tamesis.

McNair, Alexander J. 2003. "Re-evaluating Herrera's Sonnet XXXIII: Notes on Sense and Intellect in the Lyric Persona of *Algunas Obras*." *Hispanic Review* 71 (4): 565–84.

Mele, Eugenio. 1930. "In margine alle poesie di Garcilaso." *Bulletin Hispanique* 32 (3): 218–45.

Merrifield, Andrew. 1993. "Place and Space: A Lefebvrian Reconciliation." *Transactions of the Institute of British Geographers* 18 (4): 516–31.

Mexía, Pedro. 2003. *Silva de varia lección*. Edited by Isaías Lerner. Madrid: Castalia.

Middlebrook, Leah. 2009. *Imperial Lyric: New Poetry and New Subjects in Early Modern Spain*. University Park, PA: Penn State University Press.

Miele, Michele, ed. 1995. *Le origine della Madonna dell'Arco: Il "Compendio dell'historia, miracoli e gratie" di Arcangelo Domenici (1608)*. Naples: Domenicana Italiana.

Minkowski, Eugène. 1967. *Vers une cosmologie, fragments philosophiques*. Paris: Aubier-Montaigne.

Mira Caballos, Esteban. 1994. "Las licencias de esclavos negros a Hispanoamérica (1544–1550)." *Revista de Indias* 54 (201): 273–97.

Montero, Juan. 1987. *La controversia sobre las Anotaciones herrerianas*. Seville: Servicio de Publicaciones del Excmo. Ayuntamiento de Sevilla.

Morillo. María Dolores. 2019. "Pedro de Urdemalas/Nicolás de los Ríos o el polítropolingüístico: Multiplicidad y heteronomía en *Pedro de Urdemalas*." *Cervantes: Bulletin of the Cervantes Society of America* 39 (1): 29–45.

Morley, S. Griswold, and Courtney Bruerton. 1940. *The Chronology of Lope de Vega's Comedias*. New York: Modern Language Association.

Morrás, María. 2020. "Saints Textual: Embodying Female Exemplarity in Spanish Literature." In *Gender and Exemplarity in Medieval and Early Modern Spain*, edited by María Morrás, Rebeca Sanmartín, and Yonsoo Kim, 1–39. Leiden: Brill.

Morris, David B. 1985. "Gothic Sublimity." *New Literary History* 16 (2): 299–319.

Morris, Marcia A. 2018. *Writing in the Time of Troubles: False Dmitry in Russian Literature*. Boston: Academic Studies Press.

Mortimer, Ian. 2016. *Millenium: From Religion to Revolution. How Civilization Has Changed over a Thousand Years*. New York/London: Pegasus Books.

Müller-Bochat, Eberhard. 1984. "Las ideas de Cervantes sobre el teatro y su síntesis en *Pedro de Urdemalas*." *Arbor* 119:225–36.

Nadeau, Carolyn. 2013. "Transformation and Transgression at the Banquet Scene in *La Celestina*." In *Objects of Culture in the Literature of Imperial Spain*, edited by Mary E. Barnard and Frederick A. de Armas, 205–27. Toronto: University of Toronto Press.

Navarrete, Ignacio.1991. "Decentering Garcilaso: Herrera's Attack on the Canon." *PMLA* 106 (1): 21–33.

– 1994. *Orphans of Petrarch: Poetry and Theory in the Spanish Renaissance.* Berkeley: University of California Press.

Navarrete, Ignacio, and Mary Quinn. 2016. "Imagining Domesticity in Cervantes' *Novelas ejemplares* and *Don Quijote.*" *Bulletin of Spanish Studies* 93 (7–8): 1181–1203.

Navarro Ledesma, Francisco. 1973. *Cervantes: The Man and the Genius.* Translated by Don and Gabriela Bliss. New York: Charterhouse.

Neusner, Jacob, trans. 1985. *Genesis Rabbah: The Judaic Commentary to the Book of Genesis, Parashiyyot One through Thirty-Three.* Vol. 1. Atlanta: Scholars Press.

Nieves Baranda, Anne J. Cruz, ed. 2018. *The Routledge Research Companion to Early Modern Spanish Writers.* London: Routledge.

Nieves Baranda Leturio, Anne J. Cruz, and María Carmen Marín Pina. 2014. *Letras en la celda. Cultura escrita de los conventos femeninos en la España moderna.* Madrid: Vervuert.

Nirenberg, David. 2014. "'Judaism,' 'Islam,' and the Dangers of Knowledge in Christian Culture, with Special Attention To the Case of Alfonso X, 'the Wise,' of Castile." In *Mapping Knowledge: Cross-Pollination in Late Antiquity and the Middle Ages,* edited by Charles Burnett and Pedro Mantas España, 253–76. Córdoba and London: Oriens Academic and The Warburg Institute.

Novísima recopilación de las leyes de España. Dividida en XII libros. Mandada formar por el señor don Carlos IV. 1805. Madrid.

Núñez Roldán, Francisco, ed. 2005. *La ciudad de Cervantes. Sevilla 1587–1600.* Seville: Ayuntamiento de Sevilla, Junta de Andalucía, Consejería de Cultura, Fundación El Monte, Caja San Fernando Obra Socia.

O'Brien, Eavan. 2010. *Women in the Prose of María de Zayas.* Woodbridge, UK: Tamesis.

Olivares, Julián. 2009. *Studies on Women's Poetry of the Golden Age: Tras el espejo la musa escribe.* Woodbridge, UK: Tamesis.

Olsen, H. Eric R. 2003. *The Calabrian Charlatan, 1598–1603. Messianic Nationalism in Early Modern Europe.* Basingstoke: Palgrave Macmillan.

Olson, Vibeke. 2017. "Blood, Sweat, Tears, and Milk: 'Fluid' Veneration, Sensory Contact, and Corporeal Presence in Medieval Devotional Art." In *Binding the Absent Body in Medieval and Modern Art: Abject, Virtual, and Alternate Bodies,* edited by Emily Kelley and Elizabeth Richards Rivenbark, 11–31. New York: Routledge.

Orlemanski, Julie. 2019. "Who Has Fiction? Modernity, Fictionality, and the Middle Ages." *New Literary History* 50 (2): 145–70.

Orobitg, Christine. 1997. *L'Humeur noire: Mélancolie, écriture et pensée en Espagne au XVIe et au XVIIe siècle.* Bethesda, MD: International Scholars Publications.

– 2010. "Melancolía e inspiración en la España del Siglo de Oro." *Bulletin of Spanish Studies* 87 (8): 17–31.

– 2014. "Del Examen de ingenios de Huarte a la ficción cervantina, o cómo se forja una revolución literaria." *Criticón* nos. 120–1, 3–39.

Orozco Díaz, Emilio. 1969. *El teatro y la teatralidad del Barroco.* Barcelona: Planeta.

Ortega y Gasset, José. 2005. *Ideas sobre el teatro y la novela.* Madrid: Alianza Editorial.

Ortiz Arza, Javier. 2015. "Dos hidalgos riojanos en el comercio atlántico y el tráfico esclavista con las Indias: Miguel Martínez de Jáuregui y Jerónimo de Jáuregui (S. XVI)." *Berceo* no. 168, 131–57.

Osorio, Alejandra B. 2017. "Courtly Ceremonies and a Cultural Urban Geography of Power in the Habsburg Spanish Empire." In *Cities and the Circulation of Culture in the Atlantic World: from the Early Modern to Modernism,* edited by Leonard von Morzé, 37–72. New York: Palgrave.

Oteiza, Blanca. 2020. "Geografías de guerra y amor en Tirso." *Criticón* no. 139, 69–78. https://doi.org/10.4000/criticon.16333.

Ovid. 1984. *Metamorphoses.* Translated by Frank Justus Miller. Revised by G.P. Goold. 2 vols. 2nd edition. Cambridge, MA: Harvard University Press.

Padrón, Ricardo. 2004. *The Spacious Word: Cartography, Literature, and Empire in Early Modern Spain.* Chicago: University of Chicago Press.

– 2020. *The Indies of the Setting Sun: How Early Modern Spain Mapped the Far East as the Transpacific West.* Chicago: University of Chicago Press.

Pardo, Italo. 1994. "On the Neapolitan Way of Death: Representations of Mourning and the Hereafter." *Journal of Mediterranean Studies* 4 (1): 143–6.

Parker, Alexander A. 1982. "Segismundo's Tower: A Calderonian Myth." *Bulletin of Hispanic Studies* 59 (3): 247–56.

Pastor Comin, Juan José. 2007. *Cervantes: Música y poesía. El hecho musical en el pensamiento lírico cervantino.* Vigo: Editorial Academia del Hispanismo.

Pavel, Thomas. 1986. *Fictional Worlds.* Cambridge, MA: Harvard University Press.

Pendergast, Mark. 2003. *Mirror, Mirror: A History of the Human Love Affairs with Reflection.* New York: Basic Books.

Perry, Mary Elizabeth. 1980. *Crime and Society in Early Modern Seville.* Hanover, NH: University Press of New England.

Petrarch. 1976. *Petrarch's Lyric Poems.* Edited and translated by Robert M. Durling. Cambridge, MA: Harvard University Press.

Philo of Alexandria. 1929. *On the Creation; Moses I and II.* Translated by F.H. Colson and G.H. Whitaker. Cambridge, MA: Harvard University Press.

Piñero Ramírez, Pedro M., and Rogelio Reyes Cano. 2013. *La imagen de Sevilla en la obra de Cervantes: Espacio y paisaje humano*. Seville: Universidad de Sevilla.

Pinet, Simone. 2016. *The Task of the Cleric: Cartography, Translation, and Economics in Thirteenth-Century Iberia*. Toronto: University of Toronto Press.

Plato. 2013. *Republic*. Translated by Chris Emlyn-Jones and William Preddy. Cambridge, MA: Harvard University Press.

Pliny the Elder. 1855. *The Natural History of Pliny*, II. Translated by John Bostock and H.T. Riley. London: Henry G. Bohn.

Porter, James. 2016. *The Sublime in Antiquity*. Cambridge: Cambridge University Press.

Precht, Raoul. 1988. "Artificio y verdad en la comedia *Pedro de Urdemalas* de Cervantes." *Pliegos de Cordel* 3:51–71.

Predmore, Richard. 1973. *Cervantes*. London: Thames & Hudson.

Presberg, Charles D. 1998. "Precious Exchanges: The Poetics of Desire, Power, and Reciprocity in Cervantes's *La gitanilla*." *Cervantes* 18 (2): 53–73.

Pulido Serrano, Ignacio, y William Childers, dirs. 2020. *La Inquisición vista desde abajo*. Madrid/Frankfurt am Main: Iberoamericana/Vervuert.

Pythian Ode." In *Embodied Voices: Representing Female Vocality in Western Culture*, edited by Leslie C. Dunn and Nancy A. Jones, 17–34. Cambridge: Cambridge University Press.

Quintero, María Cristina. 1999. *Poetry as Play: "Gongorismo" and the "Comedia."*Amsterdam: John Benjamins Publishing Company.

Rallo Gruss, Asunción. 1978. "El sevillano Pedro Mexía, historiador de Carlos V." In *Actas del Primer Congreso de Historia de Andalucía. Andalucía moderna (siglos XVI-XVII)*, vol. 2, 307–14. Córdoba: Monte de Piedad y Caja de Ahorros de Córdoba.

– 1983. *Misceláneas del Siglo de Oro*. Madrid: Planeta.

– 1984. "Las misceláneas: Conformación y desarrollo de un género renacentista." *Edad de Oro* 3:159–80.

Ramachandran, Ayesha. 2015. *The Worldmakers: Global Imagining in Early Modern Europe*. Chicago: University of Chicago Press.

Refini, Eugenio. 2012. "Longinus and Poetic Imagination in Late Renaissance Literary Theory." In *Translations of the Sublime: The Early Modern Reception and Dissemination of Longinus Peri Hupsous in Rhetoric, the Visual Arts, Architecture and Theater*, edited by Caroline van Eck, Stijn Bussels, Maarten Delbeke, and Jurgern Pieters, 33–53. Boston: Brill.

Rhodes, Elizabeth. 2011. *Dressed to Kill. Death and Meaning in Zayas's "Desengaños."* Toronto: University of Toronto Press.

Ricapito, Joseph V. 1996. *Cervantes's "Novelas ejemplares": Between History and Creativity*. West Lafayette, IN: Purdue University Press.

Riva, Fernando. 2019. *"Nunca mayor sobervia comidió Luçifer." Límites del conocimiento y cultura claustral en el "Libro de Alexandre."* Madrid: Iberoamericana-Vervuert.

– 2020. "'La carne es la tierra': Microcosmic Adam, Cartographic Christ in the *Libro de Alexandre.*" *Journal of Medieval Iberian Studies* 12 (1): 44–69.

Rivers, Elias L., ed. and trans. 1966. *Renaissance and Baroque Poetry of Spain.* New York, Dell.

– ed. 1974. *Garcilaso de la Vega: Obras completas con comentario.* Madrid: Castalia.

Rochberg, Francesca. 2012. "The Expression of Terrestrial and Celestial Order in Ancient Mesopotamia." In *Ancient Perspectives: Maps and Their Place in Mesopotamia, Egypt, Greece and Rome,* edited by Richard J.A. Talbert, 9–46. Chicago: University of Chicago Press.

Rodríguez, Alfred, and Daniel Villa. 1990. "*Pedro de Urdemalas* de Lope de Vega: El disfraz varonil y el 'trickster.'" *Romance Notes* 31 (1): 53–57.

Rodríguez Cacho, Lina. 1993. "La selección de lo curioso en 'silvas' y 'jardines': Notas para la trayectoria del género." *Criticón* no. 58, 155–68.

Rojas, Fernando de. 2011. *La Celestina.* Edited by Francisco J. Lobera and Guillermo Serés. Madrid: Real Academia Española.

– 2012. *Celestina.* Translated by Margaret Sayers Peden. New Haven, CT: Yale University Press.

Rose, Gillian. 1993. *Feminism and Geography: The Limits of Geographical Knowledge.* Minneapolis: University of Minnesota Press.

Rossi, Paolo. 2006. *Logic and the Art of Memory.* Translated by Stephen Clucas. New York: Continuum.

Roth, Norman. 1978. "The 'Theft of Philosophy' by the Greeks from the Jews." *Classical Folia* 32 (1): 52–67.

Rowland, Ingrid. 1997. "The Intellectual Background of the School of Athens: Tracking Divine Wisdom in the Rome of Julius II." In *Raphael's "School of Athens,"* edited by Marcia Hall. Cambridge: Cambridge University Press.

Rubiera Fernández, J. 2002. "La movilidad espacial en la comedia española. El espacio itinerante." In *Actas del VI Congreso de AISO,* edited by Francisco Domínguez Matito and María Lusia Lobato López, vol. 2, 1545–54. Madrid/Frankfurt am Main: Iberoamericana/Vervuert.

Ruiz Pérez, Pedro. 1996. *El espacio de la escritura: en torno a una poética del espacio del texto barroco.* Bern: Lang.

Ryan, Marie-Laure. 2012. "Space." In *The Living Handbook of Narratology,* edited by Jan Christoph Meister. 13 Jan. 2021. https://www-archiv.fdm.uni -hamburg.de/lhn/node/55.html. Accessed 7 Oct 2022.

Ryan, Marie-Laure, Kenneth Foote, and Maoz Azaryahu. 2016. *Narrating Space/Spatializing Narrative: Where Narrative Theory and Geography Meet.* Columbus: Ohio State University Press.

Sabat de Rivers, Georgina. 1986. "Voces del convento: Sor Marcela, la hija de Lope." *Actas AIH* IX:591–600.

– 1993. "Soledades de sor Marcela." *La Torre* 25:17–35.

Sáez, Adrián. 2014. "Elementos religiosos en *Pedro de Urdemalas*." *e-Spania: Revue Interdisciplinaire d'Études Hispaniques Médiévales et Modernes* 18: n.p. https://journals.openedition.org/e-spania/23725.

Salstad, Louise M. 1998. "The Influence of Sacred Oratory on María de Zayas: A Case in Point, *La fuerza del amor*." *Modern Language Notes* 113 (2):426–32.

Salucio del Poyo, Damián. 2023. *El rey muerto*. Edited by C. George Peale. Introduction by Christopher B. Weimer. Santa Barbara: *eHumanista*. https://ehumanista.ucsb.edu/sites/default/files/sitefiles/publications /monographs/elrey%20ha%20muerto.pdf.

San Román Espinosa, Teresa. 2010. *La diferencia inquietante*. Madrid: Siglo XXI de España.

Sánchez, Magdalena. 1998. *The Empress, the Queen, and the Nun: Women and Power at the Court of Philip III of Spain*. Baltimore: Johns Hopkins University Press.

Sánchez Ortega, María-Helena. 1988. *La inquisición y los gitanos*. Madrid: Taurus.

Sánchez Hernández, Leticia. 2014a. "La capilla de Guadalupe en el monasterio de las Descalzas Reales de Madrid." In *Herederas de Clío: Mujeres que han impulsado la historia*, edited by Gloria Ángeles Franco Rubio, María Ángeles Pérez Samper, and María Victoria López-Cordón Cortezo, 493–514. Seville: Mergablum.

– 2014b. "Servidoras de Dios, Leales al Papa. Las Monjas de los Monasterios Reales." *Librosdelacorte.es* 1:293–318.

Sánchez León, José, and Pablo Recio Sánchez. 2024. "The Bizarre History of the Astrological Vault *El Cielo de Salamanca*. *Journal for the History of Astronomy* 55 (1): 31–46.

Sauter, Michael. 2019. *The Spatial Reformation: Euclid Between Man, Cosmos, and God*. Philadelphia: University of Pennsylvania Press.

Sawday, Jonathan. 1995. *The Body Emblazoned: Dissection and the Human Body in Renaissance Culture*. London: Routledge.

Scham, Michael. 2014. *Lector Ludens: The Representation of Games and Play in Cervantes*. Toronto: University of Toronto Press.

Schatzberg, Eric. 2018. *Technology: Critical History of a Concept*. Chicago: University of Chicago Press.

Schiesari, Juliana. 1992. *The Gendering of Melancholia: Feminism, Psychoanalysis, and the Symbolics of Loss in Renaissance Literature*. Ithaca, NY: Cornell University Press.

Schlau, Stacey. 1998. *Viva al Siglo, Muerta al Mundo. Selected Works/Obras escogidas de María de San Alberto (1568–1640)*. New Orleans: University Press of the South.

Schmidt, Rachel. 2011. *Forms of Modernity: Don Quixote and Modern Theories of the Novel*. Toronto: University of Toronto Press.

Schwartz, Lía. 2016. "Amor y deseo en textos de Fernando de Herrera, humanista, poeta neoplatónico y estoico." *Criticón* no. 128, 53–68.

Segal, Charles. 1989. *Orpheus: The Myth of the Poet*. Baltimore: Johns Hopkins University Press.

– 1994a. *Singers, Heroes, and Gods in the Odyssey*. Ithaca, NY: Cornell University Press.

– 1994b. "The Gorgon and the Nightingale: The Voice of Female Lament and Pindar's Twelfth *Pythian Ode*." In Embodied Voices: Representing Female Vocality in Western Culture, edited by Lesley A. Dunn and Nancy C. Jones, 17–34. Oxford: Oxford University Press.

Sela, Shlomo. 2003. *Abraham Ibn Ezra and the Rise of Medieval Hebrew Science*. Leiden: Brill.

Selig, Karl-Ludwig. 1962. "Concerning the Structure of Cervantes' *La Gitanilla*." *Romanistisches Jahrbuch* 13 (1): 273–6.

Shakespeare, William. 2016. *Hamlet*. In *The Norton Shakespeare. Tragedies*, 3rd ed., edited by Stephen Greenblatt et al., 345–499. New York: W.W. Norton.

Shuger, Dale. 2011. "Framing Interiority: *El coloquio de los perros* and Inquisitorial Certainty." *Cervantes: Bulletin of the Cervantes Society of America* 31 (2): 185–211.

Sierra Matute, Víctor. 2023. "Material Methodologies in Early Modern Iberian Treatises." *Romanic Review* 114 (2): 237–58.

– ed. 2025. *Soundscapes of the Early Modern Hispanophone and Lusophone Worlds*. London: Routledge.

Silk, Michael. 2013. Review of *The Sublime from Antiquity to the Present*, edited by Timothy M. Costelloe. In *The American Journal of Philology* 134 (3): 517–21.

Simpson, Paul. 2011. "Street Performance and the City: Public Space, Sociality, and Intervening in the Everyday." *Space and Culture* 14 (4): 415–30.

Sirat, Colette. 1996. *A History of Jewish Philosophy in the Middle Ages*. Cambridge: Cambridge University Press.

Sloman, Albert E. 1953. "The Structure of Calderón's *La vida es sueño*." *Modern Language Review* 48 (3): 293–300.

Smith, Bruce R. 1999. *The Acoustic World of Early Modern England: Attending to the O-Factor*. Chicago: University of Chicago Press.

Smith, Shawn O. 2005. "*Pedro de Urdemalas*: Contesting the Spanish Hapsburg Discourse of Blood." *Vanderbilt e-Journal of Luso-Hispanic Studies* 2: n.p.

Soja, Edward. 1996. *Thirdspace: Journeys to Los Angeles and Other Real-and-Imagined Places*. Oxford: Blackwell.

– 2008. *Taking Space Personally. The Spatial Turn*. London: Routledge.

Soufas, Teresa Scott. 1990. *Melancholy and the Secular Mind in Spanish Golden Age Literature*. Columbia: University of Missouri Press.

Spadaccini, Nicholas, and Jenaro Talens. 1993."On Theater as Narrativity."
    In *Through the Shattering Glass: Cervantes and the Self-Made World*, 64–108.
    Minneapolis: University of Minnesota Press.

Spain, Daphne. 1992. *Gendered Spaces*. Chapel Hill: University of North
    Carolina Press.

Spector, Matías A. 2024. "Cervantes y los servicios de inteligencia: Espías e
    informantes en 'La gitanilla.'" *Neophilologus* 108:197–212.

Stewart, Susan. 1993. *On Longing: Narratives of the Miniature, the Gigantic, the
    Souvenir, the Collection*. Durham, NC: Duke University Press.

Stoichita, Victor I. 1995. *Visionary Experience in the Golden Age of Spanish Art*.
    London: Reaktion Books.

– 1997. *The Self-Aware Image*. Cambridge: Cambridge University Press.

Stoneman, Richard, trans. 1991. *The Greek Alexander Romance*. London:
    Penguin Books.

– 2008. *Alexander the Great: A Life in Legend*. New Haven, CT: Yale University
    Press.

Surtz, Ronald E. 1980. "Cervantes' *Pedro de Urdemalas*: The Trickster as
    Dramatist." *Romanische Forschungen* 92 (1–2): 118–25.

Talley, Robert T., Jr. 2013. *Spatiality*. London: Routledge.

Taussig, Michael. 2006. *Walter Benjamin's Grave*. Chicago: Chicago University
    Press.

Teixeira de Souza, Ana Aparecida, and Carolina de Pontes Rubira. 2017.
    "Pedro de Urdemalas: un personaje proteico en el teatro cervantino." no.
    131, 157–74.

Tejero Prieto, Carlos. (n.d.). *Astronomy at the University of Salamanca at the end
    of the 15th Century: What "El Cielo de Salamanca" tells us*. https://sac.usal.es
    /wp-content/uploads/2020/11/El-cielo-de-Salamanca.pdf.

Tentori, Tullio. 1976. "An Italian Religious Feast: The *Fujenti* Rites of the
    Madonna dell'Arco, Naples." *Cultures* 3 (1): 117–40.

Teresa de Jesús. 2019. *Libro de las moradas o castillo interior*. Madrid: Editorial
    Verbum.

Terpstra, Nicholas. 2015. "Body Politics: The Criminal Body between Public
    and Private." *Journal of Medieval and Early Modern Studies* 45 (1): 7–52.

Tessicini, Dario. 2018. "Comments in Renaissance Science." In *Encyclopedia of
    Renaissance Philosophy*, edited by M. Sgarbi. Cham: Springer. https://doi
    .org/10.1007/978-3-319-02848-4_256-1.

Thacker, Jonathan. 2002. *Role-Play and the World as Stage in the "Comedia."*
    Liverpool: Liverpool University Press.

Thom, Johan, trans. 2014. *Cosmic Order and Divine Power: Pseudo-Aristotle, "On
    the Cosmos."* Tübingen: Mohr Siebeck.

Thompson, Stith. 1955–8. *Motif-Index of Folk-Literature*. Vol. 6.2. Bloomington:
    Indiana University Press.

Tiffany, Tanya. 2019. "The Infant Christ at the Spanish Court: Sor Margarita de la Cruz (1567–1633) and Sacred Material Culture." *The Sixteenth Century Journal* 50 (3): 783–820.

Tirso de Molina. 1958. *La ventura con el nombre*. In *Obras completas de Tirso de Molina*, III, edited by Blanca de los Ríos, 953–1001. Madrid: Águilar.

Toft, Evelyn. 2010. "Cecilia de Nacimiento, Second-Generation Mystic of the Carmelite Reform." In *A New Companion to Hispanic Mysticism*, edited by Hilaire Kallendorf, 231–52. Leiden: Brill.

Torquemada, Antonio de. 1982. *Jardín de flores curiosas*. Edited by Giovanni Allegra. Madrid: Cátedra.

Torres, Isabel. 2013. Love *Poetry in the Spanish Golden Age: Eros, Eris, and Empire*. Woodbridge, UK: Tamesis.

Torres Salinas, Ginés. 2019. "El nombre 'Luz' en la poesía de Fernando de Herrera: Una lectura desde el neoplatonismo renacentista." *Tonos Digital: Revista Electrónica de Estudios Filológicos* no. 36, n.p. https://digitum.um.es /digitum/handle/10201/67599.

Tuan, Yi-Fu. 1977. *Space and Place: The Perspective of Experience*. Minneapolis: University of Minnesota Press.

– 1996. *Cosmos & Hearth: A Cosmopolite's Viewpoint*. Minneapolis: University of Minnesota Press.

Usher, Peter D. 2010. *Shakespeare and the Dawn of Modern Science*. New York: Cambria Press.

Valencia, Felipe. 2021. *The Melancholy Void: Lyric and Masculinity in the Age of Góngora*. Lincoln: University of Nebraska Press.

Valerius Maximus. 2000. *Memorable Doings and Sayings*. Edited and translated by D.R. Shackleton Bailey. Cambridge, MA: Harvard University Press.

Van Bekkum, Wout Jac., trans. 1992. *A Hebrew Alexander Romance According to MS London, Jews College, No. 145*. Leuven: Peeters Press.

Vardi, Amiel. 2004. "Genre, Conventions, and Cultural Programme in Gellius' *Noctes Atticae*." In *The World of Aulus Gellius*, edited by Leofranc Holford-Strevens and Amiel Vardi, 159–86. Oxford: Oxford University Press

Velarde Lombraña, Julián. 1993. "Huarte de San Juan, Patrono de la psicología." *Psicothema* 5 (2): 451–58.

Vélez de Guevara, Luis. *El rey muerto*. Manuscript. Biblioteca Nacional de España. http://bdh-rd.bne.es/viewer.vm?id=0000239400.

Vickers, Nancy. 1982. "Diana Described: Scattered Woman and Scattered Rhyme." In *Writing and Sexual Difference*, edited by Elizabeth Abel, 95–110. Chicago: University of Chicago Press.

Vilacoba Ramos, Karen María, and Teresa Muñoz Serrulla. 2010. "Las religiosas de las Descalzas Reales de Madrid en los Siglos XVI–XX: Fuentes Archivísticas." *Hispania Sacra* 62 (125): 115–56.

Virgil. 2000. *Eclogues.. Georgics. Aeneid I–IV.* Translated by H. Rushton Fairclough. Revised by G.P. Goold. Vol. 1. Cambridge, MA: Harvard University Press.

Vollendorf, Lisa. 2001. *Reclaiming the Body: María de Zayas's Early Modern Feminism.* Chapel Hill: University of North Carolina Press.

Wagschal, Steven. 2012. "The Smellscape of *Don Quixote*: A Cognitive Approach." *Cervantes: Bulletin of the Cervantes Society of America* 32 (1): 125–62.

– 2018. "The Aesthetics of Disgust in Cervantes and Zayas." In *Beyond Sight: Engaging the Senses in Iberian Literatures and Cultures, 1200–1750*, edited by Ryan D. Giles and Steven Wagschal, 94–120. Toronto: University of Toronto Press.

Walton, Kendall. 1990. *Mimesis as Make-Believe: On the Foundations of the Representational Arts.* Cambridge, MA: Harvard University Press.

Warf, Barney, and Santa Arias, eds. 2009. *The Spatial Turn: Interdisciplinary Perspectives.* London: Routledge.

Weber, Alison. 2009. "Could Women Write Mystical Poetry?: The Literary Daughters of Juan de la Cruz." In *Studies on Women's Poetry of the Golden Age: "Tras el espejo la musa escribe,"* edited by Julián Olivares, 185–201. London: Tamesis.

Weinrich, Harald. 2004. *Lethe. The Art and Critique of Forgetting.* Translated by Steven Rendall. Ithaca, NY: Cornell University Press.

Wethey, Harold E., and Alice Suderland Wethey. 1966. "Herrera Barnuevo and His Chapel in the Descalzas Reales." *The Art Bulletin* 48 (1): 15–34.

Wheeler, Chloe. "The Tabloids of Torquemada: Shape-Shifting Women and Confession in the *Jardín de flores curiosas* (1570)." Forthcoming.

Whitmarsh, Tim. 2013. *Beyond the Second Sophistic: Adventures in Greek Postclassicism.* Berkeley: University of California Press.

Williams, Patrick. 2014. "Enrique Pimentel." In *Diccionario Biográfico electrónico*, Real Academia de la Historia, http://dbe.rah.es.

Xerez, Juan de, y Lope de Deça. 2001. *Razón de corte.* Edited by Antonio T. Reguera Rodríguez. León: Universidad de León.

Yates, Frances. 1966. *The Art of Memory.* Oxford: Routledge.

Yeo, Richard. 2007. "Lost Encyclopedias: Before and After the Enlightenment." *Book History* 10:47–65.

Yiu, Yvonne. 2005. "The Mirror and Painting in Early Renaissance Texts." *Early Science and Medicine* 10 (2): 187–210.

Zayas, María de. 2000. *Novelas amorosas y ejemplares.* Edited by Julián Olivares. Madrid: Cátedra.

Zugasti, Miguel. 2017. "Luis Vélez de Guevara y la comedia palatina." *Criticón* no. 129, 41–68. http://journals.openedition.org/criticon/3303.

Zumthor, Paul. 1993. *La mesure du monde: Représentations de l'espace au Moyen Age.* Paris: Seuil.

Contributors

Mary E. Barnard is professor of Spanish and comparative literature at Pennsylvania State University. Her research interests include visual and material culture, classical mythology, and the interplay of text and image in early modern print culture. She is the author of *The Myth of Apollo and Daphne from Ovid to Quevedo: Love, Agon, and the Grotesque*; *Garcilaso de la Vega and the Material Culture of Renaissance Europe*, selected by *Choice* as an Outstanding Academic Book for 2015; and most recently *A Poetry of Things: The Material Lyric in Habsburg Spain*. She has co-edited *Objects of Culture in the Literature of Imperial Spain*. She is currently working on a book on space in poetry, *Spaces of Performance in Early Modern Spanish Lyric*.

Marina S. Brownlee is the Robert Schirmer Professor of Spanish and Comparative Literature at Princeton University. Her books include *The Severed Word: Ovid's "Heroides" and the "Novela Sentimental"*; *The Poetics of Literary Theory in Lope and Cervantes*; and *The Cultural Labyrinth of María de Zayas*. She has co-edited a number of volumes on comparative medieval and early modern topics, including *Renaissance Encounters: Greek East and Latin West*. Her most recent medieval contribution is an essay on the origins of medieval Iberian lyric and narrative in *Literary Beginnings in the European Middle Ages*.

Keith Budner is an assistant professor at the University of Illinois Chicago who specializes in the literature and culture of medieval Iberia and early modern Spain, which he situates in conversation with Hebrew, Latin, and Greek literature. He is completing his first book on the Renaissance revival of Roman Hispania among Judaeoconverso humanists and literary authors. His chapter "Geographic Games" represents a next project on the relationship between maps, play, and literary fictionality as mutually informing modes of world-creation. Keith's research has been supported by the National Endowment for the Humanities, the Huntington Library, the Social Science Research Council, and the Free University of Berlin.

Frederick A. de Armas is Robert O. Anderson Distinguished Service Professor (now emeritus) at the University of Chicago, where he studies early modern writers such as Cervantes and Calderón often from a comparative perspective. He has served as president of the Cervantes Society of America and of AISO (Asociación Internacional Siglo de Oro). He has been awarded several NEH Fellowships and has directed several NEH Seminars. In 2018 he was awarded a doctorate *honoris causa* from the University of Neuchatel (Switzerland). His more recent books include *Cervantes Raphael and the Classics* (Cambridge UP, 1998), *Quixotic Frescoes: Cervantes and Italian Renaissance Art* (UTP, 2006), *Don Quixote Among the Saracens: A Clash of Genres and Civilizations* (UTP 2011), *El retorno de Astrea: astrología y mito en Calderón* (revised and translated version 2016), and *Cervantes' Architectures: The Dangers Outside* (UTP 2022).

Edward H. Friedman is Gertrude Conaway Vanderbilt Professor of the Humanities, emeritus, at Vanderbilt University. His primary field of research is early modern Spanish literature, with emphasis on the picaresque, Cervantes, theatre, and comparative topics. He has served as editor of the *Bulletin of the Comediantes* (1999–2017), president of the Cervantes Society of America, and director of the Robert Penn Warren Center for the Humanities at Vanderbilt.

Ryan D. Giles is a professor in the Department of Spanish and Portuguese and director of the Medieval Studies Institute at Indiana University, Bloomington. He has published more than forty essays in scholarly journals and books, co-edited four volumes, and authored two monographs: *The Laughter of the Saints: Parodies of Holiness in Late Medieval and Renaissance Spain* (UTP, 2009) and *Inscribed Power: Amulets and Magic in Early Spanish Literature* (UTP, 2017). Most recently he co-edited and co-translated the *Labyrinth of Fortune/Laberinto de Fortuna* (Harvard UP, 2025).

Rosilie Hernández is a professor of Hispanic studies at the University of Illinois Chicago. Her present research centres on early modern secular and religious women's cultural production. She has authored numerous articles and book chapters, two book-length monographs –

Bucolic Metaphors: History, Subjectivity, and Gender in the Early Modern Spanish Pastoral (2006; 2018) and *Immaculate Conceptions: The Power of the Religious Imagination in Early Modern Spain* (2019) – and has co-edited two volumes – *Disciplines on the Line: Feminist Research on Spanish, Latin American, and U.S. Latina Women* (2003; 2004) and *Women's Literacy in Early Modern Spain and the New World* (2011).

Carolyn A. Nadeau, Byron S. Tucci Professor of Spanish, teaches early modern Spanish literature and culture classes at Illinois Wesleyan University. Author of the critical edition and translation of Francisco Martínez Montiño's *Arte de cocina, pastelería, vizcochería y conservería* (1611, UTP, 2023) and the monograph *Food Matters: Alonso Quijano's Diet and the Discourse of Food in Early Modern Spain* (UTP, 2015), she is currently writing a book-length project to be entitled *Artistic Voices of the Transatlantic Exchange,* where she explores the role of literary and visual artists as catalysts of collective social memory and how food is portrayed in their works of art.

María Cristina Quintero is Fairbank Professor Emeritus in the Humanities and Spanish, Bryn Mawr College. Her publications include *Beyond Spain's Borders: Women Players in Early Modern National Theaters* (co-edited with Anne J. Cruz, Routledge, 2017) and *Gendering the Crown in the Spanish Baroque Comedia* (Ashgate, 2012). Her articles on theories of translation, gender and lyric poetry, and the politics of the *comedia* in Habsburg Spain have appeared in *MLN, Hispanic Review, Revista de Estudios Hispánicos, Bulletin of Hispanic Studies,* and in several anthologies of early modern studies.

Víctor Sierra Matute is assistant professor of Spanish and comparative literature at Baruch College, The City University of New York. His research spans early modern Iberian and colonial cultural studies, material culture, transoceanic studies, and the history of emotions. He is working on his first monograph, *A Sense of Empire: Perceptual and Material Foundations of Early Modern Iberian Colonialism.* He has edited *Soundscapes of the Early Modern Hispanophone and Lusophone Worlds* (Routledge, 2025) and has published in journals including the *Bulletin of Hispanic Studies, Latin American Research Review,* the *Bulletin of Spanish Visual Studies,* and *Romanic Review,* among others.

Matías A. Spector is currently a teaching fellow in the humanities at the University of Chicago. His research interests include early modern Iberian and colonial culture, particularly in connection with legal studies, urbanism, and classical philosophy and literature. His work has appeared in journals such as the *Bulletin of Spanish Studies* and *Neophilologus*, among others. He is currently working on his first book-length manuscript, which examines the interplay between seventeenth-century surveillance systems and literature through an interdisciplinary and transnational lens.

Christopher Weimer earned his PhD at Pennsylvania State University. He is professor of languages and literatures at Oklahoma State University, where he has taught courses in Spanish and interdisciplinary humanities since 1994. He has co-edited two volumes devoted to early modern Spanish literature, *Echoes and Inscriptions: Comparative Approaches to Early Modern Hispanic Literatures* and *"Los cielos se agotaron de prodigios": Essays in Honor of Frederick A. de Armas*. His essays have appeared in numerous journals and critical anthologies. With Barbara Simerka and James T. Abraham he co-founded the online journal *Laberinto*.

Index

Abraham Ibn Ezra, 79

Aeschylus, 35–6

Ajax, 31, 32, 35, 36, 38, 42

Albardonedo Freire, Antonio José, 97 (fig 5.1); 101 (fig 5.2); 106, 108n7, 108n8

Alcalá Galán, Mercedes, 67n4

Alfonso X El Sabio: *General Estoria* (Proverbios), 72, 75; *Libro de Juegos*, 82–3

Ana Dorotea, Sor, 6; Discalced Convent, Madrid, Habsburg family connections, 180–2; Rudolf II's influence, 189–92

Arguijo, Juan de, 5, 6

Arias Montano, Benito, 5

Ariosto, Ludovico, 34

Aristotle, Aristotelianism, 68, 74, 77, 79, 88, 89n11

Astraea, 32, 33, 36, 41

Austria, Juana de, 6

Bachelard, Gaston, 7

Barnard, Mary E., 8

Barthes: "the grain of the voice," 18, 21–2; text as cloth, 22

Bible: Proverbs, 72–5, 82; Ezekiel, 81–2

Biblioteca General Histórica (University of Salamanca), 197, 199

board games, 81–3

Bouza, Fernando, 200

Bradbury, 67n2, 67n4

Brahe, Tycho, 3

Brownlee, Marina S., 9

Bruno, Giordano, 3

Buen Retiro Palace, 5

Burke, Edmund, 35, 40

Calderón de la Barca, Pedro, 8, 31–43, 116; *La gran Cenobia*, 32; *La vida es sueño*, 8, 32–43

Cancioneiro, 197–8

Caruth, Cathy: trauma as wound, 18, 22

Carrillo, Martín, 6; *Elogios de mujeres insignes del viejo testamento*, 182, 192; doctrine of immaculacy and Marian privilege, 182–3

cartography, 4

Carvajal y Mendoza, Luisa de, 6

Cavarero, Adriana, 25, 27

Cecilia de Nacimiento, 11, 162, 166–74, 178n6, 178n7, 178n8, 178n10, 179n12

Certeau, Michel de, 7, 32–3, 162–3, 165–6, 178n4, 203; place (*lieu*) vs. space (*espace*), 163–4, 169, 173

Cervantes, Miguel de, 5, 9, 10, 31–2, 55–7, 59, 61, 63, 65–6; *Don Quijote*,

5, 9, 63, 69–71, 84–7, 128, 137, 140;
"El coloquio de los perros," 9,
93–109; "La gitanilla," 10, 110–26;
"Novela del casamiento engañoso," 98; *Ocho comedias y ocho
entremeses*, 32; *Pedro de Urdemalas*,
10, 127–41; "Rinconete y Cortadillo," 93, 106, 108n4, 110
Charles V, 4
Chaves Fernández Manuel F., and
Rafael M. Pérez García, 103–4
Circe, 25
Cleve III, Hendrik van, 39
comets, 38–9
confraternities, 224–5
convent, 161, 175; as gendered
space, 161–3, 172–4, 178;
conventual architecture/
construction, 161, 162–4,
166–7, 170, 177; *ermitas*
(hermitages),
164–5, 171–3
corral de comedias, 5
corruption, 94–6, 106
Cortés, Hernán, 4
Council of Trent, 161
Cowell, Edward Byles, 42n8

Dadson, Trevor, 200
Dante Alighieri: *Purgatorio*, 27–8;
Rime petrose, 30n10
de Armas, Frederick A., 8
Demosthenes, 31
Descalzas Reales (Convent), 6, 11,
180–3
Domus Aurea, 36

Empedocles, 34
enslavement, 102–5, 106, 109n14
Enterline, Lynn, 29n8
Escorial (monastery), 5
Euripides, 35

Examen de ingenios para las sciencias,
46, 61–2
exemplarity in female religious
identity, 184–5

Ficino, Marsilio, 30n9
Foucault, Michel, 44, 67n1, 162, 178,
178n4; heterotopia, 162–3, 177–8
Freud, Sigmund: "Mourning and
Melancholia," 23
Friedman, Edward H., 10

García Santo-Tomás, Enrique, 111
Garcilaso de la Vega, 5, 20, 21–2
Garrido Aranda, Antonio, 95–6
gaze, 110, 114–17, 121
geotagging, 93–109
Giles, Ryan D., 12
Greek Alexander Romance, 75, 80–1,
89n11
Guadalupe Chapel, 11; visual
program, 182–3
gypsies, 10

hagiography, 217, 220, 227
Hernández, Rosilie, 11
Herrera, Fernando de, 6, 8, 17–30;
"Al mar desierto," 24–6; "Serena
Luz," 26–8; "Suäve Filomela,"
17–24
Herrera Barrionuevo, Sebastián de, 6
Hesiod, 34
hippogriff, 33–5
Homer, 8, 31–2; *Iliad*, 31, 32; *Odyssey*,
24–6, 31
Huarte de San Juan, Juan, 9, 45, 46,
61–7; *Examen de ingenios para las
sciencias*, 9, 30n9, 46, 61–2
Huete (Spain), 197, 215n18
Hurtado de Mendoza, Diego, 5
Hurtado de Mendoza, Francisco, 6
Hutchinson, Steven, 96–7

idolatry, Jewish conceptions of, 71–2,
   76–9, 81–4, 87, 89n9
Inquisition, 222–3

Jameson, Frederic, 94
Jardín de flores curiosas, 46, 48, 54–60,
   61, 67
Johnson, Paul, 105
Juan de la Cruz 168–9, 178n8
Juan de Xerez, 116

La Celestina, 118
Lastanosa, Vincencio Juan de, 5
Lefebvre, Henri, 7, 44, 67n1, 162,
   166–7
Libro de Alexandre, 9, 68–70, 72, 75,
   78–9
Longinus (pseudo), 8, 31–43
Lope de Deça, 116
Lope de Vega Carpio, Félix, 6, 127,
   135, 140n2; *El caballero de Olmedo*,
   222, 228
Loyola, Ignatius of (Saint), 205

MacCarthy, Denis Florence,
   42–3n8
Madrid, 111–21
Maimonides, Moses, 77, 88, 89n10
Marcela de San Félix, 11, 162, 174–8,
   179n13, 179n14, 179n15
Margarita de la Cruz, 182
María de Ágreda, Sor: *Mística ciudad
   de Dios*, 193
María de San Alberto, 11, 162, 163–6,
   171, 174, 178n8
Mary, St, 217–21, 224–6
materiality, 214n11, 211–12
medicine, 218, 222–3
melancholy, 23
memory, 5, 18, 19, 26, 44–6, 48–54,
   59, 60, 61, 62, 63, 67
Mendoza, Mencía de, 6

Mercator, Gerardus, 4
metatheatre, 128, 135, 137
metropolises, 111, 121, 124
Mexía, Pedro, 9, 44–54, 56, 58, 62, 67;
   Silva de varia lección, 9, 45–50, 52,
   54, 56
Minkowski, Eugène, 18, 21
mirrors: portraiture and self-
   portraiture, 185–7, 190–1, 194–5;
   rise of the individual, 186–7;
   theological interpretation (*speculum vitae, speculum justitiae*, and
   speculum sine macula), 187–9;
   vanitas, 187
Monardes, Nicolás, 104–5
Murcia, 111, 121–4

Nadeau, Carolyn A., 9–10
Naples, 216–28
narrative, process, 96–8, 107
nightingale, 21–2

Orpheus, 17, 21; and Eurydice, 20
Odysseus, 25–6, 27, 29; and the
   sirens, Attic red-figured stamnos
   (fig 1.1), 28–9
Ovid, 8, 18–20, 22

Pantheon (Roman), 37
Patroclus, 31, 41–2n1
performance, 110–26, 200, 206, 211
Perry, Mary Elizabeth, 95
Petrarch, 20, 21, 23–4, 30n11
Phaeton, 35, 36, 41
Philip II of Spain, 4, 6
Philip III of Spain, 5
Philip IV of Spain, 5
Philomela, 8, 18–20, 22–4
Pimentel, Enrique (Bishop of
   Cuenca), 12, 197–8, 212
Pimentel de Herrera, Juan Alonso
   (Count of Benavente), 197

Plato, Platonism, 73, 74
presence, 198, 203, 212
Ptolemy: astronomer and geographer, 4, 79, 80, 83, 89n13; *Geographia*, 4; Macedonian King of Egypt, 79, 80, 81

Quevedo, Francisco de, 4; *El buscón*, 138, 222; *La Hora de Todos y la Fortuna con seso*, 4
Quintero, María Cristina, 11

Raphael, School of Athens, 79–81, 89n14
Recibimiento al obispo Pimentel, 12
relics, 221–3
Rilke, Rainer Maria, 17
Rojas, Fernando de, *La Celestina*, 222, 228
Roma community, 110–26
Rudolph II, 6
Ryan, Marie-Laure, 94, 107

Samuel Ibn Tibbon, Hebrew Alexander Romance, 69, 77, 81, 88, 89n11
Santillana, Marquis of, 5
Schiesari, Juliana, 23, 24
Sebastián Herrera Barnuevo, painter of the Guadalupe Chapel, 181
Sensorium, 200–1, 206
Seville, 9–10, 93–109; bribery in, 96; food insecurity 94, 96; Plaza de San Francisco, 96–7, 106; Portuguese in, 103–4; Puerta de la carne, 94–5, 108n7; Puerta de Jerez, 106, Puerta de Macarena, 106–7; slaughterhouse in, 94–6; Triana, 106, 109n16
Shakespeare, William, 3; *Hamlet*, 3, 7, 18, 21, 23
Sierra Matute, Víctor, 12
Sigüenza, José de, 5

siren: Homeric, 24–6, 28; hybrid, 26–9, 30n11
Sisyphus, 37, 41
soledad (solitude) 161, 163–5, 167–8, 174–5, 179n15
Solomon Ibn Gabirol, 73, 74
space: acoustic, 8, 18, 20–1; and libraries 5–6; of memory, 44–53, 57, 59, 61, 67; of performance, 18; narrative, 94, 96, 98, 100; soundscape, 18, 202–4, 213n7; urban, 4, 9–10, 94, 99, 100, 107, 108n4
Spector, Matias A., 10, 12
Stoichita, Victor: mirrors and portraiture, 193–4; visionary art, 183–4
strife (Eris), 34
sublime, 8, 31–43
Suspension, 117–19, 123

Teresa of Ávila: use of mirror metaphor, 164, 177, 187–8
Torquemada, Antonio de, 45, 46, 48, 54–62, 67; *Jardín de flores curiosas*, 9, 46, 48, 54–60, 61, 67
Tuan, Yi-Fu, 7, 8, 18, 35–6, 40

Valladolid, 98–9
Virgil, 17, 20–1, 28
voice: as performance, 18; of Philomela, 18–24, of the siren, 24–8; of trauma, 8, 18, 22–4

Weimer, Christopher, 10–11
Weinrich, Harald, 63
witchcraft, 222–5, 228
Wunderkammer, 5
Wyngaerde, Anton van den, 4

Zayas, María de, 12, 216–28; *La fuerza del amor*, 12
Zumthor, Paul, 7

Toronto Iberic

1 Anthony J. Cascardi, *Cervantes, Literature, and the Discourse of Politics*
2 Jessica A. Boon, *The Mystical Science of the Soul: Medieval Cognition in Bernardino de Laredo's Recollection Method*
3 Susan Byrne, *Law and History in Cervantes'* Don Quixote
4 Mary E. Barnard and Frederick A. de Armas (eds.), *Objects of Culture in the Literature of Imperial Spain*
5 Nil Santiáñez, *Topographies of Fascism: Habitus, Space, and Writing in Twentieth-Century Spain*
6 Nelson R. Orringer, *Lorca in Tune with Falla: Literary and Musical Interludes*
7 Ana M. Gómez-Bravo, *Textual Agency: Writing Culture and Social Networks in Fifteenth-Century Spain*
8 Javier Irigoyen-García, *The Spanish Arcadia: Sheep Herding, Pastoral Discourse, and Ethnicity in Early Modern Spain*
9 Stephanie Sieburth, *Survival Songs: Conchita Piquer's* Coplas *and Franco's Regime of Terror*
10 Christine Arkinstall, *Spanish Female Writers and the Freethinking Press, 1879–1926*

11 Margaret E. Boyle, *Unruly Women: Performance, Penitence, and Punishment in Early Modern Spain*

12 Evelina Gužauskytė, *Christopher Columbus's Naming in the* diarios *of the Four Voyages (1492–1504): A Discourse of Negotiation*

13 Mary E. Barnard, *Garcilaso de la Vega and the Material Culture of Renaissance Europe*

14 William Viestenz, *By the Grace of God: Francoist Spain and the Sacred Roots of Political Imagination*

15 Michael Scham, Lector Ludens: *The Representation of Games and Play in Cervantes*

16 Stephen Rupp, *Heroic Forms: Cervantes and the Literature of War*

17 Enrique Fernandez, *Anxieties of Interiority and Dissection in Early Modern Spain*

18 Susan Byrne, *Ficino in Spain*

19 Patricia M. Keller, *Ghostly Landscapes: Film, Photography, and the Aesthetics of Haunting in Contemporary Spanish Culture*

20 Carolyn A. Nadeau, *Food Matters: Alonso Quijano's Diet and the Discourse of Food in Early Modern Spain*

21 Cristian Berco, *From Body to Community: Venereal Disease and Society in Baroque Spain*

22 Elizabeth R. Wright, *The Epic of Juan Latino: Dilemmas of Race and Religion in Renaissance Spain*

23 Ryan D. Giles, *Inscribed Power: Amulets and Magic in Early Spanish Literature*

24 Jorge Pérez, *Confessional Cinema: Religion, Film, and Modernity in Spain's Development Years, 1960–1975*

25 Joan Ramon Resina, *Josep Pla: Seeing the World in the Form of Articles*

26 Javier Irigoyen-García, *"Moors Dressed as Moors": Clothing, Social Distinction, and Ethnicity in Early Modern Iberia*

27 Jean Dangler, *Edging toward Iberia*

28 Ryan D. Giles and Steven Wagschal (eds.), *Beyond Sight: Engaging the Senses in Iberian Literatures and Cultures, 1200–1750*

29 Silvia Bermúdez, *Rocking the Boat: Migration and Race in Contemporary Spanish Music*

30 Hilaire Kallendorf, *Ambiguous Antidotes: Virtue as Vaccine for Vice in Early Modern Spain*

31 Leslie J. Harkema, *Spanish Modernism and the Poetics of Youth: From Miguel de Unamuno to* La Joven Literatura

32 Benjamin Fraser, *Cognitive Disability Aesthetics: Visual Culture, Disability Representations, and the (In)Visibility of Cognitive Difference*

33 Robert Patrick Newcomb, *Iberianism and Crisis: Spain and Portugal at the Turn of the Twentieth Century*

34 Sara J. Brenneis, *Spaniards in Mauthausen: Representations of a Nazi Concentration Camp, 1940–2015*

35 Silvia Bermúdez and Roberta Johnson (eds.), *A New History of Iberian Feminisms*

36 Steven Wagschal, *Minding Animals in the Old and New Worlds: A Cognitive Historical Analysis*

37 Heather Bamford, *Cultures of the Fragment: Uses of the Iberian Manuscript, 1100–1600*

38 Enrique García Santo-Tomás (ed.), *Science on Stage in Early Modern Spain*

39 Marina S. Brownlee (ed.), *Cervantes'* Persiles *and the Travails of Romance*

40 Sarah Thomas, *Inhabiting the In-Between: Childhood and Cinema in Spain's Long Transition*

41 David A. Wacks, *Medieval Iberian Crusade Fiction and the Mediterranean World*

42 Rosilie Hernández, *Immaculate Conceptions: The Power of the Religious Imagination in Early Modern Spain*

43 Mary L. Coffey and Margot Versteeg (eds.), *Imagined Truths: Realism in Modern Spanish Literature and Culture*

44 Diana Aramburu, *Resisting Invisibility: Detecting the Female Body in Spanish Crime Fiction*

45 Samuel Amago and Matthew J. Marr (eds.), *Consequential Art: Comics Culture in Contemporary Spain*

46 Richard P. Kinkade, *Dawn of a Dynasty: The Life and Times of Infante Manuel of Castile*

47 Jill Robbins, *Poetry and Crisis: Cultural Politics and Citizenship in the Wake of the Madrid Bombings*

48 Ana María Laguna and John Beusterien (eds.), *Goodbye Eros: Recasting Forms and Norms of Love in the Age of Cervantes*

49 Sara J. Brenneis and Gina Herrmann (eds.), *Spain, the Second World War, and the Holocaust: History and Representation*

50 Francisco Fernández de Alba, *Sex, Drugs, and Fashion in 1970s Madrid*

51 Daniel Aguirre-Oteiza, *This Ghostly Poetry: History and Memory of Exiled Spanish Republican Poets*

52 Lara Anderson, *Control and Resistance: Food Discourse in Franco Spain*

53 Faith S. Harden, *Arms and Letters: Military Life Writing in Early Modern Spain*

54 Erin Alice Cowling, Tania de Miguel Magro, Mina García Jordán, and Glenda Y. Nieto-Cuebas (eds.), *Social Justice in Spanish Golden Age Theatre*

55 Paul Michael Johnson, *Affective Geographies: Cervantes, Emotion, and the Literary Mediterranean*

56 Justin Crumbaugh and Nil Santiáñez (eds.), *Spanish Fascist Writing: An Anthology*

57 Margaret E. Boyle and Sarah E. Owens (eds.), *Health and Healing in the Early Modern Iberian World: A Gendered Perspective*

58 Leticia Álvarez-Recio (ed.), *Iberian Chivalric Romance: Translations and Cultural Transmission in Early Modern England*

59 Henry Berlin, *Alone Together: Poetics of the Passions in Late Medieval Iberia*

60 Adrian Shubert, *The Sword of Luchana: Baldomero Espartero and the Making of Modern Spain, 1793–1879*

61 Jorge Pérez, *Fashioning Spanish Cinema: Costume, Identity, and Stardom*

62 Enriqueta Zafra, *Lazarillo de Tormes: A Graphic Novel*

63 Erin Alice Cowling, *Chocolate: How a New World Commodity Conquered Spanish Literature*

64 Mary E. Barnard, *A Poetry of Things: The Material Lyric in Habsburg Spain*

65 Frederick A. de Armas and James Mandrell (eds.), *The Gastronomical Arts in Spain: Food and Etiquette*

66 Catherine Infante, *The Arts of Encounter: Christians, Muslims, and the Power of Images in Early Modern Spain*

67 Robert Richmond Ellis, *Bibliophiles, Murderous Bookmen, and Mad Librarians: The Story of Books in Modern Spain*

68 Beatriz de Alba-Koch (ed.), *The Ibero-American Baroque*

69 Deborah R. Forteza, *The English Reformation in the Spanish Imagination: Rewriting Nero, Jezebel, and the Dragon*

70 Olga Sendra Ferrer, *Barcelona, City of Margins*

71 Dale Shuger, *God Made Word: An Archaeology of Mystic Discourse in Early Modern Spain*

72 Xosé M. Núñez Seixas, *The Spanish Blue Division on the Eastern Front, 1941–1945: War, Occupation, Memory*

73 Julia Domínguez, *Quixotic Memories: Cervantes and Memory in Early Modern Spain*

74 Anna Casas Aguilar, *Bilingual Legacies: Father Figures in Self-Writing from Barcelona*

75 Julia H. Chang, *Blood Novels: Gender, Caste, and Race in Spanish Realism*

76 Frederick A. de Armas, *Cervantes' Architectures: The Dangers Outside*

77 Michael Iarocci, *The Art of Witnessing: Francisco de Goya's* Disasters of War

78 Esther Fernández and Adrienne L. Martín (eds.), *Drawing the Curtain: Cervantes's Theatrical Revelations*

79 Emiro Martínez-Osorio and Mercedes Blanco (eds.), *The War Trumpet: Iberian Epic Poetry, 1543–1639*

80 Christine Arkinstall, *Women on War in Spain's Long Nineteenth Century: Virtue, Patriotism, Citizenship*

81 Ignacio Infante, *A Planetary Avant-Garde: Experimental Literature Networks and the Legacy of Iberian Colonialism*

82 Enrique Fernández, *The Image of Celestina: Illustrations, Paintings, and Advertisements*

83 Maryanne L. Leone and Shanna Lino (eds.), *Beyond Human: Decentring the Anthropocene in Spanish Ecocriticism*

84 Jennifer Nagtegaal, *Politically Animated: Non-fiction Animation from the Hispanic World*

85 Anton Pujol and Jaume Martí-Olivella (eds.), *Catalan Cinema: The Barcelona Film School and the New Avant-Garde*

86 Matthew Bailey, *Speaking Truth to Power: The Legacy of the Young Cid*

87 Hilaire Kallendorf, *Perilous Passions: Ethics and Emotion in Early Modern Spain*

88 Anita Savo, *Portraying Authorship: Juan Manuel and the Rhetoric of Authority*

89 Robin M. Bower, *In the Doorway of All Worlds: Gonzalo de Berceo's Translation of the Saints*

90 Daniel Holcombe and Frederick A. de Armas (eds.), *Bodies Beyond Labels: Finding Joy in the Shadows of Imperial Spain*

91 Susan Larson (ed.), *Comfort and Domestic Space in Modern Spain*

92 Heather Jerónimo, *Performing Parenthood: Non-Normative Fathers and Mothers in Spanish Narrative and Film*

93 Enric Bou, *Cartographies of Disappearance: Vestiges of Everyday Life in Literature*

94 Martin Repinecz, *Volatile Whiteness: Race, Cinema, and Europeanization in Spain*

95 Howard Mancing and Tatevik Gyulamiryan (eds.), *A Character Named Cervantes: On Screen, on Stage, and on the Page*

96 Daniel Holcombe, *Quixotic Quests: Salvador Dalí's First Illustrated Don Quixote*

97 Susan Byrne, *The Aesthetic Turn in Cervantes*

98 Cory A. Reed, *Cervantes, Technology, and the Novel: An Aesthetic of Instrumentality in Don Quixote*

99 Ignacio Navarrete, *Sneaking into Print: Mouvance and Narrative Culture in Spain c. 1500*

100 Heather Bamford, *Unprinted: Reading and Meaning in Early Modern Iberia*

101 Mary E. Barnard and Frederick A. de Armas (eds): *The Spatial Turn in the Literature and Art of Early Modern Spain*